Fodor's 16th Edition   P9-DCM-720

Cancún, Cozumel, Yucatán Peninsula

The Guide
for All Budgets

Completely
Updated

Where to Stay, Eat,
and Explore

On and Off
the Beaten Path

When to Go,
What to Pack

Maps, Travel Tips,
and Web Sites

Fodor's Travel Publications • New York, Toronto, London, Sydney, Auckland
www.fodors.com

Fodor's Cancún, Cozumel, Yucatán Peninsula

EDITOR: Nuha E. Ansari

Editorial Contributors: Patricia Alisau, Satu Hummasti, Julie Mazur, Shelagh McNally, Maribeth Mellin, Jane Onstott

Maps: David Lindroth, *cartographer;* Rebecca Baer and Robert Blake, *map editors*

Design: Fabrizio La Rocca, *creative director;* Guido Caroti, *art director;* Jolie Novak, *senior picture editor;* Melanie Marin, *photo editor*

Cover Design: Pentagram

Production/Manufacturing: Colleen Ziemba

Cover Photo (Izamal Convent, Yucatan): Andrea Pistolesi

Copyright

Important Tip

Although all prices, opening times, and other details in this book are based on information supplied to us at press time, changes occur all the time in the travel world, and Fodor's cannot accept responsibility for facts that become outdated or for inadvertent errors or omissions. So **always confirm information when it matters,** especially if you're making a detour to visit a specific place.

Special Sales

Fodor's Travel Publications are available at special discounts for bulk purchases for sales promotions or premiums. Special editions, including personalized covers, excerpts of existing guides, and corporate imprints, can be created in large quantities for special needs. For more information, contact your local bookseller or write to Special Markets, Fodor's Travel Publications, 280 Park Avenue, New York, NY 10017. Inquiries from Canada should be directed to your local Canadian bookseller or sent to Random House of Canada, Ltd., Marketing Department, 2775 Matheson Boulevard East, Mississauga, Ontario L4W 4P7. Inquiries from the United Kingdom should be sent to Fodor's Travel Publications, 20 Vauxhall Bridge Road, London SW1V 2SA, England.

CONTENTS

Maps

ON THE ROAD WITH FODOR'S

A TRIP TAKES YOU OUT OF YOUR-SELF. Concerns of life at home completely disappear, driven away by more immediate thoughts—about, say, what marvels will beguile the next day, or where you'll have dinner. That's where Fodor's comes in. We make sure that you know all your options, so that you don't miss something that's around the next bend just because you didn't know it was there. Mindful that the best memories of your trip might have nothing to do with what you came to **Cancún** to see, we guide you to sights large and small **all over the region**. You might set out to **relax and catch the sun on a lovely white-sand beach**, but back at home you find yourself unable to forget **the dramatic Maya pyramids and snorkeling above beautiful coral reefs.** With Fodor's at your side, serendipitous discoveries are never far away.

About Our Writers

Our success in showing you every corner of **Cancún, Cozumel, and the Yucatán Peninsula** is a credit to our extraordinary writers. Although there's no substitute for travel advice from a good friend who knows your style, our contributors are the next best thing—the kind of people you *would* poll for travel advice if you knew them.

Patricia Alisau, who updated the Caribbean Coast chapter of this book, is a psychologist turned journalist who was so drawn to the surrealism of Mexico that she moved to the capital. What began as a one-week vacation turned into a 20-year-plus sojourn. She's explored just about every nook and cranny of this marvelous country many times over and has credits as a foreign correspondent, war correspondent (in Nicaragua), and restaurant and food editor for many publications abroad. Her favorite pursuit is researching the Maya culture and scaling its lofty pyramids in near and far places of the ancient empire.

Journalist turned travel writer **Shelagh McNally** has lived on the Yucatán Peninsula since 1997, when she left her native Canada for a four-month Mexican vacation with her young daughter and de-cided to stay on and learn more about the Maya history and culture. She has covered Cancún, Cozumel, Campeche, Isla Mujeres, and elsewhere on the Caribbean coast for Fodor's and has also written for the Miami Herald, Mundo Maya Magazine, and other publications and Web sites in Mexico, Canada, the United Kingdom, and the United States.

Maribeth Mellin first visited Cozumel in on a backpacking trip in 1980, when she camped on the beach and snorkeled on the reefs. She's been back many times, and thinks it is the most romantic place in Mexico. Maribeth has received the prestigious Pluma de Plata award for her writings on Mexico, along with several awards from the Society for American Travel Writers and the Press Club.

An inveterate traveler, **Jane Onstott** has trekked extensively in Mexico and Latin America. She has survived a near plunge into a gorge in the highlands of Mexico, a knife-wielding robber in Madrid, and a financial shipwreck on one of the more remote Galápagos Islands. Jane has written and edited guidebooks to Mexico, Ecuador, and Southern California, and she updated the Mérida and the State of Yucatán and Campeche sections of this edition. She lives in San Diego.

You can rest assured that you're in good hands—and that no property mentioned in the book has paid to be included. Each has been selected strictly on its merits, as the best of its type in its price range.

How to Use This Book

Up front is **Smart Travel Tips A to Z,** arranged alphabetically by topic and loaded with tips, Web sites, and contact information. **Destination: Cancún, Cozumel, Yucatán Peninsula** helps get you in the mood for your trip. **Subsequent chapters** are arranged regionally. All city chapters begin with exploring information, with a section for each neighborhood (each recommending a good tour and listing sights alphabetically). All regional chapters are divided geographically; within each area, towns are covered in logical geographical order, and attractive stretches of road between them are indicated by the designation *En Route*. To help you decide what you'll have time to visit, all chapters begin with our writers' favorite itineraries. (Mix itineraries from several chapters, and you can put together a really exceptional trip.) The A to Z section that ends every chapter lists additional resources. At the end of the book you'll find **Background and Essentials**, including **a chronology of the Maya and Yucatán, and a Spanish vocabulary section.**

Icons and Symbols

★ Our special recommendations
✕ Restaurant
🏠 Lodging establishment
✕🏠 Lodging establishment whose restaurant warrants a special trip
⚠ Campgrounds
🔺 Archaeological site
🐤 Good for kids (rubber duck)
☞ Sends you to another section of the guide for more information
✉ Address
☎ Telephone number
🕐 Opening and closing times
💰 Admission prices (those we give apply to adults; substantially reduced fees are almost always available for children, students, and senior citizens)

Numbers in white and black circles ③ ❸ that appear on the maps, in the margins, and within the tours correspond to one another.

For hotels, you can assume that all rooms have private baths, phones, TVs, and air-conditioning unless otherwise noted and that all hotels operate on the European Plan (with no meals) if we don't specify another meal plan. We always list a property's facilities but not whether you'll be charged extra to use them, so when pricing accommodations, do ask what's included. For restaurants, it's always a good idea to book ahead; we mention reservations only when they're essential or are not accepted. All restaurants we list are open daily for lunch and dinner unless stated otherwise; dress is mentioned only when men are required to wear a jacket or a jacket and tie. Look for an overview of local dining-out habits in Smart Travel Tips A to Z and in the Pleasures and Pastimes section that follows each chapter introduction.

Don't Forget to Write

Your experiences—positive and negative—matter to us. If we have missed or misstated something, we want to hear about it. We follow up on all suggestions. Contact the **Cancún, Cozumel, Yucatán Peninsula** editor at editors@fodors.com or c/o Fodor's at 280 Park Avenue, New York, NY 10017. And have a fabulous trip!

Karen Cure

Karen Cure
Editorial Director

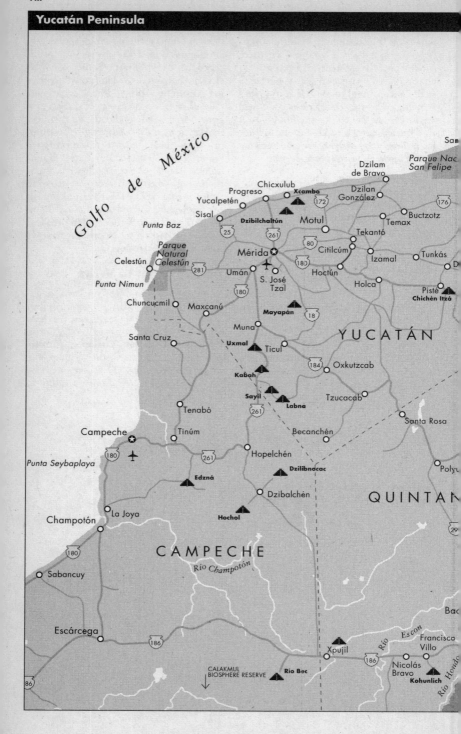

Golfo de México

Parque Nac San Felipe

Dzilam de Bravo

Chicxulub
Progreso
Xcamba
Dzilan González

Yucalpetén
Sisal
Dzibilchaltún
Motul
Temax
Buctzotz

Punta Baz
Tekantó

Celestún
Parque Natural Celestún
Mérida
Citilcúm
Izamal
Tunkás

Punta Nimun
Umán
S. José Tzal
Hoctún
Holca
Pisté
Chichén Itzá

Chuncucmil
Maxcanú
Mayapán

Santa Cruz
Muna
YUCATÁN

Uxmal
Ticul
Oxkutzcab

Kabah
Sayil
Labna
Tzucacab
Santa Rosa

Tenabó
Tinúm
Becanchén

Campeche
Hopelchén
Polyu

Punta Seybaplaya
Dzilibnocac

Edzná
Dzibalchén
QUINTAN

Champotón
La Joya
Hochol

Sabancuy
CAMPECHE
Río Champotón

Escárcega
Bac
Escon
Francisco Villo

Xpujil
Nicolás Bravo

CALAKMUL BIOSPHERE RESERVE
Río Bec
Kohunlich

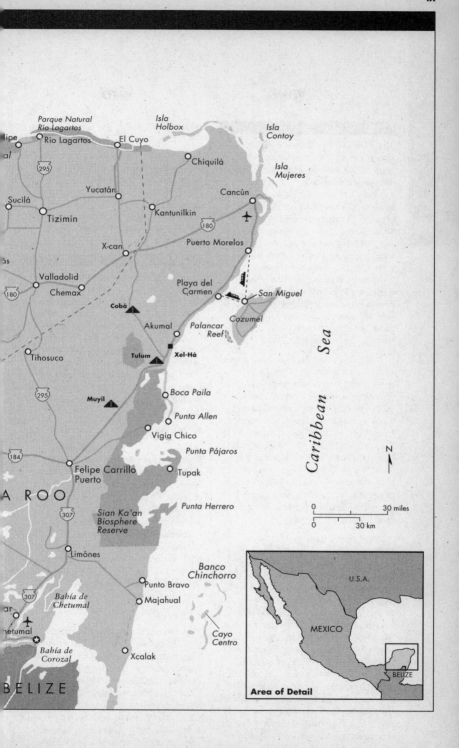

Parque Natural
Río Lagartos
Isla
Holbox
Isla
Contoy
Río Lagartos
El Cuyo
Chiquilá
Isla
Mujeres
295
Yucatán
Cancún
Sucilá
Kantunilkin
Tizimin
180
X-can
Puerto Morelos
Valladolid
180
Chemax
Playa del
Carmen
San Miguel
Cobá
Akumal
Cozumel
Palancar
Reef
Tihosuco
Tulum
Xel-Há
295
Muyil
Boca Paila
Punta Allen
Vigia Chico
Punta Pájaros
184
Felipe Carrillo
Puerto
Tupak
A R O O
307
Punta Herrero
Sian Ka'an
Biosphere
Reserve
Limónes
Banco
Chinchorro
307
Punto Bravo
Bahía de
Chetumal
Majahual
etumal
Cayo
Centro
Bahía de
Corozal
Xcalak
B E L I Z E

Caribbean Sea

N

0   30 miles
0   30 km

U.S.A.

MEXICO

BELIZE

Area of Detail

ESSENTIAL INFORMATION

ADDRESSES

The Mexican method of naming streets can be exasperatingly arbitrary, so **be patient when searching for street addresses.** Streets in the centers of many colonial cities (those built by the Spanish) are laid out in a grid surrounding the *zócalo* (main square) and often change names on different sides of the square. Other streets simply acquire a new name after a certain number of blocks. Numbered streets are usually designated *norte/sur* (north/south) or *oriente/poniente* (east/west) on either side of a central avenue. Three of these are abbreviated: Nte., Ote., and Pte. Sur is spelled out.

In many cities, streets that have proper names change names when they cross some other street—and only a map will show where one begins and the other ends. Blocks are often labeled numerically, according to distance from a chosen starting point, as in "la Calle de Pachuca," "2a Calle de Pachuca," etc. Many addresses have "s/n" for *sin número* (no number) after the street name. This is common in small towns where there aren't many buildings on a block. A *carretera* is a main highway.

Abbreviations used in addresses include the following: Av. (*avenida,* or avenue); Calz. (*calzada,* or road); Fracc. (*fraccionamiento,* or housing estate); and Int. (*interior,* which is the same in English). "Sm" stands for Super Manzana (*manzana* alone means block), or neighborhood; each usually has its own park or square. Super Manzanas in Cancún and in other cities and towns are labeled with an Sm number (Sm 23, Sm 25, etc.) The streets in Super Manzanas are horseshoe shaped with a park in the middle. Traffic enters from one end and leaves from the other. The street name is shown on each side with an arrow indicating which way the traffic should flow.

Addresses in Mexico are written with the street name first, followed by the street number. A five-digit *código postal* (postal code) precedes, rather than follows, the name of the city. Apartado Postal, abbreviated as Apdo. Postal or A.P., means post-office box.

AIR TRAVEL

Almost all flights to Cancún have stopovers at hub airports(Houston, Dallas, Miami, Chicago, Los Angeles, or Atlanta), where you must change planes and transfer luggage. Some flights go to Mexico City, where you must pass through customs before transferring to a domestic flight to Cancún. This applies to air travel from the United States, Canada, the United Kingdom, Australia, and New Zealand.

BOOKING

When you book **look for nonstop flights** and **remember that "direct" flights stop at least once.** Try to avoid connecting flights, which require a change of plane. Two airlines may operate a connecting flight jointly, so ask if your airline operates every segment of the trip; you may find that the carrier you prefer flies you only part of the way. For more booking tips and to check prices and make on-line flight reservations, log on to www.fodors.com.

CARRIERS

You can reach the Yucatán either by U.S., Mexican, or regional carriers. The most convenient flight from the United States is a nonstop one on a domestic or Mexican airline. Booking a carrier with stopovers adds several hours to your travel time. Flying within the Yucatán, although not cost efficient, saves you precious time if you are on a tight schedule. A flight from Cancún to Mérida, for example, can cost as much as one from Mexico City to Cancún. Select your hub city for exploring before making your reservation from abroad.

All the major airlines listed here fly to Cancún. Aeroméxico, American, Continental, and Mexicana also fly to Cozumel. Aeroméxico, Delta, and Mexicana fly to Mérida.

Within the Yucatán, Aerocaribe serves Cancún, Cozumel, Mérida, Chichén Itzá, Palenque, Chetumal, and Playa del Carmen. Flight service from the new Kuau airport near Pisté connects to Palenque, Cancún, and Cozumel. Aeroméxico flies to Campeche and Ciudad del Carmen from Mexico City. Aviacsa serves Cancún, Chetumal, and Mérida.

➤ MAJOR AIRLINES: Aeroméxico (☎ 800/237–6639). American (☎ 800/433–7300). Continental (☎ 800/231–0856). Delta (☎ 800/221–1212). Mexicana (☎ 800/531–3585). Northwest (☎ 800/447–4747). TWA (☎ 800/892–4141). US Airways (☎ 800/428–4322).

➤ WITHIN THE YUCATÁN: Aerocaribe ☎ 998/884–2000; 55/5536–9046 in Mexico City). Aerocozumel ☎ 998/884–2000). Aeroméxico (☎ 800/021–2622; 55/5625– 2622 in Mexico City). Aviacsa (☎ 800/711–6733). Mexicana (☎ 800/502–2000; 55/5448–0990 in Mexico City).

CHECK-IN AND BOARDING

For domestic flights, arrive at the airport at least two hours before your scheduled departure time. For international flights, plan on arriving at the airport at least 3½ hours before departure, but be sure to ask your carrier whether it requires an earlier check-in. There are three departure terminals at Cancún airport. If you are flying to Mexico City to catch a connecting flight you will be leaving from the Domestic Departures Terminal. This is at the east end of the main terminal (also known as the International Departures Terminal). Regular flights leave from the main terminal. Charter flights leave from a separate terminal, ½ km (¼ mi) west of the main terminal. During peak season give yourself plenty of time to check in, as lines can be long and slow-

moving. Be sure to ask your airline about your check-in location and departure terminal.

Assuming that not everyone with a ticket will show up, airlines routinely overbook planes. When everyone does, airlines ask for volunteers to give up their seats. In return, these volunteers usually get a certificate for a free flight and are rebooked on the next flight out. If there are not enough volunteers, the airline must choose who will be denied boarding. The first to get bumped are passengers who checked in late and those flying on discounted tickets, so **get to the gate and check in as early as possible,** especially during peak periods.

Always **bring a government-issued photo ID to the airport;** even when it's not required, a passport is best.

CUTTING COSTS

The least expensive airfares to the Yucatán Peninsula are priced for round-trip travel and must usually be purchased in advance. Airlines generally allow you to change your return date for a fee; most low-fare tickets, however, are nonrefundable. It's smart to **call a number of airlines,** and when you are quoted a good price, **book it on the spot**—the same fare may not be available the next day. Always **check different routings** and look into using alternate airports. Also, price off-peak flights, which may be significantly less expensive than others. Travel agents, especially low-fare specialists (☞ Discounts and Deals, *below*), are helpful.

Consolidators are another good source. They buy tickets for scheduled international flights at reduced rates from the airlines, then sell them at prices that beat the best fare available directly from the airlines. Sometimes you can even get your money back if you need to return the ticket. Carefully read the fine print detailing penalties for changes and cancellations, purchase the ticket with a credit card, and **confirm your consolidator reservation with the airline.**

➤ CONSOLIDATORS: Cheap Tickets (☎ 800/377–1000 or 888/922–8849, WEB www.cheaptickets.com). Discount

Airline Ticket Service (☎ 800/576–1600). **Unitravel** (☎ 800/325–2222, WEB www.unitravel.com). **Up & Away Travel** (☎ 212/889–2345, WEB www.upandaway.com). **World Travel Network** (☎ 800/409–6753).

ENJOYING THE FLIGHT

State your seat preference when purchasing your ticket, and then repeat it when you confirm and when you check in. For more legroom, you can request one of the few emergency-aisle seats at check-in, if you are capable of lifting at least 50 pounds—a Federal Aviation Administration requirement of passengers in these seats. Seats behind a bulkhead also offer more legroom, but they don't have under-seat storage. Don't sit in the row in front of the emergency aisle or in front of a bulkhead, where seats may not recline.

Ask the airline whether a snack or meal is served on the flight. If you have dietary concerns, **request special meals when booking.** These can be vegetarian, low-cholesterol, or kosher, for example. It's a good idea to pack some healthy snacks and a small bottle (plastic) of water in your carry-on bag. On long flights, try to maintain a normal routine, to help fight jet lag. At night, **get some sleep.** By day, **eat light meals, drink water** (not alcohol), and **move around the cabin** to stretch your legs. For additional jet-lag tips consult *Fodor's FYI: Travel Fit & Healthy* (available at bookstores everywhere).

Smoking policies vary from carrier to carrier. Many airlines prohibit smoking on all of their international flights; others allow smoking only on certain routes or certain departures. Ask your carrier about its policy.

Many of the larger U.S. airlines no longer offer meals on flights to the Yucatán Peninsula. The flights are considered short-haul flights because there is a stopover at a hub airport (where you can purchase your own overpriced meals). The snacks provided on such flights are measly at best, so you may want to **bring food on board** with you. Aeroméxico and Mexicana both provide full meals. All flights aboard Mexican airlines are no-smoking.

FLYING TIMES

Cancún is 3½ hours from New York and Chicago, 4½ hours from Los Angeles, 3 hours from Dallas, 11¾ hours from London, and 18 hours from Sydney. Add another 1–4 hours if you change planes at one of the hub airports and have a long layover. Flights to Cozumel and Mérida are comparable in length.

HOW TO COMPLAIN

If your baggage goes astray or your flight goes awry, complain right away. Most carriers require that you **file a claim immediately.** The Aviation Consumer Protection Division of the Department of Transportation publishes *Fly-Rights*, which discusses airlines and consumer issues and is available on-line. At PassengerRights.com, a Web site, you can compose a letter of complaint and distribute it electronically.

➤ AIRLINE COMPLAINTS: **Aviation Consumer Protection Division** (✉ U.S. Department of Transportation, Room 4107, C-75, Washington, DC 20590, ☎ 202/366–2220, WEB www.dot.gov/airconsumer). **Federal Aviation Administration Consumer Hotline** (☎ 800/255–1111).

RECONFIRMING

Check the status of your flight before you leave for the airport. You can do this on your carrier's Web site, by linking to a flight-status checker (many Web booking services offer these), or by calling your carrier or travel agent. Always confirm international flights at least 72 hours ahead of the scheduled departure time, and call your airline closer to departure time to check for delays. This is especially important if you are flying on a charter, since they often have delays and sometimes cancellations. During the rainy season, high winds, tropical storms, or hurricane warnings can delay flights.

AIRPORTS

Cancún Airport (CUN) and **Cozumel Airport** (CZM) are the area's major gateways. The inland **Hector José Vavarrette Muñoz Airport** (MID), in Mérida, is good-size and closest to the major Maya ruins. Campeche, Chetumal, and Playa del Carmen have smaller airports served primarily by domestic carriers. The ruins at Palenque and Chichén Itzá also have airstrips that handle small planes.

Fly into the airport closest to where you'll be doing most of your travel. Airfares to Cancún, Mérida, and Cozumel don't differ much, and the airports serving these three are no more than 20 minutes from downtown. Car rentals are a bit less expensive in Mérida than in Cancún and Cozumel, but not enough to warrant a four-hour drive to Cancún if it's your hub.

➤ AIRPORT INFORMATION: **Cancún Airport** (☎ 998/886–0341). **Cozumel Airport** (☎ 987/872–0485). **Mérida Airport** (☎ 999/946–1340).

DUTY-FREE SHOPPING

Cancún and Cozumel are duty-free shopping zones with more variety and better prices than the duty-free shops at the airports.

BIKE TRAVEL

Bicycling in Mexico is a rough-and-ready proposition. Most roads lack shoulders, and drivers are not used to accommodating cyclists. Bikes are especially useful for travel off the beaten track. In Yucatán, where bikes are the primary form of transportation for locals, every small town has a bike-repair shop. Be sure to **carry plenty of water and everything you might need to repair your bike.** Pack extra patch kits; shards of glass often litter the roads. If you can take your bike apart and fold it up, buses will allow you to store it in the cargo space.

Your hotel can direct you to local rental agents. You may get a new mountain bike, but it is more likely that you'll get an ordinary bicycle, nothing glamorous or high-tech. Rentals start at about $30 per day. Helmets are not widely worn or available.

➤ BIKE MAPS: There are no bicycle maps published in Mexico, but road maps created by PEMEX and Guía Roji are available at *papelerías* (stationery stores), bookstores, newspaper stands, and department stores in Mexico.

BIKES IN FLIGHT

Most airlines accommodate bikes as luggage, provided they are dismantled and boxed; check with individual airlines about packing requirements. Airlines sell bike boxes, which are often free at bike shops, for about $15 (bike bags start at $100). International travelers often can substitute a bike for a piece of checked luggage at no charge; otherwise, the cost is about $100. Domestic and Canadian airlines charge $40–$80 each way.

BIKING RESOURCES

Latin America by Bike (Mountaineer Books), by Walter Sienko, provides information on biking opportunities in Mexico as well as Central and South America. *Bicycling Mexico* (Hunter Publishing Inc.), by Ericka Weisbroth and Eric Ellman, is the bible of bicyclists, complete with maps, color photos, historical information, and a kilometer-by-kilometer breakdown of every route possible. For a list of companies that run organized bike tours of Mexico, *see* Tours and Packages, *below.*

BOAT AND FERRY TRAVEL

The Yucatán is served by a number of ferries and boats, ranging from the efficient speedboats between Playa del Carmen and Cozumel to the more modest launches between Puerto Juárez, Punta Sam, and Isla Mujeres.

FARES AND SCHEDULES

Most carriers follow schedules, with the exception of boats going to the smaller, less-visited islands. However, departure times can vary with the weather and the number of passengers.

For specific fares and schedules, *see* Boat and Ferry Travel *in* the A to Z section in each chapter.

BUSINESS HOURS

In well-traveled places such as Cancún, Mérida, and Cozumel, businesses generally are open during posted hours. In more off-the-beaten-path areas, neighbors can tell you when the owner will return.

BANKS AND OFFICES

Banks are open weekdays 9–5. Some banks open on Saturday morning. Most banks will exchange money only until noon. Most businesses are open weekdays 9–2 and 4–7.

GAS STATIONS

Most gas stations are open 24 hours.

MUSEUMS AND SIGHTS

Most museums throughout Mexico are closed on Monday and open 8–5 the rest of the week. But it's best to call ahead or ask at your hotel. Hours of sights and attractions in this book are denoted by a clock icon, ☉.

PHARMACIES

Pharmacies in Cancún and Cozumel are usually open 8 AM–10 PM and stay open through the afternoon. More and more pharmacies in Campeche and the Yucatán are staying open during lunch. The big cities have at least one 24-hour pharmacy.

SHOPS

Stores in the tourist areas such as Cancún and Cozumel are usually open 10–9 Monday through Saturday and on Sunday afternoon. Shops in more traditional areas, such as Campeche and Mérida and the Yucatán, close weekdays between 1 PM and 4 PM, opening again in the evening. They are generally closed Sunday.

BUS TRAVEL

The Mexican bus network is extensive and also the best means of getting around, since passenger trains have just about become obsolete. Service is frequent and tickets can be purchased on the spot (except during holidays and on long weekends, when advance purchase is crucial). **Bring something to eat on long trips** in case you don't like the restaurant where the bus stops; **bring toilet tissue;** and **wear a sweater,** as the air-conditioning is often set on high. Most buses play videos or television continually until midnight, so if you are bothered by noise **bring earplugs.** Smoking is prohibited on a growing number of Mexican buses, though the rule is occasionally ignored.

CLASSES

Buses range from comfortable, fast, air-conditioned coaches with bathrooms, televisions, and complimentary beverages (*especial,* deluxe, and first-class) to dilapidated "vintage" buses (second-class), which stop at every village along the way and pick up anyone who flags them from the highway. On the more rural routes passengers will include chickens, pigs, or baby goats. A second-class bus ride can be interesting if you're not in a hurry and want to see the sights and experience the local culture. The fare is usually at least 20% cheaper. For comfort's sake alone, travelers planning a long-distance haul are advised to **buy first-class or *especial* tickets.** Several truly first-class bus companies offer service connecting Mexico's major cities. ADO (Autobuses del Oriente) is the Yucatán's principal first-class bus company.

For additional city-specific bus travel information, *see* Bus Travel *in* the A to Z sections in each chapter.

FARES AND SCHEDULES

Bus travel in the Yucatán, as throughout Mexico, is inexpensive by U.S. standards, with rates averaging $2–$5 per hour depending on the level of luxury (or not). Schedules are posted at bus stations; the bus leaves more or less around the listed time.

RESERVATIONS

Most bus tickets, including first-class or *especial* and second-class, can be reserved in advance in person at ticket offices. ADO (Autobuses del Oriente) allows you to reserve tickets 48 hours in advance over the Internet.

➤ BUS INFORMATION: **ADO** (☎ 01–800/702–8000; 998/884–5542; 999/925–0910 in Mérida; WEB www.adogl.com.mx).

CAMERAS
AND PHOTOGRAPHY

Don't snap pictures of military or high-security installations anywhere in the country. It's forbidden. Ask permission before taking pictures of indigenous people. The Maya are especially sensitive about photos. Don't miss photos of the ruins at Tulum and Chichén Itzá.

The *Kodak Guide to Shooting Great Travel Pictures* (available at bookstores everywhere) is loaded with tips.

➤ PHOTO HELP: **Kodak Information Center** (☎ 800/242–2424, WEB www.kodak.com).

EQUIPMENT PRECAUTIONS

Humidity and heat are problems for cameras in this region. Always **keep your camera, film, tape, and computer disks out of the sun.** Try to **keep sand out of your camera.** After a trip to the beach be sure to clean your lens, since salt air can leave a film on the lens and grains of sand may scratch it. Keep a special cleansing solution and cloth for this purpose. **Don't pack film and equipment in checked luggage,** where it is much more susceptible to damage. X-ray machines used to view checked luggage are becoming much more powerful and therefore are much more likely to ruin your film. Try to **ask for hand inspection of film,** which becomes clouded after repeated exposure to airport X-ray machines, and **keep videotapes and computer disks away from metal detectors.** Carry an extra supply of batteries, and **be prepared to turn on your camera, camcorder, or laptop** to prove to airport security personnel that the device is real.

FILM AND DEVELOPING

Film is widely available in Cancún, Cozumel, Playa del Carmen, Campeche City, and Mérida, and all have one-hour photo development places. (Check to see that all the negatives were developed into pictures; sometimes a few are missed.) Prices are a bit more expensive than those in the United States.

VIDEOS

The local standard for videotape in Mexico is the same as in the United States. All videos are NTSC (National Television Standards Committee). Prices are a bit more expensive than those in the United States, and videotapes for newer machines may be hard to find.

CAR RENTAL

An economy car with no air-conditioning, manual transmission, and unlimited mileage begins at $50 a day or about $300 a week in Cancún; in Mérida, rates are about $35 a day or $210 a week; and in Campeche, $30 a day or $200 a week. Count on about $10 a day more with air-conditioning and automatic transmission. This does not include tax, which is 10% in Cancún and on the Caribbean coast and 15% elsewhere. The most common and least-expensive brand of car here is the Volkswagen Beetle.

➤ MAJOR AGENCIES: **Alamo** (☎ 800/327–9633; WEB www.alamo.com). **Avis** (☎ 800/331–1212; 800/272–5871 in Canada; 02/9313–6333 in Australia; 0800/65–5111 in New Zealand; 0870/606–0100 in the U.K., WEB www.avis.com). **Budget** (☎ 800/527–0700; 044/1442/28–0181 in the U.K., WEB www.budget.com). **Dollar** (☎ 800/800–3665; 0800/085–4578 in the U.K., where it's affiliated with Sixt; 02/9223–1444 in Australia; WEB www.dollar.com). **Hertz** (☎ 800/654–3131; 800/263–0600 in Canada; 020/7026–0077 in the U.K.; 3/9698–2295 in Australia; 0800/654–321 in New Zealand; WEB www.hertz.com). **National Car Rental** (☎ 800/227–7368; 020/8680–4800 in the U.K.; WEB www.nationalcar.com).

CUTTING COSTS

For a good deal, **book through a travel agent who will shop around.**

Local car rental agencies often have specials, and you can sometimes arrange for discount rates after speaking with a manager. Go with the larger, more established companies though, as their cars are newer and serviced more regularly. Smaller operations often run a popular rental scam: you agree on a price (usually too good to pass up) and put the deposit on your credit card after filling out your hotel details. The next morning you'll find your car stolen by the rental company, who had a second set of keys. Of course this can't be proven, so the car is listed as stolen and under the terms of the contract you are responsible for the deposit. The car is painted a different color and rented again. So, be cautious if you want to rent from smaller companies, and don't give out your hotel details. If you're traveling during a holiday period, make sure that a confirmed reservation guarantees you a car.

Do **look into wholesalers,** companies that do not own fleets but rent in bulk from those that do and often offer better rates than traditional car-rental operations. Prices are best during off-peak periods. Rentals booked through wholesalers often must be paid for before you leave home.

➤ LOCAL AGENCIES: **Executive** (☎ 998/886–0065 in Cancún; 999/946–1387 in Mérida; WEB www.executive.com.mx). **Localiza** (☎ 998/887–3109 in Cancún; 999/923–2040 in Mérida; WEB www.localizarentacar.com). **Monaco** (☎ 998/884–7843 in Cancún, WEB www.monacorentacar.com). **Zipp Rent a Car** (☎ 998/883–2077 in Cancún).

➤ WHOLESALER: **Kemwel** (☎ 800/678–0678 or 800/576–1590, FAX 207/842–2124, WEB www.kemwel.com).

INSURANCE

When driving a rented car you are generally responsible for any damage to or loss of the vehicle. You may also be liable for any property damage or personal injury that you may cause while driving. Before you rent, see what coverage you already have under the terms of your personal auto-insurance policy and credit cards. Be sure to read your contract carefully and ask for an explanation of any terms you don't understand.

Regardless of any coverage afforded to you by your credit-card company, you must **obtain Mexican auto-liability insurance.** This is usually sold by car-rental agencies and included in the cost of the car. Be sure that you have been provided with proof of such insurance; if you drive without it, you are not only liable for damages, but you're also breaking the law. If you are in a car accident and you don't have insurance, you may be placed in jail until you are proven innocent. If anyone is injured you will remain in jail until you make retribution to all injured parties and their families. Mexican laws favor nationals.

REQUIREMENTS AND RESTRICTIONS

In Mexico your own driver's license is acceptable, but an International Driver's Permit (IDP) is a good idea. An international permit is valid only in conjunction with your regular driver's license and is universally recognized; having one may save you a problem with local authorities. It's available from the American and Canadian automobile associations and, in the United Kingdom, from the Automobile Association or Royal Automobile Club.

SURCHARGES

Before you pick up a car in one city and leave it in another, **ask about drop-off charges or one-way service fees,** which can be substantial. Note, too, that some rental agencies charge extra if you return the car before the time specified in your contract. To avoid a hefty refueling fee, **fill the tank just before you turn in the car,** but be aware that gas stations near the rental outlet may overcharge. It's almost never a good deal to buy the tank of gas in the car when you rent it; the understanding is that you'll return it empty, but some fuel usually remains. Usually the car rental is for only one person, and the charges for additional drivers start at $10 per day. If the name on the credit card used is different from the driver's then this should be noted on the contract.

CAR TRAVEL

Though convenient, cars are not a necessity in this part of Mexico. Cancún offers excellent bus and taxi service; Isla Mujeres is too small to make a car practical. Cars are not needed in Playa del Carmen because the downtown area is quite small and the main street is blocked off to vehicles. You will need a car in Cozumel only if you wish to explore the eastern side of the island. Cars are actually a burden in Mérida and Campeche City because of the narrow cobbled streets and the lack of parking spaces. Driving is the easiest way to explore other areas of the region, especially those off the beaten track. But even then a car is not absolutely necessary, as there is good bus service.

Before setting out on any car trip, **check your vehicle's fuel, oil, fluids, tires, and lights.** Gas stations and mechanics can be hard to find, especially in more remote areas. Consult a map and have your route in mind as you drive. Be aware that there is no formal driver's education in Mexico. This makes for many bad drivers on the roads who think nothing of tailgating, speeding, and weaving in and out of traffic. **Drive defensively** and keep your cool. When stopped for traffic or at a red light, always **leave sufficient room between your car and the one ahead** so you can maneuver to safety if necessary.

EMERGENCY SERVICES

The Mexican Tourism Ministry operates a fleet of some 350 pickup trucks, known as Angeles Verdes, or the Green Angels, to render assistance to motorists on the major highways. You can call the Green Angels directly or call the Ministry of Tourism's hot line and they will dispatch them. The bilingual drivers provide mechanical help, first aid, radio-telephone communication, basic supplies and small parts, towing, and tourist information. Services are free, and spare parts, fuel, and lubricants are provided at cost. Tips are always appreciated.

The Green Angels patrol fixed sections of the major highways twice daily 8 am to dusk, later on holiday weekends. If your car breaks down, **pull as far as possible off the road,** lift the hood, hail a passing vehicle, and ask the driver to **notify the patrol.** Most bus and truck drivers will be quite helpful. Do not accept rides from strangers. If you witness an accident, do not stop to help but instead find the nearest official.

➤ CONTACT: **Green Angels** (☎ 55/ 5250– 8221, 55/5250–4637, 55/ 5250–8555 ext. 314; 800/903–9200 Ministry of Tourism hot line).

GASOLINE

PEMEX, Mexico's government-owned petroleum monopoly, franchises all gas stations, so prices throughout the Yucatán are the same. Prices tend to be about 30% higher than those in the United States; some stations in Mexico accept U.S. dollars and credit cards. Unleaded fuel, known as Magna Premio and Magna Sin (lower octane), is available at most PEMEX stations. There are no self-service stations in Mexico. When you have your tank filled, **ask for a specific amount in pesos** to avoid being overcharged. Check to make sure that the attendant has set the meter back to zero and that the price is shown. Watch the attendant check the oil as well—to make sure you actually need

it—and watch while he pours it into your car. **Never pay before** the gas is pumped, even if the attendant asks you to. Always **tip your attendant** a few pesos. Finally, **keep your gas tank full,** because gas stations are not plentiful in this area. If you run out of gas in a small village and there's no gas station for miles, ask if there is a local store that sells gas from containers.

PARKING

Always **park your car in a parking lot,** or at least in a populated area. Never leave anything of value in an unattended car. There is usually a parking attendant available, who will watch your car for a few pesos. Sometimes there are attendants who will wash your car and keep an eye on it for about $2.

ROAD CONDITIONS

The road system in the Yucatán Peninsula is extensive and generally in good repair. Route 307 parallels most of the Caribbean coast from Punta Sam, north of Cancún, to Tulum; here it turns inward for a stretch before returning to the coast at Chetumal and the Belize border. Route 180 runs west from Cancún to Valladolid, Chichén Itzá, and Mérida, then turns southwest to Campeche, Isla del Carmen, and on to Villahermosa. From Mérida, the winding, more scenic Route 261 also leads to some of the more off-the-beaten-track archaeological sites on the way south to Campeche and Francisco Escárcega, where it joins Route 186 going east to Chetumal. These highways are two-lane roads. Route 295 (from the north coast to Valladolid and Felipe Carrillo Puerto) is also a good two-lane road.

The *autopista,* or *carretera de cuota,* a four-lane toll highway between Cancún and Mérida, was completed in 1993. It runs roughly parallel to Route 180 and cuts driving time between Cancún and Mérida— otherwise about 4½ hours—by about 1 hour. Tolls between Mérida and Cancún can run as high as $24, and the stretches between highway exits are long. Be careful when driving on this road, as it retains the heat from the sun and can make your tires blow if they have low pressure or worn threads.

Many secondary roads are in bad condition—unpaved, unmarked, and full of potholes. If you must take one of these roads, the best course is to **allow plenty of daylight hours and never travel at night.** Slow down when approaching towns and villages—which you are forced to do by the *topes* (speed bumps)—because small children and animals are everywhere. Children selling oranges, nuts, or other food will almost certainly approach your car. Some people feel that it's best not to buy from them, reasoning that if the children can make money this way, they will not go to school. Others choose to buy from them on the theory that they would probably go to school if they could afford it and need the meager profits to survive. Judge for yourself.

ROAD MAPS

Maps published by PEMEX are available in bookstores and *papelerías* (stationery stores), but gas stations don't sell them.

RULES OF THE ROAD

Mileage and speed limits are given in kilometers. One kilometer is approximately %0 mi. In small towns, observe the posted speed limits, which can be as low as 20 kph (12 mph). To make a left turn on the highway, move over to the right shoulder of the road, turn your left blinker on, wait for all the traffic to pass you, and then make your turn. Be aware that drunk driving is not a crime in Mexico. **Do not drive late at night even on good roads.**

If you are stopped for speeding or other traffic violations, the police officer will say he wants to take your license or license plates to hold until you pay a fine at the local police station. This is only a ploy that involves a time-wasting trip to the station. What he really wants is to have you pay the "fine" on the spot. This is actually a small bribe, called a *mordida* (literally, "a bite"); police salaries are quite low in Mexico and this is how many officers support themselves. If you are in a hurry, pay the fine, which may be as little as $10 to $20. If you decide to dispute the charge, do so with a smile (getting angry only makes things worse) and say that you'd like to give the fine to the police captain. The officer is likely to let you go rather than go to the station.

CHILDREN IN THE YUCATÁN PENINSULA

Traveling with children opens doors in Mexico that often remain closed to single travelers. If they enjoy travel in general, your children will do well throughout the Yucatán.

If you are renting a car, don't forget to **arrange for a car seat** when you reserve. For general advice about traveling with children, consult *Fodor's FYI: Travel with Your Baby* (available in bookstores everywhere).

FLYING

If your children are two or older, **ask about children's airfares.** As a general rule, infants under two not occupying a seat fly at greatly reduced fares or even for free. When booking, **confirm carry-on allowances** if you're traveling with infants. In general, for babies charged 10% of the adult fare you are allowed one carry-on bag and a collapsible stroller; if the flight is full, the stroller may have to be checked or you may be limited to less.

Experts agree that it's a good idea to use safety seats aloft for children weighing less than 40 pounds. Airlines set their own policies: U.S. carriers usually require that the child be ticketed, even if he or she is young enough to ride free, since the seats must be strapped into regular seats. Do **check your airline's policy about using safety seats during takeoff and landing.** Safety seats are not allowed everywhere in the plane, so get your seat assignments as early as possible.

When reserving, **request children's meals or a freestanding bassinet** (not available at all airlines) if you need them. But note that bulkhead seats, where you must sit to use the bassinet, may lack an overhead bin or storage space on the floor.

FOOD

The more populated areas, such as Cancún, Mérida, Campeche City, Cozumel, and Playa del Carmen, have U.S. fast-food outlets, and most restaurants that serve tourists have a special children's menu with the usual chicken fingers, hot dogs, and spaghetti. Yucatecan cuisine also has plenty of dishes suited for children's taste buds. It's common for parents to share a plate with their children, so no one will look twice if you order one meal with two plates.

LODGING

Most hotels in the Yucatán Peninsula allow children under 12 to stay in their parents' room at no extra charge, but others charge for them as extra adults; be sure to **find out the cutoff age for children's discounts.** Most of the chain hotels offer services that make it easier to travel with children. These include connecting family rooms, wading pools and playgrounds, and kid's clubs with special activities and outings. Check with your hotel before booking to see if the price includes the services you're interested in.

➤ BEST CHOICES: **Fiesta Americana Mérida** (✉ Av. Colóon 451, at Paseo Montejo, 97000 Mérida, ☎ 999/942–1111 or 800/343–7821, WEB www.fiestaamerican.com). **Gran Caribe Real Club** (✉ Blvd. Kukulcán, Km 5.5, 77500 Cancún, ☎ 998/881–7300, WEB www.real.com.mx). **Reef Club** (✉ Carretera a Progreso Telchac, Km 32, Telchac Puerto, 97320, ☎ 999/920–4466, WEB www.interclubresorts.com).

PRECAUTIONS

Mexico has one of the strictest policies about children entering the country. All children up to 18 years of age, including infants, are considered minors and must have proof of citizenship. If the child is traveling alone, he or she must have a notarized consent form signed by both parents. Airlines also require the name, address, and telephone number of the person meeting the unaccompanied minor upon arrival in Mexico. Children traveling with one parent must also have a notarized letter from the other parent stating that the child has his or her permission to leave the home country. If the other parent is deceased or the child has only one legal parent, a notarized statement to this effect must be presented. Parents must fill out a tourist card for each child over 10 years of age traveling with them.

Since children are particularly prone to diarrhea, be especially careful with their food and beverages. Peel all fruits, cook vegetables, and stay away from ice unless it comes from a reliable source. Ice cream from vendors should also be avoided. Infants and young children may be bothered by the heat and sun; make sure they drink plenty of fluids, wear sunscreen, and stay out of the sun at midday (☞ Health, *below*).

SIGHTS AND ATTRACTIONS

The larger tourist areas have plenty of activities for children, including museums, zoos, aquariums, and theme parks. Places that are especially appealing to children are indicated by a rubber-duckie icon (☺) in the margin.

SUPPLIES AND EQUIPMENT

Fresh milk is hard to find—most of the milk sold here is reconstituted. Most other necessities, including *pañales desechables* (disposable diapers) and *fórmula infantil* (infant formula), can be found in almost every small town.

COMPUTERS ON THE ROAD

Before you plug in your computer in Mexico, invest in a Mexican surge protector, available at most electronics stores for about $45. The country experiences frequent surges and brown-outs (periods of diminished electrical power), and surge protectors used in the United States and in Canada are not effective here.

CONSUMER PROTECTION

If you are paying with a credit card, watch that your card goes through the machine only once. If there is an error and a new slip needs to be done make sure the original is destroyed before your eyes. Another favorite scam is to ask you to wait while the clerk runs next door to use their phone or verify your number. Often they are making extra copies. Don't let your card leave the store without you.

Whether you're shopping for gifts or purchasing travel services, **pay with a major credit card** whenever possible, so you can cancel payment or get reimbursed if there's a problem (and you can provide documentation). If you're doing business with a particular company for the first time, **contact your local Better Business Bureau and the attorney general's offices** in your state and (for U.S. businesses) the company's home state as well. Have any complaints been filed? Finally, if you're buying a package or tour, always **consider travel insurance** that includes default coverage (☞ Insurance, *below*).

The Mexican consumer protection agency, the Procuraduría Federal de Consumidor (PROFECO), also helps foreigners.

➤ BBBs: **Council of Better Business Bureaus** (✉ 4200 Wilson Blvd., Suite 800, Arlington, VA 22203, ☎ 703/276–0100, FAX 703/525–8277, WEB www.bbb.org). **Procuraduría Federal de Consumidor (PROFECO)** (☎ 998/884–2634 in Cancún, 55/5547–1084 in Mexico City).

CRUISE TRAVEL

Cozumel and Playa del Carmen have become increasingly popular ports for Caribbean cruises. Royal Caribbean and Norwegian cruise lines depart from Miami. Lines with Caribbean cruises stopping in the Yucatán from other Florida ports (principally Fort Lauderdale, Port Manatee, and Tampa) include Cunard, Norwegian, Princess, Regal, and Royal. Commodore and Holland America depart from New Orleans; Royal Olimpic leaves from Galveston, Texas.

To learn how to plan, choose, and book a cruise-ship voyage, consult *Fodor's FYI: Plan & Enjoy Your Cruise* (available in bookstores everywhere).

➤ CRUISE LINES: **Commodore** (☎ 800/237–5361). **Cunard** (☎ 800/221–4770). **Holland America** (☎ 800/426–0327). **Norwegian** (☎ 800/327–7030). **Princess** (☎ 800/421–0522). **Regal** (☎ 800/270–7245). **Royal** (☎ 800/227–4534). **Royal Caribbean** (☎ 800/327–6700). **Royal Olimpic** (☎ 800/872–6400).

DISCOUNT CRUISES

Usually, the best deals on cruise bookings can be found by consulting a cruise-only travel agency.

➤ AGENCY: **National Association of Cruise Only Travel Agencies** (NACOA; ✉ 3191 Coral Way, Suite 622, Miami, FL 33145, ☎ 305/446–7732, FAX 305/446–9732).

CUSTOMS AND DUTIES

When shopping abroad, **keep receipts** for all purchases. Upon reentering the country, **be ready to show customs officials what you've bought.** If you feel a duty is incorrect, appeal the assessment. If you object to the way your clearance was handled, note the inspector's badge number. In either case, first ask to see a supervisor. If the problem isn't resolved, write to the appropriate authorities, beginning with the port director at your point of entry.

It is illegal to bring tortoiseshell into the United States and several other countries. There are also some restrictions regarding black coral; to bring it into the United States you must present a certificate that shows it was purchased from a recognized dealer.

IN AUSTRALIA

Australian residents who are 18 or older may bring home A$400 worth of souvenirs and gifts (including jewelry), 250 cigarettes or 250 grams of tobacco, and 1,125 ml of alcohol (including wine, beer, and spirits). Residents under 18 may bring back A$200 worth of goods. Prohibited items include meat products. Seeds, plants, and fruits need to be declared upon arrival.

➤ INFORMATION: **Australian Customs Service** (Regional Director, ✉ Box 8, Sydney, NSW 2001; ☎ 02/9213–2000 or 1300/363263; 1800/020504 quarantine-inquiry line; FAX 02/9213–4043; WEB www.customs.gov.au).

IN CANADA

Canadian residents who have been out of Canada for at least seven days may bring in C$750 worth of goods duty-free. If you've been away fewer than seven days but more than 48 hours, the duty-free allowance drops to C$200; if your trip lasts 24 to 48 hours, the allowance is C$50. You may not pool allowances with family members. Goods claimed under the C$750 exemption may follow you by mail; those claimed under the lesser exemptions must accompany you. Alcohol and tobacco products may be included in the seven-day and 48-hour exemptions but not in the 24-hour exemption. If you meet the age requirements of the province or territory through which you reenter Canada, you may bring in, duty-free, 1.5 liters of wine or 1.14 liters (40 imperial ounces) of liquor or 24 12-ounce cans or bottles of beer or ale. If you are 19 or older you may bring in, duty-free, 200 cigarettes and 50 cigars. Check ahead of time with the Canada Customs and Revenue Agency or the Department of Agriculture for policies regarding meat products, seeds, plants, and fruits.

You may send an unlimited number of gifts (only one gift per recipient, however) worth up to C$60 each duty-free to Canada. Label the package UNSOLICITED GIFT—VALUE UNDER $60. Alcohol and tobacco are excluded.

➤ INFORMATION: **Canada Customs and Revenue Agency** (✉ 2265 St. Laurent Blvd. S, Ottawa, Ontario K1G 4K3, ☎ 204/983–3500 or 506/636–5064; 800/461–9999, WEB www. ccra-adrc.gc.ca/).

IN NEW ZEALAND

All homeward-bound residents may bring back NZ$700 worth of souvenirs and gifts; passengers may not pool their allowances, and children can claim only the concession on goods intended for their own use. For those 17 or older, the duty-free allowance also includes 4.5 liters of wine or beer; one 1,125-ml bottle of spirits; and either 200 cigarettes, 250 grams of tobacco, 50 cigars, or a combination of the three up to 250 grams. Meat products, seeds, plants, and fruits must be declared upon arrival to the Agricultural Services Department.

➤ INFORMATION: **New Zealand Customs** (Head office: ✉ The Customhouse, 17–21 Whitmore St., Box 2218, Wellington, ☎ 09/300–5399 or 0800/428–786, WEB www.customs. govt.nz.

IN THE U.K.

From countries outside the European Union, including Mexico, you may bring home, duty-free, 200 cigarettes or 50 cigars; 1 liter of spirits or 2 liters of fortified or sparkling wine or liqueurs; 2 liters of still table wine; 60 ml of perfume; 250 ml of toilet water; plus £145 worth of other goods, including gifts and souvenirs. Prohibited items include meat products, seeds, plants, and fruits.

➤ INFORMATION: **HM Customs and Excise** (✉ Portcullis House, 21 Cowbridge Rd. E, Cardiff CF11 9SS, ☎ 029/2038–6423 or 0845/010–9000, WEB www.hmce.gov.uk).

IN THE U.S.

U.S. residents who have been out of the country for at least 48 hours (and who have not used the $400 allowance or any part of it in the past 30 days) may bring home $400 worth of foreign goods duty-free; the duty-free allowance drops to $200 for fewer than 48 hours.

U.S. residents 21 and older may bring back 1 liter of alcohol duty-free. In addition, regardless of your age, you are allowed 200 cigarettes and 100 non-Cuban cigars. Antiques, which the U.S. Customs Service defines as objects more than 100 years old, enter duty-free, as do original works of art done entirely by hand, including paintings, drawings, and sculptures. You may also send packages home duty-free, with a limit of one parcel per addressee per day (except alcohol or tobacco products or perfume worth more than $5). You can mail up to $200 worth of goods for personal use; label the package PERSONAL USE and attach a list of its contents and their retail value. If the package contains your used personal belongings, mark it PERSONAL GOODS RETURNED to avoid paying duties. You may send up to $100 worth of goods as a gift; mark the package UNSOLICITED GIFT. Mailed items do not affect your duty-free allowance on your return.

➤ INFORMATION: **U.S. Customs Service** (for inquiries, ✉ 1300 Pennsylvania Ave. NW, Washington, DC 20229, WEB www.customs.gov, ☎ 202/354–1000; for complaints, ✉ Customer Satisfaction Unit, 1300 Pennsylvania Ave. NW, Room 5.5A, Washington, DC 20229; for registration of equipment, ✉ Office of Passenger Programs, 1300 Pennsylvania Ave. NW, Room 5.4D, Washington, DC 20229, ☎ 202/927–0530).

IN THE YUCATÁN PENINSULA

Entering Mexico, you may bring in personal items needed for your stay, along with: 400 cigarettes or 50 cigars (if you are over 18); one photographic camera and one nonprofessional film or video camera and 12 rolls of film for each; up to 20 cassettes or CDs; medicine for personal use; one personal laptop computer; camera equipment; sports equipment for personal use (golf clubs, scuba gear, a bicycle); and gift items not exceeding a combined value of $300. You are not allowed to bring meat, vegetables, plants, fruit, or flowers into Mexico. Contact the Mexican Consulate for current restrictions and requirements for bringing pets into the country.

➤ INFORMATION: **Los Angeles** (Mexican Consulate: ✉ 2401 W. 6th St., Los Angeles, CA 90057, ☎ 231/351–6800, FAX 213/389–9249, WEB www.consulmex-la.com). **New York** (Mexican Consulate: ✉ 27 E. 39th St., New York, NY 10016, ☎ 212/217–6400, FAX 212/217–6493, WEB www.consulmexny.com).

DINING

The restaurants we list are the cream of the crop in each price category. Properties indicated by an ✕🖼 are lodging establishments whose restaurant warrants a special trip.

MEALS AND SPECIALTIES

Desayuno can be either a breakfast sweet roll and coffee or milk or a full breakfast of an egg dish such as *huevos a la mexicana* (scrambled eggs with chopped tomato, onion, and chilies), *huevos rancheros* (fried eggs on a tortilla covered with tomato sauce), or *huevos con jamón* (scrambled eggs with ham), plus juice and tortillas. Lunch is called *comida* or *almuerzo* and is the biggest meal of the day. Traditional businesses close down between 2 PM and 4 PM for this meal. It usually includes soup, a main

dish, and dessert. Regional specialties include *pan de cazón* (baby shark shredded and layered with tortilla and tomato sauce), in Campeche; *pollo pibíl* (chicken marinated in sour orange and baked in banana leaves), in Mérida; and *tikinchic* (fish in a sour-orange sauce), on the coast. Restaurants in tourist areas also serve American-style food such as hamburgers, pizza, and pasta. The lighter evening meal is called *cena*.

MEALTIMES

Most restaurants are open daily for lunch and dinner during high season (December–April), but hours tend to be more erratic during the rest of the year. It's always a good idea to **phone ahead.**

Unless otherwise noted, the restaurants listed in this guide are open daily for lunch and dinner.

PAYING

Most small restaurants do not accept credit cards. Larger chain restaurants and those catering to tourists take credit cards, but their prices reflect the fee placed on all credit-card transactions.

RESERVATIONS AND DRESS

Reservations are always a good idea; we mention them only when they're essential or not accepted. Book as far ahead as you can, and reconfirm as soon as you arrive. (Large parties should always call ahead to check the reservations policy.) We mention dress only when men are required to wear a jacket or a jacket and tie.

WINE, BEER, AND SPIRITS

Almost all restaurants in the region serve beer and some also offer wine. Larger restaurants have beer, wine, and spirits. You pay more for imported liquor such as vodka, brandy, and whiskey; tequila and rum are less expensive. Small lunch places called *loncherias* don't sell liquor, but you can bring your own as long as you are discreet. Almost all corner stores sell beer and tequila; grocery stores carry all brands of beer, wine, and spirits. Liquor stores are rare and usually carry specialty items. You must be 18 to buy liquor, but this rule is often overlooked.

DISABILITIES
AND ACCESSIBILITY

For people with disabilities, traveling in the Yucatán can be both challenging and rewarding. Travelers with mobility impairments used to venturing out on their own should not be surprised if locals try to prevent them from doing things. This is mainly out of concern; most Mexican families take complete care of relatives who use wheelchairs, so the general public is not accustomed to such independence. Additionally, very few places in the Yucatán have handrails, let alone special facilities and means of access. Although some of the newer hotels are accessible to wheelchairs, not even Cancún offers wheelchair-accessible transportation. Knowing how to ask for assistance is extremely important. If you are not fluent in Spanish, be sure to **take along a pocket dictionary.** Travelers with vision impairments who have no knowledge of Spanish probably need a translator; people with hearing impairments who are comfortable using body language usually get along very well.

LODGING

Le Meridien in Cancún, the Presidente Inter-Continental Cozumel, and the Fiesta Americana Mérida are the only truly wheelchair-accessible hotels in the region. Individual arrangements must be made with other hotels.

➤ BEST CHOICES: **Fiesta Americana Mérida** (✉ Av. Colón 451, at Paseo Montejo, 97000 Mérida, Yúcatan, ☎ 999/942–1111 or 800/343–7821, WEB www.fiestaamericana.com). **Le Meridien** (✉ Retorno Del Rey, Lote 37, 77500 Cancún, Quintana Roo, ☎ 998/881–2200 or 800/543–4300, WEB www.meridiencancun.com.mx). **Presidente Inter-Continental Cozumel** (✉ Carretera Chankanaab, Km 6.5, 77600 Cozumel, Quintana Roo, ☎ 987/872–0322 or 800/327–0200, WEB www.interconti.com).

RESERVATIONS

When discussing accessibility with an operator or reservations agent, **ask hard questions.** Are there any stairs, inside *or* out? Are there grab bars next to the toilet *and* in the shower/tub? How wide is the doorway to the room? To the bathroom? For the most extensive facilities meeting the latest legal specifications, **opt for newer accommodations.** If you reserve through a toll-free number, consider also calling the hotel's local number to confirm the information from the central reservations office. Get confirmation in writing when you can.

SIGHTS AND ATTRACTIONS

Few beaches, ruins, and sites around the Yucatán are accessible for people who use wheelchairs. The most accessible museums are found in Mérida (although there are stairs and no ramp) and in Cancún. Xcaret is wheelchair accessible; special transport is available but must be arranged in advance.

TRANSPORTATION

There isn't any special transportation for travelers who use wheelchairs. Public buses are simply out of the question, there are no special buses, and some taxi drivers are not comfortable helping travelers with disabilities. Have your hotel arrange for a cab.

➤ COMPLAINTS: **Aviation Consumer Protection Division** (☞ Air Travel, *above*) for airline-related problems. **Departmental Office of Civil Rights** (for general inquiries, ✉ U.S. Department of Transportation, S-30, 400 7th St. SW, Room 10215, Washington, DC 20590, ☎ 202/366–4648, FAX 202/366–3571, WEB www.dot.gov/ost/docr/index.htm). **Disability Rights Section** (✉ NYAV, U.S. Department of Justice, Civil Rights Division, 950 Pennsylvania Ave. NW, Washington, DC 20530; ☎ ADA information line 202/514–0301, 800/514–0301, 202/514–0383 TTY, 800/514–0383 TTY, WEB www.usdoj.gov/crt/ada/adahom1.htm).

TRAVEL AGENCIES

In the United States, the Americans with Disabilities Act requires that travel firms serve the needs of all travelers. Some agencies specialize in working with people with disabilities.

➤ TRAVELERS WITH MOBILITY PROBLEMS: **Access Adventures** (✉ 206 Chestnut Ridge Rd., Scottsville, NY

14624, ☎ 716/889–9096, dltravel@
prodigy.net), run by a former physical-
rehabilitation counselor. **CareVaca-
tions** (⊠ No. 5, 5110–50 Ave., Leduc,
Alberta T9E 6V4, Canada, ☎ 780/
986–6404 or 877/478–7827, FAX 780/
986–8332, WEB www.carevacations.
com), for group tours and cruise
vacations. **Flying Wheels Travel**
(⊠ 143 W. Bridge St., Box 382,
Owatonna, MN 55060, ☎ 507/451–
5005, FAX 507/451–1685, WEB www.
flyingwheelstravel.com).

DISCOUNTS AND DEALS

Be a smart shopper and **compare all
your options** before making decisions.
A plane ticket bought with a promotional coupon from travel clubs,
coupon books, and direct-mail offers
or on the Internet may not be cheaper
than the least expensive fare from a
discount ticket agency. And always
keep in mind that what you get is just
as important as what you save.

DISCOUNT RESERVATIONS

To save money, **look into discount
reservations services** with Web sites
and toll-free numbers, which use their
buying power to get a better price on
hotels, airline tickets, even car rentals.
When booking a room, always **call
the hotel's local toll-free number** (if
one is available) rather than the
central reservations number—you'll
often get a better price. Always ask
about special packages or corporate
rates.

When shopping for the best deal on
hotels and car rentals, **look for guar-
anteed exchange rates,** which protect
you against a falling dollar. With your
rate locked in, you won't pay more,
even if the price goes up in the local
currency.

➤ AIRLINE TICKETS: ☎ **800/AIR–
4LESS.**

➤ HOTEL ROOMS: **Turbotrip.com** (☎
800/473–7829, WEB www.turbotrip.
com).

PACKAGE DEALS

Don't confuse packages and guided
tours. When you buy a package, you
travel on your own, just as though
you had planned the trip yourself.
Fly-drive packages, which combine
airfare and car rental, are often a
good deal.

ECOTOURISM

Turtle-nesting beaches in Cozumel,
Isla Mujeres, and along the Caribbean
coast are protected areas from June to
August, when the females come
ashore to lay their eggs. In September
and October special care must be
taken while driving; this is when the
blue crabs migrate from the mangroves down to the ocean to lay their
eggs, crossing the highways and roads
on their journey. Always, when camping, be considerate of the environment by packing up your garbage,
burying your waste, and following
the rules as you would in your native
country.

ELECTRICITY

Electrical converters are not necessary, because Mexico operates on the
60-cycle, 120-volt system; however,
many outlets have not been updated
to accommodate three-prong and
polarized plugs (those with one larger
prong), so **bring an adapter.** When in
Mexico **purchase a surge protector**
for valuable electronic equipment
such as computers and stereos.

EMBASSIES

➤ AUSTRALIA: **Australian Embassy**
(⊠ Rubén Darío 55, Col. Polanco,
11560 Mexico City, ☎ 55/5531–
5225 information; 55/5905–407–
1698 emergencies, FAX 55/5203–8431,
WEB www.dfat.gov.au).

➤ CANADA: **Canadian Embassy**
(⊠ Calle Schiller 529, Col. Bosques
de Chapultepec, 11560 Mexico City,
☎ 55/5724–7900, FAX 55/5724–7980,
WEB www.canada.org.mx).

➤ NEW ZEALAND: **New Zealand
Embassy** (⊠ José Luis Lagrange,
Col. Polanco, 11510 Mexico City,
☎ 55/5283–9460, FAX 55/5283–9480,
WEB www.nzemb.org).

➤ UNITED KINGDOM: **U.K. Embassy**
(⊠ Río Lerma 71, Col. Cuauhtémoc,
06500 Mexico City, ☎ 55/5207–
2089, 55/5207–2593, or 55/5207–
2449, FAX 55/5242–8517, WEB www.
embajadabritanica.com.mx).

➤ UNITED STATES: **U.S. Embassy**
(⊠ Paseo de la Reforma 305, Col.
Cuauhtémoc, 06500 Mexico City,
☎ 55/5080–2000, FAX 55/5511–9980,
WEB www.usembassy-mexico.gov).

EMERGENCIES

It's helpful, albeit daunting, to know ahead of time that you're not protected by the laws of your native land once you're on Mexican soil. However, if you get into a scrape with the law, you can call the Citizens' Emergency Center in the United States. In Mexico, you can also call the 24-hour English-speaking hot line of the Mexican Ministry of Tourism (SECTUR). The hot line can provide immediate assistance as well as general, nonemergency guidance. **In an emergency, call 06 from any phone.**

➤ CONTACTS: **Air Ambulance America of Mexico** (☎ 01–800/222–3564). **Air Evac** (☎ 800/ 421–6111), in the United States. **Citizens' Emergency Center** (☎ 202/647–5226), in the United States. **Mexican Ministry of Tourism** (SECTUR; ☎ 01–800/903–9200 or 800/482–9832). **Procuraduría de Protección al Turista** (Attorney General for the Protection of Tourists; ☎ 55/5625–8153 in Mexico City, 800/482–9832 from the U.S.).

ENGLISH-LANGUAGE MEDIA

BOOKS

There are very few English-language bookstores in the region, but Puerto Morelos and Isla Mujeres both have well-stocked stores. Mérida has bookstores with small sections in English plus an English-language library. English-language books and magazines can be found at the bookstores and also at some of the larger grocery stores, but the publications are expensive.

NEWSPAPERS AND MAGAZINES

Mexico has two major English-language newspapers, the *Mexico City Times* and the *News*. The latter is the larger of the two and contains the most complete coverage of local and international news, sports, and cultural events. Both are rather conservative in their politics. The *Miami Herald* publishes a Cancún edition with little news and lots of advertising for Xcaret.

RADIO AND TELEVISION

There are no English-language radio stations except those picked up by shortwave radio. But Mexico is well served by cable and satellite TV; for example, Direct TV offers more than 500 (mostly English-language) stations.

ETIQUETTE AND BEHAVIOR

In the United States, being direct, efficient, and succinct are highly valued traits. In Mexico, where communication tends to be more diplomatic and subtle, this style is often perceived as rude and aggressive. People will be far less helpful if you lose your temper and/or complain loudly, as such behavior is considered impolite. Remember that things move at a much slower rate here. There is no stigma attached to being late. Try to accept this pace gracefully. Learning basic phrases such as *por favor* (please) and *gracias* (thank you) in Spanish will make a big difference.

BUSINESS ETIQUETTE

Business etiquette is much more formal and traditional in Mexico than in the United States. Personal relationships always come first, so developing rapport and trust is essential. A handshake is an appropriate greeting, along with a friendly inquiry about family members. With established clients, do not be surprised if you are welcomed with a kiss on the check or full hug with a pat on the back. Mexicans love business cards—be sure to present yours in any business situation. Without a business card you may have trouble being taken seriously. In public always be respectful of colleagues and keep confrontations private. Meetings may or may not start on time, so remain patient with delays. When invited to dinner at the home of a customer or business associate, it's not necessary to bring a gift.

GAY AND LESBIAN TRAVEL

Gender roles in Mexico are rigidly defined, especially in rural areas. Openly gay couples are a rare sight, and two people of the same gender may have trouble getting a *cama matrimonial* (double bed) at hotels. All travelers, regardless of sexual orientation, should be extra cautious when frequenting gay-friendly venues, as police sometimes violently crash these clubs, and there's little recourse or sympathy available to victims. The companies below can help answer your questions about safety and travel to the Yucatán.

➤ GAY- AND LESBIAN-FRIENDLY TRAVEL AGENCIES: **Different Roads Travel** (✉ 8383 Wilshire Blvd., Suite 902, Beverly Hills, CA 90211, ☎ 323/651–5557 or 800/429–8747, FAX 323/651–3678, lgernert@tzell.com). **Kennedy Travel** (✉ 314 Jericho Turnpike, Floral Park, NY 11001, ☎ 516/352–4888 or 800/237–7 433, FAX 516/354–8849, WEB www.kennedytravel.com). **Now Voyager** (✉ 4406 18th St., San Francisco, CA 94114, ☎ 415/626–1169 or 800/255–6951, FAX 415/626–8626, WEB www.nowvoyager.com). **Skylink Travel and Tour** (✉ 1006 Mendocino Ave., Santa Rosa, CA 95401, ☎ 707/546–9888 or 800/225–5759, FAX 707/546–9891, WEB www.skylinktravel.com, serving lesbian travelers.

GUIDEBOOKS

Plan well and you won't be sorry. Guidebooks are excellent tools—and you can take them with you. You may want to check out color-photo-illustrated *Fodor's Exploring Mexico,* which is thorough on culture and history. It's available at on-line retailers and bookstores everywhere.

HEALTH

Medical clinics in all the main tourist areas have English-speaking personnel. Many of the doctors in Cancún have studied in Miami and speak English fluently. You will pay much higher prices than average for the services of English-speaking doctors or for clinics catering to tourists. Campeche and the more rural areas have few doctors who speak English.

DIVERS' ALERT

Do not fly within 24 hours of scuba diving.

FOOD AND DRINK

In the Yucatán, the major health risk is posed by the contamination of drinking water, fresh fruit, and vegetables by fecal matter, which causes the intestinal ailment known as *turista,* or traveler's diarrhea. Bad shellfish can also be a culprit. To prevent

such unpleasant interruptions to your vacation, **watch what you eat** and **always wash your hands before eating.** Stay away from ice, uncooked food, seafood that may not have been refrigerated, and unpasteurized milk and milk products, and **drink only bottled water or water that has been boiled** for several minutes. When ordering cold drinks at untouristed establishments, skip the ice—ask for your beverage *sin hielo.* (You can usually identify ice made commercially from purified water by its uniform shape and the hole in the center.) Hotels with water-purification systems post signs to that effect in the rooms. For mild cases of *turista,* try Pepto-Bismol. Drink plenty of purified water or tea; chamomile tea (*te de manzanilla,* which is readily available in restaurants throughout Mexico) is a good folk remedy for soothing the stomach. Try the BRAT diet (bananas, rice, applesauce, and dry toast). In severe cases, rehydrate yourself with a Gatorade drink or a salt-sugar solution. For children there is a special rehydrating formula available at all pharmacies. If you suspect food poisoning, see a local doctor immediately. If diarrhea persists for more than two days, see one of the local doctors. Take Lomotil or Imodium (loperamide), an antidiarrheal agent that dulls or eliminates abdominal cramps, if you must travel. Otherwise, it's often better to let the illness run its course.

Hangovers, caused by overindulgence of Mexican beer and tequila, can also be mistaken for turista. if you have been drinking give yourself one day to recover before assuming you have turista.

MEDICAL PLANS

No one plans to get sick while traveling, but it happens, so **consider signing up with a medical-assistance company.** Members get doctor referrals, emergency evacuation or repatriation, hot lines for medical consultation, cash for emergencies, and other assistance.

➤ MEDICAL-ASSISTANCE COMPANY: **International SOS Assistance** (✉ 8 Neshaminy Interplex, Suite 207, Trevose, PA 19053, ☎ 215/245–4707 or 800/523–6586, FAX 215/244–9617; ⊠ 12 Chemin Riantbosson, 1217 Meyrin 1, Geneva, Switzerland, ☎ 22/785–6464, FAX 22/785–6424; ⊠ 331 N. Bridge Rd., 17-00, Odeon Towers, Singapore 188720, ☎ 338–7800, FAX 338–7611.

OVER-THE-COUNTER REMEDIES

U.S. brands of acetaminophen, ibuprofen, aspirin, and other popular medications are readily available in Mexico (as is Pepto-Bismol). Most pharmacies have a blue book that lists generic and Mexican drug names. Get the generic name of your prescription drugs before your trip. Sunscreen is available at large supermarkets, pharmacies, and department stores. Prices are slightly higher than in the United States.

PESTS AND OTHER HAZARDS

It's best to be cautious and go indoors at dusk (called the "mosquito hour" by locals). An excellent brand of *repellente de insectos* (insect repellent) called Autan is readily available; do not use it on children under age 2. If you want to bring a mosquito repellent from home, make sure it has at least 10% DEET or it won't be effective. If you're hiking in the jungle, wear repellent and long pants and sleeves; if you're camping in the jungle use a mosquito net and invest in a package of mosquito coils (sold in most stores). Another local flying pest is the deer fly, which resembles a common household fly with yellow stripes. Some people swell up after being bitten, but taking an antihistamine can help. Scorpions also live in the region; their sting is similar to a bee sting. They are not poisonous but can cause strong reactions in small children. Those who are allergic to bee stings should go to the hospital. Again, antihistamines help. Clean all cuts carefully, as the rate of infection is much higher here.

Other hazards to travelers in Mexico are sunburn and heat exhaustion. The sun is strong here; it takes fewer than 20 minutes to get a serious sunburn. Avoid the sun between 11 AM and 3 PM all year round. Wear a hat and use sunscreen. You should **drink more fluid than you do at home**—Mexico is probably hotter than what you're used to and you will perspire more. Rest in the afternoons and stay out of the sun to avoid heat exhaustion. The first signs of dehydration and heat exhaustion are dizziness, extreme irritability, and fatigue.

SHOTS AND MEDICATIONS

According to the U.S. government's National Centers for Disease Control and Prevention (CDC) there is a limited risk of malaria and dengue fever in certain rural areas of the Yucatán Peninsula, especially the states of Campeche and Quintana Roo. Travelers in mostly urban or easily accessible areas need not worry. However, if you plan to visit remote regions or stay for more than six weeks, **check with the CDC's International Travelers Hotline.** In areas where mosquito-borne diseases like malaria and dengue are prevalent, use mosquito nets, wear clothing that covers the body, apply repellent containing DEET, and use spray for flying insects in living and sleeping areas. You might **consider taking antimalarial pills,** but the side effects are quite strong and the current strain of Mexican malaria can be cured with the right medication. There is no vaccine to combat dengue, although it is not a life-threatening disease.

➤ HEALTH WARNINGS: **National Centers for Disease Control and Prevention** (CDC; National Center for Infectious Diseases, Division of Quarantine, Traveler's Health Section, ⊠ 1600 Clifton Rd. NE, M/S E-03, Atlanta, GA 30333, ☎ 888/232–3228 general information, 877/394–8747 travelers' health line, 800/311–3435 public inquiries, FAX 888/232–3299, WEB www.cdc.gov).

HOLIDAYS

The lively celebration of holidays in Mexico interrupts most daily business, including banks, government offices, and many shops and services, so plan your trip accordingly: New Year's Day; February 5, Constitution Day; May 5, Anniversary of the Battle of Puebla; September 1, the State of the Union Address; September 16, Independence Day; October 12, Day of the Race; November 1, Day of the Dead; November 20, Revolution Day;

December 12, Feast of Our Lady of Guadaloupe, and Christmas Day.

Banks and government offices close during Holy Week (the Sunday before Easter until Easter Sunday), especially the Thursday and Friday before Easter Sunday. Some private offices close from Christmas to New Year's Day; government offices usually have reduced hours and staff.

INSURANCE

The most useful travel-insurance plan is a comprehensive policy that includes coverage for trip cancellation and interruption, default, trip delay, and medical expenses (with a waiver for pre-existing conditions).

Without insurance you will lose all or most of your money if you cancel your trip, regardless of the reason. Default insurance covers you if your tour operator, airline, or cruise line goes out of business. Trip-delay covers expenses that arise because of bad weather or mechanical delays. Study the fine print when comparing policies.

If you're traveling internationally, a key component of travel insurance is coverage for medical bills incurred if you get sick on the road. Such expenses are not generally covered by Medicare or private policies. U.K. residents can buy a travel-insurance policy valid for most vacations taken during the year in which it's purchased (but check pre-existing-condition coverage). British and Australian citizens need extra medical coverage when traveling overseas.

Always **buy travel policies directly from the insurance company**; if you buy them from a cruise line, airline, or tour operator that goes out of business you probably will not be covered for the agency or operator's default, a major risk. Before making any purchase, **review your existing health and homeowner's policies** to find what they cover away from home.

➤ TRAVEL INSURERS: In the U.S.: **Access America** (✉ 6600 W. Broad St., Richmond, VA 23230, ☎ 800/284–8300, FAX 804/673–1491 or 800/346–9265, WEB www.accessamerica.com). **Travel Guard International** (✉ 1145 Clark St., Stevens Point, WI 54481, ☎ 715/345–0505 or 800/826–1300; FAX 800/955–8785; WEB www.travelguard.com).

➤ INSURANCE INFORMATION: In Australia: **Insurance Council of Australia** (✉ Level 3, 56 Pitt St., Sydney NSW 2000, ☎ 02/9253–5100, FAX 02/9253–5111, WEB www.ica.com.au). In Canada: **RBC Travel Insurance** (✉ 6880 Financial Dr., Mississauga, Ontario L5N 7Y5, ☎ 905/791–8700 or 800/668–4342, FAX 905/813–4704, WEB www.rbcinsurance.com). In New Zealand: **Insurance Council of New Zealand** (✉ Level 7, 111–115 Customhouse Quay, Box 474, Wellington, ☎ 04/472–5230, FAX 04/473–3011, WEB www.icnz.org.nz). In the U.K.: **Association of British Insurers** (✉ 51 Gresham St., London EC2V 7HQ, ☎ 020/7600–3333, FAX 020/7696–8999, WEB www.abi.org.uk).

LANGUAGE

Spanish is the official language of Mexico, although Indian languages are spoken by approximately 20% of the population, many of whom speak no Spanish at all. In the beach resorts of Cancún and Cozumel, English is understood by most people employed in tourism; at the very least, shopkeepers know numbers in English for bargaining purposes. Mexicans welcome even the most halting attempts to use their language; in Mérida, you may even be introduced to a few Maya words and phrases. For a rudimentary vocabulary of terms that travelers are likely to encounter in the Yucatán, **review the Spanish vocabulary at the end of this book.**

The Spanish that most U.S. and Canadian citizens learn in high school is based on Castilian Spanish, which is different from Latin American Spanish. In terms of grammar, Mexican Spanish ignores the *vosotros* form of the second person plural, using the more formal *ustedes* in its place. As for pronunciation, the lisped Castilian "c" or "z" is dismissed in Mexico as a sign of affectation. The most obvious differences are in vocabulary: Mexican Spanish has thousands of indigenous words and uses *¿mande?* instead of *¿cómo?* (excuse me?). Words or phrases that are harmless or commonplace in one Spanish-speaking country can take on salacious or otherwise offensive meanings in another. Unless you are lucky enough to be briefed on these nuances by a native coach, the only way to learn is by trial and error. Mexicans are very forgiving of errors and will appreciate your efforts.

LANGUAGE-STUDY PROGRAMS

Intensive Spanish classes for foreigners are offered by two schools in Mérida: Centro de Idiomas and the slightly more expensive Academia de Cultura e Idiomas de Mérida. Classes last a minimum of two weeks; advanced classes in special areas of study are available. Students stay with local families or in hotels. There is also a recommended Spanish-language study center in Playa del Carmen. Students can stay at the center or lodge with a local family.

➤ PROGRAMS: **Academia de Cultura e Idiomas de Mérida** (✉ Calle 13 No. 23, at Calle 10, Prado Nte., 97137 Mérida, Yucatán, ☎ FAX 999/944–3148). **Centro de Idiomas** (✉ Calle 57 at Calle 66, Altos, Ed. Alejandria, 97000 Mérida, Yucatán, ☎ 999/923–0954). **Playalingua del Caribe** (✉ Calle 20 Nte. between Avs. 5-A and 10-A, Playa del Carmen, ☎ 984/873–3876, WEB www.playalingua.com).

LANGUAGES FOR TRAVELERS

A phrase book and language-tape set can help get you started. *Fodor's Spanish for Travelers* (available at bookstores everywhere) is excellent.

LODGING

You have a variety of accommodations to choose from if you plan to stay in Cancún or Cozumel. Here, luxurious and expensive internationally affiliated properties, with lots of restaurants, cafés, and bars, have the latest room amenities, boutiques, and sports facilities. These beach resorts also have more-modest accommodations—usually a short walk or a shuttle ride from the water. Of course, as you get into the less-populated and -visited areas of the Yucatán, accommodations tend to be simpler and more typically Mexican: inexpensive bungalows, campsites, and beachside places to hang a hammock. The lodgings and facilities we list are the cream of the crop in each price category. When pricing accommodations, always ask what's included and what costs extra.

Assume that hotels operate on the **European Plan** (EP, with no meals) unless we specify that they use either the **Continental Plan** (CP, with a Continental breakfast) or the **Modified American Plan** (MAP, with breakfast and dinner) or are **all-inclusive** (including all meals and most activities).

APARTMENT AND VILLA RENTALS

If you want a home base that's roomy enough for a family and comes with cooking facilities, **consider a furnished rental.** These can save you money, especially if you're traveling with a group. Home-exchange directories sometimes list rentals as well as exchanges.

Local rental agencies can be found in Isla Mujeres, Cozumel, and Playa del Carmen. They specialize in renting out apartments, condos, villas, and private homes.

➤ INTERNATIONAL AGENTS: **Hideaways International** (✉ 767 Islington St., Portsmouth, NH 03801, ☎ 603/430–4433 or 800/843–4433, FAX 603/430–4444, WEB www.hideaways.com; membership $129). **Vacation Home Rentals Worldwide** (✉ 235 Kensington Ave., Norwood, NJ 07648, ☎ 201/767–9393 or 800/633–3284, FAX 201/767–5510, WEB www.vhrww.com). **Villas International** (✉ 4340 Redwood Hwy., Suite D309, San Rafael, CA 94903, ☎ 415/499–9490 or 800/221–2260, FAX 415/499–9491, WEB www.villasintl.com).

➤ LOCAL AGENTS: **Mundaca Travel** (✉ Av. Hidalgo, 77400 Isla Mujeres, Quintana Roo, ☎ 998/877–0025, FAX 998/877–0076, WEB www.mundaca. com). **Cozumel Vacation Villas** (✉ Av. Rafael E. Melgar 685, 77600 San Miguel, Quintana Roo, ☎ 987/872–0729, FAX 303/442–0380, WEB www. cozumel-villas.com). **Playa Beach Rentals** (✉ Av. 5 at Calle 8, 77710 Playa del Carmen, Quintana Roo, ☎ FAX 984/873–1354, FAX 303/442–0380, WEB www.playabeachrentals.com).

BED-AND-BREAKFASTS

B&Bs are relatively new to Mexico and consequently there are only a handful found throughout the Yucatán peninsula. The establishments listed in this guide are closer to small hotels that offer breakfast.

CAMPING

There are no official campgrounds in the Yucatán. Since all beachfront is federal property, you can legally camp on the beach. However, there are no services and this can be a dangerous practice especially for women traveling alone. Those wishing to sleep out on the beach in safety and comfort should contact Kai Luum II. Las Ruinas Camp Grounds in Playa del Carmen have palapas, tents, and RV spaces.

➤ INFORMATION: **Kai Luum II** (✉ La Posada del Capitán Lafitte, off Hwy. 307 at Km 62, 77400, Quintana Roo; reservations: **Turquoise Reef Group** ✉ Box 2664, Evergreen, CO 81439, ☎ 800/538–6802, FAX 303/674–8735, WEB www.mexicoholiday.com). **Las Ruinas Camp Grounds** (✉ Calle 2 and Av. 5 Nte., 77400 Playa del Carmen, Quintana Roo, ☎ FAX 984/ 873–0405).

HOME EXCHANGES

If you would like to exchange your home for someone else's, **join a home-exchange organization,** which will send you its updated listings of available exchanges for a year and will include your own listing in at least one of them. It's up to you to make specific arrangements.

➤ EXCHANGE CLUBS: **HomeLink International** (✉ Box 47747, Tampa, FL 33647, ☎ 813/975–9825 or 800/638–3841, FAX 813/910–8144, WEB www.homelink.org; $106 per year).

HOSTELS

No matter what your age, you can **save on lodging costs by staying at hostels.**

In some 4,500 locations in more than 70 countries around the world, Hostelling International (HI), the umbrella group for a number of national youth-hostel associations, offers single-sex, dorm-style beds and, at many hostels, rooms for couples and family accommodations. Membership in any HI national hostel association, open to travelers of all ages, allows you to stay in HI-affiliated hostels at member rates; one-year membership is about $25 for adults (C$35 for a two-year minimum membership in Canada, £13 in the U.K., A$52 in Australia, and NZ$40 in New Zealand); hostels run about $10–$30 per night. Members have priority if the hostel is full; they're also eligible for discounts around the world, even on rail and bus travel in some countries.

➤ ORGANIZATIONS: **Hostelling International—American Youth Hostels** (✉ 733 15th St. NW, Suite 840, Washington, DC 20005, ☎ 202/783–6161, FAX 202/783–6171, WEB www. hiayh.org). **Hostelling International—Canada** (✉ 400–205 Catherine St., Ottawa, Ontario K2P 1C3, ☎ 613/237–7884 or 800/663–5777, FAX 613/237–7868, WEB www.hihostels.ca). **Youth Hostel Association Australia** (✉ 10 Mallett St., Camperdown, NSW 2050, ☎ 02/9565–1699, FAX 02/9565–1325, WEB www.yha.com.au). **Youth Hostel Association of England and Wales** (✉ Trevelyan House, Dimple Rd., Matlock, Derbyshire DE4 3YH, U.K., ☎ 0870/870–8808, FAX 0169/592–702, WEB www.yha.org. uk). **Youth Hostels Association of New Zealand** (✉ Level 3, 193 Cashel St., Box 436, Christchurch, ☎ 03/379–9970, FAX 03/365–4476, WEB www. yha.org.nz).

HOTELS

In the off-season, Cancún hotels can cost one-third to one-half what they cost during peak season. Keep in mind, however, that this is also the time that many hotels undergo necessary repairs or renovations.

All hotels listed have private bath unless otherwise noted.

RESERVING A ROOM

Reservations are easy to make in this region over the Internet. If you call hotels in the larger urban areas, there will be someone who speaks English. In more remote regions you will have to make your reservations in Spanish.

➤ TOLL-FREE NUMBERS: Best Western (☎ 800/528–1234, WEB www.bestwestern.com). Choice (☎ 800/424–6423, WEB www.choicehotels.com). Doubletree and Red Lion Hotels (☎ 800/222–8733, WEB www.hilton.com). Hilton (☎ 800/445–8667, WEB www.hilton.com). Holiday Inn (☎ 800/465–4329, WEB www.sixcontinentshotels.com). Howard Johnson (☎ 800/654–4656, WEB www.hojo.com). Hyatt Hotels & Resorts (☎ 800/233–1234, WEB www.hyatt.com). Inter-Continental (☎ 800/327–0200, WEB www.intercontinental.com). Krystal (☎ 800/ 231–9860, WEB www.krystal.com.mx). Marriott (☎ 800/228–9290, WEB www.marriott.com). Melia (☎ 888/975–3542, WEB www.solmelia.com). Le Meridien (☎ 800/543–4300, WEB www.lemeridien-hotels.com). Omni (☎ 800/843–6664, WEB www.omnihotels.com). Palace Resorts (☎ 800/636–1836, WEB www.palaceresorts.com). Ritz-Carlton (☎ 800/241–3333, WEB www.ritzcarlton.com). Sheraton (☎ 800/325–3535, WEB www.starwood.com/sheraton). Westin Hotels & Resorts (☎ 800/228–3000, WEB www.starwood.com/westin).

MAIL AND SHIPPING

Mail can be sent from your hotel or the local post office. Be forewarned, however, that mail service to, within, and from Mexico is notoriously slow and can take anywhere from 10 days to six weeks. **Never send anything of value to or from Mexico via the mail,** including checks or credit-card numbers.

OVERNIGHT SERVICES

Despite the promises, overnight courier service is rare in Mexico. It's not the fault of the courier service, which may indeed have the package there overnight. Delays occur at customs. Depending on the time of year, all courier packages are opened and inspected. This can slow everything down. You can expect one- to three-day service in Cancún and two- to four-day service elsewhere.

➤ MAJOR SERVICES: AeroMexpress (☎ 998/886–0123). DHL (☎ 998/887–1906). Estafeta (☎ 998/884–1167). Fedex (☎ 998/887–4003).

POSTAL RATES

It costs a minimum of 6 pesos to mail a postcard or letter weighing fewer than 20 grams to the United States or Canada; the cost to Great Britain is 8 pesos.

RECEIVING MAIL

Mail can be sent either to your hotel, to the post office, or, if you are an American Express card member, to the local branch of American Express. There are American Express offices in Campeche City, Mérida, Cancún, and Cozumel. Another option is the Mexican postal service's *lista de correos* service. To use this service, you must first register with the local post office where you wish to receive your mail. Mail should be addressed to: your name; a/c Lista de Correos; town name; state, postal code; Mexico. Mail is held at post offices for 10 days, and a list of recipients is posted daily. Postal codes for the main Yucatán destinations are as follows: Cancún, 77500; Isla Mujeres, 77400; Cozumel, 77600; Campeche, 24000; Mérida, 97000. Keep in mind that the mail service in Mexico is very slow and can take up to eight weeks to deliver mail.

SHIPPING PARCELS

Hotel concierges can recommend international carriers, such as DHL, Estafeta, or Federal Express, which give your package a tracking number and ensure its arrival back home.

MONEY MATTERS

Prices in this book are quoted most often in U.S. dollars. This is because the value of the peso fluctuates considerably and what costs 90 pesos today might cost 120 pesos in six months.

Mexico has a reputation for being inexpensive, particularly compared with other North American vacation spots, such as the Caribbean; the devaluation of the peso, started in late 1994, has made this especially true, though prices of the large chain hotels, calculated in dollars, have not gone down, and some restaurant owners and merchants have raised their prices to compensate for the devaluation. In general, costs vary with the when, where, and how of your travel. If you are not wedded to standardized creature comforts, you can spend as little as $25 a day on room, board, and local transportation. Speaking Spanish is also helpful in bargaining situations and when asking for dining recommendations. As a rule, region by region, costs decrease as the amount of English that people speak decreases.

Cancún is one of the most expensive destinations in Mexico. Cozumel is a bit less costly than Cancún, and Isla Mujeres in turn is slightly less expensive than Cozumel. You're likely to get the best value for your money in Mérida and the other Yucatán cities less frequented by visitors, like Campeche. For obvious reasons, if you stay at international chain hotels and eat at restaurants designed with tourists in mind (especially hotel restaurants), you may not find the Yucatán such a bargain.

Peak-season sample costs: cup of coffee, 10 pesos–20 pesos; bottle of beer, 20 pesos–50 pesos; plate of tacos with trimmings, 25 pesos–60 pesos; grilled fish platter at a tourist restaurant, 35 pesos–80 pesos; 2-km (1-mi) taxi ride, 20 pesos.

Prices throughout this guide are given for adults. Substantially reduced fees are almost always available for children, students, and senior citizens. For information on taxes, *see* Taxes, *below*.

ATMS

Cirrus and Plus are the most commonly found networks in Mexico. Many big hotels and all but the smallest Mexican towns have major banks with 24-hour ATMs. If your transaction cannot be completed—an annoyingly common occurrence—chances are that the computer lines are busy or being serviced and you'll have to try again later. If it's a holiday, it's possible that the machine has run out of money.

Many Mexican ATMs accept only personal identification numbers (PINs) of four or fewer digits. If your PIN is longer, ask your bank about changing it before you go; it sometimes takes a few weeks to process the change.

For cash advances, plan to use your Visa and MasterCard, as many Mexican ATMs don't accept American Express. The ATMs at Banamex, one of the oldest and perhaps the strongest of the nationwide banks, tend to be the most reliable and generally give you an excellent exchange rate. Bancomer is another bank with many *cajero automatico* (ATM) locations, but they generally provide only cash withdrawals (rather than credit-card advances). The Serfín banks have reliable ATMs that accept credit cards as well as Plus and Cirrus bank cards.

CREDIT CARDS

Large hotels, restaurants, and department stores accept credit cards readily. Most of the smaller, less expensive restaurants and shops take cash only. Credit cards are generally not accepted in small towns and villages, except in the larger hotels. When shopping, you can usually get better prices if you **pay with cash.** But if you need to rely on your credit cards, it's wise to **make sure that "pesos" is clearly marked on all credit-card receipts** to avoid fraud. Keep good, accurate records of all transactions to avoid paying for fraudulent charges that might be put through by unscrupulous hotel employees.

Throughout this guide, the following abbreviations are used: **AE**, American Express; **DC**, Diners Club; **MC**, MasterCard; and **V**, Visa.

➤ REPORTING LOST CARDS: **American Express** (☎ 800/221–7282; 301/214–8228 collect from Mexico). **Diners Club** (☎ 5/258–3220; 303/799–1504 collect from Mexico). **MasterCard**

(☎ 800/307–7309 collect from Mexico). **Visa** (☎ 800/847–2911; 410/581–3836 collect from Mexico).

CURRENCY

At press time, the exchange rate was 9.10 pesos to the U.S. dollar, 5.72 pesos to the Canadian dollar, 13 pesos to the pound sterling, 7.96 pesos to the Euro, 4.67 pesos to the Australian dollar, and 3.81 pesos to the New Zealand dollar. Because the market and prices continue to adjust, **check with your bank or the financial pages of your local newspaper for current exchange rates.**

Pesos come in denominations of 10, 20, 50, 100, 200, and 500. Coins come in denominations of 20, 10, 5, 2 and 1 pesos and 50, 20 and 10 *centavos*. Some denominations of bills and coins are very similar, so check carefully.

U.S. dollar bills, but not coins, are widely accepted in the Yucatán, particularly in Cancún, Cozumel, and Playa del Carmen. Many hotels, shops, and market vendors, as well as virtually all hotel service personnel, take them, too. Dollar bills are particularly welcome tips.

CURRENCY EXCHANGE

For the most favorable rates, **change money through banks.** Although ATM transaction fees may be higher abroad than at home, ATM rates are excellent because they are based on wholesale rates offered only by major banks. You won't do as well at exchange booths in airports or rail and bus stations, in hotels, in restaurants, or in stores. To avoid lines at airport exchange booths, **get a bit of local currency before you leave home.**

Most banks only change money on weekdays until noon (though they stay open until 5), while *casas de cambio* (private exchange offices) generally stay open until 6 or 9 and often operate on weekends. Bank rates are regulated by the federal government and are therefore invariable, while casas de cambio have slightly more variable rates. Exchange houses in the airports and in areas with heavy tourist traffic tend to have the worst rates, often considerably

lower than the banks. Some hotels also exchange money, but for providing you with this convenience they help themselves to a bigger commission than banks.

When changing money, count your bills before leaving the bank, and don't accept any partially torn, ink-marked, or taped-together bills; they will not be accepted anywhere. Also, many shop and restaurant owners are unable to make change for large bills. Enough of these encounters may compel you to request *billetes chicos* (small bills) when you exchange money.

➤ EXCHANGE SERVICES: **International Currency Express** (☎ 888/278–6628 orders). **Thomas Cook Currency Services** (☎ 800/287–7362 for telephone orders and retail locations, WEB www.us.thomascook.com).

TRAVELER'S CHECKS

Do you need traveler's checks? It depends on where you're headed. If you're going to rural areas and small towns, go with cash; traveler's checks are best used in cities. Lost or stolen checks can usually be replaced within 24 hours. To ensure a speedy refund, buy your own traveler's checks—don't let someone else pay for them: irregularities like this can cause delays. The person who bought the checks should make the call to request a refund.

OUTDOORS AND SPORTS

Water activities such as scuba diving, snorkeling, and deep-sea fishing are the main sports in the Yucatán. Scuba diving is synonymous with Cozumel, and with good reason. It's lauded as one of the best dive sites in the world. Divers also favor several spots along the Caribbean coast, which is blessed with abundant reefs. Isla Mujeres is best known for snorkeling; Cancún, Puerto Morelos, and Cozumel, for deep-sea fishing. You can bring your own equipment or rent it at the myriad rental shops. Those bound for the elusive marlin or other billfish can find boat rentals with captain, crew, and equipment readily available; Cozumel has a billfishing tournament each spring.

Cancún has several world-class golf courses, and Mérida has an 18-hole golf course on the outskirts of town.

Biking is one of the newer sports attracting a loyal following, but rental places are few and far between.

PACKING

Pack light, because you may want to save space for purchases: the Yucatán is filled with bargains on clothing, leather goods, jewelry, pottery, and other crafts.

Bring lightweight clothes, sundresses, bathing suits, sun hats or visors, and cover-ups for the Caribbean beach towns, but also pack a jacket or sweater to wear in the chilly, air-conditioned restaurants, or to tide you over during a rainstorm or an unusual cool spell. For trips to rural areas or Mérida, where dress is typically more conservative and shorts are considered inappropriate, women may want to pack one longer skirt. If you plan to visit any ruins, **bring comfortable walking shoes** with rubber soles. Lightweight rain gear is a good idea during the rainy season. Cancún is the dressiest spot on the peninsula, but even fancy restaurants don't require men to wear jackets.

Pack sunscreen, sunglasses, and umbrellas for the Yucatán. Other handy items—especially if you are traveling on your own or camping—include toilet paper, facial tissues, a plastic water bottle, and a flashlight (for occasional power outages or use at campsites). Snorkelers should consider bringing their own equipment unless traveling light is a priority; shoes with rubber soles for rocky underwater surfaces are also advised. For long-term stays in remote rural areas, *see* Health, *above.*

In your carry-on luggage, **pack an extra pair of eyeglasses or contact lenses and enough of any medication** you take to last a few days longer than the entire trip. You may also ask your doctor to write a spare prescription using the drug's generic name, since brand names may vary from country to country. In luggage to be checked, **never pack prescription drugs or valuables.** And don't forget to carry with you the addresses of offices that handle refunds of lost traveler's checks. Check *Fodor's How to Pack* (available in bookstores everywhere) for more tips.

To avoid customs and security delays, carry medications in their original packaging; don't pack any sharp objects, including knives of any size or material, scissors, manicure tools, and corkscrews, or anything else that might arouse suspicion. If you need such objects on your trip, consider shipping them to your destination or buying them there.

CHECKING LUGGAGE

How many carry-on bags you can bring with you is up to the airline. Most allow two, but not always, so make sure that everything you carry aboard will fit under your seat or in the overhead bin. Get to the gate early, so you can board as soon as possible. Note that if you have a seat at the back of the plane, you'll probably board first, while the overhead bins are still empty.

If you are flying internationally, note that baggage allowances may be determined not by piece but by weight—generally 88 pounds (40 kilograms) in first class, 66 pounds (30 kilograms) in business class, and 44 pounds (20 kilograms) in economy.

Airline liability for baggage is limited to $2,500 per person on flights within the United States. On international flights it amounts to $9.07 per pound or $20 per kilogram for checked baggage (roughly $640 per 70-pound bag) and $400 per passenger for unchecked baggage. You can buy additional coverage at check-in for about $10 per $1,000 of coverage, but it excludes a rather extensive list of items, shown on your airline ticket.

Before departure, **itemize your bags' contents** and their worth, and label the bags with your name, address, and phone number. (If you use your home address, cover it so potential thieves can't see it readily.) Inside each bag, **pack a copy of your itinerary.** At check-in, **make sure that each bag is correctly tagged** with the destination airport's three-letter code. If your bags arrive damaged or fail to arrive at all, file a written report with the airline before leaving the airport.

PASSPORTS AND VISAS

When traveling internationally, **carry your passport** even if you don't need one (it's always the best form of ID) and **make two photocopies of the data page** (one for someone at home and another for you, carried separately from your passport). If you lose your passport, promptly call the nearest embassy or consulate and the local police.

U.S. passport applications for children under age 14 require consent from both parents or legal guardians; both parents must appear together to sign the application. If only one parent appears, he or she must submit a written statement from the other parent authorizing passport issuance for the child. A parent with sole authority must present evidence of it when applying; acceptable documentation includes the child's certified birth certificate listing only the applying parent, a court order specifically permitting this parent's travel with the child, or a death certificate for the non-applying parent. Application forms and instructions are available on the Web site of the U.S. State Department's Bureau of Consular Affairs (www.travel.state.gov).

ENTERING THE YUCATÁN PENINSULA

Citizens of the United States and Canada need only a valid piece of identification (passport, certified copy of a birth certificate, or a voter registration card) for stays of 180 days. British citizens need only a valid passport, and residents of Australia and New Zealand require a multiple-entry visa to the United States in addition to a valid passport. If you are flying into the state of Quintana Roo you will be issued a 30-day tourist visa in high season and a 60-to 90-day tourist visa at all other times. Your entry fee is included in the price of your airline ticket. If you drive into Mexico, you are given a 30- to 180-day tourist visa depending on the mood of the official. Ask for 180 days up front if that's what you want.

PASSPORT OFFICES

The best time to apply for a passport or to renew is in fall and winter. Before any trip, check your passport's expiration date, and, if necessary, renew it as soon as possible.

➤ AUSTRALIAN CITIZENS: **Australian State Passport Office** (☎ 131–232, WEB www.passports.gov.au).

➤ CANADIAN CITIZENS: **Passport Office** (to mail in applications: ✉ Department of Foreign Affairs and International Trade, Ottawa, Ontario K1A 0G3; ☎ 800/567–6868 toll-free in Canada or 819/994–3500, WEB www.dfait-maeci.gc.ca/passport).

➤ NEW ZEALAND CITIZENS: **New Zealand Passport Office** (☎ 0800/22–5050 or 04/474–8100, WEB www.passports.govt.nz).

➤ U.K. CITIZENS: **London Passport Office** (☎ 0870/521–0410, WEB www.passport.gov.uk).

➤ U.S. CITIZENS: **National Passport Information Center** (☎ 900/225–5674; calls are 35¢ per minute for automated service, $1.05 per minute for operator service; WEB www.travel.state.gov).

REST ROOMS

Tourist destinations such as Cancún, Cozumel, Playa del Carmen, and Mérida generally have U.S.-style facilities with clean flush toilets, toilet paper, soap, and running water. Other places have simple but clean toilets. The more primitive rest rooms, usually in public areas with little tourist traffic, have no toilet paper and at times no water and no toilet seats. Some public places, like bus stations, charge 1 or 2 pesos to use the facility, but toilet paper is included in the fee. Because the Yucatán Peninsula is actually a limestone shelf, the whole area operates on a septic system that can't handle toilet paper. Standard procedure is to place the paper in a basket by the toilet. It's always a good idea to carry some tissue or toilet paper with you.

SAFETY

When visiting the Yucatán, even in such resort areas as Cancún and Cozumel, use common sense. Wear a money belt, make use of hotel safes when available, and carry your own baggage whenever possible unless you are checking into a hotel. Put jewelry and other valuables in the hotel safe when you go on sightseeing excursions. Leave expensive jewelry at home, since it often entices thieves and will mark you as a *"rico turista"* who can afford to be overcharged.

When traveling with all your money, be sure to distribute your cash and any valuables between a deep front pocket, an inside jacket or vest pocket, and a hidden money pouch. Do not reach for your money pouch once in public. If you carry a purse, choose one with a zipper and a thick strap that you can drape across your body; adjust the length so that the purse sits in front of you at or above hip level. Fortunately purse snatchers, pickpockets, and muggers are rare in the area. Theft usually occurs when bags or purses are left unattended.

Reporting a crime to the police is often a frustrating experience unless you speak excellent Spanish and have a great deal of patience.

WOMEN IN THE YUCATÁN PENINSULA

A woman traveling alone will be the subject of much curiosity, since traditional Mexican women do not venture out unless accompanied by family members or friends. Violent crimes against women are rare here, but you should still be cautious. Part of the machismo culture is being flirtatious and showing off in front of *compadres,* and lone women are likely to be subjected to catcalls, although this is less true in the Yucatán than in other parts of Mexico. While annoying, it is essentially harmless. The best way to get rid of unwanted attention is to simply ignore the advances. Avoid direct eye contact with men on the streets—it invites further acquaintance. It's best not to enter into a discussion with harassers, even if you speak Spanish. When the suitor is persistent say "no" to whatever is said, walk briskly, and leave immediately for a safe place, such as a nearby store. Dressing conservatively may help; clothing that seems innocuous to you, such as brief tops or Bermuda shorts, may be inappropriate in more conservative rural areas. **Never go topless on the beach** unless it is a recognized nude beach with lots of other people.

SENIOR-CITIZEN TRAVEL

To qualify for age-related discounts, **mention your senior-citizen status up front** when booking hotel reservations (not when checking out) and before you're seated in restaurants (not when paying the bill). Be sure to have identification on hand. When renting a car, ask about promotional car-rental discounts, which can be cheaper than senior-citizen rates.

➤ EDUCATIONAL PROGRAMS: **Elder-hostel** (✉ 11 Ave. de Lafayette, Boston, MA 02111-1746, ☎ 877/426–8056, FAX 877/426–2166, WEB www.elderhostel.org). **Interhostel** (✉ University of New Hampshire, 6 Garrison Ave., Durham, NH 03824, ☎ 603/862–1147 or 800/733–9753, FAX 603/862–1113, WEB www.learn.unh.edu).

SHOPPING

Shopping is convenient in Cancún and Cozumel, but often you pay top peso for items that you can find in smaller towns for less money. Bargaining is widely accepted in the markets, but keep in mind that in many small towns residents earn their livelihoods from the tourist trade. Rarely are the prices outrageous. If you feel the price quoted is too high, start off by offering no more than half the asking price and then slowly go up, usually to about 70% of the original price. Bargaining is not accepted in most shops, except at times when you are paying cash instead of using a credit card.

It is illegal to take out of the country pre-Hispanic artifacts and paintings by such Mexican masters as Diego Rivera and Frida Kahlo, which are defined as part of the national patrimony.

KEY DESTINATIONS

Cozumel is famous for its jewelry, and there are many good deals to be found on diamonds and other precious gemstones. For authentic arts and crafts, you must journey inland to Mérida and Campeche. To buy hammocks, shoes, and pottery directly from artisans go to the the tiny village of Ticul, one hour south of Mérida. Perhaps the richest source of crafts and the least visited area is La Ruta de Artesanos in Campeche along Route 180. Here you will find villages filled with beautiful crafts: Calkini, famed for its lovely pottery; Nunkini, known for its beautiful woven mats and rugs; Pomuch, with its famous bakery; and Becal, where the renowned Panama hats are woven by locals.

SMART SOUVENIRS

T-shirts and other commonplace souvenirs abound in the area. But there are also some unique gifts to be found. This area is well known for its vanilla. There is also a special variety of bees on the peninsula that produces rich, aromatic honey that is much sought after. Supermarkets and outdoor markets carry a variety of brands, which are priced considerably less than in the United States.

The Yucatecan hammock is considered the finest in the world and comes in a variety of sizes, color, and materials. You can find the best hammocks from street vendors or at the municipal markets. Prices start from $16 and go up to $60. Don't pass up any opportunity to purchase a Panama hat—most start around $35. A hand-embroidered *huipile* (the traditional dress of Maya women) or a *guayabera* shirt both make lovely souvenirs. Prices depend on the material and amount of embroidery done. The simplest dresses and shirts start at $20 and can go as high as $150. You can also pick up handwoven shawls for under $20.

Mexico is also famous for its amber. Most of the amber sold by street merchants is plastic, but there are several fine amber shops to be found in Playa del Carmen. Prices depend on the size of the amber.

WATCH OUT

Although Cuban cigars are readily available, American visitors will have to enjoy them while in Mexico. However, Mexico has been producing some fine alternatives to Cuban cigars. If you plan to bring any Mexi-can cigars back to the States, make sure they have the correct Mexican seals on both the individual cigars and on the box. Otherwise they may be confiscated. Cowboys boots, hats, and sandals made from the leather of endangered species such as crocodiles will be taken from you at customs. Anything made from sea turtles is also contraband. You will need a certificate from an authorized dealer to bring back anything made from black coral. However, it is recommended that you don't buy any black coral, since it is almost an endangered species.

SIGHTSEEING GUIDES

In the states of Quintana Roo and the Yucatán most of the tour guides found outside the more popular ruins are not official guides. Some are professionals, but others make it up as they go along (which can be highly entertaining). Official guides will be wearing a name tag and identification issued by **INAH, Instituto Nacional de Antropología e Historia** (National Institute of Anthropology and History). These guides are excellent and can teach you about the architecture and history of the ruins. At the smaller ruins, guides are usually part of the research or maintenance teams and can give you an excellent tour. All guides in Campeche have been trained by the state and very knowledgeable. They must be booked through the Campeche tourist office. Costs vary. At the smaller sites usually a $5 to $10 tip will suffice. At the larger ruins the fees can run as high as $30. Those charging more are scam artists. The larger ruins have the more aggressive guides. Turn them down with a very firm *No, gracias,* and if they persist, lose them at the entrance gate.

STUDENTS IN THE YUCATÁN PENINSULA

➤ IDs and Services: **Council Travel** (✉ 205 E. 42nd St., 15th floor, New York, NY 10017, ☎ 212/822–2700 or 888/226–8624, FAX 212/822–2719, WEB www.counciltravel.com). **Travel Cuts** (✉ 187 College St., Toronto, Ontario M5T 1P7, Canada, ☎ 416/979–2406 or 888/838–2887, FAX 416/979–8167; WEB www.travelcuts.com).

TAXES

AIRPORT TAXES

An air-departure tax of $18 or the peso equivalent must be paid at the airport for international flights from Mexico. For domestic flights the departure tax is around $10. It's important that you save a little cash for this transaction, as traveler's checks and credit cards are not accepted.

HOTELS

Hotels in the state of Quintana Roo charge a 12% lodging tax; in Yucatán and Campeche, expect a 17% lodging tax.

VALUE-ADDED TAX (VAT)

Mexico has a value-added tax (VAT), or IVA (*impuesto de valor agregado*), of 15% (10% along the Cancún–Chetumal corridor). Many establishments already include the IVA in the quoted price. Occasionally (and illegally) it may be waived for cash purchases.

TELEPHONES

In November 2001, all of Mexico experienced a total overhaul of area codes. Except for the three largest cities (Mexico City, Monterrey, and Guadalajara), towns and cities of all sizes now have three-digit area codes (LADAs) and seven-digit phone numbers. However, many of the numbers in brochures and other literature will undoubtedly be written in the old style.

AREA AND COUNTRY CODES

The country code for Mexico is 52. When dialing a Mexico number from abroad, drop the initial 0 from the local area code.

COLLECT CALLS

To place a collect or person-to-person international call, first **dial 09** and wait (sometimes a very long time) for the bilingual long-distance operator to pick up. Then give the operator the number you want to call and your name or card number, as appropriate.

Collect calls can also sometimes be placed from *casetas de larga distancia*, a telephone service usually operated out of a store, for a fee; look for the phone symbol on the door. Casetas may cost more to use than pay phones, but you have a better chance of immediate success. To make a direct long-distance call from a caseta, tell the person on duty the number you'd like to call, and he or she will give you a rate and dial for you. Casetas generally charge 50¢–$1.50 to place a collect call (some charge by the minute); it's usually better to **call por cobrar (collect) from a pay phone.**

DIRECTORY AND OPERATOR ASSISTANCE

Throughout Mexico, you can **dial 040 for information.**

INTERNATIONAL CALLS

International phone calls can be made from many hotels, but excessive taxes and surcharges—on the order of 60% to 70%—usually apply. It's better to buy a phone card to use in one of the many TELMEX phones. Other types of phones charge exorbitant rates.

When calling direct to the United States or Canada, **dial 001** before the area code and phone number (the country code for the United States and Canada is 1). When calling Europe, Latin America, or Japan, dial 00 before the country and city codes. (The country for Australia is 61; it's 64 for New Zealand and 44 for the United Kingdom.) For long-distance calls within Mexico, **dial 01,** then the area code and the local number.

LOCAL CALLS

To place a local call, dial only the seven-digit local number, without the area code. See individual chapters for an explanation of the telephone numbers in that area.

Throughout the book, toll-free numbers that work in the United States are simply listed as 800/123–4567; those that work in Mexico only appear as 01–800/123–4567.

LONG-DISTANCE SERVICES

AT&T, MCI, and Sprint access codes make calling long distance relatively convenient, but you may find the local access number blocked in many hotel rooms. First ask the hotel operator to connect you. If the hotel operator balks, ask for an international operator, or dial the international operator yourself. One way to improve your odds of getting connected to your long-distance carrier is to travel with more than one company's calling card (a hotel may block Sprint, for example, but not MCI). If all else fails, call from a pay phone.

➤ ACCESS CODES: **AT&T Direct** (☎ 01–800/288–2872 or 800/462–4240). **MCI WorldPhone** (☎ 800/674–7000). **Sprint International Access** (☎ 800/877–8000).

PHONE CARDS

Public telephones are operated by TELMEX and are found in every village no matter how small. These phone accept prepaid phone cards, called Ladatel cards, sold in blocks of 30, 50, 100, and 200 pesos (about $3, $5, $10, and $20, respectively) at newsstands and pharmacies. Many pay phones accept only these cards, and coin-only pay phones are usually broken. To use a Ladatel card, simply insert it in the slot of the phone, dial 001 (for calls to the States and Canada) or 01 (for long-distance calls in Mexico), followed by the area code and number you're trying to reach. Credit is deleted from the card as you use it, and your balance is displayed on the phone's small screen.

TIME

Mexico has two time zones. The west coast and middle states are on Pacific Standard Time. The rest of the country is on Central Standard Time, which is one hour behind Pacific Time.

TIPPING

At restaurants it's customary to leave a 10%–15% tip (make sure, however, that a service charge hasn't already been added to your bill). Give bellhops and porters $1 to $2; hotel maids, $1 to $2 per day, per room. Tour guides should get $1 per person for a half-day tour and $2 for a full day. Tour-bus drivers should receive $1 per person per day. Car watchers and windshield washers (usually young boys), as well as gas-station attendants and theater ushers, should be satisfied with 3 to 5 pesos. Taxi drivers and shoe shiners do not expect tips, although a few pesos are always appreciated.

TOURS AND PACKAGES

Because everything is prearranged on a prepackaged tour or independent vacation, you spend less time planning—and often get it all at a good price.

BOOKING WITH AN AGENT

Travel agents are excellent resources. But it's a good idea to collect brochures from several agencies, as some agents' suggestions may be influenced by relationships with tour and package firms that reward them for volume sales. If you have a special interest, **find an agent with expertise in that area**; the American Society of Travel Agents (ASTA; ☞ Travel Agencies, *below*) has a database of specialists worldwide.

Make sure your travel agent knows the accommodations and other services of the place being recommended. Ask about the hotel's location, room size, beds, and whether it has a pool, room service, or programs for children, if you care about these. Has your agent been there in person or sent others whom you can contact?

Do some homework on your own, too: local tourism boards can provide information about lesser-known and small-niche operators, some of which may sell only direct.

BUYER BEWARE

Each year consumers are stranded or lose their money when tour operators—even large ones with excellent reputations—go out of business. So **check out the operator.** Ask several travel agents about its reputation, and try to **book with a company that has a consumer-protection program.** (Look for information in the company's brochure.) In the United States, members of the National Tour Association and the United States Tour Operators Association are required to set aside funds to cover your payments and travel arrangements in the event that the company defaults. It's also a good idea to choose a company that participates in the

American Society of Travel Agents' Tour Operator Program (TOP); ASTA will act as mediator in any disputes between you and your tour operator.

Remember that the more your package or tour includes the better you can predict the ultimate cost of your vacation. Make sure you know exactly what is covered, and **beware of hidden costs.** Are taxes, tips, and transfers included? Entertainment and excursions? These can add up.

➤ TOUR-OPERATOR RECOMMENDATIONS: **American Society of Travel Agents** (☞ Travel Agencies, *below*). **National Tour Association** (NTA; ✉ 546 E. Main St., Lexington, KY 40508, ☎ 859/226–4444 or 800/682–8886, WEB www.ntaonline.com). **United States Tour Operators Association** (USTOA; ✉ 275 Madison Ave., Suite 2014, New York, NY 10016, ☎ 212/599–6599 or 800/468–7862, FAX 212/599–6744, WEB www.ustoa.com).

THEME TRIPS

➤ ADVENTURE: **TrekAmerica** (✉ Box 189, Rockaway, NJ 07866, ☎ 973/983–1144 or 800/221–0596, FAX 973/983–8551, WEB www.trekamerica.com).

➤ ART AND ARCHAEOLOGY IN THE YUCATÁN: **Ceiba Adventures** (✉ Box 2274, Flagstaff, AZ 86003, ☎ 520/527–0171, FAX 520/527–8127). **Destino Maya** (✉ Av. Miguel Alemán 162, Altos 106, 24000 Campeche, ☎ 981/811–0934, FAX 981/811–0934). **Far Horizons Archaeological & Cultural Trips** (✉ Box 91900, Albuquerque, NM 87199-1900, ☎ 505/343–9400 or 800/552–4575, FAX 505/343–8076, WEB www.farhorizon.com). **Maya-Caribe Travel** (✉ 7 Davenport Ave., 3F, New Rochelle, NY 10805, ☎ 914/235–2221). **Sanborn's Viva Tours** (✉ 2015 S. 10th St., McAllen, TX 78505, ☎ 956/682–9872 or 800/395–8482, FAX 956/682–0016, WEB www.sanborns.com). From the U.K.: **Journey Latin America** (✉ 16 Devonshire Rd., Chiswick, London W4 2HD, ☎ 020/8747–8315, FAX 020/8742–1312).

➤ BICYCLING: **Aventuras Tropicales de Sian** (✉ 37 S. Clearwater Rd., Grand Marais, MN 55604, ☎ 218/388–9455 or 800/649–4166, WEB www.

boreal.org/yucatan). **Backroads** (✉ 801 Cedar St., Berkeley, CA 94710-1800, ☎ 510/527–1555 or 800/462–2848, FAX 510/527–1444, WEB www.backroads.com).

➤ ECOTOURISM: **Ecoturismo Yucatán** (✉ Calle 3 No. 235, between Calles 32-A and 34, Col. Pensiones, 97219 Mérida, ☎ 999/925–2187 or 999/925–2187, FAX 999/925–9047, WEB www.mexonline.com/ecoyuc.htm). **Emerald Planet** (✉ 4076 Crystal Court, Boulder, CO 80304, ☎ 919/401–9593 or 800/883–3260, FAX 303/541–9683, WEB www.emeraldplanet.com).

➤ FISHING: **Costa de Cocos** (✉ 2 km [1 mi] outside of Xcalak, Quintana Roo, ☎ FAX 983/831–0110, WEB www.costadecocos.com). **Cutting Loose Expeditions** (✉ Box 447, Winter Park, FL 32790, ☎ 407/629–4700 407/740–7816). **Fishing International** (✉ Box 2132, Santa Rosa, CA 95405, ☎ 707/539–3366 or 800/950–4242, FAX 707/539–1320). **Rod & Reel Adventures** (✉ 2294 Oakmont Way, Eugene, OR 97401, ☎ 800/356–6982, FAX 541/242–0742, WEB rodreeladventures.com).

➤ SPAS: **Spa-Finders** (✉ 91 5th Ave., Suite 301, New York, NY 10003-3039, ☎ 212/924–6800 or 800/255–7727).

TRAIN TRAVEL

Trains in southeast Mexico have a somewhat bad reputation—they're notoriously run-down and late, and they're a haven for thieves. Most of the train lines in the Yucatán have been discontinued.

TRANSPORTATION AROUND THE YUCATÁN PENINSULA

Forget train travel. Buses are efficient and cheap and go to just about every location in the Yucatán. Traveling by car gives you lots of freedom and flexibility: primary roads are excellent throughout the region, and most secondary roads are in good condition (with some potholes). Short-distance flights are offered by a variety of companies, and while more expensive than ground transportation, they can be a good alternative for those with limited time.

TRAVEL AGENCIES

A good travel agent puts your needs first. Look for an agency that has been in business at least five years, emphasizes customer service, and has someone on staff who specializes in your destination. In addition, **make sure the agency belongs to a professional trade organization.** The American Society of Travel Agents (ASTA)—the largest and most influential in the field with more than 26,000 members in some 170 countries—maintains and enforces a strict code of ethics and will step in to help mediate any agent-client disputes involving ASTA members if necessary. ASTA (whose motto is "Without a travel agent, you're on your own") also maintains a Web site that includes a directory of agents. (If a travel agency is also acting as your tour operator, see Buyer Beware in Tours and Packages, above.)

➤ LOCAL AGENT REFERRALS: American Society of Travel Agents (ASTA; ✉ 1101 King St., Suite 200, Alexandria, VA 22314 ☎ 800/965–2782 24-hr hot line, FAX 703/739–7642, WEB www.astanet.com). Association of British Travel Agents (✉ 68–71 Newman St., London W1T 3AH, U.K., ☎ 020/7637–2444, FAX 020/7637–0713, WEB www.abtanet.com). Association of Canadian Travel Agents (✉ 130 Albert St., Suite 1705, Ottawa, Ontario K1P 5G4, Canada, ☎ 613/237–3657, FAX 613/237–7052, WEB www.acta.ca). Australian Federation of Travel Agents (✉ Level 3, 309 Pitt St., Sydney NSW 2000, Australia, ☎ 02/9264–3299, FAX 02/9264–1085, WEB www.afta.com.au). Travel Agents' Association of New Zealand (✉ Level 5, Tourism and Travel House, 79 Boulcott St., Box 1888, Wellington 6001, New Zealand, ☎ 04/499–0104, FAX 04/499–0827, WEB www.taanz.org.nz).

VISITOR INFORMATION

➤ IN THE U.S.: Mexican Government Tourist Office (MGTO; ☎ 800/446–3942; ✉ 21 E. 63rd St., 3rd fl., New York, NY 10021, ☎ 212/821–0314, FAX 212/821–0367; ✉ 300 N. Michigan Ave., 4th fl., Chicago, IL 60601, ☎ 312/606–9252, FAX 312/606–9012; ✉ 2401 W. 6th St., 5th fl., Los Angeles, CA 90057, ☎ 213/351–20675,

FAX 213/351–2074; ✉ 10103 Fondren St., Suite 555, Houston, TX 77042, ☎ 713/772–2581, FAX 713/772–6058); ✉ 1200 NW 78th St., Miami, FL 33126, ☎ 305/718–4098, FAX 305/718–4091).

➤ IN CANADA: Mexican Government Tourist Office (MGTO; ✉ 1 Pl. Ville Marie, Suite 1510, Montréal, Québec H3B 2B5, ☎ 514/871–1052, FAX 514/871–3825; ✉ 2 Bloor St. W, Suite 1502, Toronto, Ontario M4W 3E2, ☎ 416/925–0704, FAX 416/925–6061; ✉ 999 W. Hastings St., Suite 1610, Vancouver, British Columbia V6C 2WC, ☎ 604/669–2845, FAX 604/669–3498).

➤ IN THE U.K.: Mexican Government Tourist Office (MGTO; ✉ 41 Trinity Square, Wakefield House, London EC3N 4DJ, ☎ 207/488–9392 or 207/265–0705, FAX 207/265–0704).

➤ U.S. GOVERNMENT ADVISORIES: U.S. Department of State (✉ Overseas Citizens Services Office, Room 4811, 2201 C St. NW, Washington, DC 20520, ☎ 202/647–5225 interactive hot line or 888/407–4747, WEB www.travel.state.gov); enclose a business-size SASE.

WEB SITES

Do check out the World Wide Web when planning your trip. You'll find everything from weather forecasts to virtual tours of famous cities. Be sure to **visit Fodors.com** (www.fodors.com), a complete travel-planning site. You can research prices and book plane tickets, hotel rooms, rental cars, vacation packages, and more. In addition, you can post your pressing questions in the Travel Talk section. Other planning tools include a currency converter and weather reports, and there are loads of links to travel resources.

There are two official Web sites for Mexico: www.mexico-travel.com and www.visitmexico.com have information on tourist attractions and activities, and an overview of Mexican history and culture. If you would like to get a feel for the country's political climate, check out the president's site at www.presidencia.gob.mx; he also has a site for children (www.elbalero.gob.mx). For more information specifically on the Yucatán Peninsula, try www.yucatantoday.com, www.mayan-riviera.com, or www.cancun.com. All are fairly comprehensive sites with information on nightlife, hotel listings, archaeological sites, area history, and other useful information for travelers.

WHEN TO GO

High season along the Mexican Caribbean runs from mid-December through the week after Easter. The most popular vacation times are Semana Santa (Holy Week, the week leading up to Easter) and the week from Christmas to New Year's. Most hotels are booked well in advance for these holiday periods, when prices are at their highest and armies of travelers swarm popular attractions. Resorts popular with college students (i.e., any place with a beach) tend to fill up in the summer months and during spring-break season (generally March through April).

Off-season price changes are considerable at the beach resorts but are less pronounced in Mérida, Campeche, and other inland regions. To avoid crowds, and high prices, the best times to go are October and March through May.

CLIMATE

From November through March, winter temperatures hover around 80°F. Occasional winter storms can bring blustery skies and high winds, but it is generally sunny. During the early spring months (April–May) there is a period of intense heat that tampers off in June. The hottest months with temperatures reaching up to 110°F start mid-July and last until the end of September when the rainy season starts. The rainy season lasts until mid-November. Officially the tropical storm/hurricane season starts in June but usually doesn't hit the area until mid-September. Inland regions tend to be 10 to 15° warmer than the coast, which is perfect in winter but can be quite uncomfortable in the spring and summer months.

➤ FORECASTS: **Weather Channel Connection** (☎ 900/932–8437), 95¢ per minute from a Touch-Tone phone.

CLIMATE IN CANCÚN

Jan.	84F	29C	May	91F	33C	Sept.	87F	31C
	66	19		73	23		75	24
Feb.	85F	29C	June	92F	33C	Oct.	87F	31C
	68	20		75	24		73	23
Mar.	88F	31C	July	91F	33C	Nov.	86F	30C
	69	21		73	23		71	22
Apr.	88F	31C	Aug.	91F	33C	Dec.	84F	29C
	71	22		75	24		66	19

FESTIVALS AND SEASONAL EVENTS

➤ JAN. 6: **El Día de Los Reyes** (Three Kings' Day/Feast of the Epiphany) is the day Mexican children receive gifts brought by the three kings (the Mexican version of Santa Claus). It also coincides with Mérida's **Founding Day,** the anniversary of the 1542 founding of the city. There, traditional gift-giving is combined with parades, fireworks, and outdoor parties.

➤ JAN. 17: **El Día de San Antonio de Abad** (St. Anthony the Abbot Day) is a religious holiday when animals are taken to churches to be blessed.

➤ FEB. 2: **La Candeleria** is the date of the final Christmas fiesta, hosted by whoever got the small plastic doll called *El Niño* (literally "the child," for Baby Jesus) in his or her piece of *Rosca de Reyes* (Kings' Ring) cake on January 6.

➤ FEB. 24: **El Día de Bandera** (Flag Day) is a national holiday honoring the Mexican flag.

➤ FEB.–MAR.: **Carnival** festivities take place the week before Lent, with parades, floats, outdoor dancing, music, and fireworks; they're especially spirited in Mérida, Cozumel, Isla Mujeres, Campeche, and Chetumal.

➤ MAR. 21: **Aniversario de Benito Juárez** (Benito Juárez's Birthday) is the celebration of the birthday of one of Mexico's greatest heroes; parades are held on this national holiday. On the **Equinoxes** (Mar. 21 and Sept. 21), shadows on the steps of the temple at Chichén Itzá create a snake that appears to be slithering down to earth.

➤ EASTER WEEK: Easter is the most important holiday in Mexico. Fiestas, parades, visits to the family, and numerous religious processions and services mark the event.

➤ APR. 28–MAY 3: **Holy Cross Fiestas** in Chumayel, Celestún, and Hopelchén—all in Yucatán state—include cockfights, dances, and fireworks.

➤ LATE APR.–EARLY MAY.: The **Sol a Sol International Regatta,** launched from St. Petersburg, Florida, arrives in Isla Mujeres, sparking regional dances and a general air of festivity.

➤ LATE APR.–JUNE: **Billfish tournaments** take place in Cozumel, Puerto Aventuras, Puerto Morelos, and Cancún.

➤ MAY 1: **Día del Trabajo** (Day of Work) is an official government holiday celebrated with a big parade.

➤ MAY 5: **Cinco de Mayo** is the Mexican national holiday that honors the Mexican defeat of the French army at Puebla de los Angeles in 1862.

➤ MAY 10: **El Día de Madres** (Mother's Day) is an important holiday because of the special role mothers have in Mexico.

➤ MEMORIAL DAY WEEKEND: The **Cancún Jazz Festival,** an annual event since 1991, has featured such top musicians as Wynton Marsalis and Gato Barbieri.

➤ JUNE 1: **El Día de Péon** (Navy Day) is an official Mexican holiday.

➤ AUG. 18–24: **Founder's Day** celebrates the founding of Isla Mujeres with six days of races, folk dances, music, and regional cuisine.

➤ SEPT. 14: *Vaquerías* (traditional cattle-branding feasts) attract aficionados to rural towns for bullfights, fireworks, and music.

➤ SEPT. 14–28: **Fiesta de San Román** attracts 50,000 people to Campeche to view the procession carrying the Black Christ of San Román—the city's most sacred patron saint—through the streets.

➤ SEPT. 15–16: **Día de Independencia** (Independence Day), the commemoration of a historic speech, known as the *grito* (shout), by Independence leader Padre Miguel Hidalgo, is celebrated throughout Mexico with fireworks and parties.

➤ SEPT. 27: **Fiesta de Cristo de las Ampollas** (Our Lord of the Blisters) begins two weeks or more of religious events and processions in Mérida; dances, bullfights, and fireworks take place in Ticul and other small villages.

➤ OCT. 18–25: **Fiesta del Cristo de Sitilpech** in Izamal, an hour from Mérida, heralds a week of daily processions in which the image of Christ is carried from Sitilpech village to Izamal; dances and fireworks accompany the walks.

➤ NOV. 1–2: On **Día del Muerto** (Day of the Dead, or All Saints' Day), Mexicans all over the country visit cemeteries to construct marigold-strewn altars on the graves of loved ones and ancestors and to symbolically share a meal with them by leaving offerings and having graveside picnics. Bakers herald the annual return of the departed from the spirit world with pastry skulls and candy.

➤ NOV. 20: **Día de la Revolución Mexicana** (Day of the Mexican Revolution) is an official Mexican holiday celebrating the Mexican Revolution of 1910.

➤ NOV. 29–DEC. 8: **Fiesta de Isla Mujeres** honors the island's patron saint, the Virgin of the Immaculate Conception, as members of various guilds stage processions, dances, and bullfights.

➤ NOV. 30–DEC. 8: **Fiesta de la Virgen de Concepción** (Feast of the Virgin Conception) is held each year in Champotón, Campeche.

➤ EARLY DEC.: The **Feria de Cancún** (Cancún Fair) serves as a nostalgia trip for provincials who now live along the Caribbean shore but still remember the small-town fiestas back home.

➤ DEC. 3–9: **Fiesta de la Concepción Immaculada** (Festival of the Immaculate Conception) is observed for six days in the villages across Quintana Roo, with processions, folkloric dances, fireworks, and bullfights.

➤ DEC. 12: **Fiesta de Nuestra Señora de Guadalupe** (Festival of Our Lady of Guadalupe) is celebrated throughout Mexico. Pilgrims who journeyed to the Basilica of the Virgin of Guadalupe in Mexico City return home via bicycles or on foot in time for a midnight Mass followed by dance performances and fiestas.

➤ DEC. 8–12: The **Aquatic Procession** highlights festivities at the fishing village of Celestún, west of Mérida.

➤ DEC. 16–25: **Navidad** (Christmas) is celebrated in the Yucatán villages with processions culminating in the breaking of candy-filled piñatas. The most important day of the holiday season is December 24, **Nochebuena** (Holy Night), when families gather to eat a traditional midnight dinner.

1 DESTINATION: CANCÚN, COZUMEL, YUCATÁN PENINSULA

A PLACE APART

The Yucatán Peninsula has captivated travelers since the early Spanish explorations. "A place of white towers, whose glint could be seen from the ships . . . temples rising tier on tier, with sculptured cornices" is how the expeditions' chroniclers described the peninsula, then thought to be an island. Rumors of a mainland 10 days west of Cuba were known to Columbus, who obstinately hoped to find "a very populated land," and one that was richer than any he had yet discovered. Subsequent explorers and conquistadors met with more resistance there than in almost any other part of the New World, and this rebelliousness continued for centuries.

Largely because of their geographic isolation, Yucatecans tend to preserve ancient traditions more than many other indigenous groups in the country. This can be seen in such areas as housing (the use of the ancient Maya thatched hut, or *na*); dress (*huipiles* have been made and worn by Maya women for centuries); occupation (most modern-day Maya are farmers, just as their ancestors were); language (while the Maya language has evolved considerably, basically it is very similar to that spoken at least 500 years ago); and religion (ancient deities persist, particularly in the form of gods associated with agriculture, such as the *chacs*, or rain gods, and festivals to honor the seasons and benefactor spirits maintain the traditions of old).

This vast peninsula encompasses 113,000 square km (43,630 square mi) of a flat limestone table covered with sparse topsoil and scrubby jungle growth. Geographically, it comprises the states of Yucatán, Campeche, and Quintana Roo, as well as Belize and a part of Guatemala (these two countries are not discussed in this book). Still one of the least Hispanicized (or Mexicanized) regions of the country, Yucatán catapulted into the tourist's vocabulary with the creation of its most precious manmade asset, Cancún.

Mexico's most popular resort destination owes its success to its location on the superb eastern coastline of the Yucatán Peninsula, which is washed by the exquisitely colored and translucent waters of the Caribbean and endowed with a semitropical climate, unbroken stretches of beach, and the world's second-longest barrier reef, which separates the mainland from Cozumel. Cancún and, to a lesser extent, Cozumel incarnate the success formula for sun-and-sand tourism: luxury hotels, sandy beaches, water sports, nightlife, and restaurants that specialize in international fare.

Although Cancún is no longer less expensive than its Caribbean neighbors, it can be reached via more nonstop flights and it offers a far richer culture. With the advent of Cancún, the peninsula's Maya ruins—long a mecca for archaeology enthusiasts—have become virtual satellites of that glittering star. The proximity of such compelling sites as Chichén Itzá, Uxmal, and Tulum allows Cancún's visitors to explore the vestiges of one of the most brilliant civilizations in the ancient world without having to journey too far from their base.

Yucatán offers a breathtaking diversity of other charms, too. The waters of the Mexican Caribbean are clearer and more turquoise than those of the Pacific; many of the beaches are unrivaled. Scuba diving (in natural sinkholes, caves, and along the impressive barrier reef), snorkeling, deep-sea fishing, and other water sports attract growing numbers of tourists. They can also go birding, camp, spelunk, and shop for Yucatán's splendid handicrafts. There is a broad spectrum of settings and accommodations to choose from: the highrise, pricey strip of hotels along Cancún's Paseo Kukulcán; the less showy properties on Cozumel, beloved of scuba divers; and the relaxed ambience of Isla Mujeres, where most lodgings consist of rustic bungalows with ceiling fans and hammocks.

There are also the cities of Yucatán. Foremost is Mérida, wonderfully unaltered by time, where Moorish-inspired, colonnaded colonial architecture blends handsomely with turn-of-the-century pomposity. In Mérida, café life remains an art, and the Maya still live proudly as Maya. Campeche, one of the few walled cities in North America, possesses an eccentric charm; it is slightly out of step with the rest of the country and not the least bothered by the fact. Down on the border with Belize stands Chetumal, a modest commercial center that is pervaded by the hybrid culture of coastal Central America and the pungent smell of the sea. Progreso, at the other end of the peninsula on the Gulf of Mexico, is Chetumal's northern counterpart, an overgrown fishing village turned commercial port. Hotels in these towns, while for the most part not as luxurious as the beach resort properties, range from the respectable if plain 1970s buildings to the undated fleabags so popular with filmmakers and writers exploring the darker side of Mexico (one thinks of *Under the Volcano* by Malcolm Lowry). As a counterpoint to this, deeper into Yucatán, the countryside now shines with magnificently restored haciendas turned into luxury lodgings.

Wildlife is another of Yucatán's riches. Iguanas, lizards, tapirs, deer, armadillos, and wild boars thrive on this alternately parched and densely foliated plain. Flamingos and herons, manatees and sea turtles, their once-dwindling numbers now rising in response to Mexico's newly awakened ecological consciousness, find idyllic watery habitats in and above the coastline's mangrove swamps, lagoons, and sandbars, acres of which have been made into national parks. Both Río Lagartos and the coast's Sian Ka'an Biosphere Reserve sparkle with Yucatán's natural beauty. Orchids, bougainvillea, and poinciana are ubiquitous; dazzling reds and pinks and oranges and whites spill into countless courtyards—effortless hothouses. And while immense palm groves and forests of precious hardwood trees slowly succumb to fire and disease, the region's edible tropical flora—coconuts, limes, papaya, bananas, and oranges—remains a succulent ancillary to the celebrated Yucatecan cuisine.

But perhaps it is the colors of Yucatán that are most remarkable. From the stark white, sun-bleached sand, the sea stretches out like some immense canvas painted in bands of celadon greens, pale aquas, and deep dusty blues. At dusk the sea and the horizon meld in the sumptuous glow of a lavender sunset, the sky just barely tinged with periwinkle and violet. Inland, the beige, gray, and amber stones of ruined temples are set off by riotous greenery. The colors of newer structures are equally intoxicating: tawny, gray-brown thatched roofs sit atop white oval huts. Colonial mansions favor creamy pastels of bisque, salmon, and coral tones, again highlighted by elegant white: white arches, white balustrades, white rococo porticos. Brilliant colors glimmer in carved hardwood doors, variegated tile floors, brown and green pottery and rugs affixed to walls, and snatches of bougainvillea rushing down the sides of buildings.

Yucatán's color extends beyond the physical to the historical. From the conquistadors' first landfall off Cape Catoche in 1517 to the bloody skirmishes that wiped out most of the Indians to the razing of Maya temples and burning of their sacred books, the peninsula was a battlefield. Pirates wreaked havoc off the coast of Campeche for centuries. Half the Indian population was killed during the 19th-century uprising known as the War of the Castes, when the enslaved indigenous population rose up and massacred thousands of Mexicans; Yucatán was attempting to secede from Mexico, and dictator Porfirio Díaz sent in his troops. These events, like the towering Maya civilization, have left their mark throughout the peninsula: in its archaeological museums, its colonial monuments, and the opulent mansions of the hacienda owners who enslaved the natives to cultivate their henequen.

But despite the past's violent conflicts with foreigners, the people of Yucatán treat today's visitors with genuine hospitality and friendliness, especially outside the beach resorts. If you learn a few words of Spanish, you will be rewarded with an even warmer welcome.

— Updated by Patricia Alisau
and Shelagh McNally

WHAT'S WHERE

Cancún

The rhinestone of Mexico's Caribbean coast, Cancún, in the upper eastern portion of the Yucatán Peninsula, is currently

Mexico's most popular destination. A slender, 14-mi-long barrier island called the Hotel Zone is lined with lush, landscaped resorts, which welcome more than 2 million visitors a year. The fun comes in all varieties, from outdoorsy to raucous to culturally enriching. With the Caribbean on one side and the Laguna de Nichupté on the other, water-sports are a major draw. So are clear, turquoise vistas and soft white sand. When the sun sets, Cancún gets down. Club-hopping and tequila-sampling attract throngs of merrymakers. Performances of the Ballet Folklórico de Cancún (Folkloric Ballet of Cancún) give you a taste of Mexican culture, and you can venture farther, to El Centro, downtown Cancún, for some real Mexican-Maya flavor in the markets and restaurants.

Isla Mujeres

Only 8 km (5 mi) across the bay from Cancún, Isla Mujeres is light-years away in temperament, a laid-back, less crowded, and less expensive counterpoint to the big resorts' flash. Key diversions are sunning on the white-sand beaches, snorkeling and diving, eating fresh seafood, or just lazing under a *palapa* (thatched roof).

Cozumel

A mere 20 km (12 mi) offshore from the Caribbean Coast, Cozumel is older and mellower than Cancún, hipper than Isla Mujeres, and draws the best from both worlds. More than anything, its raison d' être is diving. Cozumel's reefs are the finest in the Americas, and many of them are protected as national parks. Parque Chankanaab is the showpiece, where you can meet a Maya rain god under the waves or a golden iguana resplendent by a blue-green lagoon. Reef, ruins, and retailers can fill your days here, but there's plenty of action for night owls, too, at Cozumel's rocking dance clubs and bars.

The Caribbean Coast

South of Cancún, golf carts and tennis shops practically disappear and the number of acres of beach per visitor skyrockets. And what beaches. The shores are strands of dazzling white with waters multilayered blues and greens, beckoning to sun worshipers as well as snorkelers, divers, birders, and beachcombers, and anyone else who likes the ocean clear and seascapes

no taller than the surrounding jungle. The Riviera Maya, a slice of coast about 113 km (70 mi) long a few miles south of Cancún on the eastern shore of Yucatán, is becoming increasingly popular with visitors as well as developers. Accommodations come in every style, from jungle lodges and campgrounds to extravagant resorts. Playa del Carmen is a Cancún-in-the-making with plentiful dining options and a lively nightlife. But the natural beauty of the coast is its biggest draw. Eco-tourists head for the intriguing Sian Ka'an Biosphere Reserve, a giant UNESCO showpiece where you can see Yucatán as it was when the Maya flourished. Visit Tulum, truly a ruin with a view, or mighty, jungle-clad Cobá, with its towering imperial pyramids.

Mérida and the State of Yucatán

The ancient ruins here best reflect the grandeur of the ancient Maya civilization. There's the spectacular Chichén Itzá, a world-famous site, and elegant Uxmal, known for its understated beauty. Indeed, the Maya never really left Yucatán. The old deities receive their due, and religious pageants adroitly meld Christian and pre-Hispanic beliefs. All this makes the old Maya capital city of Mérida the perfect base for exploring. Maya meets colonial here, weaving a rich cultural and visual tapestry. The music, dance, and museums are the best Yucatán, and farther west along the coast, the flamingo watching is memorable.

Campeche

Yucatecan life is at its mellowest in Campeche, which lies off the west coast of the Yucatán Peninsula caressing the Gulf of Mexico. Here the Maya imprint is intoxicating. In Becal, artisans still weave traditional hats known as *jipis*, and the ancient ruins are architecturally diverse and richly detailed. The regal city of Calakmul in southern Campeche is primeval rain forest, protected as the Calakmul Biosphere Reserve, where jaguar, ocelot, and puma still roam free. Spanish colonial heritage is most palpable in Campeche City, notably at Fuerte San José, which warded off pirate attacks in the days of the buccaneers.

PLEASURES AND PASTIMES

Archaeological Sites

Amateur archaeologists will find heaven in the Yucatán, where the ancient Maya most abundantly left their mark. Pick your period and your preference, whether for well-excavated sites or overgrown, out-of-the-way ruins barely touched by a scholar's shovel. The major Maya sites are Cobá, Tulum, Chichén Itzá and Uxmal, but smaller sites scattered throughout the peninsula are often equally fascinating.

Ek Balam, 20 km (12 mi) north of Valladolid in Yucatán state, is one of the more rewarding Maya sites in Yucatán. Only a few structures have been excavated, but the magnitude of overgrown ruins is impressive. Among the restored structures is a dazzling pyramid tower with huge stucco monster masks, which was the mausoleum for a Maya king. Buried with him were precious jewels, gold, jade, and perforated seashells, among other riches.

The opening of the first of several planned environmentally friendly jungle lodges in the Xpuhil area of the state of Campeche has made possible extended visits to the ruins at Becán, Xpujil, Hormiguero, Río Bec, and Calakmul, all of which are undergoing restoration. Another such lodge has opened near the site of Kohunlich along the Caribbean coast, enabling adventurous visitors to experience direct links with the ancient past.

Beaches

Cancún and the rest of Yucatán offer a wonderful variety of beaches. You'll find white sands, rocky coves and promontories, curvaceous bays, and murky lagoons. Resorty Playa Chacmool and Playa Tortugas are on the bay side of Cancún, which is calmer if less beautiful than the windward side. Go to the north end of Isla Mujeres to Playa Norte for great sunsets. Beaches on Cozumel's east coast—once used by buccaneers—are rocky, and the swimming is treacherous, but they offer privacy. On the relatively sheltered leeward side are the widest and best sand beaches.

The Caribbean coast abounds with exquisite hidden beaches and coves, as well as not-so-hidden beaches. There are also long stretches of white sand, usually filled with sunbathers, at Puerto Morelos, Akumal, and especially Playa del Carmen.

Travelers to Campeche and Progreso will find the waters of the Gulf of Mexico deep green, shallow, and tranquil. Such beaches as Payucán, Sabancuy, and Isla del Carmen are less visited by North Americans and facilities are minimal; Telchac Puerto is more developed.

Bird-Watching

The Yucatán Peninsula is one of the finest areas for birding in Mexico. Habitats range from wildlife and bird sanctuaries to unmarked lagoons, estuaries, and mangrove swamps. Frigates, tanagers, warblers, and macaws inhabit Isla Contoy (off Isla Mujeres) and the Laguna Colombia on Cozumel; an even greater variety of species is to be found in the Sian Ka'an Biosphere Reserve on the Boca Paila peninsula south of Tulum. Along the north and west coasts of Yucatán—at Río Lagartos, Laguna Rosada, and Celestún—flamingos, herons, ibis, cormorants, pelicans, and peregrine falcons thrive.

Dining

The mystique of Yucatecan cooking has a lot to do with the generous doses of local spices and herbs, although generally the food tends not to be too spicy. In the early days, it was tremendously influenced by French, Cuban, and New Orleans cooking because of continual cultural contact. This multi-cultural approach resulted in such distinctive specialties as *pollo pibíl* (chicken marinated in a sour orange and annatto seed sauce and baked in banana leaves); *poc chuc* (Yucatecan pork marinated in a sour-orange sauce with pickled onions); *tikinchic* (fried fish prepared with sour orange); *panuchos* (fried tortillas filled with black beans and topped with diced turkey, chicken, or pork as well as pickled onions and avocado); *papadzules* (tortillas rolled up with hard-boiled eggs and drenched in a sauce of pumpkin seed and fried tomato); and *codzitos* (rolled tortillas in pumpkin-seed sauce). *Achiote* (annatto), cilantro (coriander), and the fiery *chile habañero* are zesty condiments. Along the gulf coast, there's nothing finer than a dish of fresh blue crab, or baby shrimp.

Yucatecans are renowned for—among other things—their love of idiosyncratic beverages. *Yztabentún,* a liqueur made of fermented honey and anise, dates back to the ancient Maya; like straight tequila, it's best drunk in small sips between bites of fresh lime. Local brews, such as the dark bock León Negra and the light Montejo, are excellent but hard to find in peninsular restaurants. On the healthier side, *chaya* is the bright-green local plant resembling spinach, often made into juice or cooked. Yucatecan *horchata,* a favorite all over Mexico, is made from milled rice and water flavored with vanilla.

Fishing

Sportfishing is popular in Cozumel and throughout the Caribbean coast. The rich waters of the Caribbean and the Gulf of Mexico support hundreds of species of tropical fish, making the Yucatán coastline and the outlying islands a paradise for deep-sea fishing, fly-fishing, and bonefishing. Particularly between the months of April and July, the waters off Cancún, Cozumel, and Isla Mujeres teem with sailfish, marlin, red snapper, tuna, barracuda, and wahoo, among other denizens of the deep. Billfishing is so rich around Cozumel that it holds an annual tournament.

Farther south, along the Boca Paila peninsula, bone fishing for these feisty little critters and light-tackle saltwater fishing for banana fish, shad, permit, and sea bass are the hands-down favorites, while oysters, shrimp, and conch lie on the bottom of the Gulf of Mexico near Campeche and Isla del Carmen. At Progreso, on the north coast, sportfishing for grouper, dogfish, and pompano is quite popular.

Scuba Diving and Snorkeling

Underwater enthusiasts come to Cozumel, Akumal, Xcalak, Xel-Há, and other parts of Mexico's Caribbean coast for the clear turquoise waters, the colorful and assorted tropical fish, and the exquisite coral formations along the Palancar reef system. Currents allow for drift diving, and both reefs and offshore wrecks lend themselves to dives, many of which are safe enough for neophytes. The peninsula's cenotes, or natural sinkholes, and underwater caverns provide an unusual dive experience. Individual chapters will direct you to the dive sites that will best suit you.

Water Sports

All manner of water sports—jet skiing, catamaran sailing, sailboarding, waterskiing, sailing, and parasailing—are practiced in Cancún, Cozumel, Playa del Carmen, and other places along the Caribbean coast, where you'll find well-equipped watersports centers.

FODOR'S CHOICE

Archaeological Sites

Chichén Itzá. This best-known Maya site was the most important city in Yucatán from the 11th to the 13th century. Its eclectic architecture shows a complex intermingling of ancient cultures.

Cobá. Once a central city-state in the Maya domain, this site has long languished in a lush, tropical setting. Only about 5% of its more than 6,000 structures have been excavated.

Edzná. Archaeologists consider this remote, little-explored, and remarkably intact ruin crucial for its transitional role in Maya architectural development.

Uxmal. The lovely Uxmal style includes ornate stone friezes, intricate cornices, and soaring arches.

Beaches

Akumal. Long stretches of this popular section of the Caribbean coast are filled with shells, crabs, and migrant birds. Protected coves with tranquil water are ideal for swimming or snorkeling.

Playa Norte. A white sand beach on the northern tip of Isla Mujeres, Playa Norte—sometimes called Cocoteros or Cocos—is both scenic and social.

Punta Celerain. The lighthouse at the southern end of Cozumel affords wonderful views of pounding waves, swamps, and jungle.

Xcalak Peninsula. One of the Caribbean coast's still-remote spots, this peninsula is lush with mangrove swamps, tropical flowers, and wildlife.

Dining

Maria Bonita, Cancún. A lively restaurant reminiscent of a Mexican hacienda, Maria Bonita has an enclosed patio with an ocean view. It is the perfect place to enjoy the best of Mexican cuisine. $–$$$

La Bella Epoca, Mérida. At this gracious converted mansion, diners indulge in platters of Middle Eastern specialties along with well-prepared versions of French and Yucatecan dishes. $$

Casa Cenote, Mexico's Caribbean coast. This unique restaurant near the ruins of Tulum allows diners to plunge into a large natural pool before enjoying tasty American and Mexican fare. $$

La Choza, Cozumel. The superfresh Mexican entrées at this friendly, family-run place include chicken mole and grilled lobster; tortillas are baked on the premises. $$

Marganzo, Campeche. The food at this popular, low-key place typifies the distinctive seafood dishes known as *estillo campechano* (Campeche style) all over Mexico. $

Velazquez, Isla Mujeres. This quintessential palapa-style eatery is right on the beach. Don't be misled by the simple, rustic ambience; here you'll find the best seafood on the island. $

Lodging

Presidente Inter-Continental Cozumel. A great water-sports center, a fine beach for snorkeling, and bright, contemporary-style rooms make this the luxury-class choice on Cozumel. $$$$

Ritz-Carlton Cancún. The Cancún link of this international chain adds class to the beachfront hotel zone. Its facilities and restaurants are superb. $$$$

Na Balam, Isla Mujeres. The rooms here are attractive in a simple, folk-art fashion, and their proximity to sea and sand is hard to beat. $$$

Gran Hotel, Mérida. The oldest hotel in Mérida combines character—an Art Nouveau courtyard and balconied rooms—with reasonable prices. $$

Ramada Ecovillage Resort, Campeche. Comfort and even a bit of luxury can be found at this jungle lodge on the fringe of the Calakmul rain forest and near a little-explored archaeological zone. $$

Villa Arqueológica Cobá, Mexico's Caribbean coast. Sleep among the ruins at this Club Med, about 10 minutes away from Cobá. The lakeside setting is lovely, and the food is the best in the area. $$

Nature Reserves and Natural Beauty

Isla Contoy. An unspoiled island preserve off the coast of Isla Mujeres, Isla Contoy is especially notable for its birds; more than 70 species pass through in the fall.

Laguna de Bacalar. The second-largest lake in Mexico is known as the "Lake of Seven Colors" because of the stunning hues that a mix of seawater, freshwater, and seaweed produce.

Loltún Caves. This largest of the many limestone caverns that honeycomb the central Yucatán Peninsula has colorful rock formations as well as pictographs left by the Maya, who lived here for thousands of years.

Parque Natural del Flamenco Mexicano. One of the biggest colonies of flamingos in North America rests here from September through April; deer and armadillo roam this huge wildlife preserve, too.

Sian Ka'an Biosphere Reserve. At this 1.3-million-acre preserve you can see half-submerged Maya ruins in mangrove canals or bird-watch for exotic species in the jungle.

Nightlife

Azucar, Cancún. Locals and visitors of all ages gather at this hot nightspot for the best live salsa in Cancún.

Dady'O, Cancún. Though it's been around for a while, this is still *the* place to come if you need a cure for Saturday Night Fever.

Joe's Lobster House, Cozumel. Beginning about 9 PM, live rollicking reggae and hot salsa spice up the music menu here. This quaint nightspot, popular with locals, hops into the wee hours.

YaYa's, Isla Mujeres. Live rock and Texas-style chili dogs have proved a winning combination here.

Shopping

Los Cinco Soles, Cozumel. Cruise-ship passengers with limited time to shop can find a large array of well-priced clothing and crafts here.

Mercado de Artesanías "García Rejón," Mérida. Come to this handicrafts market for hammocks, Panama hats, baskets, and other Yucatán souvenirs.

Mercado Municipal, Mérida. The best general market in Yucatán sells everything from live birds and food to intricate local crafts.

GREAT ITINERARIES

Highlights of Yucatán

9 to 10 Days

The Yucatán Peninsula is so diverse that you can visit islands, a biosphere, follow the footsteps of the ancient Maya at their ceremonial centers, dive at one of the world's best reefs systems, play at beachcombing, learn about conservation efforts at UNESCO's biggest Mexican forest reserve—and all this in a single trip. Start your visit in Cancún, on the storied Caribbean coast, and use it as your hub for a few days.

Isla Mujeres (*1 day*). There are plenty of white sand beaches, or you can go snorkeling at the El Garrafón underwater park, teeming with reef life. In the 17th century, the same reefs hid lusty pirates lying in wait for passing Spanish galleons and before that, the Maya worshiped a moon deity on a windy bluff overlooking the sea. The shrine to the deity is still standing while the small inns and restaurants remind you that Isla is still a peaceful Mexican retreat. ☞ Chapter 3.

Tulum, Xel-Há (*1 day*). Tulum, as part of the great trading dynasty of the ancient Maya, became a walled city to protect precious cargo. Nearby Xel-Há, with its natural coves and inlets was a Maya port of call, and is now a swimmer's paradise. Together they make a perfect day's outing. ☞ Tulum, Xel-Há in Chapter 5.

Sian Ka'an Biosphere Reserve (*1 day*). This 1.3 million-acre UNESCO site was first settled in the 5th century AD and has one of the last undeveloped coasts in North America. Conservation is at the forefront here. Take a tour and see villagers saving the spiny lobster, explore watery channels once used as part of a trade route to the sea, and share space with hundreds of wild birds, who've made it

their haven. ☞ Sian Ka'an Biosphere Reserve in Chapter 5.

Cozumel (*2 days*). Otherworldly and serene, Cozumel's first pilgrims were pregnant women who beseeched the Maya goddess of fertility for a blessed birth. Today it's a scuba diving mecca, one of the top five dive spots on the globe. In fact, Jacques Cousteau made it his headquarters during many an underwater exploration. Grab a wet suit and plumb fabulous reefs filled with caves, canyons, tunnels, and archways. If you're not a diver, the island also has snorkeling, handicrafts shops, sportfishing, and nightlife. ☞ Chapter 4.

Mérida (*2 days*). The splendid architecture of this capital of the state of Yucatán taps into Spanish, Moorish, and French influences but states its case clearly. It was, and remains, a Maya city. The Maya dialect can be heard on the streets and many women wear traditional *huipil* dresses. If you arrive on Sunday, spend it in the festive main plaza where free performances of folk music and dance are given throughout the day. Visit the Indian markets, hammock makers, and small cafés filled with the local intelligentsia, or just stroll long the avenues gazing at the wonderfully detailed colonial buildings. Drop in to the Museum of Anthropology prior to your trip to the ruins at Chichén Itzá for a preview. ☞ Mérida in Chapter 6.

Chichén Itzá (*1 day*). First settled in AD 432, Chichén Itzá was later abandoned and then rediscovered by the Itzás in 868. Under their rule and subsequent alliances, it rose to become the most important city in Yucatán from the 10th through the 12th centuries. The area is dominated by the spectacular El Castillo (the Castle), a pyramid on top of which stands a temple dedicated to Kukulcán. ☞ Chichén Itzá in Chapter 6.

Campeche City (*1 day*).Tour the 16th century colonial downtown and the impressive remains of the San Juan Fortress with its light-and-sound show. You'll also have time to travel to the Maya site of Edzná outside town with its multistory pyramid. ☞ Campeche City in Chapter 7.

Maya Sites

10 to 12 Days

With a history spanning 3,000 years, the Maya are one of the greatest civilizations the world has ever known. In this tour you can travel through time to the glories of Mayan dynasties, their sacred cities, architectural and engineering feats, and art and culture.

Mérida (*2 days*). Mérida was a thriving Maya city before the arrival of the Spanish conquistadores in the 16th century. It remains an important commercial hub of the Yucatán Peninsula, bringing untold wealth into the city coffers. The wealth built stately mansions and palaces, many of which can be viewed today. Visit a town where the modern-day Maya fuse past with present in custom and dress and where museums and cultural offerings are the best on the Peninsula. Surrounded by archaeological sites, nature reserves, and other colonial cities, it's the perfect base from which to explore the region. Make day trips to Chichén Itzá and Uxmal from here. ☞ Mérida in Chapter 6.

Chichén Itzá (*1 day*). One of the most famous Maya sites in the world, Chichén Itzá covers several square miles punctuated by temples and pyramids. Thousands gather each spring and autumn equinox for special ceremonies honoring Kukulcán, the mystical plumed serpent god. Walk through a ball court, scale the tall El Castillo pyramid, and visit Old Chichén Itzá built in the "pure Maya" style adorned with latticework and stone serpents. The light-and-sound show during a full moon is exceptional. ☞ Chichén Itzá in Chapter 6.

Uxmal and the Ruta Puuc (*1 day*). Uxmal rose to prominence during the Late Classical period of the 7th and 9th centuries. The city celebrates the Puuc style of architecture with its subtle elegance and long, quadrangle-shape buildings. Note details such as elaborate stone mosaic latticework and cornices with curled noses representing the rain god Chaac. The highest structure is the mysterious elliptical–shaped Pyramid of the Magicians, soaring 125 ft into the heavens. The most famous is the Nun's Quadrangle, which served as the living quarters of a high lord of the Maya. ☞ Uxmal and the Puuc Route in Chapter 6.

Campeche City (*1 day*). In the colonial era, Campeche City became a prominent shipping port for goods bound for Spain. To thwart pirates, it then became a walled city—the only one in New Spain. You can tour the colonial downtown, climb the ramparts of the San Juan Fortress, and visit a museum loaded with stupendous jade artifacts. Stop at the Maya ruins at Edzná, which reached its apex from the 7th to 10th centuries. Then book a tour in Campeche City to the ruins in the southern part of the state. ☞ Campeche City in Chapter 7.

Xpuhil, Becán, Hormiguero, and Chicanná (*1 day*). You will experience the dramatic Chenes and Río Bec styles of Maya architecture at these sites. Doorways fashioned into fascinating monster mouths; pyramid towers; fortified walls; sculpted faces and reliefs of the rain god Chaac stand out in the isolated jungle setting. Plan to stay overnight in order to have time to visit Calakmul. ☞ Xpuhil, Becán, Hormiguero, and Chicanná in Chapter 7.

Calakmul Biosphere Reserve (*1 day*). Skirting the Guatemala border, Calakmul was a formidable Maya military power until the 7th century AD. It is one of the largest cities of the Maya empire, and, together with its surrounding biosphere reserve, stretches over 1.8 million acres. Thousands of structures in Calakmul have yet to be excavated, but its awesome size and the dramatic beauty of the surrounding landscape is apparent everywhere. Return to Campeche City after your visit. ☞ Calakmul Biosphere Reserve in Chapter 7.

Cancún (*1 day*). A vibrant seaside resort city, Cancún has non-stop activity from dusk to dawn. Enjoy spun-sugar sandy beaches; myriad water-sports; sophisticated restaurants and bars; first-class hotels; and shopping (some in duty-free shops). Use Cancún as your hub for trips to Tulum and Cobá. ☞ Cancún in Chapter 2.

Tulum, Xel-Há (*1 day*). Tulum draws millions of tourists every year, making it the most visited archaeological site in Mexico. Perched on a cliff overlooking the multitoned turquoise waters of the Caribbean, the view is outstanding. As part of the great trading dynasty of the ancient Maya, Tulum became a walled city to protect the precious cargo brought from near and far. Nearby Xel-Há, with natural coves and inlets, is a remarkable self-contained aquatic park with dolphins, transparent lagoons, and small Maya ruins. Shake off the dust of the ruins with a plunge into cool waters. ☞ Tulum, Xel-Há in Chapter 5.

Cobá, Pac Chen (*1 day*). Cobá is the largest Maya site in the northern sector of the Caribbean coast, at one time encompassing 27 square mi. Once a close ally of Tikal in Guatemala, its enormous temples are the highest in the region reaching more than 100 ft. Built around five lakes, most of the site is covered in dense jungle (only 5% of the estimated 6,500 structures have been uncovered). Well-marked footpaths lead to the excavated temples with their plazas, stucco motifs, ball courts, and sacbés or Maya roads made of limestone, which carried trade goods to neighboring cities. You'll also have time to visit the settlement of Pac Chen, to get a glimpse of the life of the modern-day Maya in a primitive setting combined with soft adventure activities. ☞ Cobá, Pac Chen in Chapter 5.

Kohunlich, Laguna de Bacalar (*1 day*). You'll want to lodge overnight in the area, either in Chetumal or at any of a number of jungle lodges found here. Kohunlich is outstanding for its series of giant stucco masks embedded in its pyramids. The site is small, rarely crowded, and can be covered in half a day. Take a boat tour later in the day at the Laguna de Bacalar, the second-largest lake in Mexico filled with saltwater and freshwater, which creates amazing aquamarine hues. ☞ Kohunlich, Laguna de Bacalar in Chapter 5.

Dzibanché, Kinichná (*1 day*). Dzibanché and Kinichná are two smaller sites a few miles apart. The Temple of the Owl and temples dedicated to Itzamná, the Maya god of the sun, can be explored in the pristine stillness of the surrounding jungle. Before leaving the region, visit the Museum of the Maya Culture in Chetumal, the best exhibit on the life and times of this ancient culture anywhere in the country. ☞ Dzibanché and Kinichná in Chapter 5.

2   CANCÚN

The rhinestone of Mexico's Caribbean coast, Cancún is Mexico's biggest dazzle-for-dollar destination. The Hotel Zone is lined with high-rise resorts, glitzy discos, air-conditioned malls, and gorgeous beaches. For a taste of the real Mexico, go downtown, where you can sample Yucatecan specialties at casual eateries.

Updated
by Shelagh
McNally

FLYING INTO CANCÚN, you see nothing but green treetops for miles. It's clear from the air that this resort was literally carved out of the jungle. When development began here in the early 1970s, the beaches were deserted except for birds and iguanas. Now luxury hotels, shopping malls, and restaurants line Cancún's oceanfront. More vacationers come here than to any other part of Mexico, and many come again and again for the white-sand beaches, crystalline turquoise waters, sizzling nightlife, numerous restaurants, and the proximity of Maya ruins throughout the Yucatán peninsula.

Cancún has two very different sides. On the mainland is the actual Ciudad Cancún (Cancún City), the commercial center that is also informally known as El Centro. The other half, the Zona Hotelera (Hotel Zone), is the tourist heart. The Zone is actually a 22½-km (14-mi) barrier island off the Yucatán Peninsula. A separate northern strip called **Punta Sam,** north of Puerto Juárez (where the ferries to Isla Mujeres depart), is sometimes considered part of the Zone and is unofficially referred to as the Northern Hotel Zone. Both areas have been designed to please average American tastes: most people speak English, and there are fast-food outlets, brand-name stores, and cable TV. Shopping, eating, and lounging in the year-round tropical warmth are the main activities. (The sun shines an average of 240 days a year, reputedly more than at almost any other Caribbean spot. Temperatures linger at about 80°F.) At night you can enjoy activities such as knocking back tequila slammers at a bar, listening to great music at clubs, watching folkloric dance performances, and sampling Yucatecan food.

But there is more to Cancún than plopping yourself down under a *palapa* (thatch roof). Downtown offers a more authentic glimpse into the sights and sounds of Mexico. For diving and snorkeling, the reefs off Cancún and nearby Cozumel, Puerto Morelos, and Isla Mujeres are among the best in the world. Cancún also makes a relaxing base for venturing to the stupendous ruins of Chichén Itzá, Tulum, and Cobá, remnants of the area's rich Maya heritage.

As for Cancún's history, not much was written about it before its birth as a resort. The Maya people did settle the area during the Late Preclassic era, around AD 200, and remained until the 14th or 15th century, but little is known about them. Other explorers seem to have overlooked the barrier island—it doesn't appear on early navigators' maps. It was never heavily populated, perhaps because its terrain of mangroves and marshes (and resulting swarms of mosquitoes) discouraged settlement. Some minor Maya ruins were discovered in the mid-19th century, but archaeologists didn't get around to studying them until the 1950s.

In 1967, the Mexican government, under the leadership of Luis Echeverría, commissioned a study to pinpoint the ideal place for an international Caribbean resort. The computer chose Cancún, and the Cinderella transformation began. At the time the area's only residents were the three caretakers of a coconut plantation. In 1972 work began on the first hotel, and the island and city grew from there.

As is typical of any tourist resort area, Cancún first attracted the jet set, gradually welcoming less affluent tourists. Today the Zona Hotelera alone has more than 25,000 hotel rooms, many filled with package-tourists and college students, particularly during spring break, when hordes of tanned young bodies fill the beaches and restaurants.

But Cancún's success has not come without a price. Its lagoons and mangrove swamps have been polluted; a number of species, such as conch and lobster, are dwindling; and parts of the coral reef are dead. And although the beaches still appear pristine for the most part, an increased effort will have to be made in order to preserve the physical beauty that is the resort's prime appeal.

Pleasures and Pastimes

Archaeological Sites

Cancún is dotted with the vestiges of a Maya settlement from 900 to 1520. Magnificent Chichén Itzá and Tulum are easy day trips from the resort.

Beaches

The Mexican government might have designed the resort, but nature provided its most striking features—its cool, white, porous limestone sand and clear turquoise waters. Except for the tip of Punta Cancún, Cancún Island is one long beach. The windward beaches that fringe the Bahía de Mujeres have the calmest water and are ideal for water sports and swimmers of all levels. The east coast faces the open sea; the waves are bigger here, and there are serious currents and riptides. The more popular beaches, such as Playa Chacmool and Playa Tortugas, have restaurants, bars, and sports facilities. On the less trafficked eastern strand, Playa Delfines has spectacular views. All beaches are federal property and are open to everyone.

Dining

One of the best things about Cancún is its diversity of restaurants. Many present a hybrid cuisine that combines fresh fish from local waters, elements of Yucatecan and Mexican cuisines, and a fusion of French, Italian, and American influences. Fiesta dinners are a weekly staple at many hotels, so you can sample Mexican favorites without venturing out. If you enjoy high drama at dinner, there are places where waiters artistically prepare meals table-side or mix flaming cocktails with great flourish.

Lodging

There are more than 25,000 hotel rooms in Cancún and well over 110 hotels. The resort's architecture, especially in the Hotel Zone, tends to be a cross between Mediterranean style and a developer's interpretation of Maya style. In many cases the combination yields an appealing, if kitschy, look. Typical Mediterranean structures—low, solid, rectangular, with flat, red-tile roofs; Moorish arches; and white stucco walls covered with exuberantly pink bougainvillea—take on palapas and such ornamental devices as colonnettes, latticework, and beveled cornices. Inside are contemporary-style furniture and pastel hues.

Boulevard Kukulcán is the main thoroughfare, on which most of the hotels are located. It is a two-lane road, artfully landscaped with palm trees, sculpted bushes, waterfalls, and tiered pools. The hotels pride themselves on delivering endless opportunities for fun. Water sports, marinas, golf, tennis, kids' clubs, fitness centers, spas, shopping, entertainment, dining, and tours and excursions are all offered, along with warm Mexican hospitality and attentive service. Of course, you pay for all of this—the Hotel Zone can be quite expensive. Downtown is more modest, and local color far outweighs resort facilities.

Nightlife

Cancún is a party town. From early evening to dawn the whole Zone pulses with music. Salsa, reggae, hip-hop, mariachi, jazz, classical, disco, rock and roll—it's all here. Such local discos as Coco Bongo and La Boom give you the chance to dance the night away, while ubiquitous American chain entertainers such as the Hard Rock Cafe and Pat

O'Briens offer both food and music. Many hotel lobby bars have two-for-one drink deals at happy hour, and bar-hopping in the big resorts is a great way to check out the different hotel interiors. To see how the locals party, head to the Latin clubs. For a taste of old Mexico, take in the Folkloric Ballet dinner show at the convention center. Or dine and dance under the stars aboard the *Cancún Queen* or the *Columbus*.

Water Sports

Cancún is one of the water-sports capitals of the world, and, with the Caribbean on one side of the island and the still waters of Laguna Nichupté on the other, it's no wonder. The most popular activities are snorkeling and diving along the coral reef just off the coast, where schools of colorful tropical fish and other marine creatures live. If you want to view the mysterious underwater world but don't want to get your feet wet, a glass-bottom boat or "submarine" is the ticket. You can also fish, sail, jet-ski, parasail, or windsurf.

EXPLORING CANCÚN

Cancún's Zona Hotelera is a small island shaped roughly like the numeral seven. The top extends east from the mainland into the Caribbean; the Punta Cancún–Punta Nizuc strip has a slight north–northeast arc. Hotel development began at the north end (close to the mainland), headed east toward Punta Cancún, and then moved south to Punta Nizuc. At the south end of the Hotel Zone, the road curves west toward the highway and airport. Downtown Cancún—El Centro—is 4 km (2½ mi) west of the Hotel Zone on the mainland.

A system of lagoons separates the Hotel Zone from the mainland. Nichupté, the largest (about 29 square km, or 18 square mi), contains both fresh- and saltwater. Bojórquez is nestled inside the northeastern elbow. Laguna Río Inglés is south of Nichupté. Bahía de Mujeres lies north of the Zone; the bay, which is 9 km (5½ mi) wide, separates Cancún from Isla Mujeres.

Boulevard Kukulcán is the main drag in the Hotel Zone, and because the island is so narrow—less than 1 km (½ mi) wide—you can see both the Caribbean and the lagoons from either side of it. Regularly placed kilometer markers alongside Boulevard Kukulcán indicate where you are. The first marker (Km 1) is near downtown on the mainland; Km 20 lies at the south end of the Zone at Punta Nizuc. The area in between consists entirely of hotels, restaurants, shopping complexes, marinas, and time-share condominiums. It's not the sort of place you can get to know by walking, although there is a bicycle–walking path that starts downtown at the beginning of the Hotel Zone and continues through to Punta Nizuc. The beginning of the path parallels a grassy strip of Boulevard Kukulcán decorated with reproductions of ancient Mexican art, including the Aztec calendar stone, a giant Olmec head, the Atlantids of Tula, and a Maya Chacmool (reclining rain god).

South of Punta Cancún, Boulevard Kukulcán becomes a busy road, difficult to cross on foot, punctuated by steeply inclined driveways that turn into the hotels, most of which are set at least 100 yards from the road. The lagoon side of the boulevard consists of scrubby stretches of land alternating with marinas, shopping centers, and restaurants. Because there are so few sights, there are no orientation tours of Cancún: just do the local bus circuit to get a feel for the island's layout.

When you first visit El Centro, the downtown layout might not be self-evident. It is not based on a grid but rather on a circular pattern. The whole city is divided into districts called Super Manzanas (abbreviated

Sm in this book), each with its own central square or park. The main streets curve around the manzanas, and the smaller neighborhood streets curl around the parks in horseshoe shapes. Avenida Tulum is the main street—actually a four-lane road with two northbound and two southbound lanes. The inner north and south lanes, separated by a meridian of grass, are the express lanes. Along the express lanes, smaller roads lead to the outer lanes, where local shops and services are located. This setup makes for some amazing traffic snarls, and it can be quite dangerous crossing at the side roads. Instead, cross at the speed bumps placed along the express lanes that act as pedestrian walkways.

Avenidas Bonampak and Yaxchilán are the other two major north–south streets that parallel Tulum. The three major east–west streets are Avenidas Cobá, Uxmal, and Chichén. They are marked along Tulum by huge roundabouts, each set with a piece of sculpture.

Numbers in the text correspond to numbers in the margin and on the Cancún map.

A Good Tour

Cancún's scenery consists mostly of its beautiful beaches and crystal-clear waters, but there are also a few intriguing historical sites tucked away among the modern hotels. In addition to the attractions listed below, two modest vestiges of the ancient Maya civilization are worth a visit, but only for dedicated archaeology buffs. Neither is identified by name. On the 12th hole of Pok-Ta-Pok golf course (Boulevard Kukulcán, Km 6.5)—the name means "ball game" in Maya—stands a ruin consisting of two platforms and the remains of other ancient buildings. And the ruin of a tiny Maya shrine is cleverly incorporated into the architecture of the Hotel Camino Real, on the beach at Punta Cancún.

You don't need a car in Cancún, but if you've rented one to make extended trips, start in the Southern Hotel Zone at **Ruinas del Rey** ①. Drive north to **Yamil Lu'um** ②, and then stop in at the **Cancún Convention Center** ③, with its small anthropology and history museum, before heading west to **El Centro** ④.

Sights to See

③ Cancún Convention Center. This strikingly modern venue for cultural events is the jumping-off point for a 1-km (½-mi) string of shopping malls that extends west to the Presidente Inter-Continental Cancún.

The **Instituto Nacional de Antropología e Historia** (National Institute of Anthropology and History; ☎ 998/883–0305), a small museum on the ground floor of the convention center, traces Maya culture with a fascinating collection of 1,000- to 1,500-year-old artifacts collected throughout Quintana Roo. Looking through it is a great way to spend a rainy afternoon. Admission to the museum is about $3 (free Sunday); it's open Tuesday–Sunday 9–7. Guided tours are available in English, French, German, and Spanish. ✉ *Blvd. Kukulcán, Km 9, Hotel Zone,* ☎ *998/883–0199.*

④ El Centro (Downtown Cancún). Markets, instead of malls, offer a glimpse into a more provincial Mexico. The main street, **Avenida Tulum,** is easily recognizable for the huge seashell sculpture in the roundabout, which adds drama to the city when lit up at night. It has many restaurants and shops, including **Ki Huic,** the largest crafts market in Cancún. If you're looking for shopping bargains, however, the parallel **Avenida Yaxchilán** usually has better prices, particularly in the Mercado Veintiocho (Market 28). Just off Avenidas Yaxchilán and Sunyaxchén, this is the hub of downtown, filled with shops and restaurants frequented by locals.

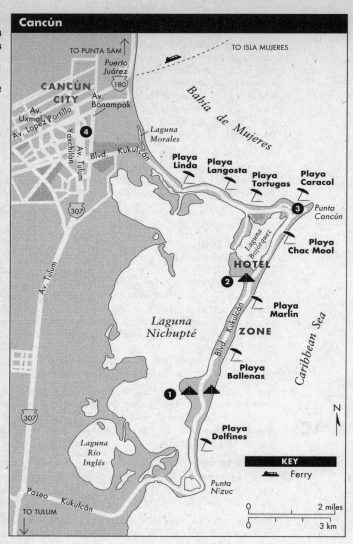

Cancún

TO PUNTA SAM

Puerto
Juárez

TO ISLA MUJERES

CANCÚN
CITY

Av.
Bonampak

Av.
Uxmal

Av. López Portillo

Blvd. Kukulcán

Av. Yaxchilán

Av. Tulum

4

Laguna
Morales

Bahía de Mujeres

**Playa
Linda**

**Playa
Langosta**

**Playa
Tortugas**

**Playa
Caracol**

3

Punta
Cancún

Laguna
Bojórquez

**Playa
Chac Mool**

HOTEL

2

**Playa
Marlín**

*Laguna
Nichupté*

Blvd. Kukulcán

ZONE

Caribbean Sea

**Playa
Ballenas**

1

*Laguna
Río
Inglés*

**Playa
Delfines**

Punta
Nizuc

N

Paseo Kukulcán

TO TULUM

KEY	
⛴	Ferry

0 — 2 miles
0 — 3 km

NEED A
BREAK? If you're looking to satiate your sweet tooth and learn about Mexican pastries at the same time, **Le Bombón** (⊠ Av. Xel-há 71, in front of San Francisco de Asís at Mercado Veintiocho, Sm 26, ☎ 998/887–1317) is the place to come. Although it's actually a bakery, you can buy slices of cake to take away or eat at the stand-up counter. The cakes are remarkably fresh and sinfully delicious. It's open Monday–Saturday 10–8.

⛴ **1** **Ruinas del Rey** (Ruins of the King). Large signs on the Zone's lagoon side, roughly opposite the Playa de Oro and El Pueblito hotels, point out these small ruins, which have been incorporated into the Caesar Park Beach & Golf Resort complex. First entered into Western chronicles in a 16th-century travelogue, then sighted in 1842 by American explorer John Lloyd Stephens and his draftsman, Frederick Catherwood, the ruins were finally explored by archaeologists in 1910, though excavations did not begin until 1954. In 1975 archaeologists, along with the Mexican government, began the restoration of the Ruinas del Rey and San Miguelito.

Del Rey may not be particularly impressive when compared to major archaeological sites such as Tulum or Chichén Itzá, but it is the largest ruin in Cancún, and it's definitely worth a look. Dating from the 3rd to 2nd century BC, del Rey is notable for its unusual architecture: two main plazas bounded by two streets—most other Maya cities contained only one plaza. The pyramid here is topped by a platform, and inside its vault are paintings on stucco. Skeletons interred both at the apex and at the base indicate that the site may have been a royal burial ground. Originally named Kin Ich Ahau Bonil, Maya for "king of the solar countenance," the site was linked to astronomical practices in the ancient Maya culture.

Now its only residents are iguanas, which lounge sleepily in the midafternoon sun. The grounds are covered with flowering trees, creating a cool, tranquil refuge that's a stark contrast to the zooming traffic just outside the gates. If you don't have time to visit the other major sites, this one will give you an idea of what the ancient Maya cities were like. ⊠ *Blvd. Kukulcán, Km 17, Hotel Zone,* ☎ *no phone.* 🎫 *About $3, free Sun.* ☉ *Daily 8–5.*

🔺 ❷ **Yamil Lu'um.** A small sign at the Sheraton directs you to a dirt path leading to this site, which stands on the highest point of Cancún—the name Yamil Lu'um means "hilly land." Although it comprises two structures—one probably a temple, the other probably a lighthouse—this is the smallest of Cancún's ruins. Discovered in 1842 by John Lloyd Stephens, the remains date from the late 13th or early 14th century. ⊠ *Blvd. Kukulcán, Km 12, Hotel Zone,* ☎ *no phone.* 🎫 *Free.*

BEACHES

Cancún Island is one long, continuous beach. By law the entire coast of Mexico is federal property and open to the public. In reality, hotel security guards discourage locals from using the beaches outside hotels. Some all-inclusive hotels distribute neon wristbands to guests, and only people wearing the bands are allowed to use the facilities. Those without a wristband are not actually prohibited from being on the beach—just from entering or exiting via the hotel. Everyone is welcome to walk along the beach, as long as you get on or off from one of the public points. Unfortunately, these points are often miles apart. One way around the situation is to find a hotel open to the public, go into the lobby bar for a drink or snack, and afterward go for a swim along the beach. This usually eliminates any problems with hotel security.

Most hotel beaches have lifeguards, but, as with all ocean swimming, use common sense—even the calmest-looking waters can have currents and riptides. Overall, the beaches on the windward stretch of the island—those facing the Bahía de Mujeres—are best for swimming; farther out, the undertow can be tricky. *Don't* swim when the red or black danger flags fly (swimmers ignoring these warnings have been known to drown); yellow flags indicate that you should proceed with caution, and green or blue flags mean the waters are calm.

Two popular public beaches, **Playa Tortugas** (Km 7) and **Chacmool** (Km 10), have restaurants and changing areas, making them especially appealing for vacationers who are staying at the beachless downtown hotels. Be careful of strong waves at Chacmool, where it's tempting to walk far out into the shallow water. South of Chacmool are the usually deserted beaches of **Playa Marlin** or **Playa Ballenas** (between Km 15 and Km 16) and **Playa Delfines** (between Km 20 and Km 21), noted for its expansive views. Swimming can be treacherous in the rough surfs of Ballenas and Delfines, but the beaches are breezy, restful places for solitary sunbathing.

Be sure to protect yourself from the intense tropical sun. The sea breeze can trick you into thinking it's much cooler than it really is, but you can burn *badly* in fewer than 20 minutes during peak sunlight hours (11–3). Wear a hat, use sunscreen or sunblock, and avoid prolonged exposure.

DINING

With more than 1,200 restaurants in Cancún, finding the right dining spot might be the hardest work you do while on vacation. Both the Hotel Zone and downtown have plenty of great places to eat. There are some pitfalls: restaurants that line Avenida Tulum are often noisy and crowded with gas fumes, detracting from the romantic ambience of the outdoor cafés. In the Hotel Zone, restaurants often cater to what they assume is a tourist preference for bland food.

One key to eating well in Cancún is to find the local haunts, most of which are in the downtown area. Parque de las Palapas, just off Avenida Tulum, is where locals go for expertly prepared Yucatecan-style food. Farther into the city center, you can find the freshest seafood and other traditional Mexican fare at Mercado Veintiocho. Dozens of small restaurants there serve great food at reasonable prices.

Large breakfast and brunch buffets are among the most popular meals in the Hotel Zone. With prices ranging from $3 to $15 per person, they are a good value—eat on the late side and you won't need to eat again until dinner. They are especially pleasant at palapa restaurants on the beach.

Unless otherwise stated, restaurants serve lunch and dinner daily.

What to Wear

Dress is casual in Cancún, but many restaurants do not allow bare feet, short shorts, bathing suits, or no shirt. At upscale restaurants, pants, skirts, or dresses are favored over shorts at dinnertime.

CATEGORY	COST
$$$$	over $30
$$$	$21–$30
$$	$10–$20
$	under $10

per person, for a main course at dinner

Hotel Zone

$$$$ ✕ **Club Grill.** The dining rooms of Cancún's Ritz-Carlton are the hands-down favorite for romantic dining. Everything is quietly elegant with rich wood, fresh flowers, crisp linens, and courtyard views. Classic dishes have been given a distinctly Mexican flavor. The sautéed foie gras with caramelized mango is a good starter, followed by the bean and lentil soup with *habañero* chili. The tasting menu offers a small selection of all the courses paired with wines followed by wickedly delicious desserts. Cynthia Davis, one of Cancún's top jazz vocalists, entertains nightly. ✉ *Blvd. Kukulcán (Retorno del Rey 36), Hotel Zone,* ☎ *998/885–0808. AE, MC, V. No lunch.*

Cancún Hotel Zone Dining and Lodging

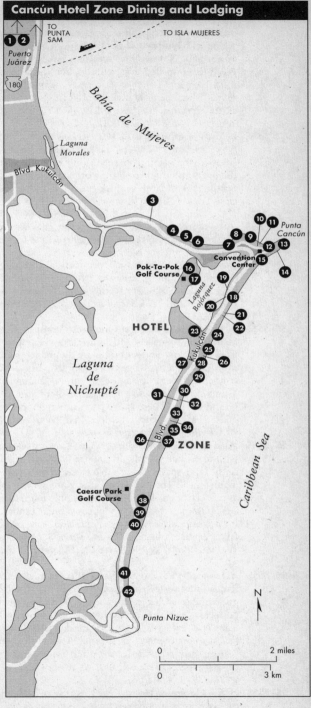

$$$–$$$$ ✕ **Côté Sud.** Dining is relaxed and stylish in the main restaurant at Le
★   Meridien hotel. Decorated with fresh green-and-taupe plaids, white linen,
and contemporary table settings, it offers dishes from France's Provence
region with creative twists. Try the duck breast in a potato *galette* (buck-
wheat pancake) and lavender sauce or Moroccan-style rack of lamb.
Fresh fish is grilled to perfection, and the wine list is extensive. "The
Fifth Element"—a chocolate extravaganza designed to look like the
planet Mars, dripping with strawberry sauce—should not be missed.
⊠ *Le Meridien, Blvd. Kukulcán, Km 14 (Retorno del Rey 37), Hotel
Zone,* ☎ *998/881–2260. AE, DC, MC, V.*

$$$–$$$$ ✕ **The Porterhouse Grill.** With its beige walls, wooden floors, and sim-
ple yet elegantly set tables, this eatery resembles a New York steak house.
Choose your steak from the display case and watch as it's prepared in
the open-grill kitchen. If the Porterhouse or filet mignon is too much,
try the rack of lamb or duck breast. The only greens served are in the
crisp Caesar salad. The wine list is superb, as are the martinis. ⊠ *Blvd.
Kukulcán, Km 12, Hotel Zone,* ☎ *998/848–9300. MC, V.*

$$$ ✕ **La Madonna.** An elegant restaurant with impeccable service, La
Madonna is a good place for sophisticated Italian food "with a Swiss
twist." The interior is dramatic, with large statues reminiscent of Greek
caryatides and a massive reproduction of the Mona Lisa dominating
the dining room. There is an extensive wine list and the bar serves a
large selection of martinis and cigars. ⊠ *La Isla Shopping Village, Blvd.
Kukulcán, Km 12.5, Hotel Zone,* ☎ *998/883–4837. Reservations essential. AE, MC, V.*

$$–$$$$ ✕ **Blue Bayou.** The first Cajun restaurant in Mexico, Blue Bayou was
an immediate success and continues to be popular with locals and vis-
itors alike. Five levels of intimate dining areas are decorated in wood,
rattan, and bamboo against a backdrop of cascading waterfalls and a
tropical garden. Specialties include Cancún jambalaya, blackened
grouper, herb crawfish Louisiana, plantation duckling, and chicken
Grand Bayou. There is live jazz every night and dancing on the week-
ends. ⊠ *Hyatt Cancún Caribe, Blvd. Kukulcán, Km 10.5, Hotel Zone,*
☎ *998/883–0044. Reservations essential. AE, DC, MC, V. No lunch.*

$$–$$$$ ✕ **La Casa de las Margaritas.** This is truly a Mexican theme restaurant,
with the country's folk art and traditional textiles adorning every inch
of the large space. There's live music nightly so this is not the place for
a quiet meal. The kitchen creates contemporary Mexican cuisine, such
as marinated chicken strips with tequila flambé, and for dessert, sweet-
ened pumpkin casserole with brown sugar, orange, and Mexican spices.
It's a great place to stop for dinner and margaritas while visiting the La
Isla Shopping Village. ⊠ *La Isla Shopping Village, Blvd. Kukulcán, Km
12, Hotel Zone,* ☎ *998/883–3222,* WEB *www.lacasadelasmargaritas.com.
MC, V.*

$$–$$$$ ✕ **Lorenzillo's.** Named after a 17th-century pirate, this is one of the
handsomest waterfront restaurants in the Hotel Zone. Built on the la-
goon underneath a giant palapa roof, its indoor-outdoor terrace is the
perfect spot to watch the sunset. It has its own lobster farm, so the del-
icacy is offered year-round (at market price) and is fresh—not frozen
like at so many other restaurants. Also good are the "Treasure Chest"
(shrimp stuffed with lobster) and *los pirates* (beef medallions in a
three-peppercorn sauce). ⊠ *Blvd. Kukulcán, Km 10.5, Hotel Zone,* ☎
998/883–1254. AE, MC, V.

$$–$$$$ ✕ **The Plantation House.** The theme here is plantation-era Caribbean;
the handsome lounge resembles an elegant colonial home, and in the
dining room, tables dressed in crisp, white linen overlook the lagoon
and mangroves. The waiters wear white gloves, and there is live piano
music. All of the islands are represented in the inspired menu—have a
taste of St. Maarten with duck medallions in green-pepper sauce, or

visit St. Lucia in the fillet of beef with a two-wine sauce. Traveling has never been so delicious. ⊠ *Blvd. Kukulcán, Km 10.5, Hotel Zone,* ☎ *998/883–1433. Reservations essential. AE, MC, V. No lunch.*

$$–$$$ ✕ **Cambalache.** This boisterous Argentine steak house is renowned for mouthwatering, tender, juicy steaks. Other highlights include suckling pig on a stick, salads, and a well-stocked bar. Meat eaters are not likely to come away disappointed. Vegetarians, on the other hand, may wish to go elsewhere—the only vegetables on the menu are potatoes. ⊠ *Forum-by-the-Sea, Blvd. Kukulcán, Km 9.5, Hotel Zone,* ☎ *998/883–0897. AE, MC, V.*

$$–$$$ ✕ **Casa Rolandi.** The secret to the success of this elegant sister to the Rolandi chain is its creative handling of Swiss–northern Italian cuisine. Be sure to try the carpaccio *di tonno alla Giorgio* (thin slices of fresh tuna with extra-virgin olive oil and lime juice), the homemade lasagna, or the ravioli *neri ripieni d'arargosta* (black ravioli stuffed with lobster). Appetizers are tempting as well: puff bread from a wood-burning oven, and a huge salad and antipasto bar. The restaurant's beautiful setting and attentive service make for a wonderful dining experience. ⊠ *Plaza Caracol, Blvd. Kukulcán, Km 8.5, Hotel Zone,* ☎ *998/883–2557. AE, MC, V.*

$$–$$$ ✕ **Gustino Italian Beachside Grill.** A dramatic staircase leading to a brick
★ and wood entrance is only the beginning at this graceful restaurant. Walk past the open-air kitchen into the dining room with its leather furniture, sleek table settings, and artistic lighting, and enjoy the exquisitely presented, delicious food. The black-shells mussels in a white wine sauce is a good start followed by the pasta in sweet pepper sauce or the braised veal shank served with mushroom polenta. While dining, enjoy the panoramic views and romantic violin music. Reservations are recommended. ⊠ *JW Marriott Resort, Blvd. Kukulcán, Km 14.5, Hotel Zone,* ☎ *998/848–9600 ext. 6649. AE, MC, V.*

$$–$$$ ✕ **Mikado.** Sit around the *teppanyaki* tables and watch the utensils fly as showmen chefs prepare steaks, seafood, vegetables, and rice. The menu includes Japanese classics as well as Thai specialties. Feast on the delicious Thai spring rolls, *negimaki* (rib eye and green-onion roll), or *tendon* (shrimp and vegetable tempura) and fresh sushi. The pad thai and curries are delicious and spicy. Sushi and lobster are priced at market rates. ⊠ *Marriott Casa Magna, Blvd. Kukulcán, Km 14.5, Hotel Zone,* ☎ *998/881–2000. DC, MC, V. No lunch.*

$–$$$ ✕ **The Captain's Cove.** One of the few Zone eateries open at 7 AM, this spot under the giant palapa on Laguna Nichupté serves hearty, delicious breakfasts at very low prices. In the evening the menu focuses on lobster, shrimp, and crab. ⊠ *Blvd. Kukulcán, Km 16.5, Hotel Zone,* ☎ *998/885–0016. AE, MC, V.*

$–$$$ ✕ **Iguana Wana.** This upbeat, contemporary Mexican café decorated with art from around Mexico offers an extensive, inexpensive all-you-can-eat breakfast buffet along with special vegetarian and children's menus. During the day, televised sports provide the entertainment; in the evening, there's live music. Choose from the extensive "zizzling" fajitas menu or from the "wana grill." There is also a tempting selection of beers and tequilas. ⊠ *Plaza Caracol, Blvd. Kukulcán, Km 8.5, Hotel Zone,* ☎ *998/883–0829. AE, MC, V.*

$–$$$ ✕ **La Joya.** This restaurant inside the Fiesta Americana Grand Coral hotel has three levels of stained-glass windows with a fountain, artwork, and beautiful furniture from the interior of Mexico. The food is traditional cuisine with creative twists, like the duck tamale. The lamb chops stuffed with poblano peppers and the Cornish hens in a chocolate mole sauce are also highlights and shouldn't be missed. Children under 12 dine at half price. ⊠ *Blvd. Kukulcán, Km 9.5, Hotel Zone,* ☎ *998/881–3222. DC, MC, V.*

$–$$$ ✕ **Maria Bonita.** Here is authentic Mexico in food, music, and atmo-
★ sphere. This delightful restaurant is decorated as a Mexican hacienda
with lots of green, red, and white tile work, ceramics, and paintings.
The glass-enclosed patio with an ocean view is the perfect spot to enjoy
the best of Mexican cuisine. Worth trying are the various mole dishes,
such as chicken almond mole (with chocolate, almonds, and chilies)
or any of the various Tex-Mex or grilled entrées. The menu explains
the different chilies used by the kitchen. ✉ *Hotel Camino Real, Punta
Cancún, Blvd. Kukulcán, Km 9, Hotel Zone,* ☎ 998/848–7000. AE,
MC, V. No lunch.

$–$$$ ✕ **La Sirenita.** Experience the best of Cancún at this romantic beach-
★ front restaurant in the Hilton Cancún Beach & Golf Resort, where the
flavors of East and West have been blended for spectacular gourmet
Asian cuisine. Watch the waves, listen to the trio of guitars, and enjoy
sublime oysters, mussels, sushi, sashimi, beef tenderloin, tempura, or
grilled fish. The dessert menu is divine, the coffee delicious. A soft blue
interior with ceramic shells and carved pillars enhances the whole
dreamy experience. During full moons, you can dine right on the beach
under the stars attended by the excellent staff. ✉ *Hilton Cancún,
Blvd. Kukulcán, Km 17 (Retorno Lacandones), Hotel Zone,* ☎ 998/
881–8000 ext. 72. AE, MC, V.

$$ ✕ **La Destileria.** Be prepared to have your perceptions about tequila
changed forever at this combination restaurant–tequila museum dec-
orated like an antique tequila distillery. Enjoy one of the 100 tequilas
offered or their superb margaritas. (Cheap tequila drinks will never be
the same.) The menu is traditional Mexican cuisine that includes shark
panuchos (tortillas filled with fish) and *El Chiquihuite Maximiliano*
(pastry filled with chicken and corn truffle). Afterward, you can drop
by the tequila shop and pick up your favorite brand. ✉ *Blvd. Kukul-
cán, Km 12.65 (across from Kukulcán Plaza), Hotel Zone,* ☎ 998/883–
1087. AE, MC, V.

$–$$ ✕ **Cenacolo.** Italian art and stained glass fill the relaxed interior of this
charming neighborhood restaurant, where musicians serenade you
throughout your meal. Outside is a bustling, plant-filled patio overlooking Boulevard Kukulcán. The food is consistently good, especially
the salad of mixed greens, the ricotta ravioli, the lasagna with béchamel,
and the sliced filet mignon in balsamic vinegar. The staff spoils you
completely. ✉ *Kukulcán Plaza, Blvd. Kukulcán, Km 13.5, Hotel Zone,*
☎ 998/885–3603. AE, MC, V.

$–$$ ✕ **Pacal.** Try Pascal for sophisticated renditions of regional Maya cui-
sine. To match the food there is fine linen and silverware against a backdrop of Maya carvings and stelae. Start off with the Yucatecan lime
soup followed by *Ya Hax* (duck in a fried peanut and green tomato
base). Also on the menu are the classic *cochinita pibil* (pork baked in
banana leaves) and *Tikin Xic* (fish in sour orange sauce). ✉ *Blvd. Kukulcán, Km 8.5, next to Plaza Caracol, Hotel Zone,* ☎ 998/883–2184.
AE, MC, V.

$–$$ ✕ **Rio Churrascaria Steak House.** You could easily pass over this haven
for meat lovers because of its simple look. The menu is a Brazilian specialty, based on different kinds of grilled meats. More than 20 cuts of
meat are slowly cooked on skewers over charcoal and then sliced right
onto your plate. You can pick and choose what you would like. Choices
include Angus and USDA certified beef, pork, and chicken as well as
more exotic meat. Vegetarian will not be happy here. ✉ *Blvd. Kukulcán, Km 3.5, Hotel Zone,* ☎ 998/849–9040. AE, MC, V.

$–$$ ✕ **Faro's Lighthouse.** There are spectacular sunsets at this lagoon-side
restaurant. Its distinctly nautical theme is appropriate for its menu of
fresh fish and seafood. Try the peppered swordfish in an oyster sauce
or the tequila broiled shrimp. The combination platter of lobster and

snow crab is excellent as well. ⊠ *Blvd. Kukulcán, Km 14.2, Hotel Zone,* ☎ *998/885–1107. AE, MC, V.*

$ ✕ **Johnny Rocket.** This is a transplanted American diner from the 1950s serving great hamburgers and genuine malted milk shakes. Hot dogs, sandwiches, and salads are also on the menu, along with good old-fashioned American apple pie. The jukeboxes add just the right touch. The one drawback is the slow service. ⊠ *La Isla Shopping Village, Blvd. Kukulcán, Km 12.5, Hotel Zone,* ☎ *998/883—5576. MC, V.*

$ ✕ **100% Natural.** Looking for something light and healthy? Head to one of these cheery open-air restaurants, done up with plenty of plants and modern Maya sculptures. The menus emphasize soups, fruit and veggie salads, fresh fruit drinks, and other nonmeat items, though egg dishes, sandwiches, grilled chicken and fish, and Mexican and Italian specialties are also available. *Hotel Zone:* ⊠ *Kukulcán Shopping Plaza, Blvd. Kukulcán, Km 13.5, Hotel Zone,* ☎ *998/885–2903;* ⊠ *Forum-by-the-Sea, Blvd. Kukulcán, Km 9.5, Hotel Zone,* ☎ *998/883–1180; Downtown:* ⊠ *Av. Sunyaxchén 62, Sm 25,* ☎ *99/884–3617;* ⊠ *Plaza las Américas, Av. Tulum, Super Manzana 4,* ☎ *no phone. MC, V.*

Downtown

$$–$$$ ✕ **La Habichuela** (The Green Bean). Once an elegant home, this much-★ loved restaurant is decorated with Maya sculpture among local trees and flowers. When lit up at night, the garden is especially enchanting. In the 24 years that the Pezzotti family has been running the restaurant there have been few complaints. Don't miss the famous *crema de habichuela* (a rich, cream-based seafood soup) or the *cocobichuela* (lobster and shrimp in a light curry sauce served inside a coconut). Finish off your meal with Xtabentun, a Maya liqueur made with honey and anise. ⊠ *Av. Margaritas 25, Sm 22,* ☎ *998/884–3158. AE, DC, MC, V.*

$$–$$$ ✕ **Lacanda Paolo.** Southern Italian cuisine is brought to new heights ★ of excellence in this sophisticated, innovative restaurant—considered by many to be the best Italian in Cancún. Don't even think of passing up the black pasta in calamari sauce or the penne with basil and tomato sauce. Also delicious are the steamed lobster in garlic sauce and the lemon fish. Flowers, artwork on the walls, and attentive service give the restaurant a warmth without being fussy. ⊠ *Av. Uxmal 35, Sm 3,* ☎ *998/887–2627. AE, DC, MC, V.*

$$–$$$ ✕ **La Parilla.** This Mexican grill is a favorite with both locals and tourists alike. With its palapa roof, hacienda style, and energetic waiters, it remains a Cancún classic. Popular dishes are the mixed Mexican grill, which includes chicken, steak, shrimp, and lobster, or the grilled steak Tampiqueña style. Enjoy these and many other Mexican specialties along with a wide selection of tequila. ⊠ *Av. Yaxchilán 51, Sm 24,* ☎ *998/ 887–6141. AE, MC, V.*

$$–$$$ ✕ **Perico's.** Zany and eclectic, this restaurant-bar is a big hit with travelers. Bar stools are topped with saddles, caricature busts of political figures line the walls, and waiters dressed as *zapatas* (revolutionaries) serve flaming desserts. The Mexican menu is passable, but the real draw are the mariachi and marimba bands that play every night from 7—everyone jumps up to join the conga line. Your reward for galloping through the restaurant and nearby streets is a free shot of tequila. ⊠ *Av. Yaxchilán 61, Sm 25,* ☎ *998/884–3152. AE, MC, V.*

$–$$ ✕ **El Cejas.** In the heart of the bustling, lively Mercado Veintiocho, this ★ is a neighborhood restaurant with an international reputation. The seafood is the freshest there is and it's cheaper than in the Hotel Zone. If you've had a wild night, try the *vuelva la vida,* or "return to life" (conch, oysters, shrimp, octópus, calamari, and fish with a hot tomato sauce). Equally wonderful is the ceviche and hot, spicy shrimp soup.

24

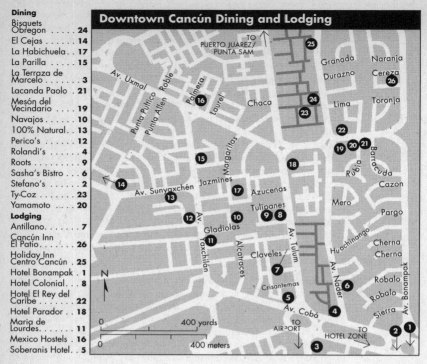

Downtown Cancún Dining and Lodging

⊠ *Mercado Veintiocho, Av. Sunyaxchén, Sm 26,* ☎ *998/887–1080. MC, V.*

$–$$ ✕ **Mesón del Vecindario.** This sweet little restaurant tucked away from the street resembles an A-frame house in the woods. The menu specializes in all kinds of cheese and beef fondues along with terrific salads, fresh pasta, and baked goods. Breakfasts are hearty and economical. It makes a pleasant change from the usual downtown fare. ⊠ *Av. Uxmal 23, Sm 3,* ☎ *998/884–8900. AE.*

$–$$ ✕ **Sasha's Bistro.** Dinner at this not-to-be-missed bistro is an experi-
★ ence you're not likely to forget. Owner Alexander (Sasha) Rudin, a Swiss master chef, knows how to play up the subtleties of his ingredients. He serves the most original and inspired menu along this coast—a fusion of Asian and European flavors—and the presentation is as artful as the food. The menu changes monthly so it's always fresh. Past masterpieces have included pork chops with a creamy porcini mushroom sauce. ⊠ *Av. Nader 118, at Av. Mojarro, Sm 3,* ☎ *998/887–9105. MC, V. Closed Sun. and Mon. No lunch.*

$–$$ ✕ **La Terraza de Marcelo.** This is a perfect place for that quiet romantic dinner, with a terrace for dining under the stars. The menu combines the flavors of Mexico and Italy to produce dishes like cambray salad (artichoke and avocado in a vinaigrette dressing, the pork loin in tamarind sauce, and the Terrasaniz breast of chicken (stuffed with ham and spices). Finish off your meal with one of the rich desserts or a fine espresso. ⊠ *Av. Labna 29, at Gacela, Sm 20,* ☎ *998/884–2056. AE, MC, V.*

$–$$ ✕ **Yamamoto.** The fresh sushi here rivals any found in the Hotel Zone. The restaurant also offers traditional Japanese dishes such as beef teriyaki and tempura for those who prefer their food cooked. ⊠ *Av. Uxmal 31, Sm 3,* ☎ *998/887–3366. MC, V.*

$ ✕ Bisquets Obregon. With its cheery colors, two levels of tables, and sit-down luncheon counter, this cafeteria-style spot is *the* place to have breakfast downtown. Begin your day with hearty Mexican classics such as *huevos rancheros* (eggs sunny-side up on tortillas, covered with tomato sauce) and do try the *cafe con leche* (coffee with hot milk)—just watching the waiters pour it is impressive. The place opens early (7 AM). ⊠ *Av. Nader 9, Sm 2,* ☎ *998/887–6876. MC, V.*

$ ✕ Navajos. Just behind the Parque de las Palapas, this outdoor restaurant serves simple, light food. Breakfast includes yogurt, sweetbreads, and fruit plates. For lunch and dinner, choose from soups, sandwiches, and salads. There are also daily specials at great prices. As the name suggests, the surroundings are along a Native American theme. It's a great place to watch all the action in this busy downtown neighborhood. ⊠ *Av. Alcatraces 18, Sm 25,* ☎ *998/887–7269. AE, MC, V.*

$ ✕ Rolandi's. The wood-burning ovens are in clear view at this bright red-and-yellow sidewalk eatery, another success in the Rolandi story. There are 15 varieties of pizza to choose from—if you can't make up your mind, try the delicious *che* pizza, with three different types of cheese. Homemade pasta dishes are also on the menu. Delivery to your hotel is available. ⊠ *Av. Cobá 12, Sm 3,* ☎ *998/884–4047. MC, V.*

$ ✕ Roots. This is a favorite hangout for both locals and tourists, who come to enjoy Cancún's fusion jazz and flamenco music scene. It also doubles as a classy café serving fresh salads, soups, sandwiches, and pastas with an international slant. Enjoy the Athens salad, Chinese chicken, Mexican fish, or German sausage. ⊠ *Av. Tulipanes 26, Sm 22,* ☎ *998/884–2437,* FAX *998/884–5547. MC, V. Closed Sun. No lunch.*

$ ✕ Stefano's. This is a cozy little bistro that offers good food at reasonable prices. Delicious and hearty pizzas are cooked in a wood oven, and pastas are prepared fresh each day. Enjoy the chicken medallions topped with crabmeat, or the spinach and cheese cannelloni. Dine inside amid European art or outside in the small patio garden. The lunch specials are quite a bargain. ⊠ *Av. Bonampak 177, Sm 4,* ☎ *998/887–9964. AE, V.*

$ ✕ Ty-Coz. Tucked behind the Comercial Mexicana and across from the bus station on Avenida Tulum, this restaurant serves excellent Continental breakfasts with croissants and freshly brewed coffee. Lunches are a combination of sandwiches and salads served on freshly baked baguettes. Pictures of the Brittany region of France adorn the walls of the bright dining room. ⊠ *Av. Tulum, Sm 2,* ☎ *no phone. No credit cards.*

LODGING

You might find it bewildering to choose among the many hotels in Cancún, not least because brochures and Web sites make them sound—and look—alike. For luxury and amenities, the Hotel Zone is the place to stay. If proximity to downtown is a priority, you probably want to stay in the north end. Many of the malls are within walking distance, and taxis downtown and to the ferries at Puerto Juárez cost less than from hotels farther south. If you prefer something more secluded, there is less development at the south end.

For the most part the downtown hotels don't offer anything near the luxury or amenities of the Hotel Zone properties. They will, however, give you the opportunity to stay in a popular resort without paying resort prices, and many places have free shuttle service to the beach. Downtown hotels are also closer to Ki Huic, Cancún's crafts market, and restaurants that are more authentic—and less costly—than those in the Zone.

Expect minibars, satellite TV, laundry and room service, private safes (check to see if there is an extra charge for safe use), and bathroom hair dryers in hotels in the $$$$ category; in addition, almost every major hotel has suites, rooms for people with disabilities, no-smoking rooms, an in-house travel agency and/or a car-rental concession, guest parking, water-sports facilities, hair salon and spa, fully equipped gymnasium, and a daily schedule of planned games and activities for guests. Unless otherwise noted, all hotels have private baths.

Boutique hotels have been springing up; these small luxury hotels usually have no more than 30 rooms, each individually decorated. Boutique hotels cater to smaller crowds and offer individual services and amenities.

Many hotels now have all-inclusive packages. For the best rates, book these ahead of time with a travel agent. In keeping with this trend, many properties are also offering theme-night parties complete with food, beverages, activities, and games. Mexican, Italian, and Caribbean themes seem to be the most popular. Take note, however, that the larger the all-inclusive resort, the blander the food is likely to be. (It's difficult to provide gourmet fare when serving hundreds of people.) For fine dining, you may need to leave the grounds.

Price categories are based on nondiscounted rates in the peak winter season, December to early May. For most of the hotels, it's best to make reservations at least one month in advance and up to three months in advance for the Christmas season. Many of the larger chain hotels also offer special Internet deals, with room rates dropping considerably when reserved on-line.

CATEGORY	COST
$$$$	over $200
$$$	$120–$200
$$	$50–$120
$	under $50

All prices are for a standard double room, excluding 12% tax.

Punta Sam

North of Puerto Juárez (where the ferries leave to Isla Mujeres), this mostly residential area is being developed into the Northern Hotel Zone. For now it remains quieter than the actual Hotel Zone or downtown but still offers a variety of services.

$$$ 🏨 **Blue Bay Club Cancún.** Nestled between the ocean and mangroves on a long, narrow strip of beach, this comfortable all-inclusive resort caters to families. Rooms are spacious with king-size beds, kitchens, pull-out sofas, and private terraces with ocean views. Water activities, gymnasium, and tennis and basketball courts are also available. Adult guests can use the facilities at Blue Bay Getaway, the sister hotel in the Hotel Zone. A complimentary shuttle bus operates between Punta Sam and the Hotel Zone. ✉ *Carretera Punta Sam, Km 1.5, Punta Sam,* ☎ *998/881–7900,* FAX *998/883–0904,* WEB *www.bluebayresorts.com. 100 rooms. 3 restaurants, kitchens, 2 tennis courts, pool, gym, basketball, 3 bars, dance club, theater, car rental. AE, DC, MC, V.*

$$ 🏨 **Chalet Maya.** These gorgeous waterfront bungalows are on the vir-
★ gin beaches of Isla Blanca—9 km (5½ mi) north of Punta Sam. With no phones or televisions, the hotel has been designed for maximum privacy and relaxation. Bungalows are individually decorated with hand-carved sculptures. A charming on-site restaurant offers moderately priced, delicious meals. The hotel offers bird-watching trips to nearby Isla Con-

toy and snorkeling or fishing trips out to the reef. ⊠ *Isla Blanca, Km 9, Punta Sam,* ☎ *998/850–4610,* FAX *998/850–4819,* WEB *www.chaletmaya. com. 20 rooms. Restaurant, pool, dock, boating. MC, V.*

The Hotel Zone

$$$$ ⊞ **Baccará.** Each suite of this gorgeous Yucatan Resorts property, a perfect ex-
★ ample of a boutique hotel, is decorated differently, with Mexican art, furniture, and textiles. All have fully equipped kitchens, living and dining rooms, and private hot tubs that overlook either the ocean or the lagoon. Downstairs is a lobby and beach bar centered on an artfully designed pool area. The attentive staff adds to the hotel's warmth. ⊠ *Blvd. Kukulcán, Km 11.5, 77500, Hotel Zone,* ☎ *998/883–2077 or 800/713–8170,* FAX *998/883–2173,* WEB *www.yucatanresorts. com. 34 rooms. 3 restaurants, in-room hot tubs, kitchens, pool, beach, 3 bars, car rental. AE, DC, MC, V.*

$$$$ ⊞ **Fiesta Americana Cancún.** A perennial favorite, this hotel has everything going for it: perfect location, gracious service, and good restaurants. It's been designed to resemble a Mexican village, with a brown and yellow color scheme. The public areas are decorated with marble from Mexico, which is offset by Guadalajara stained glass. Rooms have rattan furniture, marble floors, colorful rugs, and decorative art. All face the calm northern waters of Bahía de Mujeres (one of the best beaches for swimming). ⊠ *Blvd. Kukulcán, Km 9.5 (Box 696), 77500, Hotel Zone,* ☎ *998/881–1400 or 800/343–7821,* FAX *998/881–1401,* WEB *www.fiestaamericana.com. 236 rooms, 16 suites. 3 restaurants, pool, health club, hair salon, spa, beach, 3 bars, baby-sitting, car rental, free parking. AE, DC, MC, V.*

$$$$ ⊞ **Hilton Cancún Beach & Golf Resort.** This elegant hotel has rooms
★ done up in bright yellows and greens that complement the terra-cotta floors and rattan furniture. All rooms have a balcony or terrace with an ocean view; some have views of the resort's championship 18-hole, par-72 golf course. Seven lavish, interconnecting pools wind through palm-dotted lawns, ending at the magnificent beach. For total luxury consider staying at the Beach Club, with its 80 oceanfront villas. In the evening enjoy incredible Asian fare at the romantic seaside restaurant, Sirenita. ⊠ *Blvd. Kukulcán, Km 17 (Retorno Lacandones), 77500, Hotel Zone,* ☎ *998/881–8000,* FAX *998/881–8082,* WEB *www. hilton.com. 426 rooms, 4 suites. 3 restaurants, 18-hole golf course, 2 tennis courts, 7 pools, aerobics, gym, hair salon, hot tubs, sauna, beach, 3 bars, lobby lounge, shops, children's programs (ages 4–12), car rental. AE, DC, MC, V.*

$$$$ ⊞ **JW Marriott Cancún Resort &Spa.** This is a sister property to the Marriott Casa Magna. Large vaulted windows let the sunlight stream in and highlight the polished marble and ceramics in the lavish lobbies. Beautifully manicured lawns lead down to fountains and sumptuous outdoor pools. The ocean-view rooms are elegant in light gold, jade, and taupe tones with matching wood furnishings. Marble bathrooms add to the luxury. In the evening you can dine at the Gustino Italian Beachside Grill. ⊠ *Blvd. Kukulcán, Km 14.5, 77500, Hotel Zone,* ☎ *998/848–9600 or 800/228–9290,* FAX *998/848–9601,* WEB *www.marriott. com. 423 rooms, 36 suites. 3 restaurants, tennis court, gym, hair salon, hot tubs, spa, beach, dock, bar, shops, Internet, meeting rooms, travel services, children's programs (ages 4–12). AE, DC, MC, V.*

$$$$ ⊞ **Marriott Casa Magna.** Sweeping grounds lead up to this eclectically designed six-story hotel set with large windows, crystal chandeliers, hanging vines, and contemporary furniture. Rooms have a rose, mauve, and earth-tone color scheme with tile floors and soft rugs. All have ocean views, and most have balconies. Three restaurants overlook the handsome pool area and the ocean. In the evening, sit back and watch the chefs perform at Mikado, the hotel's fine Japanese steak house. ⊠ *Blvd. Kukulcán, Km 14.5, 77500, Hotel Zone,* ☎ *998/881–2000 or 888/ 236–2427,* FAX *998/881–2085,* WEB *www.marriott.com. 414 rooms, 36 suites. 3 restaurants, 2 tennis courts, hair salon, health club, hot tubs, sauna, beach, dock, bar, shops. AE, DC, MC, V.*

$$$$ 🏨 **Meliá Cancún.** A sheer black marble wall and a waterfall flank this boldly modern version of a Maya temple. The ultrachic atrium has lush tropical flora dappled with sunlight, which floods in from corner windows and a pyramid skylight overhead. Ivory, dusty-pink, and light-blue hues softly brighten rooms (all with private balconies or terraces), and ivory-lacquered furniture and wall-to-wall carpeting make them opulent. This is one of the largest hotels in the area and houses a convention center and six meeting halls—don't come expecting an intimate setting. ⊠ *Blvd. Kukulcán, Km 16, 77500, Hotel Zone,* ☎ *998/ 881–1100,* FAX *998/881–1140,* WEB *www.solmelia.es. 794 rooms, 64 suites. 5 restaurants, 9-hole golf course, tennis court, 2 pools, health club, spa, beach, paddle tennis, volleyball, 3 bars, baby-sitting, convention center, car rental, travel services. AE, DC, MC, V.*

$$$$ 🏨 **Le Meridien.** High on a hill, this refined yet relaxed hotel has an Art
★ Deco style with subtle Maya influences; there's lots of wood, glass, and mirrors. Rooms have spectacular ocean views. The many thoughtful extras—such as different temperature in each swimming pool—make a stay here special. The Spa del Mar is the best in the area, offering the latest European techniques along with an outdoor hot tub and waterfall. It's open to the public, so you can visit even if you're not at the hotel. Gourmet dining can be found at the wonderful Côté Sud. ⊠ *Blvd. Kukulcán, Km 14 (Retorno del Rey, Lote 37), 77500, Hotel Zone,* ☎ *998/881–2200 or 800/543–4300,* FAX *998/881–2201,* WEB *www.meridiencancun.com.mx. 213 rooms, 28 suites. 3 restaurants, 2 tennis courts, 3 pools, gym, hot tub, spa, beach, 2 bars, shops, children's programs (ages 4–12). AE, MC, V.*

$$$$ 🏨 **Presidente Inter-Continental Cancún.** It's hard to miss the striking yellow entrance of this hotel, five minutes from Plaza Caracol. Inside, lavish marble with accents of Talavera pottery decorates the hotel throughout. It has a quiet beach and a waterfall in the shape of a Maya pyramid by the pool. Larger-than-average rooms have royal-blue or beige color schemes with light wicker furniture and area rugs on stone floors. Rooms on the first floor have patios and outdoor hot tubs. The suites offer contemporary furnishings, in-room video equipment, and spacious balconies. ⊠ *Blvd. Kukulcán, Km 7.5, 77500, Hotel Zone,* ☎ *998/848–8700 or 800/327–0200,* FAX *998/883–2602,* WEB *www. interconti.com. 290 rooms, 6 suites. 2 restaurants, tennis court, 2 pools, gym, hair salon, hot tubs, beach, bar, shops. AE, MC, V.*

$$$$ 🏨 **Ritz-Carlton Cancún.** Ultraposh, ornate, and sumptuous, the Ritz ex-
★ udes opulent charm. Its thick carpets, plush furniture, European antiques, and oil paintings may lead you to forget that you are in Mexico. Rooms are decorated in shades of teal, beige, and rose, with wall-to-wall carpeting and large balconies overlooking the Caribbean. Marble bathrooms are fitted with separate tubs and showers. In the evening enjoy fine dining at the Club Grill. ⊠ *Blvd. Kukulcán, Km 14 (Retorno del Rey 36), 77500,* ☎ *998/881–0808 or 800/241–3333,* FAX *998/885– 1048,* WEB *www.ritzcarlton.com. 365 rooms, 40 suites. 3 restaurants, 3 tennis courts, pro shop, 3 pools, health club, hot tub, spa, beach, 2 bars, shops. AE, DC, MC, V.*

$$$$ 🏨 **Sheraton Cancún Resort & Towers.** At this two-hotels-in-one Sheraton there are 304 rooms with spectacular views of the ocean or lagoon. The Resort-building lobby has a contemporary black, white, and beige color scheme; rooms mirror the modern design with graceful fur-

nishings. The adjacent Tower is newer and quieter. Here the 167 rooms are done in soft Caribbean colors and private balconies facing the ocean. The main pool is surrounded by incredible gardens filled with exotic flowers, and palm trees. On the grounds is the small Maya ruin Yamil Lu'um. Several rooms overlook the ruin. ⊠ *Blvd. Kukulcán, Km 12.5, 77500, Hotel Zone,* ☎ *998/883–1988 or 888/625–5144,* FAX *998/885–0204,* WEB *www.sheraton.com. 471 rooms. 4 restaurants, 4 tennis courts, 2 pools, hair salon, health club, beach, 3 bars, shops, children's programs (ages 4–12). AE, MC, V.*

$$$$ ⊞ **Westin Regina Resort Cancún.** On the southern end of the Hotel Zone, this low-rise hotel is more secluded than most. The lobby has dramatic sculptures displayed against vivid pink or blue backdrops. Both the stylish lobby bar and restaurant have stunning ocean views. Rooms are even more elegant; cozy beds dressed in soft white linens, oak tables and chairs, and pale marble floors extending to ocean view balconies. This is one of the few hotels with direct access to both beach and Laguna Nichupté. For added privacy consider staying at its Royal Beach Club, a separate area on the grounds that has 48 rooms. ⊠ *Blvd. Kukulcán, Km 20, 77500, Hotel Zone,* ☎ *998/848–7400, 888/625–5144 in the U.S.,* FAX *998/885–0296,* WEB *www.starwood.com/westin. 278 rooms, 15 suites. 4 restaurants, 2 tennis courts, 5 pools, health club, beach, 3 bars, children's programs (ages 4–12). AE, MC, V.*

$$$ ⊞ **Avalon Grand Resort.** This beautiful resort is a sister property to the Baccará, which is a few doors down; both are run by Yucatan Resorts. A dramatic staircase entrance flanked by water fountains leads to the all-inclusive suites, which are decorated with Mexican art, ceramics, furniture, and textiles. Kitchens are fully equipped. Choose a suite with a beach or lagoon view. Some of the rooms don't require meal-plan participation. ⊠ *Blvd. Kukulcán, Km 12, 77500, Hotel Zone,* ☎ *998/883–2077,* FAX *998/883–2173,* WEB *www.yucatanresorts. com. 138 suites. 2 restaurants, kitchens, 2 pools, gym, hair salon, beach, lobby lounge, sports bar, baby-sitting, business services, meeting room, car rental. AE, DC, MC, V.*

$$$ ⊞ **Fiesta Americana Condesa.** The Condesa is easily recognized by the 118-ft tall palapa that covers it lobby. Despite the primitive roof, the hotel is quite extravagant, with lots of marble pillars, stained-glass awnings, and swimming pools joined by arched bridges. The three 7-story towers overlook an inner courtyard with hanging vines and fountains. Standard rooms share balconies with ocean views and are done up in off-white stucco with blue and pink accents. Suites have hot tubs on their terraces. ⊠ *Blvd. Kukulcán, Km 16.5, 77500, Hotel Zone,* ☎ *998/881–4200,* FAX *998/885–1800,* WEB *www.fiestaamericana.com. 476 rooms, 25 suites. 4 restaurants, some kitchenettes, 3 tennis courts, 3 pools, gym, spa, beach, 3 bars, children's programs (ages 3–12), travel services. AE, MC, V.*

$$$ ⊞ **Gran Caribe Real Resort.** This beach resort has all-inclusive packages geared to families. The bright lobby restaurants have stained-glass windows, hanging plants, and elegant furniture. Sunny, comfortable suites all have ocean views. There is plenty to keep you busy, including a gym, spa, game room, tennis courts, pools, and various watersports equipment. The children's program is among the best in Cancún. Staying here also gives you access to Costa Real Hotel & Suites in Cancún and Porto Real Resort in Playa del Carmen. Be warned: this is not the place for peace and quiet. ⊠ *Blvd. Kukulcán, Km 5.5, 77500, Hotel Zone,* ☎ *998/881–7300,* FAX *998/881–7399,* WEB *www.real.com.mx. 466 rooms, 34 suites. 2 restaurants, 2 tennis courts, 2 pools, gym, spa, beach, dock, 2 bars, theater, video game room, shops, children's programs (ages 2–12). AE, MC, V.*

$$$ ⊞ **Hyatt Cancún Caribe Villas & Resort.** This crescent-shape, intimate resort has a white marble lobby with rattan furniture in pale colors. Oceanfront rooms are decorated with contemporary Mexican accents: colorful stenciled borders on the walls, tile floors, light wood furniture, curtains and bedspreads in dusty pinks and pale green prints. Beach-level rooms have gardens. For ultimate privacy try one of the 28 beachfront rooms with their fully equipped kitchen and dining-living area. Be sure to eat at least once at the Blue Bayou restaurant. ⊠ *Blvd. Kukulcán, Km 10.5, 77500, Hotel Zone,* ☎ *998/883–0044 or 800/ 633–7313,* FAX *998/883–1514,* WEB *www.hyatt.com. 173 rooms, 28 villas. 3 restaurants, some kitchens, 3 tennis courts, 3 pools, hair salon, hot tubs, beach, dock, 2 bars, shop. AE, DC, MC, V.*

$$$ ⊞ **Hyatt Regency Cancún.** A cylindrical 14-story tower with the Hyatt trademark—a striking central atrium filled with tropical greenery and topped by a sky-lighted dome—affords a 360-degree view of the sea and the lagoon. Soothing blue, green, and beige tones prevail in the rooms. There's also an enormous two-level pool with a waterfall. Cilantro, the hotel's pretty waterfront dining room, serves a good breakfast buffet. This Hyatt is close to the convention center and several shopping malls. ⊠ *Blvd. Kukulcán, Km 8.5, 77500, Hotel Zone,* ☎ *998/883–0966 or 800/233–1234,* FAX *998/883–1349,* WEB *www.hyatt. com. 300 rooms. 2 restaurants, pool, health club, beach, 3 bars, recreation room. AE, MC, V.*

$$$ ⊞ **Krystal Cancún.** This hotel along the Punta Cancún is in the heart of the Hotel Zone, within walking distance of three major shopping malls and dozens of restaurants. The lobby is split level, with marble pillars leading to two towers where the rooms are located. All rooms have ocean views and are modestly furnished in earth tones with contemporary furniture. While the beach is small, there are three spacious pools with poolside service. The hotel houses four restaurants, as well as the popular Bull Dog Rock 'n Roll Club. ⊠ *Blvd. Kukulcán, Km 9, Lote 9, 77500, Hotel Zone,* ☎ *998/883–1133 or 800/232–9860,* FAX *998/883–1790,* WEB *www.krystal.com.mx. 322 rooms. 4 restaurants, 2 tennis courts, pool, gym, hot tub, sauna, beach, 4 bars, dance club, shops. AE, DC, MC, V.*

$$$ ⊞ **Oasis Playa Hotel.** This jewel of a hotel rests on a hilltop in the southern end of the Hotel Zone. Rooms are warm and intimate, in burnt sienna with Mexican wrought-iron furnishings. Standard rooms have either ocean or lagoon views with enclosed balconies, while "superior" rooms have ocean views and whirlpools on open terraces. The pool is two-tiered, leading to a spacious dock and one of the nicest beaches in the Hotel Zone. The gardens are magnificent, filled with flowers, bushes, and palm trees that really do turn the hotel into an oasis. ⊠ *Blvd. Kukulcán, Km 19.5, 77500, Hotel Zone,* ☎ *998/885–1111,* FAX *404/365–0666,* WEB *www.oasishotels.com. 396 rooms. 3 restaurants, some kitchenettes, golf privileges, tennis court, 2 pools, wading pool, gym, beach, bar, children's programs (ages 2–12), travel services. AE, MC, V.*

$$$ ⊞ **Omni Cancún Hotels & Villas.** This is a pleasant, pink 10-story hotel surrounded by smaller villas. The cozy lobby has marble floors, sea-green and pink color schemes, and tasteful wood furniture—a scheme that continues into the rooms. More expensive rooms have balconies; all have either ocean or lagoon views. The flexible rules allow you to choose between an all-inclusive option or European-plan rates if you prefer to eat outside the grounds. The villas have fully-equipped kitchens. Highlights of the hotel include three restaurants, three snack bars, a three-level pool, a fitness center, and a spa. ⊠ *Blvd. Kukulcán, Km 16.5, 77500, Hotel Zone,* ☎ *998/881–0600,* FAX *998/885–0059,* WEB *www.omnihotels.com. 331 rooms, 15 villas. 3 restaurants, 3 snack* *bars, 2 tennis courts, pool, gym, beach, dock, 2 bars, shops. AE, DC, MC, V.*

$$$ 🖼 **Park Royal Pirámides Cancún.** This charming hotel with its twin pyra-
★ mids has a compact but well-planned lobby done with cool beige fur-
nishings. Rooms have sea and sunset colors with original artwork
(some of it created with local sand). Standard suites have two double
beds and full baths; Ambassador suites have fully equipped kitchens,
living-dining rooms, three double beds, and full baths. Selected suites
also have private hot tubs and terraces. Some have views of the Maya
ruin, Yamil Lu'um, next door. The property has two pools joined by
a waterfall, a lovely beach, and a well-stocked, reasonably priced grocery store. ⊠ *Blvd. Kukulcán, Km 12.5, 77500, Hotel Zone,* ☎ *998/
885–1333,* ℻ *998/885–0113,* WEB *www.piramidescancun.com.mx.
232 rooms, 54 suites. Restaurant, grocery, some kitchens, 2 pools, gym,
beach, bar, shops, children's programs (ages 4–12), travel services. AE,
MC, V.*

$$$ 🖼 **El Pueblito Beach Hotel.** Built on a hill, this all-inclusive resort is de-
signed with clusters of guest rooms in tri-level units. Pathways lined
with tropical foliage lead to terraced pools with waterfalls and stone
archways; there's also a long, separate water slide for children. Rooms,
which are large for the price, have marble floors and simple rattan fur-
nishings; a few have kitchenettes. This is a good choice for families,
as the rooms are spacious and comfortable. Ask about the European
plan, which excludes meals and can lower the cost of the room. ⊠ *Blvd.
Kukulcán, Km 17.5, 77500, Hotel Zone,* ☎ *998/885–8800,* ℻ *998/
885–0422. 348 rooms. 3 restaurants, some kitchenettes, tennis court,
5 pools, beach, bar, shops, travel services. AE, MC, V.*

$$$ 🖼 **Sun Palace.** This adults-only, all-inclusive resort is set up like a camp
with daily activities posted in the lobby and coordinators to direct you
toward game rooms, tennis courts, exercise and water-sports equipment, and the pool. Rooms have ocean views but no balconies or
room service. Guest also have access to all the sister resorts, including
Beach Palace, Cancún Palace, and Moon Palace. If you book over the
Internet or through a travel agent you will get a better price ⊠ *Blvd.
Kukulcán, Km 20, 77500, Hotel Zone,* ☎ *998/885–1555 or 877/505–
5515,* ℻ *998/885–2425,* WEB *www.palaceresorts.com. 227 rooms, 19
suites. 3 restaurants, 3 tennis courts, pool, gym, hot tub, beach, billiards, Ping-Pong, recreation room. AE, MC, V.*

$$$ 🖼 **Villas Tacul.** Originally built for traveling dignitaries, these 23 vil-
las are a great place to set up home. The grounds are beautifully land-
scaped with well-trimmed lawns and gardens that lead down to a
private beach. All villas have kitchens and from two to five bedrooms,
making them ideal for families or couples traveling together. They
have red-tile floors, authentic Mexican colonial–style furniture, wagon-
wheel chandeliers, and tinwork mirrors. You can also have a house-
keeper who cleans and serves breakfast. Less expensive rooms without
kitchen facilities are also available. ⊠ *Blvd. Kukulcán, Km 5.5, 77500,
Hotel Zone,* ☎ *998/883–0000 or 800/842–0193,* ℻ *998/883–0349,*
WEB *www.cancun.com/hotels/villastacul. 23 villas. Restaurant, kitchens,
2 tennis courts, pool, basketball, beach, bar. AE, DC, MC, V.*

$$ 🖼 **Holiday Inn Express.** Within easy walking distance of the Pok-Ta-
Pok golf course, this clean, pleasant hotel was built to resemble a
Mexican hacienda—but with a pool instead of a courtyard at its center. Rooms are bright with blues and reds and modern furniture and
have either patios or small balconies that overlook the pool and deck.
While not luxurious, it's perfect for families in which Dad wants to
golf, Mom wants to shop, and the kids want to hit the beach. A complimentary shuttle bus takes you to the shops and beaches five minutes away; taxis are inexpensive alternatives. ⊠ *Paseo Pok-Ta-Pok,*

77500, Hotel Zone, ☎ *998/883–2200,* FAX *998/883–2532,* WEB *www. holidayinncancun.com.mx. 119 rooms. Restaurant, pool. AE, MC, V.*

$$ 🖭 **Suites Sina.** These economical suites are in the heart of the Hotel Zone in front of Laguna Nichupté and close to the golf course. Each suite is equipped with comfortable furniture, kitchenette, dining-living room with sofa bed, balcony or terrace, television, and double beds. Outside is a central pool and garden. Perhaps the best deal in the Hotel Zone, these suites are particularly affordable if you rent for a few weeks or share with someone. ⊠ *Club de Golf, Calle Quetzal 33, 77500, Hotel Zone,* ☎ *998/883–1017 or 877/666–9837,* FAX *998/883–2459,* WEB *www. cancunsinasuites.com.mx. 33 suites. Kitchenettes, pool. AE, MC, V.*

Downtown

$$ 🖭 **Antillano.** On the main strip, this beautifully maintained hotel
★   stands out from the others in its league. Each room is fitted with wood furnishings, one or two double beds, a sink area separate from the bath, red-tile floors, and a small television. There is a cozy little lobby bar and decent-size pool. The quietest rooms are those facing the interior— avoid the noisier rooms that face Avenida Tulum. ⊠ *Av. Tulum at Calle Claveles, 77500, Sm 21,* ☎ *998/884–1532,* FAX *998/884–1878,* WEB *www. hotelantillano.com. 48 rooms. Pool, bar, shops, baby-sitting. AE, DC, MC, V.*

$$ 🖭 **Cancún Inn El Patio.** This charming inn has the feel of an old Mexican residence. The entrance leads off a busy street into a central patio, landscaped with trees, flowers, and a lovely tiled fountain. Off to one side is a comfortable dining-living room. Upstairs, large, airy rooms are furnished with Spanish-style furniture and Mexican photos and ceramics. Downtown attractions are within walking distance, and the helpful owners, who live on-site, can direct you to the best spots in the area. ⊠ *Av. Bonampak 51, 77500, Sm 2,* ☎ *998/884–3500,* FAX *998/ 884–3540,* WEB *www.cancun-suites.com. 18 rooms. MC, V.*

$$ 🖭 **Holiday Inn Centro Cancún.** This is the place to stay if you want to
★   pay modest rates and be near the restaurants and shops but still have luxury hotel amenities. The attractive pink four-story building is reminiscent of a hacienda and has modern rooms with mauve and blue color schemes and Mexican ceramics and textiles. All rooms overlook a large pool surrounded by tropical plants. Its sister hotel, Margaritas Cancún, at Avenida Yaxchilán 41 (☎ 998/884–9333), also downtown, has pretty rooms with balconies and the same amenities and is a little less expensive. ⊠ *Av. Nader 1, 77500, Sm 2,* ☎ *998/887–4455 or 800/465–4329,* FAX *998/884–7954,* WEB *www.sixcontinentshotels.com/ holiday-inn. 246 rooms. 2 restaurants, tennis court, pool, gym, hair salon, 2 bars, nightclub, laundry facilities, car rental, travel services. AE, DC, MC, V.*

$$ 🖭 **Hotel Bonampak.** Named after one of the famous Maya ruins, this comfortable hotel is on the edge of the Hotel Zone, just minutes away from the beach by bus or taxi. The bullring and open-air markets are within walking distance. Rooms are basic, with a rose and taupe color scheme. There are no patios or terraces, but the windows do look out onto the medium-size pool and garden below. Each floor has a large, bright, airy sitting area. The staff is quite helpful. Salad lovers can find sustenance at the Ensalada Rico restaurant, right on the premises. ⊠ *Av. Bonampak 225, 77500, Sm 4,* ☎ FAX *998/884–0280. 80 rooms. Restaurant, pool, laundry service, free parking. AE, MC, V.*

$$ 🖭 **Hotel El Rey del Caribe.** A marvel in downtown Cancún, El Rey del
★   Caribe has been designed to have zero impact on the environment, in part by using solar energy for electricity, a water recycling plan, and special composting toilets. And its luxuriant garden, which blocks the

heat and noise of downtown, makes it an oasis. Hammocks hang poolside, and wrought-iron tables and chairs are placed throughout the grounds. Rooms are on the small side but are pleasant and have convenient kitchenettes. The hotel is within walking distance of all downtown shops and restaurants. ⊠ *Avs. Uxmal and Nader, 77500, Sm 2,* ☎ *998/884–2028,* FAX *998/884–9857,* WEB *www.reycaribe.com. 26 rooms. Kitchenettes, pool, hot tub. AE, MC, V.*

$ 🏨 **Hotel Colonial.** This small economy hotel in the colonial style has rooms centered on a charming fountain and garden. Rooms are comfortable but simple, each with a double bed, dresser, and bathroom. What it lacks in luxury it makes up for in price and location; you are within walking distance of all the downtown concerts, clubs, restaurants, shops, and attractions. ⊠ *Av. Tulipanes 22, 77500, Sm 21,* ☎ *998/884–1535,* FAX *998/884–1535. 46 rooms. Restaurant, free parking. MC, V.*

$ 🏨 **Maria de Lourdes.** This budget hotel offers a lot of luxury at ex-
★ tremely reasonable rates. Basic rooms are furnished with two queen-size beds, television, and bath. A well-maintained, decent-size swimming pool is surrounded by tables, where guests gather to play cards and chat. The staff is as amiable as the surroundings. It's within walking distance of shops and restaurants along Tulum. ⊠ *Av. Yaxchilán 31, 77500, Sm 22,* ☎ *998/884–4744,* FAX *998/884–1242. 50 rooms. Restaurant, pool, bar. MC, V.*

$ 🏨 **Mexico Hostels.** Four blocks from the main bus terminal and open
★ 24 hours, this hostel is absolutely *the* cheapest place to stay in Cancún. The pleasant space has four beds per room, private lockers, access to a full kitchen, a lounge area, and Internet access. Those who want to sleep outdoors can share a space with 20 others under a palapa roof. ⊠ *Calle Palmera 30 (off Av. Uxmal, beside the BMW dealership), 77500, Sm 23,* ☎ *998/887–0191 or 212/699–3825 ext. 7860,* FAX *425/ 962–8028,* WEB *www.mexicohostels.com. 50 beds. No credit cards.*

$ 🏨 **Soberanis Hotel.** This is both a hostel and a hotel. Rooms are ele-
★ gant and uncluttered, with modern furniture and white tile floors. Downtown banks, shops, and restaurants are within walking distance. The hostel section has four bunks to a room, each with its own locker, for $12 per night. A Continental breakfast is included in the price. This is one of the best deals in Cancún. ⊠ *Av. Cobá, Calle 5 y 7, 77500, Sm 22,* ☎ *998/884–4564,* FAX *998/884–5138,* WEB *www.soberanis.com. mx. 78 rooms. Restaurant, room service, cable TV, Internet, meeting room, free parking. MC, V.*

NIGHTLIFE AND THE ARTS

The Arts

The **Casa de Cultura** (⊠ Prolongación Av. Yaxchilán, Sm 26, ☎ 998/ 884–8364) hosts local cultural events, including art exhibits, dance performances, plays, and concerts, throughout the year.

Festivals

Cancún's **Jazz Festival** is an annual weeklong event in late May that draws a huge international crowd from the United States, South America, and Europe. The Cancún Hotel Association (☎ 998/884–7083) can provide information about this popular gathering.

Each fall the city of Cancún hosts a festival of music and dance. Past events have included **Caribbean Culture Festival** and the **Viva Mexico Festival.** Artists and musicians from all over Mexico and the Caribbean come to participate in events that range from dance to music to poetry readings, and restaurants participate by offering special dishes. Consult your hotel for details.

Film

Most movies that play in Cancún are Hollywood blockbusters shown in English with Spanish subtitles, although some of the more popular movies are now being dubbed into Spanish. Look for "*En Español*" displayed alongside the title on the marquee or in newspaper listings. The clerk usually tells you when you are buying a ticket for a Spanish movie instead of an English one. All children's movies are dubbed in Spanish.

In the Hotel Zone, **Cinemark Cancún** (⊠ La Isla Shopping Village, Blvd. Kukulcán, Km 12.5, Hotel Zone, ☎ 998/883–5604 or 998/883–5603, WEB www.cinemark.com.mx) has five large screens. Admission starts at $3.50.

Downtown, at Plaza las Americas, **Cinepolis** (⊠ Av. Tulum, Sm 4 and Sm 9, ☎ 998/884–4056) has the largest selection of movies, with 12 large screens. **Tulum Plus** (⊠ Av. Tulum 10, Sm 2, ☎ 998/884–3451) is a small movie theater with six large screens and cheaper prices than at many other, newer theaters. It gives the traditional Mexican halftime intermission.

Performances

Every weeknight the **Teatro de Cancún** (⊠ El Embarcadero, Blvd. Kukulcán, Km 4, Hotel Zone, ☎ 998/849–4848) presents two shows: *Voces y Danzas de Mexico* (*Voices and Dances of Mexico*), a colorful showcase of popular songs and dances from different cities in Mexico, as well as *Tradución del Caribe* (*Caribbean Tradition*), which highlights the rhythms, music, and dance of Cuba, Puerto Rico, and other Caribbean destinations. Tickets for each performance are $29. Dinner packages are also available.

Nightlife

Nightlife happens all over Cancún and in a variety of different settings. Many restaurants do double duty as party centers; discos offer music (sometimes taped, sometimes live) and light shows; and most nightclubs have live music and dancing. Sometimes the lines between the three get blurred.

Dinner Cruises

AquaWorld's **Cancún Queen** (⊠ AquaWorld Marina, Blvd. Kukulcán, Km 15.2, Hotel Zone, ☎ 998/848–8300) is the only paddle wheeler in Mexico. It offers cruises of the lagoon, complete with a three-course dinner. The 62-ft galleon **Columbus** (⊠ Royal Yacht Club, Blvd. Kukulcán, Km 16.6, Hotel Zone, ☎ 998/849–4621) offers Lobster Dinner Cruises at sunset (5 PM) and Star Cruises at 8 PM. On the **Capitán Hook** (⊠ El Embarcadero, Blvd. Kukulcán, Km 4.5, Hotel Zone, ☎ 998/849–4451 or 998/849–4452) you can watch a pirate show and enjoy a lobster dinner aboard a replica of an 18th-century Spanish galleon.

Discos

Cancún wouldn't be Cancún without its glittering discos, which generally start jumping about 10:30. **La Boom** (⊠ Blvd. Kukulcán, Km 3.5, Hotel Zone, ☎ 998/883–1152) is always the last place to close; it has a video bar with a light show and regular weekly events. The **Bull Dog Rock 'n Roll Cafe** (⊠ Krystal Cancún hotel, Blvd. Kukulcán, Km 9, Lote 9, Hotel Zone, ☎ 998/883–1793) has an all-you-can-drink bar and the latest dance music with an impressive laser light show. The wild,

wild **Coco Bongo** (⊠ Blvd. Kukulcán, Km 9.5, across the street from Dady'O, Hotel Zone, ☎ 998/883–5061) has no chairs, and everyone dances on the spot or on top of the tables. **Dady'O** (⊠ Blvd. Kukulcán, Km 9.5, Hotel Zone, ☎ 998/883–3333) has been around for a while but is still very "in" with the younger set. Next door to Dady'O, **Dady Rock** (⊠ Blvd. Kukulcán, Km 9.5, Hotel Zone, ☎ 998/883–3333) draws a high-energy crowd with live music, a giant TV screen, contests, and food specials. **Fat Tuesday** (⊠ Blvd. Kukulcán, Km 6.5, Hotel Zone, ☎ 998/849–7199), with its large daiquiri bar and live and taped disco music, is another place to go and dance the night away. **Ma'Ax'O** (⊠ Blvd. Kukulcán, Km 1.5, Hotel Zone, ☎ 998/883–5599), in La Isla Shopping Village, is a club-bar with the latest music and a wild dance floor. Also in La Isla Shopping Village, **Myth/El Alebrije** (⊠ Blvd. Kukulcán, Km 1.5, Hotel Zone, ☎ 998/883–4525) has fantasy decorations and continual laser shows but a small dance floor. **Up and Down** (⊠ Hotel Oasis, Blvd. Kukulcán, Km 15.5, Hotel Zone, ☎ 998/885–0867) holds foam parties popular with spring-breakers.

Music
To mingle with locals and hear great music for free, head down to the **Parque de las Palapas** (⊠ bordered by Avs. Tulum, Yaxchilán, Uxmal, and Cobá, Sm 22). Every Friday night at 7:30 there is live music that ranges from jazz to salsa to Caribbean.

Azucar (⊠ Hotel Camino Real, Blvd. Kukulcán, Km 9, Hotel Zone, ☎ 998/883–7000) showcases the very best Latin American bands. Go just to watch the locals dance (the beautiful people don't turn up here until *really* late) and enjoy the hot salsa. Proper dress is required—no jeans or sneakers. **Batacha** (⊠ Hotel Miramar Misión, Blvd. Kukulcán, Km 9.5, Hotel Zone, ☎ 998/883–1755) is a terrific, down-to-earth spot for Latin American and Mexican music, as well as a great place to practice your salsa moves. The **Blue Bayou Jazz Club** (⊠ Hyatt Cancún Caribe, Blvd. Kukulcán, Km 10.5, Hotel Zone, ☎ 998/883–0044) has nightly jazz in the lobby bar. The classy downtown **Roots Bar** (⊠ Av. Tulipanes 26, near Parque de las Palapas, Sm 22, ☎ 998/884–2437) is the place for jazz, fusion, flamenco, and blues.

Restaurant Party Centers
While the food at the following restaurants is usually decent, the real draw at each spot is the nightly parties that usually have live music until dawn.

At **Carlos 'n' Charlie's** (⊠ Blvd. Kukulcán, Km 5.5, Hotel Zone, ☎ 998/849–4124) zany waiters perform on stage with live rock bands. **Champions** (⊠ Marriott Casa Magna hotel, Blvd. Kukulcán, Km 14.5, Hotel Zone, ☎ 998/881–2000 ext. 6341) has a giant sports screen with 40 monitors, a live DJ, pool tables, cold beer, and dancing until the wee hours. **Kelly's Irish Pub & Sports Bar** (⊠ Avalon Grand Resort, Blvd. Kukulcán, Km 12, Hotel Zone, ☎ 998/848–9300) has the largest sports memorabilia in Mexico and has a different theme evenings with contests, live music, and cold beer. **Mango Tango** (⊠ Blvd. Kukulcán, Km 12.5, Hotel Zone, ☎ 998/883–0303) has a Las Vegas–style dinner-theater show with Caribbean music and dance. **Pat O'Briens** (⊠ Blvd. Kukulcán, Km 11.5, Hotel Zone, ☎ 998/883–0418) brings the New Orleans party scene to the Zone with live rock bands and its famous cocktails. **Señor Frog's** (⊠ Blvd. Kukulcán, Km 12.5, Hotel Zone, ☎ 998/883–1092) is known for its crazy souvenir drinks.

OUTDOOR ACTIVITIES AND SPORTS

Bullfighting

The Cancún **bullring** (✉ Blvd. Kukulcán at Av. Bonampak, Sm 4, ☎ 998/884–8372 or 998/884–8248), a block south of the Pemex station, hosts year-round bullfights. A matador, charros, a mariachi band, and flamenco dancers entertain during the hour preceding the bullfight (from 2:30 PM). Tickets cost about $40. Fights are held Wednesday at 3:30.

Go-Carts

About a 20-minute ride south of Cancún, **Karting International Cancún** is a great place for speed demons. The Honda-engine go-carts reach speeds of up to 120 kph (70 mph) on the racetrack. There's a smaller track with slower carts for children. Your choice of cart and track determines the price, which is by the hour. If you don't have a car to get here, a taxi ride should run about $5 to $10 from downtown and considerably more from the Hotel Zone. Buses leave every 20 minutes from the downtown terminal and cost about $1.20. Check to make sure your bus is not a direct route and will let you off. ✉ *Cancún–Puerto Morelos Hwy./Hwy. 307, Km 7.5, Bonfil,* ☎ *998/882–1275.* ☉ *Daily 10–10.*

Golf

The main golf course is at **Pok-Ta-Pok** (✉ Blvd. Kukulcán, between Km 6 and Km 7, Hotel Zone, ☎ 998/883–1230), a club with fine views of both sea and lagoon; its 18 holes were designed by Robert Trent Jones, Sr. The club also has a practice green, a swimming pool, tennis courts, and a restaurant. The greens fees start at $80 ($45 after 2 PM); electric cart, $30; and caddies, $20. Playing hours are 6 AM–5 PM (last tee-off is at 4). There is an 18-hole championship golf course at the **Hilton Cancún Beach & Golf Resort** (✉ Blvd. Kukulcán, Km 17, Hotel Zone, ☎ 998/881–8016); greens fees are $100 ($65 for hotel guests), carts are included, and club rentals run from $20 to $30. The 13-hole executive course (par 53) at the **Hotel Meliá Cancún** (✉ Blvd. Kukulcán, Km 12, Hotel Zone, ☎ 998/885–1160) forms a semicircle around the property and shares its beautiful ocean views. The greens fee is about $20.

Health Clubs

Most deluxe hotels have health clubs. Check them out carefully, as some are quite small and not open to the public. For a club downtown with good equipment and trainers, try **Gymnasio Cancún** (✉ Av. Ixcun 1, Sm 32, ☎ 998/884–6948).

Running

If the idea of jogging in the intense heat of Cancún sounds appealing, there is a 14-km (9-mi) track that extends along half the island, running parallel to Boulevard Kukulcán from the Punta Cancún area into Cancún City. Every December Cancún puts on an international marathon called the **Most Beautiful Marathon in the World.** The route goes through both the Hotel Zone and downtown. For more information contact Posso Promotions (✉ Box 291018, Tampa, FL, 33655, ☎ 813/980–3345, ℻ 813/985– 4386).

Water Sports

There are lots of ways to get your adrenaline going while getting wet in Cancún. You can find places to go parasailing (about $35 for eight minutes), waterskiing ($70 per hour), or jet-skiing ($70 per hour, or $60 for Wave Runners, double-seated Jet Skis). Paddleboats, kayaks, catamarans, and banana boats are readily available, too.

El Embarcadero (✉ Blvd. Kukulcán, Km 4, Hotel Zone), at Playa Linda, is the largest marina complex where most water tours depart. At the dock you can find the Garrafon Ferry, the Isla Mujeres Tour

Boat, the *Capitán Hook* galleon, the Nautibus, the Aquabus, and He-liTours. Inside the complex are Xcaret ticket booths, a folkloric mu-seum, an artists' flea market, two restaurants, a rotating scenic tower, and the Teatro Cancún, where there are nightly performances.

Aqua Fun (⊠ Blvd. Kukulcán, Km 16.5, Hotel Zone, ☎ 998/885–2930) maintains a full-service marina with large fleets of water toys such as Wave Runners, Jet Skis, speedboats, kayaks, and Windsurfers. **Aqua-World** (⊠ Blvd. Kukulcán, Km 15.2, Hotel Zone, ☎ 998/848–8300), a full-service marina, rents boats and water toys to thousands of peo-ple a day. If you would like to swim with the dolphins or feed some sharks without leaving the Hotel Zone, head over to the **Interactive Aquarium** (⊠ Blvd. Kukulcán, Km 12.5, Hotel Zone, ☎ 998/883–5725), at La Isla Shopping Village. Prices start at $65 for a half-hour dip with the dolphins, $29.95 sans dolphins. **Parque Nizuc** (⊠ Blvd. Kukulcán, Km 25, Hotel Zone, ☎ 998/881–3030) is the area's newest marine park. Your entry fee gets you into the Wet 'n Wild water park and free snorkeling at Baxal-Há Snorkel area, where you will find gentle sharks and manta rays. There is an extra charge to swim or play with the dol-phins at the Atlántida Aquarium. Visitors are asked not to bring food or beverages into the park.

FISHING

Some 500 species of tropical fish, including sailfish, wahoo, bluefin, marlin, barracuda, and red snapper, live in the waters adjacent to Can-cún. Deep-sea fishing boats and gear may be chartered from outfitters starting at about $350 for four hours, $450 for six hours, and $550 for eight hours. Charters generally include a captain and first mate, gear, bait, and beverages. The following all have charter boats for deep-sea fishing at competitive prices: **Aqua Tours** (⊠ Blvd. Kukulcán, Km 6, Hotel Zone, ☎ 998/849–4444); **Marina Punta del Este** (⊠ Blvd. Kukulcán, Km. 10.3, Hotel Zone, ☎ 998/883–1210); **Marina del Rey** (⊠ Blvd. Kukulcán, Km 15.5, Hotel Zone, ☎ 998/885–0273); **Mundo Marina** (⊠ Blvd. Kukulcán, Km 5.5, Hotel Zone, ☎ 998/849–7257).

MARINAS

There are a number of marinas throughout the Hotel Zone. They in-clude the following: **Aqua II** (☎ 998/884–1057); **Aqua Fun** (☎ 998/885–2930); **Aqua Tours** (☎ 998/849–4444); **AquaWorld** (☎ 998/848–8300); **Barracuda** (☎ 998/885–3444); and **Cancún Marina Club** (☎ 998/883–2165).

SNORKELING AND SCUBA DIVING

Snorkeling is best at Punta Nizuc, Punta Cancún, and Playa Tortugas, although you should be especially careful of the strong currents at the last. You can generally rent gear for $10 per day from many of the scuba-diving places, and most hotels and resorts have their own gear for rent. If you've brought your own snorkeling gear and want to save money, take a city bus down to Punta Nizuc.

Barracuda Marina (⊠ Blvd. Kukulcán, Km 14, Hotel Zone, ☎ 998/885–3444) has a two-hour Wave Runner jungle tour through the man-groves, which ends with snorkeling at the Punta Nizuc coral reef. The $38.50 fee includes snorkeling equipment, life jackets, and refreshments.

Scuba diving has gained in popularity in Cancún. A word of caution about one-hour "resort" courses offered as freebies by the resorts: this does not prepare you to dive in the ocean, no matter what the high-pressure concession operators tell you. A one-hour lesson in a controlled environment such as a pool differs vastly from one in the open ocean. If you have caught the scuba bug, invest in a few more lessons and prepare yourself properly so you can enjoy the experience. Remember that scuba-diving accidents can be fatal.

The secret of a good scuba company is personal attention, which is more often found at the smaller companies. Ask to meet the dive master and check out the company's equipment and certifications thoroughly. **Manta Divers** (✉ Blvd. Kukulcán, Km 6.5, Hotel Zone, ☎ 998/849–4050) is owned and operated by Daniel and Michelle Quezada, who offer specialized dive trips in Cancún and surrounding areas. **Scuba Cancún** (✉ Blvd. Kukulcán, Km 5, Hotel Zone, ☎ 998/849–4736) specializes in diving trips and offers NAUI, CMAS, and PADI instruction. It's operated by Luis Hurtado, who has more than 35 years of experience. A two-tank dive starts at $60. **Solo Buceo** (✉ Blvd. Kukulcán, Km 9, Hotel Zone, ☎ 998/883–3979) charges $50 for two-tank dives, with NAUI, SSI, and PADI instruction. The outfit goes to Cozumel, Akumal, Xpu-ha, and Isla Mujeres. Extended diving trips are available from $180.

SHOPPING

Resort wear and handicrafts are the most popular purchases in Cancún, but the prices are higher than in other cities and the selection is limited. If your vacation includes visits to other Mexican locales, it's best to postpone your shopping spree until then. Still, it is possible to find Mexican specialties such as handwoven textiles, leather goods, and jewelry handcrafted from silver and local coral. Cancún is most noted for luxury items. Many stores are "duty-free," selling designer goods at reduced prices, sometimes as much as 30%–40% off the usual retail price.

A note of caution about tortoiseshell products: the turtles from which they're made are an endangered species, and it is illegal to bring tortoiseshell into the United States and several other countries. Simply refrain from buying anything made from tortoiseshell. Also be aware that there are some restrictions regarding black coral. You must purchase it from a recognized dealer.

Throughout Mexico you often get better prices by paying with cash (pesos or dollars) or traveler's checks. This is because Mexican merchants frequently tack the 3%–6% credit-card company commission on to your bill. If you can do without plastic, you may even get the 12% sales tax lopped off. If you are just window-shopping, use the phrase "*Sólo estoy mirando, gracias*" (*so*-lo ess-*toy* mee-*ran*-do, *gras*-yas; I'm just looking, thank you). This will ease the high-pressure sales pitch that you invariably get in most stores.

Most prices are fixed in shops, but bargaining is expected at markets. Never settle for the offered price. Start by offering half the price, and let the haggling begin. Shopping around is a good idea, too, because the crafts market is very competitive. And always examine merchandise closely: some "authentic" items—particularly jewelry—might be poor imitations.

In Cancún, shopping hours are generally weekdays 10–1 and 4–7, although more and more stores are staying open throughout the day rather than closing for siesta between 1 and 4. Many shops keep Saturday-morning hours, and some are now open on Sunday until 1. Shops in the malls tend to be open weekdays 9 AM or 10 AM–8 PM or 10 PM.

Shopping Districts, Streets, and Malls

Shopping can be roughly categorized by location: mall or market. The *centros comerciales* (shopping malls) in Cancún are as well kept as similar establishments in the United States or Canada. Fully air-conditioned, they sell just about everything: designer clothing, beachwear, sportswear, jewelry, music, video games, household items, shoes, and books. Some even have the same terrible mall food that is standard north of the border. Prices are generally—but not always—higher than in the shops and markets downtown.

While mall shopping is more orderly, market shopping is more colorful. Stores are jumbled together in a chaotic fashion with the beautiful beside the ugly, quality alongside junk. Shopping is lively, and time-consuming—try out your bargaining skills to pick up some real deals.

Downtown

There are large numbers of shops downtown along Avenida Tulum (between Avenidas Cobá and Uxmal). **Fama** (⊠ Av. Tulum 105, Sm 21, ☎ 998/884–6586) is a department store that sells clothing, English books and magazines, sports gear, toiletries, liquor, and *latería* (crafts made of tin). The oldest and largest of Cancún's crafts markets is **Ki Huic** (⊠ Av. Tulum 17, between Bancomer and Bital, Sm 3, ☎ 998/884–3347). It is open daily 9 AM–10 PM and houses about 100 vendors. **Mercado Veintiocho** (Market 28), just off Avenidas Yaxchilán and Sunyaxchén, is a popular market filled with shops selling many of the same souvenir items found in the Hotel Zone but at half the price. **Ultrafemme** (⊠ Av. Tulum and Calle Claveles, Sm 21, ☎ 998/885–1402) is a popular downtown store that carries duty-free perfume, cosmetics, and jewelry. It also has branches in the Hotel Zone at Plaza Caracol, Plaza Flamingo, Kukulcán Plaza, and La Isla Shopping Village.

Plaza las Americas (⊠ Av. Tulum, Sm 4 and Sm 9, ☎ 998/887–3863) is the largest shopping center in downtown Cancún. Its 50-plus stores, three restaurants, eight movie theaters, video arcade, fast-food outlets, and five large department stores will—for better, for worse—make you feel right at home.

Plaza Bonita (⊠ Av. Tulum 260, Sm 7, ☎ 998/884–6812) is a small outdoor plaza next door to Mercado Veintiocho (Market 28). It has many wonderful specialty shops carrying Mexican goods and crafts.

Hotel Zone

There is only one open-air market in the Hotel Zone. **Coral Negro,** next to the convention center, is a collection of about 50 stalls selling crafts items. It's open daily until late evening. Everything here is overpriced, but bargaining does work.

Flamingo Plaza (⊠ Blvd. Kukulcán, Km 11.5, across from the Hotel Flamingo, Hotel Zone, ☎ 998/883–2945) is a small plaza beautifully decorated with marble. Inside are a few designer emporiums, duty-free shops, an exchange booth, sportswear shops, restaurants, and boutiques selling Mexican handicrafts.

Forum-by-the-Sea (⊠ Blvd. Kukulcán, Km 9.5, Hotel Zone, ☎ 998/883–4425) is a sparkling, three-level entertainment-shopping plaza in the Zone. There is a large selection of brand-name stores and restaurants here, all in a circuslike atmosphere.

The glittering, ultratrendy, and ultra-expensive **La Isla Shopping Village** (⊠ Blvd. Kukulcán, Km 12.5, Hotel Zone, ☎ 998/883–5025) is on the Nichupté Lagoon under a giant canopy. A series of canals and small bridges is designed to give the place a Venetian look. In addition to shops, the mall has a marina, an aquarium, a disco, restaurants, and movie theaters. You won't find any bargains here, but it's a fun place to window-shop.

Kukulcán Plaza (⊠ Blvd. Kukulcán, Km 13, Hotel Zone, ☎ 998/885–2304) is a mall that never seems to end, with around 130 shops (including Benetton and Harley Davidson boutiques), 12 restaurants, a bar, a liquor store, a bank, bowling lanes, and a video arcade. The plaza is also notable for the many cultural events and shows that take place in the main public area.

Leading off Plaza Caracol is the oldest and most varied commercial center in the Zone, **Mayafair Plaza** (⊠ Blvd. Kukulcán, Km 8.5, Hotel Zone, ☎ 998/883–0571). Mayafair has a large open-air center filled with shops, bars, and restaurants, including El Mexicano. An adjacent indoor shopping mall is decorated to resemble a rain forest, complete with replicas of Maya stelae.

The largest and most contemporary of the malls, **Plaza Caracol** (⊠ Blvd. Kukulcán, Km 8.5, Hotel Zone, ☎ 998/883–2961) is north of the convention center. It houses about 200 shops and boutiques, including two pharmacies, art galleries, a currency exchange, and folk art and jewelry shops, as well as a café and restaurants. Boutiques include Benetton, Bally, Gucci, and Ralph Lauren, with prices lower than those of their U.S. counterparts. You can rest your feet upstairs at the café, where there are often afternoon concerts, or have a meal at one of the fine restaurants.

Specialty Shops

Galleries

The **Huichol Collection** has three locations: Plaza Kukulcán (⊠ Blvd. Kukulcán, Km 13, Hotel Zone, ☎ 998/883–6078), Plaza Caracol (⊠ Blvd. Kukulcán, Km 8.5, Hotel Zone, ☎ 998/883–5059), and La Isla Shopping Village (⊠ Blvd. Kukulcán, Km 12.5, Hotel Zone, ☎ 998/883–5025). Each store sells handcrafted beadwork and embroidery made by the Huichol Indians of the West Coast. You can also watch a visiting tribe member doing this amazing work. The **Iguana Wana** restaurant (⊠ Plaza Caracol, Blvd. Kukulcán, Km 8.5, Hotel Zone, ☎ 998/883–0829) displays a small collection of art for sale. The **Modern Art Café** (⊠ La Isla Shopping Village, Blvd. Kukulcán, Km 12.5, Hotel Zone, ☎ 998/883–4511) is decorated with a revolving exhibit of works by local and international artists, all for sale. The **Renato Dorfman Gallery** (⊠ La Isla Shopping Village, Blvd. Kukulcán, Km 12.5, Hotel Zone, ☎ 998/883–5573, ⒻⒶⓍ 998/883–0359) carries Dorfman's original pieces as well as his hand-carved replicas of Maya art and stelae.

Grocery Stores

The few grocery stores in the Hotel Zone tend to be expensive. It's better to shop for groceries downtown. **Chedraui** (⊠ Av. Tulum, Sm 21; Plaza las Americas, Av. Tulum, Sm 4 and Sm 9; ☎ 998/887–2111) is a popular department store with two central locations. **Comercial Mexicana** (⊠ Avs. Tulum and Uxmal, Sm 2; Av. Kabah at Av. Yaxchilán, Sm 21; ☎ 998/880–9164) is one of the major Mexican grocery store chains, with three locations. The most convenient is at Avenues Tulum and Uxmal, across from the bus station; its largest store is farther north on Avenue Kabah. If you are a member in the States, you can visit **Costco** (⊠ Av. Kabah at Av. Yaxchilán, Sm 21, ☎ 998/881–0250). **Sam's Club** (⊠ Av. Cobá, Lote 2, Sm 21, ☎ 998/881–0200) has plenty of bargains on groceries and souvenirs. Most locals shop at **San Francisco de Asís**

(✉ Av. Tulum 18, Sm 3; ✉ Mercado Veintiocho, Avs. Yaxchilán and Sunyaxchén, Sm 26; ☎ 998/884–1155) for its many bargains on food and other items. **Wal-Mart** (✉ Av. Cobá, Lote 2, Sm 21, ☎ 998/884–1383) is a popular shopping spot.

CANCÚN A TO Z

To research prices, get advice from other travelers, and book travel arrangements, visit www.fodors.com.

ADDRESSES
In Cancún addresses, "Sm" stands for Super Manzana, literally a group of houses All neighborhoods are classified with an Sm number (Sm 23, Sm 25, etc.). Each Sm has its own park or square, and the area streets are fashioned around the park.

AIR TRAVEL TO AND FROM CANCÚN
Aeroméxico flies nonstop to Cancún from Houston, Miami, and New York. American has nonstop service from Dallas and Miami. Continental offers daily direct service from Houston. Mexicana's nonstop flights are from Los Angeles, Miami, and New York. From Cancún, Mexicana subsidiaries Aerocaribe and Aerocozumel fly to Cozumel, the ruins at Chichén Itzá, Mérida, and other Mexican cities. AeroCosta flies to cities, ruins, and haciendas on the mainland. If you are coming from the mid-West or Canada, your flight will stopover in either Atlanta, Dallas, Miami, or Houston.
➤ AIRLINES AND CONTACTS: **Aerocaribe/Aerocozumel** (☎ 998/884–2000 downtown; 998/886–0083 airport). **AeroCosta** (☎ 998/884–2000 downtown). **Aeroméxico** (☎ 998/884–1097 downtown; 998/886–0003 airport). **American** (☎ 998/883–4460 airport). **Continental** (☎ 998/886–0006 airport). **Mexicana** (☎ 998/887–4444 downtown; 998/886–0068 airport).

AIRPORTS AND TRANSFERS
Cancún International Airport is 16 km (9 mi) southwest of the heart of Cancún and 10 km (6 mi) from the southernmost point of the Hotel Zone. There are three terminals. The main terminal is the largest building and handles international departures as well as domestic arrivals and departures. Next door to the main terminal is a smaller building where all regular international flights arrive. A separate terminal, 1 km (½ mi) south of the main terminal, handles all international charter flights.
➤ AIRPORT INFORMATION: **Cancún International Airport** (✉ Cancún–Puerto Morelos Hwy./Hwy. 307, Km 9.5, ☎ 998/886–0073).

AIRPORT TRANSFER
The public-transport options are taxis or *colectivos* (vans); buses are not allowed into the airport due to an agreement with the taxi union. A counter at the airport exit sells colectivo and taxi tickets; prices range from $15 to $40, depending on the destination. Getting back to the airport for your departure is less expensive; taxi rates to the airport range from about $15 to $22. Hotels post current rates. Be sure to agree on a price before getting into the taxi.

BOAT AND FERRY TRAVEL
From Playa Linda, Plaza Caracol, and Playa Tortuga on Cancún, you can take a shuttle boat to the main dock at Isla Mujeres. Municipal ferries carry vehicles and passengers between Cancún's Punta Sam and Isla's dock. (*See* Chapter 3 for more information about boat travel to and from Isla Mujeres.)

Aquabus, a water-taxi service in the Hotel Zone, travels from the hotels to various restaurants and shops; a one-way fare is $3, a day pass is $15, and a week pass is $35.

➤ WATER-TAXI INFORMATION: **Aquabus** (☎ 998/883–3155 or 998/883–5649).

BUS TRAVEL TO AND FROM CANCÚN

First-class and second-class buses arrive at the downtown bus terminal from all over Mexico. ADO, Mayab, and Playa Express are the main companies servicing the coast. Buses leave every 20 minutes for Puerto Morelos and Playa del Carmen. Check the bus schedule for departure times for Tulum, Chetumal, Cobá, Valladolid, Chichén Itzá, and Mérida.

➤ BUS INFORMATION: **ADO** (☎ 998/884–5542). **Bus terminal** (✉ Avs. Tulum and Uxmal, Sm 23, ☎ 998/887–1149). **Playa Express** (☎ 998/884–0994).

BUS TRAVEL WITHIN CANCÚN

Public buses run between the Hotel Zone and downtown from 6 AM to midnight; the cost is 5 pesos. There are designated bus stops—look for blue signs with white buses in the middle—but you can also flag down drivers along Boulevard Kukulcán. The service is frequent and quite reliable. Take Ruta 8 (Route 8) to reach Puerto Juárez and Punta Sam for the ferries to Isla Mujeres. Take Ruta 1 (Route 1) to and from the Hotel Zone. Buses from the Zone do not go into downtown Cancún but will drop you off anywhere along Avenida Tulum, from where you can catch a connecting bus that takes you into the city. Taking the bus can save you a considerable amount of money on taxis, particularly if you are staying in the Hotel Zone.

CAR RENTAL

Cars are available at Cancún International Airport or from any of a dozen agencies in town. Most of the agencies have several locations in the area: Avis, Thrifty, and Localiza Rent a Car have five each; Hertz has nine; and National has seven. The telephone numbers given here are for the airport locations.

Most rental cars are standard-shift subcompacts and Jeeps; air-conditioned cars with automatic transmissions should be reserved in advance (though bear in mind that some smaller car-rental places have only standards). Rates average around $55 per day but can be as high as $75 daily if you haven't reserved a car; you can save a great deal on a rental by booking before you leave home, particularly over the Internet. It's also a good idea to shop around. In addition to the rental agencies, the Car Rental Association can help you arrange a rental.

➤ MAJOR AGENCIES: **Avis** (✉ Cancún International Airport, ☎ 998/886–0222). **Hertz** (✉ Cancún International Airport, ☎ 998/884–1326). **National** (✉ Cancún International Airport, ☎ 998/886–0152). **Thrifty** (✉ Cancún International Airport, ☎ 998/886–0333).

➤ LOCAL AGENCIES AND CONTACTS: **Car Rental Association** (☎ 998/887–3109 or 998/884–7569). **Econorent** (✉ Avs. Bonampak and Cobá, Sm 4, ☎ 998/887–6487). **Executive** (✉ Av. Yaxchilán 160, Sm 20, ☎ 998/884–2699). **Localiza Rent a Car** (✉ Av. La Costa 128, Sm 30, ☎ 998/887–3109). **Zipp Rental Cars** (✉ Baccará hotel, Blvd. Kukulcán, Km 11.5, Hotel Zone, ☎ 998/883–2077).

CAR TRAVEL

Driving any kind of vehicle in Cancún is not for the faint of heart. Traffic moves at a breakneck speed; adding to the danger are the many one-way streets, traffic circles (*glorietas*), sporadically working traffic lights, ill-placed *topes* (speed bumps), numerous pedestrians, and large potholes. Be sure to observe speed limits in the Hotel Zone and downtown. The traffic police are quite vigilant and eager to hand out tickets. In addition, car travel becomes expensive, as it entails tips for valet parking as well as gasoline and rather costly rental rates.

Although driving in Cancún is not recommended, you might want a car to explore the surrounding areas on the peninsula. The roads are excellent within a 100-km (62-mi) radius.

Route 180 runs from Matamoros at the Texas border through Campeche, Mérida, Valladolid, and into Cancún. The trip from Texas can take up to three days. Route 307 runs south from Cancún through Puerto Morelos, Tulum, and Chetumal, then into Belize. Gas stations are only located in the major cities and towns, so keep your tank full. Route 307 has three Pemex stations between Cancún and Playa del Carmen. When approaching any village, town, or city, watch out for the numerous speed bumps—hitting them at top speed can ruin your transmission and tires.

COMPUTERS ON THE ROAD
If you are traveling with your laptop, watch it carefully. The biggest danger, aside from theft, is the constantly fluctuating electricity, which will eventually damage your hard drive. Invest in a Mexican surge protector that can handle the frequent brown-outs and fluctuations in voltage—the standard plug-in strip you use at home won't give you much protection. It's best to leave repairs until you are back home.

CONSUMER PROTECTION
The Consumer Protection Agency may help you with hassles with companies or consumer goods.
➤ CONTACT: **Consumer Protection Agency** (✉ Av. Cobá 9, 2nd floor, Sm 22, ☎ 998/884–2634).

E-MAIL
Many hotels have complimentary Internet service; a number of places in Cancún offer access for a small fee. Compu Copy, in the Hotel Zone, is open daily 9–9. Downtown, the Internet Café is open Monday–Saturday 11–10, and Infonet is open daily 10 AM–11 PM. Rates are about $3.50–$5 per hour.
➤ SERVICES: **Compu Copy** (✉ Kukulcán Plaza, Blvd. Kukulcán, Km 13, Hotel Zone, ☎ 998/885–0055). **Infonet** (✉ Plaza las Americas, Av. Tulum, Sm 4 and Sm 9, ☎ 998/887–9130). **Internet Café** (✉ Av. Tulum, behind Comercial Mexicana, across from the bus station, Sm 2, ☎ 998/887–3167).

EMBASSIES AND CONSULATES
The consulates in Cancún operate with skeleton staffs, and for complicated problems you need to contact the offices in Mérida. The U.S. Consulate, in the Hotel Zone, is open weekdays 9–1; the Mérida offices are open weekdays 7:30–4.

The Canadian Consulate is open daily 9–5. Should you have an emergency when the embassy is closed, contact the Canadian Embassy in Mexico City.
➤ CANADA: **Consulate** (✉ Plaza Caracol 11, 3rd floor, Hotel Zone, ☎ 998/883–3360, 800/706–2900 emergencies, FAX 998/883–3232). **Embassy** (☎ 55/5724–7900 in Mexico City).
➤ UNITED STATES: **Consulate** (✉ Plaza Caracol, 3rd floor, Hotel Zone, ☎ 998/883–0272, FAX 998/883–1372).

EMERGENCIES

In case of medical emergency, the safest bet is the American Medical Centre, run by Dr. Michael McFall with his wife, Lisa McFall, from the United States.

Cancún has a lot of pharmacies. Among those that offer delivery service are Canto, Farmacia Cancún, and Paris (all downtown) and, in the Hotel Zone, Roxsanna's. Paris delivers around the clock.

➤ DOCTORS AND DENTISTS: **American Medical Centre** (✉ Blvd. Kukulcán, Km 8, Hotel Zone, ☎ 998/883–1001, 998/883–0113, 998/887–1455 pager PIN 10844).

➤ EMERGENCY SERVICES: **Emergencies** (☎ 06). **Fire Department** (☎ 998/884–9480). **Highway Police** (☎ 998/884–1107). **Immigration Office** (☎ 998/884–1749). **Municipal Police** (☎ 998/887–3435). **Red Cross** (✉ Avs. Xcaret and Labná, Sm 21, ☎ 998/884–1616). **Traffic Police** (☎ 998/884–0710).

➤ PHARMACIES: **Farmacia Cancún** (✉ Av. Tulum 17, Sm 22, ☎ 998/884–1283). **Paris** (✉ Av. Yaxchilán 32, Sm 3, ☎ 998/884–3005). **Roxsanna's** (✉ Plaza Flamingo, Kukulcán Blvd., Km 11.5, Hotel Zone, ☎ 998/885–1351, 998/885–0860 delivery service).

LODGING

The Cancún Hotel Association can provide information on area lodging but *not* reservations.

➤ CONTACT: **Cancún Hotel/Motel Association** (✉ Plaza San Angel, Ave. Acanceh, Sm 15, 77500, ☎ 998/884–9347, FAX 998/887–7683).

MAIL AND SHIPPING

The post office (*correos*) is open weekdays 8–5 and Saturday 9–1; there's also a Western Union office in the building and a courier service. Bear in mind, however, that postal service to and from Mexico is extremely slow and may take four weeks or more. Avoid sending or receiving parcels—and never send checks or money through the mail. Invariably they are stolen.

You can receive mail at the post office if it's marked "Lista de Correos, Cancún, 77500, Quintana Roo, Mexico." If you have an American Express card, you can have mail sent to you at the American Express Cancún office for a small fee. The office is open weekdays 9–6 and Saturday 9–1.

➤ SERVICES: **American Express** (✉ Av. Tulum 208, at Calle Agua, Sm 4, ☎ 998/881–4020). **Post office** (✉ Av. Sunyaxchén at Av. Xel-há, Sm 26, ☎ 998/884–1418). **Western Union** (✉ Av. Sunyaxchén at Av. Xel-há, Sm 26 ☎ 998/884–1529).

MEDIA

NEWSPAPERS AND MAGAZINES

You can pick up many helpful publications at the airport, malls, tourist kiosks, and many hotels. Indeed, you can't avoid having them shoved into your hands. Most are stuffed with discount coupons offering some savings. The best of the bunch is *Cancún Tips,* a free pocket-size guide to hotels, restaurants, shopping, and recreation. Although it's loaded with advertising and coupons, the booklet, published twice a year in English and Spanish, has some useful information. The accompanying *Cancún Tips Magazine* has informative articles about local attractions. The *Mapa Pocket Guide* is handy for its Hotel Zone map and some local contact information. Since the folks who own Xcaret, Xel-ha, El Embarcadero, and Garrafon publish this guide, they often leave out information on any competitors while heavily promoting their own interests. *Passport Cancún* is for serious coupon junkies only.

MONEY MATTERS

Generally, banks in Cancún are open weekdays 9–5, with money-exchange desks open 9–1:30. Downtown locations are along Avenida Tulum; some of the larger banks have branches in the Hotel Zone as well. All have automatic teller machines that dispense Mexican money. The ATMs at the smaller banks are often out of order, but the larger banks generally have working machines. If your PIN (personal identification number) has more than four digits, you may have trouble using the ATMs. Also, don't delay in taking your card out of the machine. ATMs are quick to eat up cards, and it takes a visit to the bank and a number of forms to get them back. If your transactions require a teller, go early to avoid long lines.

Banamex and Bital both have offices downtown and in the Hotel Zone and can exchange or wire money. Other banks include Banca Serfin, Banco del Sureste, Bancomer, Scotiabank Inverlat, and Santander Mexicano.

➤ BANKS: **Banamex** (Downtown: ✉ Av. Tulum 19, next to City Hall, Sm 1, ☎ 998/884–6403; Hotel Zone: ✉ Plaza Terramar, Blvd. Kukulcán, Km 37, ☎ 998/883–3100). **Banca Serfin** (Downtown: ✉ Av. Cobá at Av. Tulum, Sm 3, ☎ 998/884–4850). **Banco del Sureste** (Downtown: ✉ Avs. Yaxchilán and Sunyaxchén, Sm 24, ☎ 998/881–4991). **BBVA Bancomer** (Downtown: ✉ Av. Tulum 20, Sm 3, ☎ 998/884–3288; Hotel Zone: ✉ Plaza El Parián, Blvd. Kukulcán, Km 9.5, next to the convention center, ☎ 998/883–0802). **Bital** (Downtown: ✉ Av. Tulum 15, Sm 4, ☎ 998/881–4103; Hotel Zone: ✉ Plaza Caracol, Blvd. Kukulcán, Km 8.5, ☎ 998/883–4652). **Santander Mexicano** (Downtown: ✉ Av. Tulum 173, Sm 3, ☎ 998/884–0629). **Scotiabank Inverlat** (Downtown: ✉ Av. Tulum 26, Sm 3, ☎ 998/884–1333).

MOPED TRAVEL

Mopeds are extremely dangerous, and you risk your life using one in either the Zone or downtown. If you have never ridden a moped or a motorcycle before, *this is not the place to learn*. Mopeds rent for about $25 a day; you are required to leave a credit-card voucher for security. You should receive a crash helmet, which by law you must wear. Read the fine print on your contract; companies will hold you liable for all repairs or replacement in case of an accident and will not offer any insurance to protect you.

TAXIS

Taxi rides within the Hotel Zone cost $5–$7; between the Hotel Zone and downtown, $8 and up; and to the ferries at Punta Sam or Puerto Juárez, $15–$20 or more. Prices depend on distance, your negotiating skills, and whether you pick up the taxi in front of a hotel or decide to save a few dollars by going onto the avenue to hail one yourself (look for green city cabs). Most hotels list rates at the door; confirm the price with your driver *before* you set out. If you lose something in a taxi or have questions or a complaint, call the Sindicato de Taxistas.

➤ INFORMATION: **Sindicato de Taxistas** (☎ 998/888–6985).

TELEPHONES

Most hotels charge the equivalent of between 50¢ and $1 for each local call you make from your room. In addition, there is usually a hefty service charge on long-distance calls, and it can add up quickly. In order to make a phone call—local or long distance—from any public phone, you must purchase a Ladatel phone card, sold in blocks of about $3, $5, $10, and $20. An alternative to the phone card is the *caseta de larga distancia*—the long-distance telephone office. There are casetas in Plaza Kukulcán, Plaza Mayafair, and Plaza Caracol and one at the down-

town bus terminal. These places have specially designed booths where
you take your call after the number has been dialed by a clerk. A service fee of $3.50–$5 is added on top of the steep long-distance charge.
The booths do, however, offer more privacy and comfort than many
public-phone booths.

INTERNATIONAL CALLS
For calls to the United States or Canada, dial 001, followed by the area
code and number. To make a collect call, dial 090 for the international
operator.

LOCAL CALLS
For local calls, the 8 of Cancún's 998 area code must be dialed first.
Bear in mind that some of the older printed material on Cancún does
not reflect this change and shows the telephone numbers written in the
old style.

LONG-DISTANCE CALLS
For long-distance calls within Mexico, dial 01, followed by the area
code (sometimes called the city code) and number.

TOURS

BOAT TOURS

Day cruises to Isla Mujeres are popular. They generally include snorkeling, shopping downtown, lunching at an open-bar buffet, and listening to music or lounging at Playa Norte. Plenty of tour operators offer
such trips. Pirate's Night offers a trip to Treasure Island on Isla Mujeres aboard a sailboat that is decked out like a pirate ship. Prices start
at $35. Capitán Hook also runs an Isla Mujeres day tour that departs
at 10 AM from El Embarcadero Marina on Boulevard Kukulcán and
returns at 5 PM; it costs about $55. Dolphin Discovery sails daily from
Playas Langosta and Tortugas to the company's dock on Isla Mujeres;
its program includes an instruction video, a 30-minute swim session
with the dolphins, and time to explore the island. Tickets start at $75.
Turimex offers a three-day, two-night cruise from Cancún to Havana
for $189.
➤ FEES AND SCHEDULES: **Capitán Hook** (✉ El Embarcadero, Blvd.
Kukulcán, Km 4.5, Hotel Zone, ☎ 998/883–3736). **Dolphin Discovery** (✉ Playa Langosta, Local 16, Blvd. Kukulcán, Km 3, Hotel Zone
☎ 998/883–0779 or 998/883–0780). *Pirate's Night* (✉ Playa Langosta
Dock, Blvd. Kukulcán, Km 5.5, Hotel Zone, ☎ 998/849–4621).
Turimex Travel (✉ Plaza America, Av. Cobá 5, Suite B-7, Sm 4, ☎
998/887–4038, FAX 998/887–1936, WEB www.turimex.com/cuba.html).

ECOTOURS
While many claim to have ecological tours, few outfits actually deliver
truly ecological experiences in authentic jungle settings. An exception
is Reserva Ecológica El Edén, established by one of Mexico's leading
naturalists, Arturo Gómez-Pompa, and his nephew, Marco Lazcano-
Barrero. The 500,000-acre reserve, 48 km (30 mi) northwest of Cancún, is dedicated to research for biological conservation in Mexico. It
offers excursions for people interested in experiencing the reserve's wet-
lands, mangrove swamps, sand dunes, savannas, and tropical forests.
"Eco-scientific" tours include bird-watching, animal-tracking, stargaz-
ing, crocodile ecology, and cenote and archaeological explorations. Prices
include transportation between Cancún and the reserve, one to two
nights' accommodation at La Savanna Research Station, meals, cocktails, guided nature walks, and all tours. Two-day, one-night excursions
start at $235 per person, three-day, two-nights at $315.

➤ FEES AND SCHEDULES: **Reserva Ecológica El Edén** (✉ Box 770, Cancún, Quintana Roo 77500, ☎ FAX 998/880–5032, WEB www.ucr.edu/pril/peten/images/el_eden/Home.html).

PLANE TOURS
Promocaribe flies one-day tours between Cancún and Guatemala City, continuing on to Flores and the ruins at Tikal. A round-trip fare of $267 includes all ground transfers, departure taxes, entrance to ruins, a tour guide, and lunch.
➤ FEES AND SCHEDULES: **Promotora Caribena** (✉ Plaza Centro, Av. Nader 8, Sm 5, ☎ 998/884–9073, WEB www.promocaribe.com).

SUBMARINE TOURS
Sub See Explorer is a "floating submarine" that takes you for a one-hour reef cruise. Experience the beauty of Cancún's reef and watch the exotic fish while staying dry. The $35 price includes lunch and refreshments. Tours leave on the hour daily 9–3 PM. Call AquaWorld for information.
➤ FEES AND SCHEDULES: *AquaWorld* (☎ 998/848–8300).

TRANSPORTATION AROUND CANCÚN
Motorized transportation of some sort is necessary, as Cancún is somewhat spread out. Public bus service is good, and taxis are relatively inexpensive.

TRAVEL AGENCIES
Mayaland Tours, Intermar Caribe (IMC), and Olympus Tours all offer day trips. You can shop around for the best price or call the Travel Agency Association for further information.
➤ LOCAL AGENT REFERRAL: **Travel Agency Association** (✉ Plaza México, Av. Tulum 200, Suite 301, Sm 5, ☎ 998/887–1670, FAX 998/884–3738).
➤ LOCAL AGENTS: **Intermar Caribe** (✉ Av. Tulum at Av. Cobá, Sm 4, ☎ 998/884–0584). **Mayaland Tours** (✉ Av. Robalo 30, Sm 3, ☎ 998/988–0870). **Olympus Tours** (✉ Av. Bonampak 107, Sm 3, ☎ 998/887–2417).

VISITOR INFORMATION
➤ TOURIST INFORMATION: **State Tourism Information Center** (✉ Av. Tulum 26, Sm 5, ☎ 998/884–8073). **State Tourism Office—Quintana Roo** (SECTUR; ✉ Government Palace, Av. Tulum, Sm 1, ☎ 998/881–9000; 800/903–9200 toll free in Mexico).

3 ISLA MUJERES

Only 8 km (5 mi) across the bay from
Cancún, Isla Mujeres is an ocean away in
attitude, as sleepy and unassuming as its
neighbor is outgoing and flashy. Snorkeling,
exploring the remnants of the island's past,
eating fresh seafood, and lazing under a
thatched roof are about as lively as it gets.

Updated
by Shelagh
McNally

SLA MUJERES (*ees*-lah moo-*hair*-ayce) has a magic of its own that seems to defy change. It makes this tiny, fish-shape island 8 km (5 mi) off Cancún a tranquil alternative to its bustling western neighbor. Only about 8 km (5 mi) long by 1 km (½ mi) wide, Isla has flat, sandy beaches on its northern end and steep, rocky bluffs to the south.

The name means "Island of Women," although no one is exactly sure who dubbed it that. Many believe it was the ancient Maya, who used the island as a religious center for worshiping Ixchel (ee-*shell*), the Maya goddess of rainbows, the moon, and the sea, and the guardian of fertility and childbirth. Another popular legend has it that the Spanish conquistador Hernández de Córdoba named the island when he landed here in 1517 and found hundreds of female-shape clay idols dedicated to Ixchel and her daughters. Others say the name dates from the 17th century, when Isla was a haven for buccaneers and smugglers. Pirates would stash their women here before heading out to rob the high seas.

After its popularity waned with brigands, Isla settled into life as a quiet fishing village. In the 1950s it became a favorite vacation spot for Mexicans. Americans discovered it shortly afterward, and in the 1960s Isla became well known among hippies and backpackers. As Cancún grew so did Isla. During the late 1970s, the number of day-trippers coming over from the mainland increased, bringing Isla's hotel, restaurant, and shop owners more business than ever. Boatloads were streaming off the ferries for quick lunches followed by frenzied shopping, and thus the island became a small-scale tourist haven.

Like the rest of the area, Isla is being developed, but it manages to keep its character as a peaceful retreat with its own local history and culture centered on the sea. And it continues to be a favorite of people who prefer such seaside pleasures as scuba diving, snorkeling, and relaxing on the beach to spending time in Cancún's fast-food joints and rollicking discos. Islanders (Isleños; pronounced ees-*lay*-nyos) largely wish to continue the legacy of the late Ramon Bravo, the shark expert, ecologist, and filmmaker who fought to preserve the island's ecology so that Isla would remain a peaceful, authentically Mexican getaway.

Pleasures and Pastimes

Beaches
The island's finest and most popular beach is Playa Norte, where you can wade far out in placid waters or relax at congenial *palapa* (thatch-roof) bars with drinks and snacks. At sunset the view here is spectacular. Playa Paraíso and Playa Lancheros on the western shore are both pleasant spots for swimming and sunning. On Sunday both these beaches are filled with locals enjoying their day off.

Bird-Watching
About 45 minutes north of Isla Mujeres, Isla Contoy (Isle of Birds) is a national wildlife park and bird sanctuary. The tiny island is a beautiful, unspoiled spot with sand dunes, mangroves, and coconut trees. It's a favorite of birders, who come to see the 70-plus local species.

Dining
Food on Isla Mujeres is what you would expect on a small island: plenty of fresh grilled lobster, shrimp, conch, and fish. It also offers pleasant variations on pasta, pizza, steak, and sandwiches. Bright mornings, sweet fruits, fresh coffee, and baked goods make breakfast on Isla a treat.

Fishing

Blue marlin and sailfish are popular catches in spring and early summer, when the warm currents around Isla attract big game fish. The island's billfish tournament held in mid-May attracts an international following. During the rest of the year, you can fish for barracuda and tuna, as well as shad, sailfish, grouper, red snapper, and wahoo.

Lodging

The small hotel reigns here, but with more than 45 lodging places, Isla offers a surprisingly broad range of options—from charming beachfront properties to simpler, less expensive accommodations in the heart of town.

Snorkeling and Scuba Diving

Despite the widespread concern over loss of reef (some reef sections, particularly at El Garrafón National Park, are dead), the underwater spectacle here is still impressive for its abundance of fascinating sea life. In spring and summer, fish are attracted to the mild temperatures and calm waters that prevail between 8 AM and 3 PM. The slightly cooler water in winter means less algae and better visibility.

EXPLORING ISLA MUJERES

To get your bearings, think of Isla Mujeres as an elongated fish, the head being the southeastern tip, the northwest prong the tail. The minute you step off the boat, you see how small Isla is. Directly in front of the ferry piers is the island's only town, known simply as El Pueblo. It extends the full width of Isla's northern "tail" and is sandwiched between sand and sea to the south, west, and northeast, with no high-rises to block the view.

The main road is Avenida Rueda Medina, which runs the length of the island; southeast of a village known as El Colonia, it eventually turns into Carretera El Garrafón. The smaller street names and addresses don't matter much here.

Past the T-shirt and souvenir shops is the island's true gathering spot—El Pueblo's main square. Bounded by Avenidas Morelos, Bravo, Guerrero, and Hidalgo, the *zócalo* (main square) is the ideal place to take in daily town life. In the evenings, locals congregate in front of the church while their children run around the playground or play basketball. On holidays and weekends the square is set up for dances, concerts, and fiestas.

Numbers in the text correspond to numbers in the margin and on the Isla Mujeres map.

A Good Tour

The best way to explore the entire island is to take a taxi or rent either a moped or golf cart. You can walk to Isla's historic **Cemeterio** ① by going northwest from the ferry piers on Avenida López Mateos. Then head southeast (by car or other vehicle) along Avenida Rueda Medina past the piers to reach the Mexican naval base, where you can see the the flag ceremonies at sunrise and sunset. Just don't take any photos—it's illegal to photo any military sites in Mexico. Continue southeast out of town; 2½ km (1½ mi) farther down the road is **Laguna Makax** ②, on the right.

At the southeast end of the lagoon, a dirt road to the left leads to the remains of the **Hacienda Mundaca** ③. About a block southeast of the hacienda, turn right off the main road at the sign that says SAC BAJO to a smaller, unmarked side road, which loops back northwest. Ap-

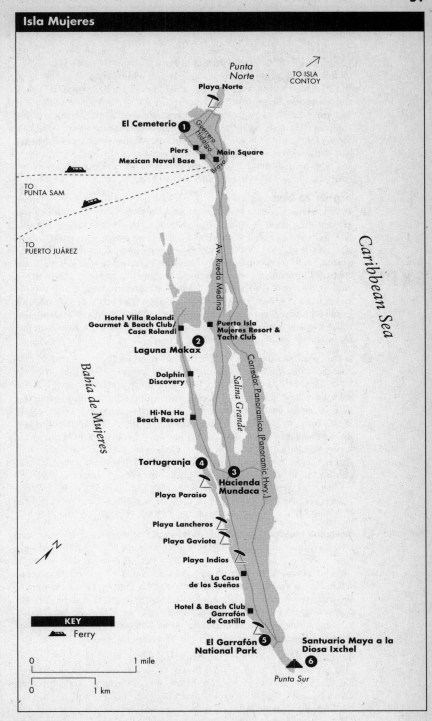

Punta Norte

TO ISLA CONTOY

Playa Norte

El Cemeterio ❶

Guerrero
Hidalgo

Piers ▪ **Main Square**
Mexican Naval Base ▪

Bravo

TO PUNTA SAM

Av. Rueda Medina

TO PUERTO JUÁREZ

Caribbean Sea

Bahía de Mujeres

Hotel Villa Rolandi
Gourmet & Beach Club/ ▪ ▪ **Puerto Isla**
Casa Rolandi **Mujeres Resort &**
Yacht Club

Laguna Makax ❷

Corredor Panorámico (Panoramic Hwy.)

Dolphin ▪
Discovery

Salina Grande

Hi-Na Ha ▪
Beach Resort

Tortugranja ❹ ❸
Hacienda
Mundaca
Playa Paraíso

Playa Lancheros ⚲

Playa Gaviota ⚲

Playa Indios ⚲

La Casa
de los Sueños ▪

Hotel & Beach Club ▪
Garrafón
de Castilla

KEY
⛴ Ferry

El Garrafón ❺
National Park

Santuario Maya a la
Diosa Ixchel
▲ ❻

0 ———————— 1 mile

0 ———————— 1 km

Punta Sur

proximately ½ km (¼ mi) farther on the left is the entrance to the **Tortugranja** ④.

Return to Avenida Rueda Medina and continue southeast past Playa Lancheros to **El Garrafón National Park** ⑤. Slightly more than ½ km (¼ mi) farther along the same road, on the windward side of the tip of Isla Mujeres, sit the remains of a small Maya ruin dedicated to Ixchel, the **Santuario Maya a la Diosa Ixchel** ⑥. Although little of the ruin is left, the ocean and bay views from here are well worth seeing. Follow the paved eastern perimeter road northwest back into town. Known as the Corredor Panorámico (Panoramic Highway), this is a beautiful, scenic drive with a few pull-off areas along the way, perfect for a secluded picnic. Swimming is not recommended along this coast because of the strong currents and rocky shore.

Sights to See

❶ El Cemeterio (Cemetery). Isla's unnamed cemetery, with its century-old gravestones, is on Avenida López Mateos, the road that runs parallel to Playa Norte. Filled with carved angels and flowers, the most beautiful of the decorated tombs are those in memory of children. Hidden among them is the tomb of the notorious Fermín Mundaca. This 19th-century slave trader—who's often billed more glamorously as a pirate—carved his own skull-and-crossbones tombstone with the ominous epitaph: AS YOU ARE, I ONCE WAS; AS I AM, SO SHALL YOU BE. Mundaca's grave is empty, however; his remains lie in Mérida, where he died. The monument is not easy to find—ask a local to point out the unidentified marker. ⊠ *Av. López Mateos.*

❺ El Garrafón National Park. Much of the coral reef at this national marine park has died—a result of too many snorkelers—and so the fish have to be bribed with food. There isn't much for snorkelers, but the park does have kayaks and ocean playground equipment, as well as a three-floor facility with restaurants, bathrooms, and gift shops. Despite these efforts to keep visitors entertained, you should bring a book if you intend to spend the day. (The Garrafón Beach Club, next door, is a much less expensive alternative and the snorkeling is equal to if not better than that in the park.) Marine-park tickets are available at any kiosk in Cancún and in Playa del Carmen; you can also get tickets at the park entrance. ⊠ *Carretera El Garrafón, 2½ km (1½ mi) southeast of Playa Lancheros,* ☎ *998/883-3233 in Cancún, 984/473-2801 in Playa del Carmen,* WEB *www.garrafon.com.* ⊠ *$19.95.* ⊙ *Daily 8:30-6:30.*

❸ Hacienda Mundaca. A dirt drive and stone archway mark the entrance to the remains of the mansion that 19th-century slave trader–cum–pirate Fermín Mundaca de Marechaja built. When the British navy began cracking down on slavers, Mundaca settled on the island. He fell in love with a local beauty nicknamed La Trigueña (The Brunette). In order to woo her, Mundaca built a sprawling estate with verdant tropical gardens. Apparently unimpressed, La Trigueña married a young islander—and Mundaca went slowly mad waiting for her to change her mind. He finally died in a brothel in Mérida.

There is little to see of the actual hacienda; it has simply vanished. Locals say the government tore it down, or merely neglected its upkeep. All that remains are a small crumbling guardhouse, a rusted cannon, an arch, and a well. The most interesting things to see here are the ruined stone archway and triangular pediment, which is carved with the following inscription: HUERTA DE LA HACIENDA DE VISTA ALEGRE MDCC-CLXXVI (Orchard of the Happy View Hacienda 1876). The gardens are well kept, lush, and colorful with tropical flora. ⊠ *East off Av. Rueda Medina (take main road southeast from town to S-curve at the end of*

Laguna Makax and turn left onto dirt road), ☎ *no phone.* 🎫 *$1.50.* ☼ *Daily 9 AM–dusk.*

2 Laguna Makax. Pirates are said to have anchored their ships in this lagoon as they lay in wait for the hapless vessels plying the Spanish Main (the geographical area in which Spanish treasure ships trafficked). These days the lagoon houses a local shipyard and is a safe harbor for boats during hurricane season. The lagoon is off of Avenida Rueda Medina about 2½ km (1½ mi) south of town, across the street from a Mexican naval base and some *salinas* (salt marshes).

6 Santuario Maya a la Diosa Ixchel (Sanctuary of the Goddess Ixchel). The sad vestiges of a Maya temple once dedicated to Ixchel are about 1 km (½ mi) southeast of El Garrafón National Park, at Isla's tip. Though Hurricane Gilbert walloped the ruin and succeeded in blowing most of it away in 1988, part of it has since been restored. A lovely walkway around the remains continues down to a natural arch underneath the ruin. The view from here, of the open ocean on one side and the Bahía de Mujeres (Bay of Women) on the other, is spectacular. Adjacent is a **lighthouse.** The official word is that climbing to the top is no longer allowed, but a small tip and your powers of persuasion may convince the keeper to let you up to see the incredible view. The ruin is at the point where the road turns northeast into the Corredor Panorámico.

4 Tortugranja (Turtle Farm). Run by an outfit called Eco Caribe, this facility is dedicated to the study and preservation of sea turtles. During hatching season (May–September) upwards of 6,000 turtles hatch along the coast of Quintana Roo. Some are brought to the farm to be raised until they are large enough to survive at sea. You can view hatchlings and young turtles of various species in outdoor tanks, go on a tour led by one of the biologists, and watch feedings. A small but well-designed museum explains the various stages of turtle life and different parts of the coral reef. ✉ *Take Av. Rueda Medina south of town; about a block southeast of Hacienda Mundaca, take the right fork (the smaller road that loops back north); the entrance is about ½ km (¼ mi) farther, on the left,* ☎ *998/877–0595.* 🎫 *$2.* ☼ *Daily 9–5.*

NEED A BREAK?	Walk northwest from Tortugranja, along the lovely beach, to reach **Hacienda Gomar** ($; ☎ 998/877–0541), a good Mexican restaurant with a buffet lunch and marimba music. A number of crafts stalls here sell local goods, and you can rest under a beach palapa. If you walk south from Tortugranja, you can eat excellent barbecued grouper, snapper, or barracuda at the restaurants along Playa Lancheros, which also has handicraft shops, a beach bar, and small palapas for shade.

BEACHES

The superb **Playa Norte,** known for its congenial atmosphere, is easy to find: simply head north on any of the north–south streets in town until you hit it. The turquoise sea is as calm as a lake, and you can wade out for 40 yards in waist-deep water. According to Isleños, Hurricane Gilbert's only good deed was to widen this and other leeward-side beaches by blowing sand over from Cancún. You can have a drink or snack at one of several palapa bars; Buho's is popular with locals and tourists, who gather to chat, eat fresh seafood, drink cold beer, and watch the sun set. Tarzan Water Sports rents out snorkeling gear, Jet Skis, floats, and sailboards.

The beaches between Laguna Makax and El Garrafón National Park, including **Playa Paraíso**, are good spots for having lunch or for shopping at the small stands that sell local handicrafts, souvenirs, and T-shirts. Some pet sea turtles and harmless *tiburones gatos* (nurse sharks) are housed in sea pens at **Playa Lancheros.** You can have your picture taken with one of the sharks. (These sharks are tamer than the *tintoreras,* or blue sharks, which live in the open seas. They have seven rows of teeth and weigh up to 1,100 lbs.)

DINING

As in the rest of Mexico, locals eat their main meal during siesta hours, between 1 and 4, and then have a light dinner in the evening. Unless otherwise stated, restaurants are open daily for lunch and dinner. Some restaurants open late and close early on Sunday; others are closed on Monday.

Generally, restaurants on the island are informal, though shirts and shoes are required in most indoor dining rooms. Some, but not all, outdoor terraces and palapas request that swimsuits and feet be covered.

CATEGORY	COST
$$$$	over $30
$$$	$21–$30
$$	$10–$20
$	under $10

per person, for a main course at dinner

$$-$$$$ ✕ **Casa Rolandi.** Part of the Rolandi family of restaurants, this Casa
★ Rolandi has the Swiss–northern Italian menu that won high marks at its Cancún location. The carpaccio *di tonno alla Giorgio* (thin slices of fresh tuna with extra-virgin olive oil and lime juice) is particularly good, as are the pastas—including lasagna and shrimp-filled black ravioli. The restaurant is part of the Hotel Villa Rolandi lobby and extends out to an open-air deck that juts out over the beach. The sunset views are spectacular. ⊠ *Hotel Villa Rolandi Gourmet & Beach Club, Fracc. Laguna Mar Makax, Sm 7,* ☎ *998/877–0100. AE, MC, V.*

$-$$$ ✕ **Lo Lo Lorena.** The innovative menu at this restaurant, one of the is-
★ land's best, changes daily according to what's available. However, because of their popularity, a few of the dishes created by Lolo, the flamboyant chef-owner, have become permanent fixtures, including "Lover's Salad," with conch and ginger, and a fantastic tart Tatin. Lolo also puts on an entertaining show in the open kitchen. Wooden shutters, a wide porch, wicker furniture, and pastel colors give the old wooden house a lovely Caribbean flavor. ⊠ *Av. Guerrero 7,* ☎ *no phone. MC, V. Closed Mon. No lunch.*

$-$$ ✕ **Isla Sol.** The local boat crowd tends to gather at this casual restaurant and bar for its 10-peso beers and delicious, large burritos. The basic cheese, bean, and chicken burrito is enough to keep you going for the evening. The fully stocked bar with its comfortable couches and a variety of great music, from classical rock to the top ten, make it a popular late-night hangout. ⊠ *Avs. Hidalgo and Matamoros 19-A,* ☎ *no phone. MC, V.*

$-$$ ✕ **Leopard Lounge.** Enjoy fresh sushi at this outdoor restaurant-bar, which
★ combines the hip style of Hollywood's Rat Pack with a tropical island atmosphere. Pull up a stool at the palapa bar and order a cold martini. If your taste doesn't run to sushi, try the teriyaki beef and chicken instead, or the tempura vegetables. There is live music here until 1 AM. ⊠ *Plaza Los Almendros, between Avs. Hidalgo and Guerrero at Av. Matamoros,* ☎ *998/877–0679. MC, V. Closed Sun.–Mon. No lunch.*

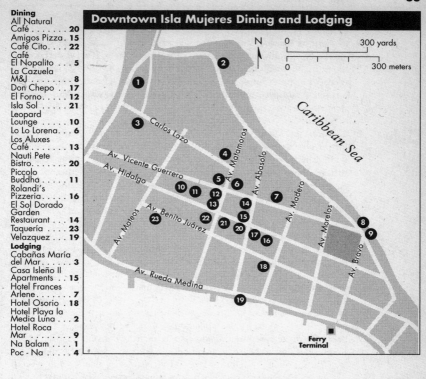

Downtown Isla Mujeres Dining and Lodging

$–$$ ✕ **Nauti Pete Bistro.** This sister restaurant of the adjacent All Natural Café opens in the evening to offer a menu of grilled meats and fish. The grilled tuna is especially fresh and done to perfection and is served with wasabi on the side. The salads are fresh and crispy. The beer is cold, especially on Monday night, which is U.S. football night and attracts sports fans from around the world. ⊠ *Centro Hidalgo, Plaza Karlita,* ☎ *998/877–0720. MC, V. No lunch.*

$–$$ ✕ **Rolandi's Pizzeria.** Like its sister operation in Cancún, this restaurant offers consistently good Italian food, such as lobster pizzas, calzones, and pastas. The grilled fresh fish and shrimp are recommended, as is the garlic bread—a puffed pita oozing butter and garlic. The tone is friendly and casual. Since it's in the heart of downtown, this is a great place to stop for a drink and people-watch. ⊠ *Av. Hidalgo 110, between Avs. Francisco Madero and Abasolo,* ☎ *998/877–0430. AE, MC, V.*

$–$$ ✕ **Velazquez.** This family-owned restaurant on the beach is open until
★ dusk and serves the freshest seafood on the island. You haven't eaten Yucatecan until you've tried the regional specialty *tikinchic*—fish marinated in a sour-orange sauce and achiote paste, wrapped in banana leaves, and cooked over an open flame. Feasting on a fantastic fish meal while you sit outside and watch the boats go by is the true Isla experience. ⊠ *Av. Rueda Medina (2 blocks northwest of ferry docks),* ☎ *no phone. No credit cards.*

$ ✕ **Los Aluxes Cafe.** Enjoy an early morning or late-night cappuccino or espresso with a freshly baked dessert. Sit at one of the charming café tables or get your java to go. The prices here are among the cheapest on the island. ⊠ *Av. Matamoros 87,* ☎ *no phone. No credit cards.*

$ ✕ **All Natural Café.** This haven for vegetarians serves breakfast, lunch, and light dinners. Try the fresh juice mixes along with salads, soups, and veggie sandwiches served on baguettes. For dinner you can also try next door at the Nauti Pete Bistro, the sister restaurant to the café. ⊠ *Centro Hidalgo, Plaza Karlita,* ☎ *998/877–0720. MC, V.*

$ ✕ **Amigos Pizza.** The place for the pizza connoisseur, Amigos offers classic combinations with some interesting twists. Pick your favorite from 14 varieties, or opt for one of several fresh pasta dishes. There is also a simple but satisfying breakfast menu. The dining room has basic plastic tables and chairs and paper napkins, which help to keep the prices among the lowest in town. ⊠ *Av. Hidalgo between Avs. Matamoros and Abasolo,* ☎ *no phone. No credit cards.*

$ ✕ **Café Cito.** Cito is one of the prettiest cafés on the island, done in bright blue and white, with simple watercolor paintings adorning the walls, shell-decorated table tops, and wind chimes dangling from the rafters. Breakfast choices include fresh waffles, fruit-filled crepes, and egg dishes, as well as great cappuccino and espresso. For lunch the chef whips up different daily specials. You can join the island's Harley Davidson Club here, or visit Sabrina next door for a tarot reading. ⊠ *Avs. Juárez and Matamoros,* ☎ *998/877–0438. No credit cards.*

$ ✕ **Café El Nopalito.** The eggs are done to perfection, the coffee is aromatic, the bread homemade, the juices fresh, and the fruit sweet at this delightful breakfast café. You can also indulge in French toast, yogurt, and granola. There's no need to rush; you can sit for a while and chat with owner Anneliese Warren, or shop at the crafts store next door. ⊠ *Av. Guerrero 17,* ☎ *998/877–0555. No credit cards. No dinner.*

$ ✕ **La Cazuela M&J.** At this oceanfront eatery next to the Hotel Roca Mar, a fresh breeze and a spectacular Caribbean view are the backdrops for the terrific food. In addition to the freshly ground, dark Colombian coffee, breakfast offerings include fruit, crepes, and omelets. Or try "La Cazuela," the house specialty created by chef-owner Marco Fraga; it's somewhere between an omelet and a soufflé. Grilled chicken with homemade barbecue sauce and thick, juicy hamburgers are on the lunch menu. ⊠ *Calle Nicolas Bravo, Zona Maritima,* ☎ FAX *998/ 877–0101. No credit cards. Closed Mon. No dinner.*

$ ✕ **Don Chepo.** Mexican grill cuisine (tacos, fajitas, and steak) is offered in this lively restaurant with good service. The "Arracera" is a fine cut of meat that's grilled and served with rice, salad, baked potato, warm tortillas, and beans. The beer is cold and delicious, and other domestic drinks are also served. ⊠ *Av. Hidalgo at Av. Francisco Madero,* ☎ *no phone. MC, V.*

$ ✕ **El Forno.** Pick up a piece of authentic Italian pizza cooked by an Italian ex-patriot. The substantial pizzas here have thick crusts and are smothered in cheese and fresh vegetables or pepperoni. For dessert there are slices of apple pie. It's a great place for a quick and filling snack. ⊠ *Av. Matamoros 85,* ☎ *no phone. No credit cards.*

$ ✕ **Piccolo Buddha.** The pasta here is handmade and prepared fresh before your eyes by an Italian expatriot. It will be hard to choose your dish, since they are all delicious. Try the Gorgonzola pasta with four different cheeses, the ravioli stuffed with cheese, or the tomato penne. It's a great place for a satisfying, economical lunch or dinner. ⊠ *Plaza Los Almendros, between Avs. Hidalgo and Guerrero at Av. Matamoros,* ☎ *no phone. No credit cards. Closed Sun.*

$ ✕ **El Sol Dorado Garden Restaurant.** Decorated with a sun motif, this funky restaurant serves great food morning, noon, and night. For breakfast consider coffee and hotcakes; for lunch, soup and salad; and for dinner, fresh-grilled fish or chicken. Out back is a delightful garden oasis. A pool table and a giant TV screen showing the latest blockbuster film are inside, so it's not surprising that this is a popular hangout for locals. ⊠ *Av. Abasolo between Avs. Guerrero and Hidalgo,* ☎ *no phone. MC, V.*

$ ✕ **Taquería.** For an inexpensive and delicious meal of Yucatán specialties including *sabutes* (fried corn tortillas smothered in chicken and salsa), *tortas* (sandwiches), *panuchos* (beans, chicken, and avocado over fried tortillas), and tamales, check out this small hole in the wall, open daily 10–10. The two sisters who do the cooking are a treat. They don't speak English but communicate with you using sign language and their version of Spanglish. ⊠ *Av. Juárez, 1 block south of cemetery,* ☎ *no phone. No credit cards.*

LODGING

Isla has plenty of hotels. Generally the older, more modest places are in town, and the newer, more expensive resorts tend to front the beach around Punta Norte or the peninsula near the lagoon. Many hotels have consciously made an effort to keep their rooms simple in order to have visitors experience the true tranquillity of Isla. Consequently most hotels have ceiling fans, and some have air-conditioning, but few have TVs or phones. Local travel agents can provide information about luxurious, self-contained time-share condominiums, which are another option.

CATEGORY	COST*
$$$$	over $100
$$$	$70–$100
$$	$40–$70
$	under $40

All prices are for a standard double room, excluding 12% tax.

$$$$ ⊞ **La Casa de los Sueños.** Tucked away at Isla's south end, this dazzling residence turned bed-and-breakfast is honeymoon-perfect. A large interior courtyard leads to a sunken, open-air living room decorated in sunset colors, which extends to a terrace with a cliff-side swimming pool overlooking the ocean. All rooms are individually decorated, with artwork and wooden furniture, and have ocean-view terraces. The master bedroom also has a Jacuzzi with a sunset view. Note that two Great Danes live in the house and like to mingle with the guests. ⊠ *Carretera El Garrafón, 77400,* ☎ *998/877–0651 or 800/551–2558,* FAX *998/877–0708,* WEB *www.lossuenos.com/. 9 rooms. Dining room, fans, pool, beach, dock, snorkeling, boating, bicycles; no room phones, no kids, no smoking. AE, MC, V.*

$$$$ ⊞ **Hotel Villa Rolandi Gourmet & Beach Club.** This compact hotel is ★ as posh as any Cancún property. A private yacht delivers you to the island, where 20 elegant suites await. Decorated in bright colors, all suites have ocean views, king-size beds, and a sitting area that leads to the balcony with its heated whirlpool bath. The showers have six adjustable heads and convert into a sauna. Both the Casa Rolandi restaurant and the lovely garden pool overlook the Bahía de Mujeres and lead down to an intimate beach. Room rates include Continental breakfast and lunch or dinner. ⊠ *Fracc. Laguna Mar Makax, Sm 7, Mz 75, 77400,* ☎ *998/877–0100,* FAX *998/877–0700,* WEB *www.rolandi. com. 20 suites. Restaurant, in-room hot tubs, pool, gym, spa, beach, dock, boating; no smoking, no kids under 13. AE, MC, V.*

$$$–$$$$ ⊞ **Na Balam.** This intimate hotel on Playa Norte may satisfy all your tropical-paradise fantasies. Each room in the main building has a palapa roof, eating area, large bathroom, and either a patio or balcony facing the ocean. Decorated with Mexican folk art or photographs, the rooms are simple yet elegant. Across the street are eight more spacious rooms, each with a balcony, sitting area, double bed, and palapa roof. There's also a swimming pool, garden, meditation room, and a TV lounge. Breakfast at the restaurant is a delightful way to kick off the day. ⊠ *Calle Zazil-Ha 118, 77400,* ☎ *998/877–0279 or 800/552–4550,*

FAX *998/877–0446,* WEB *www.nabalam.com. 31 rooms. Restaurant, pool, beach, bar; no room TVs, no room phones. AE, MC, V.*

$$$–$$$$ ☷ **Puerto Isla Mujeres Resort & Yacht Club.** The best-kept secret on Isla overlooks the lagoon. Each of the five villas and 21 suites has a private terrace, living-room area, small refrigerator, private whirlpool bath, and stereo. The grounds are spacious, with lots of room for wandering, and the pool contains a fountain and a swim-up bar off to the side. If you miss the ocean, a water taxi can shuttle you over to the property's deluxe beach club, which includes a pool and a restaurant. Families are warmly welcomed. The best part is that all this comfort comes at a relatively reasonable rate. ⊠ *Puerto de Abrigo, Laguna Makax, 77400,* ☎ *998/877–0093 or 800/960–4752,* FAX *998/877–0093,* WEB *www.puerto-isla.com/resort.htm. 21 suites, 5 villas. Some kitchenettes, refrigerators, in-room VCRs, pool, beach, dock, marina. AE, MC, V.*

$$$ ☷ **Cabañas María del Mar.** There is an eclectic mix of rooms here. The less expensive rooms, farther away from the beach, are simply furnished bungalows, with patios that face a garden and pool. Rooms in the Tower are decorated with Mexican folk art and have ocean-view balconies, refrigerators, and large beds. Castle rooms are right on the beach and have hand-carved wood furnishings and Mexican tiles; all have refrigerators and a large terrace overlooking Playa Norte. Rates include a Continental breakfast. ⊠ *Av. Arq. Carlos Lazo 1, 77400,* ☎ *998/877–0179 or 800/223–5695,* FAX *998/877–0213,* WEB *www.cabanasdelmar.com. 42 rooms, 14 bungalows. Restaurant, some refrigerators, pool, bar, travel services, motorbikes; no room TVs. MC, V.*

$$$ ☷ **Hotel Playa la Media Luna.** This charming and breezy three-story bed-and-breakfast is on Half-Moon Beach, just south of Playa Norte. All 18 guest rooms are done in soft pastel colors with king-size beds and balconies or terraces that look out onto the ocean and pool. Thatch roofs and wooden walkways give the place a castaway feel. Breakfast is served in a sunny dining room. ⊠ *Sección Rotas, Punta Norte, 77400,* ☎ *998/877–0759 or 800/223–5695,* FAX *998/877–1124,* WEB *www. cabanasdelmar.com/medialuna.htm. 18 rooms. Dining room, refrigerators, pool, beach; no room TVs, no room phones. AE, MC, V.*

$$–$$$ ☷ **Casa Isleño II Apartments.** These fully equipped apartments are private and quiet yet only minutes from the main pier and downtown. Perfect for setting up home, they come with a full kitchen, small sitting areas, king-size beds, and hammocks. ⊠ *Av. Guerrero Nte. 3-A,* ☎ FAX *998/877–70265,* WEB *www.isla-mujeres.net/casaisleno/home.htm. 3 apartments. Kitchenettes, microwaves; no TV, no room phones. No credit cards.*

$$–$$$ ☷ **Hotel Roca Mar.** The turquoise sea is the star here, as this is one of ★ the few downtown hotels overlooking the water. You can see, smell, and hear the ocean as soon as you step into your room. The private balcony, the wooden slats on the windows, and the simple furnishings—all are designed to be inconspicuous. Of course, the lovely courtyard, which is filled with plants, birds, and strategically placed benches, overlooks the ocean, too. ⊠ *Calle Nicolas Bravo, Zona Maritima, 77400,* ☎ FAX *998/877–0101,* WEB *www.mjmnet.net/HotelRocaMar/home.htm. 31 rooms. Restaurant, fans, pool, beach, snorkeling; no air-conditioning in some rooms, no room TVs, no room phones. AE, MC, V.*

$$ ☷ **Hotel & Beach Club Garrafón de Castilla.** The snorkeling at the beach club of this small family-owned hotel next door to El Garrafón National Park is better than what you're likely to experience at the park. Plus, the beach here is bigger, with easy water access. The rooms have balconies that look out onto the water and double beds; some rooms have refrigerators. Decor is kept to a minimum, but the overall effect is bright, cheery, and comfortable. ⊠ *Carretera Punta Sur, Km 6, 77400,* ☎ *998/877–0107,* FAX *998/877–0508,* WEB *www.isla-mujeres.*

net/castilla/home.htm. 14 rooms. Snack bar, minibars, some refrigerators, beach, dive shop, snorkeling, motorbikes; no room TVs, no room phones. MC, V.

$$ ★ 🏨 **Playa Gaviota.** The real plus at this hilltop hotel sandwiched between a garden and the ocean is the private beach with its barbecue, palapas, coconut trees, white sand, and gorgeous sunset views. Each of the 10 suites, decorated in basic blue and white, has a fully equipped kitchenette, two queen-size beds, a small eating area, and a large terrace facing the ocean. Three smaller, older (but still comfortable) cabins on the beach are for rent as well. The owners, a quiet Mexican family, live on site. ⊠ *Carretera El Garrafón, Km 4.5, 77400,* ☎ 🖷 *998/877–0216,* 🆆🅴🅱 *http://playagaviotasuite.cjb.net/. 10 suites, 3 cabins. Fans, kitchenettes, beach; no room phones. No credit cards.*

$ 🏨 **Hotel Frances Arlene.** This small hotel is a perennial favorite with visitors. The Magaña family takes great care to maintain both the property and its ambience—signs everywhere remind you of the rules. Rooms center on a pleasant courtyard and are fitted with double beds, bamboo furniture, and refrigerators. Some have kitchenettes. The beach and downtown are a short stroll away. ⊠ *Av. Guerrero 7, 77400,* ☎ *998/877–0430,* 🖷 *998/877–0429. 11 rooms. Fans, some kitchenettes, refrigerators; no room TVs. AE, MC, V.*

$ 🏨 **Hi-Na-Ha Beach Resort.** This intimate and luxurious hotel faces the Bahía de Mujeres with the Laguna Makax at the back. Suites have queen-size beds and ocean-view balconies. Villas have two bedrooms, fully equipped kitchens, dining rooms, and balconies. Cable television is available upon request, at an additional charge. With a lovely garden, pool, restaurant, and dock, it's a perfect retreat for families. ⊠ *Fracc. Laguna Mar Makax, Sm 7, Mz 75,* ☎ 🖷 *998/877–0615,* 🆆🅴🅱 *www.hinaha. com. 10 suites, 2 villas. Restaurant, fans, kitchenettes, massage, beach, boating, bar, Internet, travel services; no room phones. MC, V.*

$ 🏨 **Hotel Osorio.** This heart-of-town hotel is one of Isla's least expensive. Rooms are basic but clean and comfortable—with two double beds, a private bathroom, and ceiling fans. All open onto a central courtyard. The shops, restaurants, and bars are steps away. ⊠ *Avs. Juárez and Francisco Madero, 77400,* ☎ *998/877–0056. 18 rooms. Fans; no air-conditioning, no room TVs, no room phones. No credit cards.*

$ 🏨 **Poc-Na.** The island's coed youth hostel remains one of the best deals in El Pueblo. Poc-Na has hammocks and mattresses in a dormitory that sleeps 14. Proximity to Playa Norte and shops, restaurants, and bars is a bonus. ⊠ *Av. Matamoros 15, 77400,* ☎ *998/877–0090 or 998/877–0059. 14 beds. Dining room; no air-conditioning, no room TVs, no room phones. No credit cards.*

NIGHTLIFE AND THE ARTS

The Arts

The island celebrates many religious holidays and festivals in the main square, usually with live entertainment. Carnival is in February and is spectacular fun. Other popular events include the springtime regattas and fishing tournaments. Founding Day, August 17, marks the island's official founding by the Mexican government. During the **Isla Mujeres International Music Festival,** held the second week in October, the island fills with music and dancers from around the world. The Isla Mujeres tourist office (☎ 998/877–0767) can provide further information about the festival.

Casa de la Cultura (⊠ Av. Guerrero, ☎ 998/877–0639) has art, drama, yoga, and folkloric-dance classes year-round. It's open Monday–Saturday 9–1 and 4–8.

Nightlife

Plaza Isla Mujeres at Avenidas Hidalgo and Guerrero has become the official nightlife spot, with a number of bars and restaurants open until the wee hours. **Buho's** (✉ Cabañas María del Mar, Av. Arq. Carlos Lazo 1, ☎ 998/877–1479) remains the favorite restaurant on Playa Norte for a relaxing sunset drink. There is a small bar and a large television at **Chiles Loco** (✉ Plaza Isla Mujeres, Av. Hidalgo 81, Local A-4, ☎ no phone). **Isla Tequila** (✉ Avs. Hidalgo and Matamoros 19-A, ☎ no phone) has cheap beer and burritos. **Jax Bar & Grill** (✉ Av. Rueda Medina 42, near the lighthouse, ☎ no phone) has live music, cold beer, and snack food. The **Leopard Lounge** (✉ Plaza Los Almendros, between Avs. Hidalgo and Guerrero at Av. Matamoros, ☎ 998/877–0679) has live music until 1 AM. The liveliest (and loudest) bar in the area is **Slices** (✉ Plaza Isla Mujeres, Av. Hidalgo 82, ☎ no phone), where you can enjoy a live DJ and cold drinks.

OUTDOOR ACTIVITIES AND SPORTS

For water sports, Playa Norte is the calmest beach.

Fishing

If you're interested in participating in the **Red Cross Billfish Tournament,** held in April, contact Michael Creamer (☎ FAX 998/877–0443, WEB www.mjmnet.net/redcross/fishing.htm).

Captain Anthony Mendillo Jr. (✉ Av. Arq. Carlos Lazo 1, ☎ 998/877–0213, FAX 998/877–0156) offers specialized fishing trips aboard his 29-ft vessel, the *Keen M*, starting at $600 a day. **Sea Hawk Divers** (✉ Av. Arq. Carlos Lazo, Playa Norte, ☎ 998/877–0296) runs fishing trips—for barracuda, snapper, and smaller fish—that start at $150 for a half day. The **Sociedad Cooperativa Turistica** (☎ 998/877–0274) offers four hours of fishing close to shore for $100; eight hours farther out is $240.

Marinas

Marina y Club Yates (✉ Av. Rueda Medina, 2 blocks north of ferry terminal, ☎ 998/877–0211) is a small marina off Isla's downtown, with room for 30 yachts up to 48 ft in length. It includes a full-service dock for gas and diesel fuel and a small store with a palapa-style restaurant.

Puerto Isla Mujeres Resort & Yacht Club (✉ Puerto de Abrigo, Laguna Makax, ☎ 998/877–0093), the only place along the coast to get your boat repaired, has a full-service marina for vessels up to 170 ft. Daily mooring costs are $1.50 for vessels up to 89 ft and $2 for vessels 90 ft and over. The marina offers a full-service fuel station, a 150-ton lift, customs assistance, 110/220 V single and three-phase hookups, crew services, 24-hour security, and laundry, interior cleaning, and boatyard services. If you need to sleep over on land, the luxury resort is steps away from the docks.

Snorkeling and Scuba Diving

DIVE SITES

The famous coral reefs at **El Garrafón National Park** have suffered tremendously because of human negligence, boats' dropping anchors (now outlawed), and the effects of Hurricane Gilbert in 1988. Most of the reef is dead, far from its past splendor, but there are still some sights to be seen farther out from shore. Some good snorkeling can be had near Playa Norte on the north end.

Isla is a good place to learn how to dive, since the snorkeling is close to shore. Offshore, there's excellent diving and snorkeling at **Xlaches** (pronounced *ees*-lah-chayss) reef, due north on the way to Isla Contoy. One of Contoy's most alluring dives is the **Cave of the Sleeping Sharks,** east of the northern tip. The caves were discovered by an island fisherman known as Vulvula and extensively explored by Ramon Bravo, a local diver, cinematographer, and Mexico's foremost expert on sharks. *National Geographic* and the late Jacques Cousteau had also studied the curious phenomenon of the snoozing black tip, bull, and lemon sharks. The theories about why the sharks sleep here vary; they cover everything from the amount of salt in the water to the lack of carbon dioxide in the caves. It's a fascinating 150-ft dive for experienced divers only.

At the extreme southern end of the island on the leeward side lies **Los Manchones.** At 30 ft–40 ft deep and 3,300 ft off the southwestern coast, this coral reef is a good dive site. During the summer of 1994, an ecology group hoping to divert divers and snorkelers from El Garrafón commissioned the creation of a 1-ton, 9¾-ft bronze cross, which was sunk here. Named the Cruz de la Bahía (Cross of the Bay), it is a tribute to all the people who have died at sea. Together the cross and the reef make for a dramatic, fascinating dive. **Los Cuevones,** to the southwest near La Bandera, reaches a depth of 45 ft. On the windward side of the islet north of Mujeres is an unnamed site with two sunken galleons. Dive shops are able to direct you to this spot and others. Most area dive spots are also described in detail in *Dive Mexico,* a colorful magazine readily available in local shops.

DIVE SHOPS

Coral Scuba Dive Center (⊠ Av. Matamoros 13-A, ☎ 998/877–0371) offers two-tank dives for $39; shipwreck dives or photo dives for $59; and snorkel trips for $14. **Mundaca Divers** (⊠ Av. Francisco Madero 10, ☎ 998/877–0607, FAX 998/877–0601) rents tanks starting at $45 along with snorkeling gear for $5 a day. **Sea Hawk Divers** (⊠ Av. Arq. Carlos Lazo, Playa Norte, ☎ 998/877–0296) rents two tanks for $40; it also has dive gear and snorkeling equipment. It will also set up accommodations for divers in pleasant rooms starting at $35 per day. **Tarzan Watersports** (⊠ Playa Norte, past Cabañas María del Mar, ☎ 998/877–0679) offers PADI courses, dive trips, and family snorkeling trips. It also rents out Wave Runners, Hobie Cats, and kayaks. All dive shops have trips to reefs and the Cave of the Sleeping Sharks.

Water Parks
Dolphin Discovery (☎ 998/883–0777 or 998/883–0779) offers humans the chance to play with the delightful sea mammals in a small, supervised group in a pool. There are four swims daily, at 9, 11, 1, and 3. Each session consists of a 30-minute instruction video and 30 minutes in the water. The cost is $134 and includes the boat ride from Cancún and an all-you-can-eat Mexican buffet.

SHOPPING

Shopping on Isla Mujeres is a mixture of stores selling T-shirts, suntan lotion, beer, and groceries and those that sell Mexican crafts, including silver and jewelry, folk art, textiles, and clothes. Most shops accept credit cards. Hours are generally Monday–Saturday 10–1 and 4–7, although quite a few stores stay open during siesta hours (1–4).

Crafts
Many local artists display their works at the public **Artesanias Market** (⊠ Av. Matamoros and Av. Arq. Carlos Lazo, ☎ no phone), which offers plenty of bargains.

Artesanias El Nopal (⊠ Av. Guerrero at Av. Matamoros, ☎ 998/877–
0555) has an excellent selection of fine Mexican handicrafts from
across the country, hand-picked by the owner.

Casa Isleño II (⊠ Av. Guerrero Nte. 3-A, ☎ FAX 998/877–0265) offers
handpainted T-shirts in beautiful colors as well as a collection of shells
and crafts.

Grocery Stores

For fresh produce, the **Mercado Municipal** (municipal market; ⊠ Av.
Guerrero Nte., near the post office, ☎ no phone) is your best bet. It's
open daily until noon. **Panadería La Reina** (⊠ Avs. Francisco Madero
and Juárez, ☎ 998/877–0419), open Monday–Saturday starting at 7
AM, has terrific breads and baked sweets. **Super Express** (⊠ Av. Morelos 3, in the plaza, ☎ 998/877–0127), Isla's main grocery store, is well
stocked with all the basics.

Specialty Stores

Cosmic Cosas (⊠ Av. Matamoros 82, ☎ 998/877–0806) is the only
English-language bookstore on the island. The friendly shop offers two-
for-one book trades (no Harlequin romances) and e-mail and computer
services. It also rents out board games—great for children on rainy days.
Jewelry on Isla ranges from tasteful creations to junk. Bargains are to
be found, but beware the street vendors—most of their wares, especially the amber, are fake. On the other hand, **Van Cleef & Arpels** (⊠
Avs. Juárez and Morelos, ☎ 998/877–0331) offers an incredible selection of rings, bracelets, necklaces, and earrings in 18K gold mounted
with precious stones such as diamonds, Colombian emeralds, sapphires, rubies, and tanzanite. Many of the designs are innovative and
the prices lower than in the United States. Across the street is the sister sterling-silver shop, which offers designer pieces at bargain prices.

SIDE TRIP TO ISLA CONTOY

Some 30 km (19 mi) north of Isla Mujeres, Isla Contoy (Isle of Birds)
is a national wildlife park and bird sanctuary. Six and a half kilometers (4 miles) long and less than 1 km (about ½ mi) wide, the island is
a protected area—the number of visitors is carefully regulated in order
to safeguard the flora and fauna. Isla Contoy has become a favorite
among birders, snorkelers, and nature lovers, who come to enjoy its
unspoiled beauty.

More than 70 bird species—everything from gulls, pelicans, petrels,
and cormorants to cranes, ducks, flamingos, herons, frigates, sea swallows, doves, quail, spoonbills, and hawks—fly this way in late fall, some
of them to nest and breed. Although the number of species is dimin-
ishing—partly as a result of human traffic, partly from the effects of
Hurricane Gilbert—Isla Contoy is still a rare treat for bird-watchers.

There is an abundance of sea life around the island as well. Snorkelers can see brilliant coral and fish. Manta rays, which average about
5 ft across, are visible in the shallow waters. Surrounding the island
are large numbers of shrimp, mackerel, barracuda, flying fish, and trum-
pet fish. In December, lobsters pass through in great (though dimin-
ishing) numbers, on their southerly migration route.

Sand dunes inland on the east coast rise as high as 70 ft above sea level.
Black rocks and coral reefs fringe the island's east coast, which drops
off abruptly 15 ft into the sea. The west coast is fringed with sand, shrubs,
and coconut palms. At the north and the south you find nothing but
trees and small pools of water.

The island is officially open to visitors from 9 to 5:30; overnight visits are not allowed. Other than the birds and the dozen or so park rangers who make their home here, the island's only denizens are iguanas, lizards, turtles, hermit crabs, and boa constrictors.

Everyone landing on Isla Contoy must purchase a $5 authorization ticket; the price is usually included in the cost of a guided tour. Check with your tour operator to make sure that you will be landing on the island. Many of the larger companies simply cruise past. The best tours tend to be those that leave directly from Isla Mujeres; these operators know the area and therefore are more committed to protecting Isla Contoy (☞ Tours *in* Isla Mujeres A to Z, *below*). Tours that leave from Cancún can charge up to three times as much for the same tours that run from Isla Mujeres.

Once on shore, be sure to visit the outdoor museum, which has a small display of animals along with photographs of the island. Climb the nearby tower for a bird's-eye view. Remember to obey all the rules in order to protect the island: it's a privilege to be allowed here. Government officials may at some point stop all landings on Isla Contoy in order to protect its fragile environment.

ISLA MUJERES A TO Z

To research prices, get advice from other travelers, and book travel arrangements, visit www.fodors.com.

AIR TRAVEL

The island has a small landing strip for private planes and military aircraft, so the Cancún airport is really the only option.

Three companies can pick you up at the Cancún airport in an air-conditioned van and deliver you to the ferry docks at Puerto Juárez: AGI Tours, Executive Services, and Best Day. Fares start at $12 one-way ($24 round-trip); reservations are recommended.
➤ AIRPORT TRANSFERS: **AGI Tours** (☎ 998/877–6967). **Best Day** (☎ 998/881–7037). **Executive Services** (☎ 998/877–0959).

BIKE AND MOPED TRAVEL

You can rent bicycles on Isla, but keep in mind that it's very hot here and the road conditions aren't great (especially those unexpected speed bumps). Don't ride at night; many roads don't have streetlights, so drivers have a hard time seeing you. Most of the moped rental places carry bicycles starting at about $5.50 an hour.

Mopeds are the most popular mode of of transportation on Isla and are available at a number of rental agencies. Most places charge $22–$27 a day, or $5.50–$11 per hour, depending on the moped make and year.
➤ RENTALS: **Ciro's Motorent** (⊠ Av. Guerrero Nte. 11, at Av. Matamoros, ☎ 998/877–0578). **El Sol** (⊠ Av. Francisco Madero 5, ☎ 998/877–0068). **P'pe's Rentadora** (⊠ Av. Hidalgo 19, ☎ 998/877–0019). **R Cardenas** (⊠ Av. Guerrero 107, ☎ 998/877–0079).

BOAT AND FERRY TRAVEL

Speedboats and passenger ferries run between the main dock on Isla and Puerto Juárez on the mainland. Faster and more expensive shuttles to Isla's main dock leave from Cancún's Hotel Zone. Other departure points include Playa Linda, Plaza Caracol, and Playa Tortuga. Municipal ferries carry vehicles and passengers between Isla's dock and Cancún's Punta Sam.

The passenger ferries (*Sultana del Mar* and *Blanca Beatriz*) are the least expensive option. A one-way ticket is $1.60 and the trip takes at least 45 minutes. Delays and crowding aren't unknown, but often there is live music on board, which makes the trips festive.

The speedboats *Caribbean Savage* and *Caribbean Lady* are air-conditioned cruisers with bar service. A one-way ticket costs $4 and the crossing takes about 20 minutes.

Passenger ferries and speedboats leave every half hour from Cancún and Isla Mujeres 6:30 AM–8:30 PM, with a final ferry at 11 PM. Always check the times posted at the dock, as the schedule is subject to change depending on the season and weather conditions. The ferryboats also leave early when they are full.

Shuttles from Cancún cost between $9.95 and $15 round-trip and take approximately 30 minutes, depending on weather conditions. Two shuttle services, *The Isla* and *Nauti Shuttle,* depart from El Embarcadero at Playa Tortugas. *Isla* leaves for the island at 9, 11, 1, and 3:45 and returns to Cancún at 10, 12:30, and 2:30. The *Nauti Shuttle* leaves Cancún at 9:30, 10:30, 11:45, 1:15, 2:30, and 5:45 and returns to Cancún at 10, 11, 2, 3:30, 5, and 6:30. The *Asterix Water Taxi* departs from Plaza Caracol at 9, 11, 1, and 3, returning at 10, noon, 2, and 5. Colon Tours has one ferry leaving Playa Linda at 9:30 and returning at 4 PM.

You don't need a car to get around on Isla, but you can bring one over on a municipal ferry. The ride takes about 45 minutes and the fare is $1.35 per person and about $27–$50 per vehicle depending on the size of your car. From Punta Sam, the ferry leaves at 8, 11, 2:45, 5:30, and 8:15. Departures from Isla are at 6:30, 9:30, 12:45, 4:15, and 7:15. Again, check the schedule. Landlubbers' note: if you have a sensitive stomach, this ferry offers the smoothest ride when the sea is rough.
➤ BOAT AND FERRY INFORMATION: **Asterix Water Taxi, Colon Tours** (☎ 998/884–5333). *Caribbean Lady, Caribbean Savage* (☎ 998/877–0254 or 998/877–0253). **Isla Ferry office** (☎ 998/877–0065). **Isla Shuttle service** (☎ 998/883–3448). **Nauti Shuttle** (☎ 998/883–3646). *Sultana del Mar, Blanca Beatriz* (☎ 998/877–0065).

BUS TRAVEL

Municipal buses run at 20- to 30-minute intervals daily between 6 AM and 10 PM, generally following the ferry schedule. The route goes from the Posada del Mar hotel on Avenida Rueda Medina out to Colonia Salinas on the windward side. Service is slow because the buses make frequent stops. Fares are about 55¢.
➤ BUS INFORMATION: **Municipal buses** (☎ 998/877–0307 on Isla, 998/884–5542 in Cancún).

CAR TRAVEL

There is little reason to bring a car to Isla Mujeres. Taxis are inexpensive and the island is small. In addition, driving can be slow going. Although the main road is paved, it has frequent speed bumps, and the remaining roads are cobblestone. The downtown square flanked by Avenidas Morelos, Juárez, Guerrero, and Matamoros is open only to pedestrian traffic, and the remaining streets are a maze of one-ways.

E-MAIL

Internet places on Isla come and go. The most consistent is Cosmic Cosas, offering Internet access starting at $3 an hour.
➤ SERVICES: **Cosmic Cosas** (✉ Av. Matamoros 82, ☎ 998/877–0349).

EMERGENCIES

The Centro de Salud (Health Center) has a 24-hour emergency service and accepts regular visits 8 AM–8 PM. Isla also has an excellent Red Cross Clinic, which is run by a British doctor. Payment is by donation (the clinic doesn't receive government funding and operates on a shoestring budget). Your hotel can also help you find an English-speaking doctor.

A couple of pharmacies are open late: Farmacia Isla Mujeres, Monday–Saturday 9 AM–10 PM and Sunday 9–3, and Farmacia Lily, daily 8 AM–11 PM, with 24-hour service available.

➤ CONTACTS: **Centro de Salud** (✉ Av. Guerrero 5, on the plaza, ☎ 998/877–0117). **Police** (☎ 998/877–0082). **Port Captain** (☎ 998/877–0095). **Red Cross Clinic** (✉ Colonia La Gloria, south side of island, ☎ 998/877–0280, WEB www.mjmnet.net/redcross/home.htm).

➤ LATE-NIGHT PHARMACIES: **Farmacia Isla Mujeres** (✉ Av. Juárez 8, ☎ 998/877–0178). **Farmacia Lily** (✉ Av. Francisco Madero 17, ☎ 998/877–0116).

ENGLISH-LANGUAGE MEDIA

Islander is a small monthly publication (free) with maps, phone numbers, history about the island, and other useful information. You can pick up a copy at the tourist office or at your hotel.

LODGING

Some of the private homes on Isla are available as long- and short-term rentals. Check with Mundaca Travel or with the Lost Oasis Property Rentals & Management.

➤ LOCAL AGENTS: **Lost Oasis Property Rentals** (WEB www.lostoasis.net/). **Mundaca Travel & Real Estate** (☎ 998/877–0025 or 998/877–0026, FAX 998/877–0076, WEB www.mundacarealestate.com/properties.asp).

MAIL AND SHIPPING

The post office is open weekdays 8–7 and Saturday 9–1. You can have mail for you sent to "Lista de Correos, Isla Mujeres, Quintana Roo, Mexico"; the post office will hold it for 10 days, but it will take up to 12 weeks to arrive.

➤ POST OFFICE: (✉ Av. Guerrero at Av. López Mateos, ½ block from market, ☎ 998/877–0085).

MONEY MATTERS

Bital, the only bank on the island, is open weekdays 8:30–6 and Saturday 9–2. Its ATM often runs out of cash or has a long line, especially on Sunday, so be sure to save some money for the ferry ride back to the mainland.

Bital exchanges currency Monday–Saturday 10–noon. You can also exchange money at Cunex Money Exchange, which is open weekdays 8:30–7 and Saturday 9–2.

➤ BANK: **Bital** (✉ Av. Rueda Medina 3, ☎ 998/877–0104 or 998/877–0005).

➤ EXCHANGE SERVICES: **Cunex Money Exchange** (✉ Av. Hidalgo at Av. Francisco Madero 12-A, ☎ 998/877–0421).

TAXIS

Taxis line up by the ferry dock around the clock. Fares run $1.65 to $3 from the ferry or downtown to the hotels on the north end, at Playa Norte. You can also hire a taxi for a private island tour at about $16.50 an hour.

➤ TAXI COMPANY: **Sitio de Taxis** (Taxi Syndicates; ✉ Av. Rueda Medina, ☎ 998/877–0066).

TELEPHONES

Isla's area code is 998 and in order to dial local calls you must dial 98 followed by the seven-digit telephone number. The old area code was 9877, and some printed material might not have been updated to show the new code. If you are having trouble connecting (you will get a recorded message telling you your number doesn't exist), check your area code and number.

Isla has plenty of phones. Those that encourage you to "pick up and dial 0" charge ridiculously high prices. It's better to use the TELMEX phones that accept Ladatel phone cards. You can buy the cards from local stores in blocks equivalent to $3, $5, $10, and $20. Once connected, you can dial direct anywhere in the world.

To place a collect call, dial 090 for an international operator from any phone booth (no card is required) and ask for *para cobrar* (literally, "to charge").

TOURS

Cooperativa Lanchera runs four-hour trips to the submerged Virgin statue, the lighthouse, the turtles at Playa Lancheros, the coral reefs at Los Manchones, and El Garrafón, for about $28 including lunch. Cooperativa Isla Mujeres rents boats for a maximum of four hours and six people ($120). An island tour with lunch (minimum six people) costs $19 per person.

Sundreamers offers daytime and sunset tours around the island on its 52-ft catamaran. Prices start at $49 per person and include food and drinks.

Sociedad Cooperativa Isla Mujeres and La Isleña launch boats to Isla Contoy daily at 8:30 AM and return at 4 PM. Groups are a minimum of 6 and a maximum of 12 people, depending on the size of the boat. Captain Jaime Avila Canto, a local Isla Contoy expert, offers an excellent tour for large groups aboard his boat the *Anett*.

The trip to Isla Contoy takes about 45 minutes, depending on the weather and the boat; the cost is $38–$50. Sociedad Cooperativa Isla Mujeres tour operators provide a fruit breakfast on the boat and stop at Xlaches reef on the way to Isla Contoy for snorkeling (gear is included). The tour of Contoy's leeward side includes views from the water of Bird Beach and Puerto Viejo Lagoon. Along the way your crew trolls for the lunch it cooks on the beach—you may be in for anything from barracuda to snapper (beer and soda are also included). While the catch is being barbecued, you have time to explore the island, snorkel, check out the small museum and biological station, or just laze under a palapa.

➤ FEES AND SCHEDULES: **Captain Jaime Avila Canto** (✉ Av. Lic Jesús Martínez Ross 38, ☎ 998/877–0478). **Cooperativa Isla Mujeres** (✉ Av. Rueda Medina, ☎ 998/877–0274). **Cooperativa Lanchera** (✉ waterfront near dock, ☎ no phone). **La Isleña** (✉ corner of Avs. Morelos and Juárez, ½ block from pier, ☎ 998/877–0578). **Sociedad Cooperativa Isla Mujeres** (✉ pier, ☎ 998/877–0500). **Sonadoras del Sol** (Sundreamers; ✉ Av. Juárez 9, ☎ 998/877–0736, WEB www.sundreamers. com).

TRANSPORTATION AROUND ISLA MUJERES

Many places on Isla rent golf carts, a fun way to get around the island, especially when traveling with children. Ciro's Motorent and P'pe's Rentadora both have as low as $38 for 24 hours. Most island motorists are quite accommodating, but be prepared to move to the side of the road to let vehicles pass you.

➤ RENTALS: **Ciro's Motorent** (✉ Av. Guerrero Nte. 11, at Av. Matamoros, ☎ 998/877–0578). **P'pe's Rentadora** (✉ Av. Hidalgo 19, ☎ 998/877–0019). **El Sol** (✉ Av. Francisco Madero 5, entrance off Av. Guerrero and Playa Norte, ☎ 998/877–0068).

TRAVEL AGENCIES
Mundaca Travel sells plane and bus tickets, offers Federal Express services, and arranges airport transfers, tours, and house rentals.
➤ LOCAL AGENCY: **Mundaca Travel** (✉ Av. Hidalgo, ☎ 998/877–0025, 998/877–0026, or 888/501–4952, 🅵🅰🆇 998/877–0076).

VISITOR INFORMATION
The Isla Mujeres tourist office is open weekdays 9–2 and 7–9 and has general information about Isla Contoy and the island itself. The Isla Mujeres Hotel Association has information on various rentals.
➤ TOURIST INFORMATION: **Isla Mujeres Hotel Association** (☎ 998/877–0279). **Isla Mujeres tourist office** (✉ Plaza Isla Mujeres, Av. Rueda Medina 130, ☎ 998/877–0307, 🅵🅰🆇 998/877–0307, 🆆🅴🅱 www.isla-mujeres.net).

4 COZUMEL

Mexico's largest cruise-ship port, Cozumel is at once commercial and laid back. Along with day-trippers who kick around town and then head to the beach, the island attracts those eager to explore its inland jungle and ruins. Sportfishing is a fine way to while away hours at sea, but the hands-down best things here lie under the waves: divers flock to Cozumel to wall-, drift-, and hole-dive along some of the world's most spectacular reefs.

COZUMEL STRIKES A BALANCE between Cancún and Isla Mujeres. It has the former's sophistication combined with the latter's relaxed island atmosphere. Fast-food outlets, cable

Updated by
Maribeth
Mellin

television, and English usage are widespread on Cozumel, aimed at pleasing North American tastes. While development continues, even creeping into the farthest corners, Cozumel is managing to leave some of its environment unspoiled and to protect what wildlife is left on the island. The recipe here for a good vacation includes white-sand beaches, excellent snorkeling and scuba diving, sailing and water sports, luxury resorts and modest hotels, fine dining and family eateries, great shops, and even a scattering of Maya ruins. Cozumel attracts a variety of people but none more so than underwater enthusiasts, who come for some of the world's best coral reefs. Despite the inevitable effects of docking cruise ships—shops and restaurants along the main road practically drag customers in—the island's earthy charm and tranquillity are intact.

A 490-square-km (189-square-mi) island 19 km (12 mi) east of the Yucatán peninsula, Cozumel is mostly flat, with an interior covered by parched scrub, dense jungle, and marshy lagoons. White, sandy beaches with calm waters line the island's leeward (western) side, which is fringed by a spectacular reef system, while the windward (eastern) side, facing the Caribbean Sea, has powerful surf and rocky strands. A lot of Cozumel has been developed, but a good deal of the land and the shores has been set aside as national park; a few Maya ruins provide what limited sightseeing there is aside from the island's glorious natural attractions. San Miguel is the only town.

Cozumel's name comes from the Maya Ah-Cuzamil-Peten ("land of the swallows"). For the Maya, this was a sacred island as well as a key center of trade and navigation. Pilgrims from all over Mesoamerica came to honor Ixchel, the goddess of fertility, childbirth, the moon, and rainbows. One of the oldest goddesses, considered to be mother of all other gods, Ixchel was often depicted with swallows at her feet. Every Maya woman was required to visit her site at least once in a lifetime; the women made the perilous journey from the mainland to the island by canoe. Cozumel's main exports were salt and honey, both considered more valuable than gold at the time.

In 1518 Spanish explorer Juan de Grijalva arrived on Cozumel in search of slaves. His tales of treasures inspired Hernán Cortés, Mexico's most famous Spanish explorer, to visit the island the following year. There he met Geronimo de Aguilar and Gonzales Guerrera, Spanish men who had been shipwrecked on Cozumel for a number of years, living as slaves until they were accepted by the Maya. When Cortés and his company landed, Aguilar apparently jumped into the ocean and swam to the ship, while Guerrera refused to leave his Maya wife and children. Aguilar joined forces with Cortés, becoming a deadly foe to the local people; he helped set up a military base on Cozumel and used his knowledge of the Maya to defeat them. On the other hand, Guerrera died defending his adopted community and is considered a hero by the Maya. By 1570 most of the Maya islanders had been massacred or killed by disease, and by 1600 the island was abandoned.

During the 17th and 18th centuries pirates discovered that Cozumel made a perfect hideout. The notorious Jean Laffite and Henry Morgan favored the island's safe harbors and hid their treasures in the catacombs and tunnels dug by the Maya. These bandits laid siege to numerous cargo ships, many of which still lie in the briny depths close to the island. By 1843, Cozumel had once again been abandoned. Five years later, 20 families fleeing Mexico's brutal War of the Castes re-settled the island. Many of their descendants still live on Cozumel.

Around the turn of the 20th century the island began to capitalize on its abundant supply of *zapote* (sapodilla) trees, which produce chicle, prized by the chewing-gum industry (think Chiclets). Shipping routes began to include Cozumel, whose deep harbors made it a perfect stop for large vessels. Forays into the jungle in search of chicle led to the discovery of ruins, and soon archaeologists began visiting the island. Some of the ruins still stand, but Cozumel's importance as a seaport and a chicle-producing region diminished with the arrival of the air-plane and the invention of synthetic chewing gum.

For decades Cozumel was just another backwater where locals fished, hunted alligators and iguanas, and worked on coconut plantations to produce *copra,* the dried kernels from which coconut oil is extracted. Cozumeleños subsisted largely on the fruits of the sea, which remain staples of the economy. During World War II, the U.S. army built an airstrip and maintained a submarine base on the island. Unfortunately it also dismantled some of the larger Maya ruins, not realizing what was being destroyed. In the 1950s Cozumel eked out an existence as a health resort for wealthy Yucatecans. It was the famous underwater explorer Jacques Cousteau who helped make Cozumel the vacation des-tination that it is today. After his first visit, in 1961, word of the is-land's incredible reefs spread among scuba divers and viewers of Cousteau's popular television show. It's now one of the most popular dive locations in the world.

Pleasures and Pastimes

Beaches
Inviting, sandy beaches line the leeward side of the island. The most popular, Playa San Francisco, a 5-km (3-mi) expanse, has restaurants, a bar, and water-sports equipment for rent. Cozumel's windward side is pounded by the rough surf of the Caribbean. Its rocky coves and narrow beaches are fine for sun worshiping but are usually too rough for swimming.

Dining
Restaurants here serve a wide range of cuisines, from Yucatecan and Mexican specialties to Italian, Cajun, French, and Mediterranean, and just about everything in between. The emphasis is on seafood: lobster, shrimp, king crab, grouper, and red snapper are among the highlights.

Fishing
The waters off Cozumel swarm with more than 230 species of fish, which makes this one of the world's best places for deep-sea fishing. During billfish migration season, from late April through June, blue marlin, white marlin, and sailfish are plentiful and world-record catches aren't uncommon.

Deep-sea fishing for tuna, barracuda, wahoo, and dorado is good year-round. Fishing enthusiasts also can opt for bottom fishing for grouper, yellowtail, and snapper on the shallow sand flats at the north end of the island, where they also fly-fish for bonefish, tarpon, snook, grouper, and small sharks.

Lodging
Cozumel's hotels are found in three areas. Lavish resorts line the north and south beaches, inexpensive hotels are closer to town, and the true budget places are in San Miguel. There's no shortage of luxury ac-

commodations, but the number of economical hotels has dwindled. All-inclusive resorts are all the rage and line the far south shore.

Scuba Diving and Snorkeling

Because of the diversity of coral formations and the dramatic underwater peaks and valleys, divers consider Cozumel's Palancar Reef to be one of the top five in the world. With more than 30 charted reefs whose depths average 50–80 ft and water temperatures around 75°F–80°F (24°C–27°C) during peak diving season (June–August, when hotel rates are coincidentally at their lowest), Cozumel is far and away *the* place to dive in Mexico. Sixty thousand divers come here each year to explore the underwater coral formations, caves, sponges, sea fans, and tropical fish.

Snorkeling falls just behind diving among the island's popular sports. There's good snorkeling off the piers at the Presidente Inter-Continental and La Ceiba hotels. The shallow reefs in Chankanaab Bay, Playa San Francisco, and the northern beach near Plaza Las Glorias also offer good views of brilliantly colored fingerlings, parrot fish, sergeant majors, angelfish, and squirrel fish, along with elk coral, conch, sea fans, and sand dollars.

Shopping

Shopping is an even bigger industry for Cozumel than diving, thanks to the number of passengers who pour off cruise ships. (Cozumel is Mexico's largest cruise-ship port.) Thousands of tourists disembark at the three cruise-ship docks and swarm San Miguel every Wednesday. In response, Cozumel is undergoing a shopping-mall building boom—a mall housing a large variety of stores opened in December 2001. Prices in Cozumel are relatively high compared to those in, say, Mérida, but the variety of folk art ranges from downright shoddy curios to some fine silver jewelry, pottery, painted balsa-wood animals, blown glass, handcrafted textiles, and *huipiles* (embroidered cotton dresses).

EXPLORING COZUMEL

Cozumel is 53 km (33 mi) long and 15 km (9 mi) wide and, aside from the road leading to Punta Molas, has excellent paved roads. Beware of flash flooding during the rainy season; the dirt roads can become difficult to navigate in minutes.

Aside from the 15% of the island that has been developed, Cozumel is made up of expanses of sandy or rocky beaches, quiet little coves, palm groves, lagoons and swamps, scrubby jungle, and a few low hills (the maximum elevation is 45 ft). Brilliantly feathered tropical birds, lizards, armadillos, coati, deer, and small foxes populate the undergrowth and mangroves. Several minor Maya ruins dot the eastern coast of the island. One of them, El Caracol, served as an ancient lighthouse. There are also a couple of minuscule ruins—El Mirador (The Balcony) and El Trono (The Throne)—identified by roadside markers.

The town of San Miguel was given its name a century ago when workers digging near the current airport found a statue of St. Michael on September 29, which happens to be the saint's holy day. Thought to have been a gift to the locals from Juan de Grijalva, the first Spanish explorer to the island in 1518, the statue is now displayed in the church of San Miguel.

Cozumel's main road is Avenida Rafael E. Melgar, which runs parallel to the waterfront, down the western shore. South of town it is called Carretera Chankanaab (also known as Carretera Sur), which runs past hotels, shops, and the international cruise-ship terminals. After

Parque Chankanaab, it runs past several gorgeous beaches and a cluster of all-inclusive resorts. When it reaches the most southern point on the island it takes a turn northeast and is referred to simply as the coastal road. On the north side of San Miguel, Avenida Rafael E. Melgar becomes Carretera Costera Norte along the North Hotel Zone, and ends near the Cozumel Country Club.

Alongside Avenida Rafael E. Melgar in San Miguel is the 14-km (9-mi) walkway called the *malecón,* which is congested with shops and restaurants and can be impossible to navigate when the cruise ships are in. Avenida Benito Juárez is the other major road. It stretches east from the pier for 16 km (10 mi), dividing both the town and the island into north and south.

San Miguel is laid out in a typical Mexican grid fashion. *Avenidas* are roads that run north or south; they're numbered in increments of five (5, 10, 15, etc.). A road that starts out as an "avenida norte" turns into an "avenida sur" when it crosses Benito Juárez. *Calles* are streets that run east–west; those north of Benito Juárez have even numbers (Calle 2 Nte., Calle 4 Nte., etc.) while those south have odd numbers (Calle 1 Sur, Calle 3 Sur, etc.).

Plaza Central is the main square. Most often simply called *la plaza,* it's directly across from the docks—hard to miss. The square is the heart of San Miguel, where everyone congregates in the evening, especially on Sunday, when there's a free concert at 8. Shops and restaurants abound here. Heading inland (east) takes you away from the tourist zone and toward the residential sections. The heaviest commercial district is concentrated between Calle 10 Norte and Calle 11 Sur as far up as Avenida Pedro Joaquin Coldwell.

Numbers in the text correspond to numbers in the margin and on the Cozumel map.

A Good Tour

Taxis have become so costly on the island that it's worth renting a vehicle for a day or two to explore Cozumel. Be forewarned that most car-rental companies have a policy that voids your insurance when you leave the paved roads and journey to Punta Molas or other off-road points. Most dirt roads are not maintained, so proceed with great caution (if at all), especially after rain.

Head south from **San Miguel** ① and in about 15 minutes you come to **Parque Chankanaab** ②. Continue past the park to reach the beaches: Playa Corona, Playa San Clemente, Playa San Francisco, and Playa Sol. If you stay on this road you eventually reach, on your left, the turnoff for the ruins of **El Cedral** ③. Look for the red arch alongside the road announcing the turnoff.

Back on the main coast road, continue south until you reach the turnoff for Playa del Palancar, where the famous reef lies offshore. Continue to the point where the road swings north—the most southern point of the island—and you come to the **Parque Punta Sur** ④ entrance. The park encompasses Laguna Colombia and Laguna Chunchacaab as well as an ancient Maya lighthouse, El Caracol, and the modern lighthouse, Faro de Celarain. You have to leave your car at the gate and use either the bicycles or public bus provided by the park.

At Punta Sur the coast road turns north. Not far from the Parque Punta Sur entrance are the minuscule ruins of **El Mirador** and **El Trono.** This road also passes one beach after another: Playa Paraíso, Punta Chiqueros, Playa de San Martín, and Punta Morena. At Punta Este, the coast road intersects with Avenida Benito Juárez, which crosses the is-

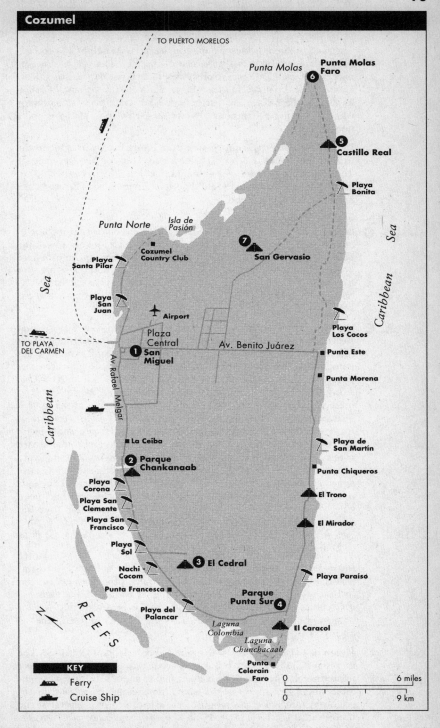

Cozumel

TO PUERTO MORELOS

Punta Molas

Punta Molas Faro

6

5 Castillo Real

Playa Bonita

Punta Norte

Isla de Pasión

Cozumel Country Club

7

San Gervasio

Playa Santa Pilar

Playa San Juan

✈ Airport

Plaza Central

1 San Miguel

Av. Benito Juárez

Playa Los Cocos

Punta Este

Punta Morena

Caribbean Sea

Sea

Caribbean

Av. Rafael Melgar

La Ceiba

2 Parque Chankanaab

Playa de San Martín

Playa Corona

Playa San Clemente

Playa San Francisco

Punta Chiqueros

El Trono

El Mirador

Playa Sol

Nachi Cocom

3 El Cedral

Punta Francesca

Playa del Palancar

Parque Punta Sur

4

Playa Paraíso

Laguna Colombia

El Caracol

Laguna Chunchacaab

R E E F S

Punta Celerain Faro

N

KEY

🚢 Ferry

🚢 Cruise Ship

0 ——— 6 miles

0 ——— 9 km

land to the opposite coast. You can take this road back into San Miguel or continue toward Punta Molas.

The road to Punta Molas is quite rough, and only half of it is accessible by car—you must walk the rest of the way. The beaches on this part of the island are marvelously deserted: Ixpal Barco, Los Cocos, Hanan Reef, Ixlapak, and then Playa Bonita, with the small **Castillo Real** ⑤, another Maya site. Farther north are a number of other minor ruins, including a lighthouse, **Punta Molas Faro** ⑥, at the island's northern tip.

If you take Avenida Benito Juárez from Punta Este, you come to the turnoff (just past the army airfield) for the ruins of **San Gervasio** ⑦. Turn right and follow this well-maintained road for 7 km (4½ mi) to get to the ruins. To return to San Miguel, return to Avenida Benito Juárez and continue driving west.

Sights to See

⑤ **Castillo Real** (Royal Castle). A Maya site on the coast near the northern tip of the island, the *castillo* (castle) includes a lookout tower, the base of a pyramid, and a temple with two chambers capped by a false arch. The waters here harbor several shipwrecks, and it's a fine spot for snorkeling, because there are few visitors to disturb the fish. Note, however, that the surf can get quite strong, so pick a time when the sea is tranquil.

③ **El Cedral.** Once the hub of Maya life on Cozumel, this was the first site found by Spanish explorers in 1518. It was also the island's first official city, founded in 1847. These days it's a quaint farming community with small houses and gardens that show little evidence of its past glory. Conquistadors tore down much of the temple, and the U.S. Army Corps of Engineers destroyed the rest during World War II to make way for the island's first airport. All that remains of the ruins is a small structure with an arch; be sure to look inside to see the faint traces of paint and stucco. Alongside is a green-and-white cinder-block church, decorated inside with crosses shrouded in embroidered lace where, reportedly, the first Mass in Mexico was celebrated. Every May there's a fair here, with dancing, music, bullfights, and a cattle show, celebrating the area's agricultural roots. Hidden in the surrounding jungle are other small ruins, but you need a guide to find them. Check with the locals near the ruins who offer excellent tours on horseback. ⊠ *Turn at Km 17.5 off Carretera Sur or Av. Rafael E. Melgar, then drive 3 km (2 mi) inland to the site,* ☎ *no phone.* ⊡ *Free.* ☉ *Daily dawn–dusk.*

Isla de Pasión (Passion Island). In Abrigo Bay, east of Punta Norte, this tiny island is part of a state reserve. It's quite difficult to get to, and its beaches are extremely secluded. Fishing is permitted, but there are no facilities on the island. If you're interested in bird-watching or want to spend time on a deserted island, ask one of the tour companies to arrange a visit.

🔄 **Museo de la Isla de Cozumel** (Museum of the Island of Cozumel). The museum is housed on two floors of what was once the island's first luxury hotel. The first floor is dedicated to natural history, with exhibits about the origins of the island, its endangered species, its topography, and an explanation of coral-reef ecology. Upstairs, the history of Cozumel is illustrated with Maya artifacts, cannons and swords of the conquistadors, and maritime instruments. Another upstairs room has a pictorial display of Cozumel during the 20th century. Guided tours are available. ⊠ *Av. Rafael E. Melgar, between Calles 4 and 6 Nte.,* ☎ *987/872–1475.* ⊡ *$3.* ☉ *Daily 9–6.*

Next to Parque Chankanaab is **Playa Corona,** which shares access to the Yucab reef and offers the same brilliant marine fauna and wonderful flora as the park. Snorkeling equipment is available for rent, and the restaurant here serves conch and shrimp ceviche. The crowds that visit Chankanaab haven't yet discovered this tranquil neighbor. The next beach south of Playa Corona, **Playa San Clemente** has wide, sandy beaches and shallow waters, and it has managed to retain its laid-back feel.

South of Parque Chankanaab and Playa San Clemente is **Playa San Francisco,** an inviting 5-km (3-mi) stretch of sandy beach that's considered one of the longest and finest on Cozumel. It encompasses the beaches known as Playa Maya and Santa Rosa and usually is packed with cruise-ship passengers during high season. On Sunday locals flock here to eat fresh fish and hear live music. Its amenities include two outdoor restaurants, a bar, dressing rooms, gift shops, volleyball nets, beach chairs, and water-sports equipment for rent. Divers also use this beach as their jumping-off point for the San Francisco reef and the Santa Rosa wall. However, the abundance of turtle grass in the water makes this a less-than-ideal spot for swimming.

Playa Sol (✉ Carretera Sur, Km 15.5, ☎ 987/872–9030) is a serious tourist trap but has enough attractions to make a visit worthwhile. The beach is beautiful and excellent for swimming or snorkeling; as an added attraction, snorkelers can view the underwater archaeological park with replicas of famous structures in the major Maya sites. The park has a small zoo, kayak and sailboat rentals, nearly every water toy you can imagine, and a decent restaurant. The entrance prices are high and you must first pass through a maze of aggressive souvenir shops to get to the beach. With lots of planned activities and loud music, this beach isn't exactly tranquil, but it's a great place to go for a party. Come early to avoid most of the crowds. The admission to use the facilities is $6; the package including all you can drink and eat is $35.

Nachi-Cocom (☎ 987/872–0555), south of Playa Sol, has a wide, uncluttered, and shallow beach; a freshwater pool; lounge chairs; a dive shop; and a restaurant and beach bar. It gets around charging an admission by having a food-or-beer minimum of $10 per adult and $5 per child.

South of all the resorts lies the mostly ignored (and therefore serene) Punta Francesca, on the outskirts of **Playa del Palancar.** Offshore is the famous Palancar Reef. There's also a water-sports center and a bar-café. Playa del Palancar has kept its prices down in order to keep drawing divers, who are generally more bargain-minded than other visitors. The beach is more mellow than many of the other beaches.

Windward Beaches

The east coast of Cozumel presents a splendid succession of mostly deserted rocky coves and narrow, powdery beaches poised dramatically against the turquoise Caribbean. Swimming can be treacherous here if you go too far out—in some parts there's a deadly undertow that can sweep you out to sea in minutes. But these beaches are perfect for solitary sunbathing.

Note that Playa Bonita can refer to two different areas, depending on whom you talk to. This is what the locals call the beach at Punta Chiqueros, where there's a restaurant that also goes by the name Playa Bonita. Officially, however, the name refers to the beach near the Castillo Real ruins.

Playa Paraíso (also known as Playa Bosh) begins at El Mirador and is the southernmost of Cozumel's windward beaches. This windswept place is good for beachcombing or sunbathing; you can cool off with a cold beer at the restaurant-bar.

North of Playa Paraíso, **Punta Chiqueros** is a moon-shape cove sheltered from the sea by an offshore reef. Part of a longer stretch of beach that most locals, confusingly, call Playa Bonita, it has fine sand, clear water, and moderate waves. You can swim here, watch the sun set and the moon rise, and eat fresh fish at a restaurant, also called Playa Bonita.

Not quite 5 km (3 mi) north of Punta Chiqueros begins a long stretch of beach where the Chen Río Reef is located. Turtles come to lay their eggs on the section known as **Playa de San Martín** (some people call it Chen Río, after the reef). During full moons in May and June, the beach is blocked by soldiers or ecologists whose goal is to prevent the poaching of the turtle eggs. Directly in front of the Chen Río Reef is a small bay with clear waters and a surf that isn't too strong, thanks to a rock formation protecting the bay. This is a particularly good spot for swimming. You can dine here on excellent fresh fish, shrimp, and lobster dishes, at a restaurant called Chen Río. Nearly 1 km (½ mi) north of here, the island road becomes hilly, providing a panoramic view of the ocean.

Surfers and boogie-board lovers have adopted **Punta Morena,** north of Playa de San Martín, as their official hangout. The pounding surf makes for great waves, and the local restaurant serves typical surf food (think hamburgers, hot dogs, and french fries).

The beach at **Punta Este** has been nicknamed Mezcalitos, after a much-loved restaurant here. (The Mezcalito Café offers seafood and beer and has a very pleasant staff.) The beach is a typical windward beach—great for beachcombing but unsuitable for swimming.

Where the paved road toward Punta Molas Faro ends and the dirt takes over starts a long stretch of deserted beaches, including **Playa Bonita,** which extends to Punta Molas at the island's northern tip. It's unspoiled and quite beautiful—perfect for sunbathing and communing with nature—and well worth the serious effort it takes to get up here.

DINING

Dining options on Cozumel reflect the nature of the place as a whole: breezy and relaxed with the occasional harmless pretensions. The downtown core has more than 80 restaurants, so you can choose among fast food, great regional dishes, and fresh seafood. Many restaurants accept credit cards; café-type places generally don't. A dining tip: don't follow the suggestions of cab drivers, who may be paid to recommend restaurants.

Reservations and Dress

Casual dress and no reservations are the rule in most $ and $$ Cozumel restaurants. In $$$ and $$$$ restaurants you wouldn't be out of place if you dressed up, and reservations are advised.

CATEGORY	COST*
$$$$	over $30
$$$	$21–$30
$$	$10–$20
$	under $10

per person, for a main course at dinner

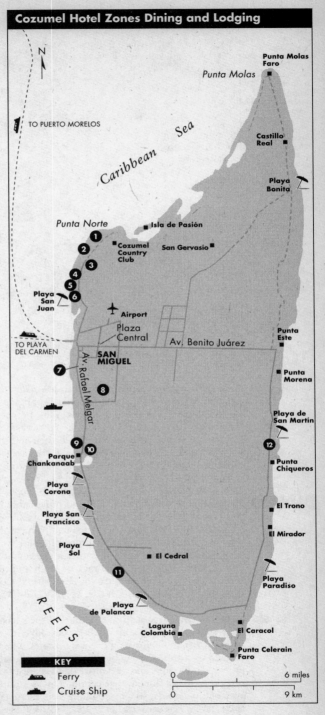

Cozumel Hotel Zones Dining and Lodging

KEY

Ferry

Cruise Ship

San Miguel Dining and Lodging

Main Dock

Plaza

$$–$$$$ ✕ **La Cabaña del Pescador Lobster House.** Walk the gangplank to this palapa restaurant with seashells and nets hanging from the walls. Yes, it's kitschy but worth it if you're looking for the freshest lobster on the island. There really isn't a menu—just crustaceans sold by weight (at market prices). You pay for the lobster, and the rest of your meal is included in the price. Another local favorite is La Cabaña's sister establishment, the less expensive El Guacamayo King Crab House, which is next door. ⊠ *Carretera Costera Norte, Km 4, across from Playa Azul Hotel,* ☎ *987/872–0795. AE, MC, V. No lunch.*

$$–$$$ ✕ **Arrecife.** A well-trained staff and impeccably prepared dishes put this casually elegant hotel restaurant in a class by itself. Tall windows providing excellent views of the sea complement the stylish interior of potted palms, white wicker furniture, and pink walls. Live music adds to the romantic mood. Specialties include delicious lobster, shrimp, conch, and other local seafood. The rack of lamb and the homemade pasta dishes are also exceptional. ⊠ *Presidente Inter-Continental Cozumel, Carretera Chankanaab, Km 6.5,* ☎ *987/872–0322. AE, DC, MC, V. No lunch.*

$$–$$$ ✕ **Pepe's Grill.** Practically a landmark, Pepe's has a nautical air, complete with ship wheels and weather vanes covering the walls and model ships on display. The dining room is upstairs, where tall windows provide an exceptional view of the sunsets. Start with the Caesar salad prepared table-side, and then move on to chateaubriand, T-bone steaks, or prime rib, all done to perfection. This is a popular place with the cruise-ship crowds, so expect a long line. ⊠ *Av. Rafael E. Melgar, at Calle Adolfo Rosada Salas,* ☎ *987/872–0213. Reservations not accepted. AE, MC, V. No lunch.*

$–$$$ ✕ **Costa Brava.** This casual café on a side street serves excellent fresh seafood from the catch of the day to garlic conch and king crab. Go for the simplest preparations. You can't go wrong with grilled fish *mojo* *de ajo* (with butter and garlic), or anything garlicky, including the soup. The breakfast special is a great deal. ⊠ *Calle 7 Sur 57 (between Avs. Melgar and 5 Sur),* ☎ *987/872–3549. AE, MC, V.*

$–$$$ ✕ **Pancho's Backyard.** The fresh margaritas here are famous and the food fabulous. Good choices include *corazón de filete de chipotle* (beef tenderloin with chili) and the fish, which arrives on its own little grill. *Flan de café al rompope* (coffee flan laced with liqueur) is a nice ending to the meal. You can sit inside, in the gorgeous Mexican interior, or outside, in the lush garden terrace with a water fountain. ⊠ *Av. Rafael E. Melgar 27, between Calles 8 and 10,* ☎ *987/872–2141. AE, MC, V.*

$–$$$ ✕ **La Veranda.** This charming wooden Caribbean house with com-
★ fortable rattan furniture, soft lighting, and good music oozes romance. You can sit and enjoy the evening on the outside terrace, or inside. Choices include poblano chilies stuffed with goat cheese, cilantro ravioli with jalapeño pesto, and coconut shrimp; the flambé desserts are sensational. ⊠ *Calle 4 Nte. 140, between Avs. 5 and 10 Nte.,* ☎ *987/ 872–4132. AE, MC, V. No lunch.*

$$ ✕ **French Quarter.** This restaurant introduced Louisiana-Cajun cuisine to the island. Owner Mike Slaughter is here nightly making sure that everyone is happy. The options include home-style gumbo, jambalaya, and crawfish étouffée, as well as the more exotic glazed frogs' legs in a Cajun marinade. You can dine outside on the spacious terrace or inside with the colorful murals. The bar is comfortable and well stocked. ⊠ *Av. 5 Sur, between Calle Adolfo Rosada Salas and Calle 3,* ☎ *987/ 872–6321. AE, MC, V.*

$–$$ ✕ **Azul Cobalto Restaurant and Bar.** Paintings by local artists are showcased at this restaurant, where the menu combines Chilean and Mexican flavors. The squid Pil Pil (in garlic butter sauce) is delicious, as are the pizzas, which are baked in a wood-burning oven. The outdoor tables edge the pedestrian walkway, where the people-watching is great. ⊠ *Av. Benito Juárez 181, between Avs. 5 and 10 Nte.,* ☎ *987/ 872–3318. No credit cards. Closed Mon.*

$–$$ ✕ **Chen Río Restaurant.** The best fish on Cozumel is served here, on
★ the east side of the island at Playa de San Martín. The restaurant is run by a Maya family whose sons go out in the morning to catch the fish they serve for lunch. Relax under the coconut trees, watch the surf, or go for a swim while you wait for your meal to arrive. The combo plate—with shrimp, lobster, fish, rice, and vegetables—is a phenomenal bargain. ⊠ *East-coast road, Km 28,* ☎ *no phone. No credit cards.*

$–$$ ✕ **La Choza.** Purely Mexican in design and cuisine, this family-owned restaurant is a favorite for *mole rojo* (a spicy sauce with cinnamon and chilies), *chiles rellenos*, and *cochinita pibíl* (marinated pork baked in banana leaves). Leave room for the chilled chocolate pie, or go for the avocado pie if you're feeling adventurous. ⊠ *Calle Adolfo Rosado Salas 198, at Av. 10,* ☎ *987/872–0958. MC, V.*

$–$$ ✕ **La Cocay.** The name is Maya for "firefly," and, like its namesake,
★ this place is a bit magical. The chef creates a menu every four to five weeks; dishes might include spiced-nut-crusted chicken breast, pumpkin-stuffed *medialunas* (half-moon pasta) with sage and Parmesan butter sauce, and rack of lamb with a red-onion sauce. The sophisticated restaurant has wood tables, wrought-iron chairs, soft lighting, and an open-air kitchen that lets you watch the staff do its magic. Desserts are fantastic, and the wine list has a nice selection. ⊠ *Av. 17 Sur 1000, at Av. 25,* ☎ *987/872–5533. No credit cards. Closed Sun. and Oct. No lunch.*

$–$$ ✕ **Cucina Italiana.** The homemade pastas at this charming restaurant are exceptional. But that's not surprising; the owners, the Tarroni family, brought their family recipes with them when they moved to Cozumel from their village near Venice, Italy. The kitchen also does its best to accommodate anyone on a special diet—vegan and low-cholesterol menus are available. ⊠ *Calle 2 Nte. and Av. 10-A,* ☎ *987/872–5230. AE, MC, V.*

$–$$ ✕ **Guido's.** Top-quality pasta dishes and pizzas, including lasagna and the "Four Seasons" pie (with ham, zucchini, mushrooms, and black olives), are the draw here. Guido's, still called Rolandi's by locals who've been coming here for decades, also has some good daily specials. Tables in the dining room facing the malecón tend to be noisy; request one on the garden patio out back, where you can sit beneath a tree and sip sangria. ⊠ *Av. Rafael E. Melgar 23, between Calles 6 and 8 Nte.,* ☎ *987/872–0946. AE, MC, V. Closed Sun.*

$–$$ ✕ **Prima.** The pastas are wonderful, salads exemplary, and the steaks
★   juicy and tender at this breezy second-floor terrace restaurant. Try the salad with blue cheese, pasta with pesto, shrimp stuffed with crab, or an Angus steak. Coffee and key lime pie are the perfect end to a perfect meal. There can be lines during the busy season (even if you have a reservation), but you can wait for your table downstairs in the cigar–sports bar. ⊠ *Calle Adolfo Rosado Salas 109-A,* ☎ *987/872–6567. AE, MC, V. No lunch.*

$–$$ ✕ **Las Tortugas.** The motto at this simple eatery is "delicious seafood at accessible prices," and Las Tortugas lives up to it in a big way. The menu lists only the freshest fish, lobster, and conch caught by local fishermen. This means daily special changes according to what's available. Fajitas and other traditional Mexican dishes also are available. This is a great place to experience the hospitality of Cozumel. ⊠ *Av. Coldwell at Calle 19 Sur,* ☎ *987/872–1242. MC, V.*

$ ✕ **Café Caribe & Backyard.** Coffee junkies and folks with a serious sweet tooth flock to this sweet café for its mouthwatering selection of coffees (Cuban, Irish, espresso, cappuccino) and for its Belgian waffles, yogurt, ice cream, freshly baked cakes, pies, and muffins, and great sandwiches. The cheery interior is decorated with colorful art posters, and there's an engaging courtyard out back. It's a perfect spot for both breakfast and after-dinner coffee and dessert. ⊠ *Av. 10 Sur 215,* ☎ *987/872–3621. No credit cards. Closed Sun.*

$ ✕ **Casa Denis.** This little yellow house near the plaza has long been the purview of budget travelers seeking Yucatecan *pollo pibíl* (spiced chicken baked in banana leaves) and other local favorites. Sit at one of the outdoor tables and watch the shoppers dash about as you relax. ⊠ *Calle 1 Sir 132 between Avs. 5 and 10,* ☎ *987/872–0067. No credit cards.*

$ ✕ **Cocos Cozumel.** Divers and anglers fuel up for the day on eggs with cheese and chilies, bowls of yogurt and fruit, and good old American breakfast with bacon, potatoes, and eggs. The clientele is friendly and chatty. You're sure to pick up some tips if you eat at the counter. ⊠ *Av. 5 Sur 180,* ☎ *987/872–0241. No credit cards. Closed Mon. and Oct.*

$ ✕ **El Foco.** Here's a fun spot to grab a *cerveza* (beer) and a bite to eat. This traditional Mexican joint is essentially a *taquería* (taco stand), offering soft tacos stuffed with pork, chorizo, cheese, or chilies. The graffiti on the walls provides the entertainment. ⊠ *Av. 5 Sur 13-B, between Calles Adolfo Rosado Salas and 3 Sur,* ☎ *no phone. No credit cards.*

$ ✕ **Jeanie's Waffle House.** A great way to start the day, Jeanie's serves light, fluffy waffles in more variations than you can imagine. Also on the menu are eggs, omelets, hash browns, fresh juice, and coffee. Jeanie's is open 6 AM–3 PM and 4 PM–9 PM. ⊠ *Av. Rafael E. Melgar, in the Vista del Mar hotel,* ☎ *987/872–4145. No credit cards.*

$ ✕ **Plaza Leza.** The best fajitas and ceviche in town are served in this unpretentious Mexican sidewalk café. You can let the hours slip away while enjoying the great food and watching the action in the square.

For more privacy, go indoors to the somewhat secluded, cozy inner patio for everything from *poc chuc* (pork chops grilled Yucatecan style with hot spices), enchiladas, and lime soup to chicken sandwiches and coconut ice cream. You can get breakfast here, too. ⊠ *Calle 1 Sur, south side of Plaza Central,* ☎ *987/872–1041. AE, MC, V.*

$ ✕ **Rock 'n Java Caribbean Café.** Healthful is the key word here. The
★ extensive breakfast menu offers such delights as whole-wheat French toast and cheese blintzes. For lunch or dinner, consider the vegetarian tacos or linguini with clam sauce, or choose from the selection of more than a dozen salads. To balance things out there are scrumptious pies, cakes, and pastries baked daily on the premises. Enjoy your healthy meal or sinful snack while sitting on the wrought-iron studio chairs. ⊠ *Av. Rafael E. Melgar 602-6,* ☎ *987/872–4405. No credit cards. Closed Sun.*

$ ✕ **El Turix.** Off the beaten track, about 10 minutes by cab from down-
★ town, this simple place is worth the trip for a chance to experience true Yucatecan cuisine served by the amiable owners, Rafael and Maruca. Don't miss the pollo pibíl or the poc chuc. There are also daily specials, and paella on request (call 24 hours ahead). ⊠ *Av. 20 Sur, between Calles 17 and 19,* ☎ *987/872–5234. No credit cards. No lunch.*

LODGING

All of Cozumel's hotels are on the leeward (west) and south sides of the island. Hotels north and south of San Miguel tend to be the larger resorts, while less expensive places are in town. Because of the proximity of the reefs, divers and snorkelers tend to congregate at the southern properties, while swimmers prefer the hotels to the north, where the beaches are better.

Cozumel has more than 3,600 hotel rooms plus private homes, condos, villas, and apartments to rent. Before booking you should call around or surf the Internet; you can find many bargains in the form of air, hotel, and dive packages, especially in the off-season (April to June and September to November). Make Christmas reservations at least three months ahead.

The majority of the resort hotels (north and south of town) are affiliated with international chains and have all the usual amenities; they usually rent water-sports equipment and can arrange excursions. The more costly properties generally have air-conditioning, no-smoking rooms, and on-site travel agencies and transportation rentals and furnish guest rooms with in-room hair dryers, safes, minibars, satellite TV, and telephones.

CATEGORY	COST*
$$$$	over $200
$$$	$120–$200
$$	$50–$120
$	under $50

Prices are for a high-season standard double room, excluding tax and service charge.

North Hotel Zone

$$$–$$$$ 🏨 **Coral Princess Hotel & Resort.** Tasteful and artistic, this hotel's lobby resembles an art gallery. Princess Villas have two bedrooms, two bathrooms, kitchen, and terrace; Coral Villas have one bedroom, a kitchen-dining area and terrace. Except for 61 studios, all rooms overlook the ocean. There isn't much of a beach, but there's a spacious pool. The celestial-theme bar is perfect for a romantic drink before dinner at El

Galeón restaurant. ⊠ *Carretera Costera Norte, Km 2.5, 77600,* ☎ *987/ 872–3200 or 800/253–2702,* FAX *987/872–2800,* WEB *www.coralprincess. com. 100 rooms, 37 villas, 2 penthouses. Restaurant, pool, dive shop, dock, snorkeling, fishing, volleyball, bar, car rental. AE, MC, V.*

$$$–$$$$ ⊡ **Paradisus Cozumel.** A long white-sand beach with clear, shallow water
  ★   fronts this all-inclusive gem at the far end of the north coast, right across the street from the golf course. The spacious rooms are cool and comfortable and have ocean-view balconies. Families congregate around the kid's club and pool; there's also a gym, water-sports center, and horseback riding. The meals are very good and the staff extremely helpful. Up to two children under 12 stay and eat free with their parents. ⊠ *Carretera Costera Norte, Km 5.8, 77600,* ☎ *987/872–0411 or 800/336–3542,* FAX *987/872–1599,* WEB *www.solmelia.com. 150 rooms. 2 restaurants, snack bar, 2 pools, 2 tennis courts, gym, dive shop, windsurfing, kayaking, 4 bars, car rental. AE, MC, V.*

$$$ ⊡ **Playa Azul Hotel.** This boutique hotel filled with artistic touches is
  ★   the perfect place for romantic getaways. The bright, airy rooms face the ocean or tropical gardens and have wicker furnishings and sun-filled terraces. Master suites have private hot tubs. Small palapas are shade lounge chairs on the perfect beach, and Carlos Scuba offers snorkeling, and diving trips from Playa Azul's own dock. The Palma Azul restaurant serves delicious Continental meals. Greens fees at the Cozumel Country Club are included in the room rate. ⊠ *Carretera Costera Norte, Km 4, 77600,* ☎ *987/872–0199,* FAX *987/872–0110,* WEB *www.playa-azul. com. 34 rooms, 16 suites. Restaurant, pool, some in-room hot tubs, massage, dive shop, dock, snorkeling, fishing, billiards, 2 bars, car rental. AE, MC, V.*

$$–$$$ ⊡ **El Cozumeleño Beach Resort.** This all-inclusive resort is geared toward families (children under seven stay free), with lots of activities— especially on the wonderful beach. Rooms are large and fitted with contemporary pine furniture; most have ocean views and terraces. Included in the package: all meals and drinks, snorkel and scuba lessons, miniature golf, tennis, kayaking, windsurfing, a game room, and children's camp. There is an additional charge for dive trips to the reefs. ⊠ *Carretera Costera Norte, Km 4.5, 77600,* ☎ *987/872–0050 or 800/437– 3923,* FAX *987/872–0381,* WEB *www.elcozumeleno.com. 252 rooms. 2 restaurants, snack bar, tennis court, 5 pools, health club, 6 hot tubs, dive shop, boating, 2 bars, children's programs (ages 2–12), car rental. AE, MC, V.*

$$–$$$ ⊡ **Sol Cabañas del Caribe.** Long-time guests don't want anything to change at this old-fashioned charmer, where the idyllic beach, casual rooms, hammocks under palms, and seaside restaurant all hark back to the good old days on the island. ⊠ *Carretera Costera Norte, Km 5.1, 77600,* ☎ *987/872–0411 or 888/341–5993,* FAX *987/872–1599,* WEB *www.solmelia.com. 39 rooms, 9 cabañas. Restaurant, pool, dive shop, bar, car rental, travel agency. AE, MC, V.*

South Hotel Zone

$$$$ ⊡ **Presidente Inter-Continental Cozumel.** Luxury, comfort, service, and
  ★   privacy are hallmarks of the Presidente. The stylish rooms are done in bright, contemporary colors with white cedar furnishings and private terraces; a majority of the rooms overlook the ocean. Mature landscaping adds to the exotic, tropical feel. The pool is modest, but the beach is the nicest on the island and has great snorkeling: fish swim in the waters a few feet off the beach. There's a dive and water-sports center, tennis courts, and a serene botanical garden. The restaurants are highly recommended. ⊠ *Carretera Chankanaab, Km 6.5, 77600,* ☎ *987/872– 0322 or 800/327–0200,* FAX *987/872–1360,* WEB *www.interconti.com. 253 rooms. 2 restaurants, 2 tennis courts, pool, gym, hot tub, dive shop,*

3 bars, shops, children's programs (ages 4–12), meeting rooms, car rental. AE, DC, MC, V.

$$$ ⛫ **Fiesta Americana Cozumel Dive Resort.** Well-situated for divers, this hotel sits across the road from the water; a pedestrian walkway over the road provides easy access to the dive shop, dock, beach, pool, and restaurant. Standard rooms are large, with light-wood furnishings; all have oceanfront balconies. The 56 casitas set along jungle paths have balconies with hammocks and outdoor lockers for dive gear. This is an excellent choice for those spending lots of time in the water. ⊠ *Carretera Chankanaab, Km 7.5, 77600,* ☎ *987/872–2622 or 800/343–7821,* FAX *987/872–2666,* WEB *www.fiestamexico.com. 172 rooms, 56 villas. 3 restaurants, 2 tennis courts, 2 pools, dive shop, dock, 3 bars, car rental, travel services. AE, MC, V.*

$$–$$$ ⛫ **Iberostar.** This all-inclusive resort at the southernmost point of Cozumel has managed to keep the local flora and fauna intact in a jungle setting. Rooms are small but pleasantly decorated with wrought iron and have either a king-size bed or two queen-size beds; all have terraces or patios. There isn't much privacy, since paths through the resort wind around the rooms. There are plenty of activities to keep the whole family busy. ⊠ *Carretera Chankanaab, Km 17, 77600 (past El Cedral turnoff),* ☎ *987/872–9900,* FAX *987/872–9909,* WEB *www. iberostar.com. 300 rooms. 3 restaurants, 2 tennis courts, 2 pools, hair salon, gym, dive shop, dock, boating, 3 bars, theater, children's programs (ages 4–12), car rental. AE, MC, V.*

$$–$$$ ⛫ **Villablanca Garden Beach Hotel.** Beautiful architecture carries
★ through from the hotel's white facade into the rooms, which have archways separating sleeping and living areas. Suites have refrigerators, sunken bathtubs, and private terraces. La Veranda, the restaurant, is very accommodating and can prepare special meals for those with dietary restrictions. The hotel has a beach club, pool, tennis courts, and a huge garden. Excellent dive packages are available at bargain prices. ⊠ *Carretera Chankanaab, Km 3, 77600,* ☎ *987/872–0730,* FAX *987/ 872–0865,* WEB *www.villablanca.net. 25 rooms, 25 suites. Restaurant, refrigerators (some), tennis court, pool, dock. AE, MC, V.*

$$ ⛫ **Casa del Mar.** The cheerful rooms at this three-story hotel are decorated with Mexican artwork and yellow-tile headboards; each has a small balcony. The bilevel cabañas, which sleep three or four, are a good deal. The hotel accommodates divers with an excellent in-house dive shop and gear storage areas. The beach is across the street. ⊠ *Carretera Chankanaab, Km 4, 77600,* ☎ *987/872–1900 or 800/435–3240,* FAX *987/872–1855,* WEB *www.cozumel-hotels.net/casa_del_mar/. 98 rooms, 8 cabañas. 1 restaurant, pool, hot tub, dive shop, 2 bars, car rental, travel services. AE, MC, V.*

Downtown Hotels

$$–$$$ ⛫ **Casa Mexicana.** The dramatic staircase leading up to the windswept lobby and the clever architecture of the rooms make this place a standout. Rooms are decorated in subtle blues and yellows. Some face the ocean while others overlook the pool and terrace. A full breakfast is included in the price. Sister properties Hotel Bahía and Suites Colonial offer equally comfortable but less expensive suites with kitchenettes (the Bahía has ocean views; the Colonial is near the square). You can contact all three hotels using the central reservation number. ⊠ *Av. Rafael E. Melgar 457 Sur, between Calles 5 and 7, 77600,* ☎ *987/872–0209 or 877/228–6747,* FAX *987/872–1387,* WEB *www.casamexicanacozumel. com. 90 rooms. Pool, gym, business services. AE, MC, V.*

$$ ⛫ **Casa Martillo Condos.** At this luxurious condo complex all units face the pool and have full kitchens, dining-living areas, sofa beds, and balconies or patios. There's a minimum three-night stay, and many guests

stay a week or more. The staff is wonderful and pays a lot of attention to details while keeping the place spotless. If you share, these condos are a great bargain. ⊠ *Calle 19 Sur and Av. 15 Sur, 77600,* ☎ *987/872–3139 or 877/627–8455,* FAX *530/623–2671,* WEB *www.casamartillo.com. 6 condos. Kitchens, pool, laundry facilities. MC, V.*

$$ 🖵 **Hotel Flamingo.** Since 1986, this colonial-style hotel has been a popular destination for international travelers. Three blocks from the ferry, the hotel has a charming courtyard and rooftop sundeck. Large rooms are done in bright colors; some have air-conditioning. Those at the front have balconies but can be noisy. The hotel offers Spanish lessons, dive packages, and Internet use. ⊠ *Calle 6 Nte. 81 (near the Cozumel Museum), 77600,* ☎ *987/872–1264 or 800/806–1601,* WEB *www.hotelflamingo.com. 21 rooms. Fans, Internet; no air-conditioning in some rooms. AE, MC, V.*

$ 🖵 **Charrita's.** This charming bed-and-breakfast is a delightful change
★ from standard hotels. Its quiet location in a residential neighborhood 11 blocks from the beach gives you a chance to experience the real Mexico. Each of the five rooms is extremely comfortable, with individual decorations a private bath. Upstairs there's a terrace for sunbathing or taking in sunsets. Guests rave about the huge Mexican breakfast included in the rate. ⊠ *Calle 11 at Av. 55 Bis, 77600,* ☎ *987/872–4760,* WEB *www.cozumelbandb.com. 5 rooms. No credit cards.*

$ 🖵 **Hotel Pepita.** One of Cozumel's first hotels, this bargain hotel offers basic, clean rooms with air-conditioning, cable TV, and refrigerators and a courtyard with plants and places to sit. Discounts are given for longer stays. ⊠ *Av. 15 Sur 120, 77600,* ☎ *987/872–0098,* FAX *987/872–0098. 15 rooms. Fans, refrigerators. No credit cards.*

$ 🖵 **Safari Inn.** Located above the Aqua Safari dive shop on the downtown waterfront, this small hotel offers divers (and non-divers) comfy beds, powerful hot-water showers, air-conditioning, and the camaraderie of fellow fanatics. ⊠ *Av. Rafael E. Melgar at Calle 5, 77600,* ☎ *987/872–0101,* FAX *987/872–0661,* WEB *www.aquasafari.com. 12 rooms. Dive shop. MC, V.*

$ 🖵 **Tamarindo Bed & Breakfast.** The owners of this five-room charmer have created a place that combines the flavor of Mexico with the elegance of France. Rooms are gracefully decorated with individual touches. Breakfast consists of fresh breads, fruits in season, homemade yogurt, and French pressed coffee. The staff arranges diving expeditions, and there's a rinse tank and gear storage facility on the premises. ⊠ *Calle 4 Nte. 421, between Avs. 20 and 25, 77600,* ☎ FAX *987/872–3614,* WEB *www.cozumel.net/bb/tamarind. 5 rooms. Fans, massage, bicycles, baby-sitting, laundry service. MC, V.*

NIGHTLIFE AND THE ARTS

The Arts

The arts scene on Cozumel tends to focus on the local culture; every Thursday during high season there's a folkloric dance performance at the **Fiesta Americana** (☎ 987/872–2622). The whole island explodes with music, costumes, dancing, parades, and parties for Carnival, which takes place just before the start of Lent. Visitors from around the world are encouraged to dress up and catch the fever.

Movies

Locals say the best thing to happen in years is the opening of **Cineopolis** (⊠ Av. Rafael E.Melgar, ☎ 987/869–0799). The modern, multiscreen theater shows current hit films in Spanish and English and has afternoon matinees and nightly shows. You can see the latest blockbusters (generally in English) at **Cine Cozumel** (⊠ Av. Rafael E. Melgar, between Calles 2 and 4 Nte., ☎ 987/872–0766).

Nightlife

Cozumel offers enough daytime activities to make you want to retire early, but that doesn't keep the island from hopping late into the night. A word to the wise: avoid the temptation to buy or use drugs here. Mexican drug laws are draconian and the jails positively medieval.

Bars
Cactus (⊠ Av. Rafael E. Melgar 145, ☎ 987/872–5799) has a disco, live music, and a bar that stays open until 5 AM. Serious bar hoppers like the wild, raucous, and at times obnoxious **Carlos 'n' Charlie's** (⊠ Av. Rafael E. Melgar 11, between Calles 2 and 4 Nte., ☎ 987/872–0191). This popular spot may move to the new Punta Langosta shopping mall, or at least open a branch there. Sports fiends can catch all the news on ESPN at **Sports Page Video Bar and Restaurant** (⊠ Av. 5 Nte. and Calle 2, ☎ 987/872–1199).

Discos
The oldest disco on the island, **Neptune Dance Club** (⊠ Av. Rafael E. Melgar at Av. 11, ☎ 987/872–1537) still lets you boogie into the night. **Viva Mexico** (⊠ Av. Rafael E. Melgar, ☎ 987/872–0799) has a DJ who spins dance music until the wee hours. There's also an extensive snack menu.

Live Music
Cafe Salsa (⊠ Av. 10, ☎ no phone) has live tropical music nightly at 10:30 and is the best place in town for Latin dancing. For sophisticated jazz, smart cocktails, and great cigars, check out the **Havana Club** (⊠ Av. Rafael E. Melgar, between Calles 6 and 8, second floor, ☎ 987/872–1268). Beware of ordering imported liquors such as vodka and scotch, as the drink prices are very high. The food isn't the draw at **Joe's Lobster House** (⊠ Av. 10 Sur 229, between Calles Adolfo Rosada Salas and 3 Sur, ☎ 987/872–3275), but the reggae and salsa bring in the crowds nightly, from 10:30 until dawn. Sunday evenings 8–10, locals head for the *zócalo*, or *la plaza* (the plaza), to hear mariachis and island musicians playing tropical tunes.

OUTDOOR ACTIVITIES AND SPORTS

Most people come to Cozumel for the water sports—scuba diving, snorkeling, and fishing are particularly popular. Services and equipment rentals are available throughout the island, especially through major hotels and water-sports centers such as **Scuba Du** (⊠ at the Presidente Inter-Continental and El Cozumeleño hotels, ☎ 987/872–0050).

Fishing

Regulations forbid commercial fishing, sportfishing, spear fishing, and collecting any marine life in certain areas around Cozumel. It's illegal to kill certain species within marine reserves, including billfish, so be prepared to return prize catches back to the sea. (Regular participants in the annual billfish tournament have seen some of the same fish caught over and over again.) U.S. Customs allows you to bring up to 30 pounds of fish back into the country.

Charters
You can charter high-speed fishing boats for $400 for a half day or $500 for a full day (maximum six people). **Albatros Deep Sea Fishing** (☎ 987/872–2390 or 888/333–4643) is a local outfit specializing in

fishing trips. **Marathon Fishing & Leisure Charters** (☎ 987/872–1986) is popular with fishermen. Full-day rates for both places include the boat and crew, tackle and bait, and lunch with beer and soda. Your hotel can help you arrange daily charters—some hotels have special deals, with boats leaving from their own dock.

Golf

The **Cozumel Country Club** (✉ Carretera Costera Norte, Km 5.8, ☎ 987/872–9670, WEB www.cozumelcountryclub.com.mx) is home to the island's first championship golf course. The gorgeous fairways set amid mangroves and a lagoon are the work of the Nicklaus Design Group. The greens fees is $110 including golf cart; many hotels are offering golf packages.

Miniature Golf

If you're not a fan of miniature golf, **Cozumel Mini-Golf** (✉ Calle 1 Sur, No. 20, ☎ 987/872–6570) might just convert you. The jungle-theme course with its banana trees and birds has two fountains and a waterfall. You can order drinks via walkie-talkies and they'll be delivered as you try for that hole in one. Admission is $5; it's open Monday–Saturday 10–11 and Sunday 5 PM–11.

Scuba Diving

The options for divers in Cozumel include deep dives, drift dives, shore dives, wall dives, and night dives, as well as theme dives focusing on ecology, archaeology, sunken ships, and photography. With so many shops to choose from (there are now more than 100), divers should look for high safety standards and documented credentials. The best places are those that offer small groups and individual attention. Avoid places that care only about volume. Next to your equipment, your dive master is the most important aspect of your dive, particularly if you're new to diving. Make sure your dive master has PADI or NAUI certification (or FMAS, the Mexican equivalent). All reputable shops require all divers to show their certification cards. Make sure you don't forget to bring it along. You will not be allowed to dive without your card. Diving requires that you be reasonably fit. Be sure to listen to your instructor and don't attempt anything that you're not comfortable doing. If you have any strange feelings during or after your dive, be sure to alert the dive master, who may refer you to one of the island's medical centers specializing in dive-related problems.

There's a reputable recompression chamber at the **Buceo Medico Mexicano** (✉ Calle 9 Sur 21-B, ☎ 987/872–2387; 987/872–1430 24-hr hot line). The **Cozumel Recompression Chamber** (✉ San Miguel Clinic, Calle 6 between Avs. 5 and 10, ☎ 987/872–3070, 987/872–2387, or 987/872–1848) is a fully equipped recompression center. These chambers, which aim for a 35-minute response time from reef to chamber, treat decompression sickness, commonly known as "the bends," which occurs when you surface too quickly and nitrogen is absorbed into the bloodstream. Recompression chambers are also used to treat nitrogen narcosis, collapsed lungs, and overexposure to the cold. Consider getting DAN (Divers Alert Network) insurance, which covers dive accidents.

Many hotels and dive shops offer Discover Scuba or other introductory dive classes, often called a "resort course." The classes usually last between two and four hours and cover the basics in using scuba gear and breathing underwater in a swimming pool. Most courses include a beach or boat dive. Once you have completed the course, you may be allowed to participate in more dives with an instructor, but you should not go deeper than 40 ft. Resort courses cost about $50–$60. Many dive shops also offer full open-water certification classes, which take at least four days of intensive classroom study and pool practice. Basic certification courses cost about $350, while advanced certification courses cost as much as $700. You can also do your classroom study at home and your training and test dives on Cozumel.

Much of the reef area off Cozumel is included in a National Marine Park. Boats are not allowed to anchor around the reefs, and you must not touch the coral or take anything from the reefs. When diving, stay at least 3 ft above the reef, not just because the coral can sting or cut you but also because coral is easily damaged and grows very slowly: it has taken 2,000 years for it to reach its present size. Some dive operators do not allow divers to wear gloves or carry dive knives as added protection for the reefs and marine life.

Dive Shops and Tour Operators

Most dive shops can provide you with all the incidentals you'll need. Equipment rental is relatively inexpensive, ranging from $6 for tanks or a lamp to about $8–$10 for a regulator and BC; underwater-camera rentals can cost as much as $35, video-camera rentals run about $75, and professionally shot and edited videos of your own dive are priced at about $160. You can choose from two-tank boat trips and specialty dives ranging from $45 to $60. Most companies also offer one-tank afternoon and night dives for $30–$35. The dive shops handle more than 1,000 divers per day; naturally, many of them run what are called "cattle boats," carrying lots of divers and gear. It's worth the extra money to go out with a smaller group on a fast boat, especially if you're an experienced diver.

Because dive shops tend to be competitive, it's well worth your while to shop around. Many hotels have their own on-site operations, and there are dozens of dive shops in town. **ANOAAT** (Aquatic Sports Operators Association; ☎ 987/872–5955, WEB www.anoaat.com) has listings of affiliated dive operations. Before signing on, ask some experienced divers about the place, check credentials, and look over the boats and equipment.

Aqua Safari (✉ Av. Rafael E. Melgar 429, between Calles 5 and 7 Sur, ☎ 987/872–0101) is one of the oldest and most professional shops on the island and offers PADI certification, classes on night diving, deep diving and other interests, and individualized dives.

Blue Bubble (✉ Av. 5 Sur at Calle 3 Sur, ☎ 987/872–1865) offers several departure times in the morning—a blessing for those who hate early wake-up calls.

Carlo Scuba (✉ Carretera Costera Norte, Km 4.5, ☎ 987/872–0199) has an office at the Playa Azul Hotel and offers personalized dives on small boats.

Del Mar Aquatics (✉ Costera Sur, Km 4, ☎ 987/872–5949) offers dive instructions and boat and shore dives. It operates at La Ceiba hotel, one of the best places for shore and night dives.

Dive Cozumel (✉ Calle Adolfo Rosado Salas 72, at Av. 5 Sur, ☎ 987/872–4167) specializes in cave diving for highly experienced divers, along with regular open water dives forthe less proficient.

Eagle Ray Dive School (✉ Avs. Chichén and Pamuul, ☎ 987/872–5735, WEB www.eagleraydivers.com) offers snorkeling trips and dive instruction.

Michelle's Dive Shop (✉ Av. 5 Sur 201, at Calle Adolfo Rosado Salas, ☎ 987/872–0947) sells a wide array of dive gear.

Pepe Scuba (✉ Carretera Costera Norte, Km 2.5, ☎ 987/872–3200) operates out of the Coral Princess Hotel and offers boat dives and several options for resort divers.

Yucatech Expeditions (✉ Av. 15 Sur 144, ☎ 987/872–5659) can take you cave diving on Cozumel and the mainland.

Reef Dives

Cozumel's reefs stretch for 32 km (20 mi), beginning at the international pier and continuing on to Punta Celarain at the southernmost tip of the island. The following is a rundown of Cozumel's main dive destinations.

CHANKANAAB REEF

This inviting reef lies just south of Parque Chankanaab, about 350 yards offshore. Here large underground caves are filled with striped grunt, snapper, sergeant majors, and butterfly fish. At 55 ft is another large coral formation that's often filled with crabs, lobster, barrel sponges, and angelfish. Drift a bit farther south to see the Balones de Chankanaab, balloon-shape coral at 70 ft. It's an excellent place for beginners.

COLOMBIA REEF

Several miles off Palancar, the reef reaches 82–98 ft and is best suited for experienced divers who want to take some deep dives. Its underwater structures are as varied as those of Palancar Reef, with large canyons and ravines to explore. Clustered near the overhangs are large groupers, jacks, rays, and even an occasional sea turtle.

MARACAIBO REEF

Considered the most difficult of all the Cozumel reefs, Maracaibo is a thrilling dive—you don't even see the ledge of the reef until you go 60 ft below the surface. At the southern end of the island, this reef lends itself to drift dives because of its length. Although there are shallow areas, only advanced divers who can cope with the current should attempt Maracaibo. Dive shops don't stop here on their regular trips, so you must make advance reservations.

PALANCAR REEF

The most famous of all the reefs on Cozumel, located 2 km (1 mi) offshore, Palancar is actually a series of varying coral formations with about 40 dive locations. It's filled with winding canyons, deep ravines, narrow crevices and archways, tunnels, and caves. Black and red coral and huge elephant-ear and barrel sponges are among the attractions at the bottom. A favorite of divers is the section called Horseshoe, where a series of coral heads form a natural horseshoe shape at the top of the drop-off. Visibility here ranges to 150 ft, making it one of the most sensational dives in the Caribbean.

PARAÍSO REEF

About 330 ft offshore, running parallel to the international cruise-ship pier, this reef averages 30–50 ft. It's a perfect spot to dive before you head for deeper drop-offs such as La Ceiba and Villa Blanca. There are impressive formations of star and brain coral as well as sea fans, sponges, sea eels, and yellow rays. It's wonderful for night diving.

PASEO EL CEDRAL

Also known as Cedar Pass, this flat reef, just northeast of Palancar Reef, has gardenlike valleys full of fish, with angelfish, lobster, and thick-lipped grouper. At depths ranging 35–55 ft, you can also spot sea turtles, moray eels, and rays.

PLANE WRECK

During a 1977 Mexican film shoot, this 40-passenger Convair airplane was sunk about 300 ft away from the La Ceiba pier. Because of its re-assuring proximity to the shore and shallow depths—only 9–30 ft—it's a favorite training ground for neophyte divers and a good spot for shore and night dives. Enormous coral structures and colorful sponges surround the wreck.

SAN FRANCISCO REEF

Considered Cozumel's shallowest wall dive (35–50 ft), this 1-km (½-mi) reef runs parallel to San Francisco Beach and has many varieties of reef fish. It requires the use of a dive boat.

SANTA ROSA WALL

A site for experienced divers, just north of Palancar, Santa Rosa is renowned for deep dives and drift dives; at 50 ft there's an abrupt yet sensational drop-off to enormous coral overhangs. The strong current drags you along the tunnels and caves, where there are huge sponges, angelfish, groupers, and rays—maybe even a shark.

TORMENTOS REEF

The abundance of sea fans, sponges, sea cucumbers, arrow crabs, green eels, groupers, and other marine life—against a terrifically col-orful backdrop—makes this a perfect spot for underwater photogra-phy. This variegated reef has a maximum depth of around 70 ft.

YUCAB REEF

South of Punta Tormentos Reef, this relatively shallow reef is close to shore, making it an ideal spot for beginners. About 400 ft long and 55 ft deep, it's teeming with queen angelfish and sea whip swimming around the large coral heads. The one drawback is the strong current, which can reach 2 or 3 knots.

Snorkeling

Snorkeling equipment is available at nearly all hotels and beach clubs as well as at Chankanaab Bay, Playa San Francisco, and Parque Sur. Gear rents for less than $10 a day.

Tour Operators

One option is to contact the dive shops to see if you can tag along when they go out to a suitable snorkeling reef. Official snorkeling tours run from $25 to $50, depending on the duration, and take in the shallow reefs off Palancar, Colombia, and Yucab. **Fiesta Cozumel** (⊠ Calle 11 Sur 598, between Avs. 25 and 30, ☎ 987/872–0725, FAX 987/872–1389) runs snorkeling tours from the 45-ft catamarans *El Zorro* and *Fury*. Rates begin at about $50 per day and include equipment, a guide, soft drinks and beer, and a box lunch. Sunset cruises aboard *El Zorro* are also available; they include unlimited drinks and live entertainment and cost about $35.

SHOPPING

Downtown shops in Cozumel are geared toward tourists. Most accept dollars as readily as pesos, and many goods are priced in dollars. You'll often get a better price if you pay with cash or traveler's checks, since some shops add a hefty surcharge on credit card bills. But if you're making a large purchase and there isn't a surcharge, you get the best exchange rate by using your credit card. MasterCard and Visa are the two most popular cards, followed by American Express. The many warn-ings you'll receive about buying from street vendors is good advice—the quality of their merchandise leaves much to be desired.

There are three cruise-ship docks (one in the center of town), and there are usually several ships in port daily. Expect the shops, restaurants, and streets to be extremely crowded and hard to maneuver between 10 AM and 2 PM. Come back later when things are calmer for leisurely dining and shopping. Traditionally, stores are open from 9 to 1 (except Sunday) and 5 to 9, but a number of them, especially those nearest the pier, tend to stay open all day and on weekends, particularly during high season. Most of the shops are closed Sunday morning.

Don't pay much attention to written or verbal offers of "20% discounts, today only" or "only for cruise-ship passengers"—they're nothing but bait to get you inside. Similarly, many of the larger stores advertise "duty-free" wares, but these are of greater interest to Mexicans from the mainland than to North Americans, since the prices tend to be higher than retail prices in the United States.

A last word of caution: don't buy black coral—it's an endangered species and really overpriced on the island. Plus, you might not be allowed to bring it to the United States and other countries.

Department Stores

Punta Langosta (⊠ Av. Melgar 551 at Calle 7), a fancy multilevel shopping mall, is across the street from the cruise-ship dock. An enclosed pedestrian walkway leads over the street from the ships to the center, which will eventually house about 90 shops, restaurants, and bars. Big-name duty-free boutiques moving in include Versace, DKNY, Nike, and Warner Bros. The restaurants will include a Señor Frog's and TGI Friday's. The center is designed to lure cruise-ship passengers into shopping in air-conditioned comfort and is likely to decrease traffic for local businesses.

Other department stores in Cozumel are relatively small and more like U.S. variety stores. **Luxury Avenue (Ultrafemme)** (⊠ Av. Rafael E. Melgar 341, ☎ 987/872–1217) sells high-end goods including watches and perfume. **Pama** (⊠ Av. Rafael E. Melgar Sur 9, ☎ 987/872–0090), near the pier, carries imported luxury items. **Viva Mexico** (⊠ Av. Rafael E. Melgar at Calle Adolfo Rosada Salas, ☎ 987/872–0791) sells souvenirs and handicrafts from all over Mexico and is your best one-stop souvenir shopping option if you're looking for standard T-shirts, blankets, and trinkets.

Shopping Districts, Streets, and Malls

Cozumel's main shopping area is downtown on the waterfront along Avenida Rafael E. Melgar and on some of the side streets around the plaza (there are more than 150 shops in this area alone). There's a **crafts market** (⊠ Calle 1 Sur, behind the plaza) in town, which sells a respectable assortment of Mexican wares. In addition, small clusters of shops can be found at **Plaza del Sol** (on the east side of the main plaza), **Villa Mar** (on the north side of the main plaza), and **Plaza Confetti** (on the south side of the main plaza). The major jewelry, electronics, and fashion shops are in **Punta Langosta** (⊠ Av. Melgar 551 at Calle 7). As a general rule, the newer, trendier shops line the waterfront, while the area around Avenida 5a houses the better crafts shops. South of the city, past Casa del Mar, is **Plaza Maya,** a collection of shops selling low-end souvenirs at high-end prices. The crafts market **Puerto Maya,** where the cruise ships dock, has some crafts at good prices. Bargains are best after the ships have departed.

For fresh produce try the **town market** (⊠ Calle Adolfo Rosada Salas, between Avs. 20 and 25 Sur, ☎ no phone), open Monday–Saturday

8–5. The main grocery store, **Chedraui** (⊠ Carretera Chankanaab, Km 1.5, and Calle 15 Sur, ☎ 987/872–3655), is open daily 8 AM–10 PM.

Specialty Stores

Clothing

Several trendy sportswear stores line Avenida Rafael E. Melgar between Calles 2 and 6. **Exotica** (⊠ Av. Benito Juárez at the plaza, ☎ 987/872–5880) has high-quality sportswear and shirts with nature-theme designs. **Lolha** (⊠ Calle 1 Sur, between Avs. 10 and 15, ☎ 987/872–7174) has a collection of Brazilian swimwear and sundresses. **Poco Loco** (⊠ Av. Rafael E. Melgar 18 and Av. Benito Juárez 2-A, ☎ 987/872–5499) sells casual wear and beach bags.

Jewelry

The opening of the Punta Langosta mall will surely change the lineup of ultra-expensive jewelry shops along Avenida Rafael E. Melgar. Look for the following shops in the mall and on the avenue. Jewelry on Cozumel is pricey, but it tends to be of higher quality than what you'll find in many other Yucatán towns. **Diamond Creations** (⊠ Av. Rafael E. Melgar Sur 131, ☎ 987/872–5330) lets you custom-design a piece of jewelry from its collection of loose diamonds, emeralds, rubies, sapphires, or tanzanite. You may also want to check out its other branches, Just for Men and Tanzanite International, two blocks north. You'll find silver, gold, and coral jewelry—bracelets and earrings especially—at **Joyeria Palancar** (⊠ Av. Rafael E. Melgar Nte. 15, ☎ 987/872–1468). Quality gemstones and striking designs are the strong points at **Rachat & Romero** (⊠ Av. Rafael E. Melgar 101, ☎ 987/872–0571). Innovative designs and top-quality stones can be found at **Van Cleef & Arpels** (⊠ Av. Rafael E. Melgar Nte., across from the ferry, ☎ 987/872–6540).

Mexican Crafts

Bugambilias (⊠ Av. 10 Sur, between Calles Adolfo Rosado Salas and 1 Sur, ☎ 987/872–6282) sells handmade Mexican linens. **Mayan Feather** (⊠ Av. 5 and Calle 2 Nte., ☎ no phone) has original paintings on feathers from birds of the area. Prices are reasonable, and many of the pictures are quite beautiful. **El Porton** (⊠ Av. 5 Sur at Calle 1 Sur, ☎ 987/872–5606) has a stunning collection of masks and unusual crafts. Look for antiques and high-quality silver jewelry at **Shalom** (⊠ Av. 10 No. 25, ☎ 987/872–3783). **Talavera** (⊠ Av. 5 Sur 349, ☎ 987/872–0171) carries beautiful ceramics from all over Mexico, including tiles from the Yucatán, masks from Guerrero, brightly painted wooden animals from Oaxaca, and carved chests from Guadalajara.

COZUMEL A TO Z

To research prices, get advice from other travelers, and book travel arrangements, visit www.fodors.com.

AIR TRAVEL

CARRIERS

Continental flies nonstop from Houston to Cozumel; US Airways flies nonstop on weekends from Charlotte, NC to Cozumel. Mexicana has nonstop service from Mexico City. AeroMéxico flies nonstop from Atlanta to Cozumel. Mexicana subsidiaries Aerocaribe and Aerocozumel fly between Cozumel and Cancún and other destinations in Mexico, including Chichén Itzá, Chetumal, Mérida, and Playa del Carmen.

➤ AIRLINES AND CONTACTS: Aerocaribe (☎ 987/872–0503). Aerocozumel (☎ 987/872–3456). Continental (☎ 987/872–0487). Mexicana (☎ 987/872–2945). **U.S. Airways** (☎ 800/622–1015 toll free in the U.S.).

AIRPORTS
The Cozumel airport is 3 km (2 mi) north of San Miguel.
➤ AIRPORT INFORMATION: **Cozumel airport** (☎ 987/872–0928).

AIRPORT TRANSFER
Because of an agreement between the taxi drivers' and bus drivers' unions, there is taxi service *to* the airport but not *from* the airport. The *colectivo*, a van that seats up to eight, takes arriving passengers to their hotels; the fare is about $7. If you want to avoid waiting for the van to fill or for other passengers to be dropped off, you can hire an *especial*—an individual van. A trip via an individual van to one of the hotel zones costs about $15; a trip to the city runs about $10. Taxis to the airport cost between $8 to $25 from the hotel zones and approximately $5 from downtown.

BOAT AND FERRY TRAVEL
Passenger-only ferries to Playa del Carmen leave Cozumel's main pier (☎ 987/872–1508) approximately every hour on the hour from 4 AM to 10 PM (no ferries at 5 and 11 AM, 1, 7, and 9 PM). They leave Playa del Carmen's dock also about every hour on the hour, from 5 AM to 11 PM (no service at 6 AM, noon, 2, and 8 PM). The trip takes 45 minutes. Call to verify the times. Bad weather often prompts cancellations.

There is a car ferry from Puerto Morelos, but travelers don't need a car on the island. The trip takes three to four hours, the ferry is infrequent, the departure times aren't convenient, and the fare is about $70 for small cars (more for larger vehicles) and $6 per passenger.
➤ BOAT AND FERRY INFORMATION: **Playa del Carmen dock** (☎ 987/873–0067).

BUS TRAVEL
Because of a union agreement with taxi drivers, public buses cannot operate in the North and South Hotel zones; local bus service runs mainly within the town of San Miguel, although there is a route from town to the airport. Service is irregular but inexpensive.

CAR RENTAL
A rental car is a great way to get around the island, particularly as taxi prices are high here. A vehicle with four-wheel drive (check to make sure that it hasn't been disconnected) is a must if you want to get to the more secluded beaches and ruins.

All the large hotels have rental offices, and most of the major car-rental companies have a location at the airport. Rental rates start at about $40 a day. Insurance doesn't cover trips off the main roads. Many of the smaller companies carry only standard transmission cars, so request an automatic in advance.
➤ MAJOR AGENCIES: **Avis** (☎ 987/872–0099 airport). **Hertz** (☎ 987/872–3888 airport).
➤ LOCAL AGENCIES: **Aguila Rentals** (⊠ Calle 11 No. 101, ☎ 987/872–0729). **Cocodrilos Car Rental** (⊠ Av. Rafael E. Melgar 601, ☎ 987/872–5030). **Rentadora Islena** (⊠ Calle 7 No. 49, ☎ 987/872–0788).

CAR TRAVEL
A car is a great way to see the island. For getting to the out-of-the-way beaches and off-the-beaten-path ruins, you need a four-wheel-drive vehicle. There are two gas stations on Cozumel: one at the corner of Avenida Benito Juárez and Avenida 30 on the way to San Gervasio, the other

at Avenidas Pedro Joaquin Coldwell and Benito Juárez. Both are open daily 7 AM–midnight.

CRUISE TRAVEL

At least a dozen cruise lines call at Cozumel and/or Playa del Carmen, including, from Fort Lauderdale, Celebrity Cruises, Cunard Line, and Princess Cruises; from Miami, Carnival Cruise Lines, Costa Cruise Lines, Norwegian Cruise Line, Premier Cruises, and Royal Caribbean; from New Orleans, Commodore Cruise Line; and from Tampa, Holland America Line.

➤ CRUISE LINES: **Carnival Cruise Lines** (☎ 800/327–9501). **Celebrity Cruises** (☎ 800/437–3111). **Costa Cruise Lines** (☎ 800/327–2537). **Cunard Line** (☎ 800/221–4770). **Holland America Line** (☎ 800/426–0327). **Norwegian Cruise Line** (☎ 800/327–7030). **Princess Cruises** (☎ 800/568–3262). **Royal Caribbean** (☎ 800/327–6700).

E-MAIL

Internet access on Cozumel is expensive. Mail Boxes Etc. and Calling Station have the most reasonable rates; they charge $3 for 30 minutes of computer usage, including Internet access.

➤ SERVICES: **Calling Station** (⊠ Av. Rafael E. Melgar 27, at Calle 3 Sur, ☎ 987/872–1417). **Mail Boxes Etc.** (⊠ Calle 3 Sur 81, at Av. Rafael E. Melgar, ☎ 987/872–7868).

EMERGENCIES

Both the Centro Medico de Cozumel (Cozumel Medical Center) and the Medical Specialties Center offer 24-hour air-ambulance service and a 24-hour pharmacy. The Centro de Salud (Health Center) offers round-the-clock emergency care.

Farmacia Dori is open daily 7 AM–midnight and offers hotel delivery service; Farmacia Joaquin is open Monday–Saturday 8 AM–10 PM and Sunday 9–1 and 5–9. Farmacias Canto, open 24 hours, delivers to hotels.

➤ CONTACTS: **Air Ambulance** (☎ 987/872–4070). **Centro Medico de Cozumel** (Cozumel Medical Center; ⊠ 1A Sur 101, corner of Av. 50, ☎ 987/872–3545 or 987/872–5370). **Centro de Salud** (⊠ Av. 20 Sur at Calle 11, ☎ 987/872–0140). The **Chiropractic Center** (⊠ Av. 5 Sur 24-A, between Calles 3 and 5, ☎ 987/872–5099). **Medical Specialties Center** (⊠ Av. 20 Nte. 425, ☎ 987/872–1419 or 987/872–2919). **Police** (⊠ Anexo del Palacio Municipal, ☎ 987/872–0409). **Recompression Chamber** (⊠ Calle 5 Sur 21-B, between Avs. Rafael E. Melgar and 5 Sur, ☎ 987/872–2387). **Red Cross** (⊠ Calle Adolfo Rosada Salas at Av. 20 Sur, ☎ 987/872–1058).

➤ LATE-NIGHT PHARMACIES: **Farmacia Dori** (⊠ Calle Adolfo Rosada Salas, between Avs. 15 and 20 Sur, ☎ 987/872–0559). **Farmacia Joaquin** (⊠ north side of plaza, ☎ 987/872–2520). **Farmacias Canto** (☎ 987/872–5377).

ENGLISH-LANGUAGE MEDIA

The tourist office and most shops and hotels around town offer the *Blue Guide to Cozumel* and *Cozumel, People & Places.* These free publications contain good information and maps of the island and downtown.

LODGING

The Cozumel Island Hotel Association has 21 member properties, and it can give you information about them and about attractions on the island. It doesn't take reservations, however.

➤ CONTACT: **Cozumel Island Hotel Association** (⊠ Calle 2 Nte. 15-A, ☎ 987/872–3132, FAX 987/872–2809).

MAIL AND SHIPPING

The local post office (*correos*), six blocks south of the plaza, is open weekdays 8–8, Saturday 9–5, and Sunday 9–1. Holders of American Express cards can receive mail at Fiesta Cozumel Holidays/American Express, which is open weekdays 8–1 and 5–8, Saturday 8–5.

➤ SERVICES: **Fiesta Cozumel Holidays/American Express** (⊠ Calle 11 Sur 598, between Avs. 25 and 30, ☎ 987/872–0725 or 987/ 872–0925). **Post office** (⊠ Calle 7 Sur at Av. Rafael E. Melgar, ☎ 987/872–0106).

MONEY MATTERS

Most of the banks are in the main square and are open weekdays 9–4 or 5. Many change currency all day.

➤ BANKS: **Banamex** (⊠ Av. 5 Nte., at the plaza, ☎ 987/872–3411). **Bancomer** (⊠ Av. 5 Nte., at the plaza, ☎ 987/872–0550). **Banco Serfín** (⊠ Calle 1 Sur, between Avs. 5 and 10 Sur, ☎ 987/872–0930). **Bancrecer** (⊠ Calle 1 Sur, between Avs. 5 and 10, ☎ 987/872–4750). **Bital** (⊠ Av. Rafael E. Melgar 11, ☎ 987/872–0142).

CURRENCY EXCHANGE

After banking hours, you can exchange money at Promotora Cambiaria del Centro, open Monday–Saturday 8 AM–9 PM.

➤ EXCHANGE SERVICE: **Promotora Cambiaria del Centro** (⊠ Av. 5 Sur between Calles 1 Sur and Adolfo Rosada Salas, ☎ no phone).

MOPED TRAVEL

Mopeds are popular here, but also extremely dangerous because of heavy traffic, potholes, and hidden stop signs; accidents happen all too frequently. Mexican law requires all riders to wear helmets (it's a $25 fine if you don't). If you do decide to rent a moped, drive slowly, check for oncoming traffic, and don't ride when it's raining or if you've had any alcoholic beverages. Mopeds rent for about $25 per day; insurance is included. RC Scooter Rentals seems to have the newest machines, and it drops them off at hotels.

➤ MOPED RENTALS: **Auto Rent** (⊠ Carretera Costera Sur, ☎ 987/872–0844 ext. 712). **RC Scooter Rentals** (⊠ Av. 30 Nte. 700, between Calles 7 and 11 Sur, ☎ 987/872–5009). **Rentadora Cozumel** (⊠ Calle Adolfo Rosada Salas 3-B, ☎ 987/872–1503; ⊠ Av. 10 Sur at Calle 1, ☎ 987/ 872–1120). **Rentadora Marlin** (⊠ Av. Adolfo López Mateos, ☎ 987/ 872–1586).

TAXIS

You can hail taxis on the street, and cabs wait at all the major hotels. The fixed rates (at press time but subject to change) run about $1.50 within town; $5–$8 between town and either hotel zone; $10 from most hotels to the airport; and about $20–$40 from the northern hotels or town to Parque Chankanaab or Playa San Francisco. The cost from the cruise-ship terminal to San Miguel is about $6. Prices quoted by the drivers should be in pesos. Tipping isn't necessary, as most drivers own their vehicles.

Despite the established taxi fares, many of the younger and quite aggressive cab drivers have begun charging double or even triple these rates. If you have to take a taxi, be firm on a price before getting into the car. If the driver refuses to give you a quote, get out of the cab immediately, as this means he is likely to overcharge when you reach your destination. Familiarize yourself with the established rates but be prepared to argue with some drivers. Taxi drivers have also been known to tell passengers that certain restaurants are closed or that certain hotels don't exist, in an effort to have you pick their alternative—from which they get a commission. If you feel you have been overcharged, misled, or mistreated in any way, contact the Sitio de Taxis (Taxi Syndicate; ☎ 987/872–0041) and report the cab driver (you need the cab number to be able to do this). Drivers are fined heavily (up to a three-day work suspension) for overcharging.

TELEPHONES

In order to accommodate a growing number of telephone lines, area codes throughout Mexico were changed in November 2001. Phone numbers in Cozumel now have a three-digit area code (987) and seven-digit local number. Some of the older printed material on Cozumel does not reflect this change.

The least-expensive way to make an international call is to buy a Ladatel phone card (sold in blocks of $3, $5, $10, and $20) and use the TELMEX public phones. The TELMEX phones can be hard to find, as they are being replaced with private services' blue and red phones that urge you to "pick up and dial 0" and have very high rates. However, you can make local calls from these phones using peso coins. Local calls start at the equivalent of about 10¢. An alternative to the phone card is the *caseta de larga distancia*—the long-distance telephone office. There's an office on Calle 1, on the south side of the plaza; it's open 8–1 and 4–9. These offices have specially designed booths where you take your call after the number has been dialed by a clerk.

More expensive than the TELMEX phones but handier is the Calling Station, at Avenida Rafael E. Melgar 27 and Calle 3 Sur. It also offers video and cell-phone rentals, currency exchange, and Internet access and is open 8 AM–11 PM daily during high season.

TOURS

ATV AND JEEP TOURS

You can travel to the northern part of the island as part of Tarzan Tours and Wild Tours' all-terrain-vehicle excursions. Rates start at $63 for a single passenger, or $96 for a driver and one passenger with Wild Tours. Rates for jeep trips offered by Tarzan Tours start at $89 a person. Both tours include a light lunch, drinks, a visit to one of the northern Maya ruins, and a beach stop. Whether you take an ATV or a jeep, the ride through the jungle is exhilarating and the scenery incredible. Tickets are available through any local travel agent.
➤ FEES AND SCHEDULES: **Tarzan Tours** (☎ 987/872–5735). **Wild Tours** (☎ 987/872–5876).

BOAT AND SUBMARINE TOURS

Atlantis Submarine runs 1½-hour submarine rides that explore the Chankanaab Reef and surrounding area; tickets for the tours are $72 for adults, $36 for children.
➤ FEES AND SCHEDULES: **Atlantis Submarines** (✉ Carretera Chankanaab, Km 4, across from Hotel Casa del Mar, ☎ 987/872–5671, WEB www. goatlantis.com). **Fiesta Cozumel Holidays/American Express** (✉ Calle 11 Sur 598, between Avs. 25 and 30, ☎ 987/872–0725).

HORSEBACK TOURS

Aventuras Naturales offers two-hour guided horseback tours. They start at $40 and visit Maya ruins and the beach. Rancho Buenavista offers four-hour horseback rides through the jungle starting at $65 per person.
➤ FEES AND SCHEDULES: **Aventuras Naturales** (✉ Av. 35 No. 1081, ☎ 987/872–1628, WEB www.aventurasnaturales.com). **Rancho Buenavista** (✉ Av. Rafael Melgar & Calle 11 Sur, ☎ 987/872–1537).

ORIENTATION

Tours of the island's sights, including the San Gervasio ruins, El Cedral, Parque Chankanaab, and the Museo de la Isla de Cozumel, cost about $45 a person and can be arranged through travel agencies. Fiesta Cozumel Holidays, which has representatives in most major hotels, and Caribe Tours sell a number of similar tours. Another option is to take a private tour of the island via taxi, which costs about $50 to $70 for the day, depending on which parts of the island you visit.

➤ FEES AND SCHEDULES: **Caribe Tours** (✉ Av. Rafael E. Melgar at Calle 5 Sur, ☎ 987/872–3100). **Fiesta Cozumel Holidays/American Express** (main office: ✉ Calle 11 Sur 598, between Avs. 25 and 30, ☎ 987/872–0725).

TRANSPORTATION AROUND COZUMEL

Taxi fares on Cozumel run very high. If you plan to visit any of the sites, you are likely to save yourself some hassles and a lot of money by renting a car or a scooter instead of using a taxi to get around. The local buses aren't a good option because they don't go to any of the tourist sights and operate only within the town's perimeter.

TRAVEL AGENCIES

A number of local travel agencies offer tours. Fiesta Cozumel Holidays and Turismo Aviomar are represented in the lobbies of several hotels.

➤ LOCAL AGENTS: **Caribe Tours** (✉ Av. Rafael E. Melgar at Calle 5 Sur, ☎ 987/872–3100). **Fiesta Cozumel Holidays/American Express** (✉ Calle 11 Sur 598, between Avs. 25 and 30, ☎ 987/872–0725). **IMC** (✉ Calle 2 Nte. 101–8, ☎ 987/872–1535). **Turismo Aviomar** (✉ Av. 5 Nte. 8, between Calles 2 and 4, ☎ 987/872–0588).

VISITOR INFORMATION

The island's official Web site is www.islacozumel.com.mx. The state tourism office is open weekdays 9–2:30. The Cozumel Island Hotel Association offers information on affiliated hotels and tour operators.

➤ TOURIST INFORMATION: **Cozumel Island Hotel Association** (✉ Calle 2 Nte. at Av. 15, ☎ 987/872–3132, FAX 987/872–2809). **Fidecomiso** (tourism office; ✉ upstairs at Plaza del Sol, at east end of main square, ☎ FAX 987/872–0972).

5 THE CARIBBEAN COAST

Although the eastern shore of the Yucatán from Cancún to Chetumal is becoming more developed, the so-called Riviera Maya still has some secluded beaches. Get your fill of the social scene and Euro beach culture in Playa del Carmen, and then head to more isolated spots like the mangrove-filled Sian Ka'an Biosphere Reserve and the tranquil Xcalak Peninsula. Visit the Maya ruins of Tulum and rub elbows with iguanas and cruise-ship passengers, or examine ancient civilizations in solitude at the Río Bec sites of Dzibanché and Kinichná.

Updated by
Patricia Alisau

ABOVE ALL ELSE, beaches are what define the east coast of the Yucatán peninsula—soft, blinding white strands of sand embracing clear turquoise waters; shorelines that curve into calm lagoons, coves, and inlets; waves that crash against cliffs; mangrove swamps with minuscule islands where only the birds hold sway alongside freshwater cenotes (sinkholes). Paralleling the coast, a magnificent coral reef teems with kaleidoscopic marine life swimming lazily among the shipwrecks and relics left by pirates. Landscapes change from savanna to wetland to scrubby limestone terrain to jungle, the flora and fauna varying with each setting. All this makes Quintana Roo's Caribbean coast a marvelous place for lovers of the outdoors.

The destinations on the coast are varied and more eccentric than Cancún, which is a big part of their allure. While Puerto Morelos still has the relaxed atmosphere of a Mexican fishing village, Playa del Carmen is filled with resorts as glitzy and hectic as those in Cancún and Cozumel, embodying the real *vida loca* of the coast. The beaches here, from Punta Tanchacté to Tulum, are beloved by scuba divers, snorkelers, birders, and beachcombers. Rustic but comfortable fishing and scuba-diving lodges on the secluded Boca Paila and Xcalak peninsulas have a well-deserved reputation for excellent bonefishing and superb diving on virgin reefs. Unfortunately, the coast continues to be under siege from developers building sprawling all-inclusive resorts, and the environment is starting to suffer.

Against this backdrop is Maya culture. While the modern Maya live in the cities and villages along the coast, their history can be seen at the ruins. At Tulum, dramatic ruins sit on a bluff overlooking the Caribbean, welcoming the sunrise each morning. Cobá, a short distance inland, has towering jungle-shrouded pyramids, testaments to its importance as a leading center of commerce in the ancient Maya world. Farther south, digs at Kohunlich have unearthed temples, palaces, and pyramids in the distinct Río Bec architectural style. They have been beautifully restored but are still largely unvisited. At the Belizean border is the capital of Quintana Roo—Chetumal. With its bright wooden houses and sultry sea air, the city feels more Central American than Mexican.

During your trek along the coast, you are likely to encounter expats from around the world, many running lodges and restaurants where you'd least expect to find them. Chat with them for a bit and find out how they succumbed to the spell of the Caribbean coast.

Pleasures and Pastimes

Archaeological Sites

This corner of the Yucatán has some fantastic archaeological treasures—Maya cities built when local people controlled the trade routes along the Caribbean. Tulum, the last city to be built, Cobá, an important trade center, and Kohunlich, a political center with majestic stucco masks, are all breathtaking. Mysterious temples with hidden chambers, stelae carved with images of deities, and the sounds of wildlife hidden in the jungles intermingle at these sites. If you plan to visit any of the ruins, don't forget to bring bug repellent.

Beaches

Caribbean-coast beaches—many blessed with white sand and clear, calm waters and fringed by dense jungle foliage—are so varied that they attract everyone from amateur archaeologists to professional divers and devoted sun worshipers.

Dining

Restaurants here vary from simple beachside affairs with outdoor tables and *palapas* (thatch roofs) to more elaborate establishments. Decor ranges from quirky to sophisticated. Casual attire is usually acceptable, and reservations generally optional. In addition to their relaxed ambience, restaurants here offer some bargains, especially when it comes to seafood. Fresh local fish, including grouper, dorado, red snapper, and sea bass, is tasty and inexpensive. On the other hand, shrimp, lobster, oysters, and other shellfish are often flown in frozen from the gulf, which makes them more expensive. Tourism and an expatriate presence mean that a variety of flavorful foods are available in some surprising places, such as Bacalar and Puerto Morelos. Playa del Carmen and Puerto Aventuras have more-urbane restaurants, as well as fast-food places serving pizza, burgers, and pasta.

CATEGORY	COST*
$$$$	over $30
$$$	$21–$30
$$	$10–$20
$	under $10

*per person for a main course at dinner

Fishing

Along with diving and snorkeling, fishing is one of the most popular activities along the coast. If you want to go fly-fishing, you can rent boats from locals who have beachside stalls. Charter captains at coastal marinas can take you out for deep-sea catches such as marlin, bonito, and sailfish. The Boca Paila Peninsula is great for a week of serious fishing, especially for the feisty bonefish.

Lodging

From Puerto Morelos down to Tulum, you can find the whole range of accommodations options: from campsites and strictly functional palapas and bungalows to mid-range hotels, luxury resorts, and condominiums. However, the coast has become one of the most expensive areas in Mexico and Central America. Many of the luxury properties are centered on Playa del Carmen, Akumal, and Puerto Aventuras.

Tulum has a number of ecological hotels that are luxurious for their tranquillity and close proximity to nature. South of Tulum accommodations are scarce, and the more-remote hotels tend to be either very primitive or very expensive. Chetumal has a respectable number of quality lodging options, as well as a few holdouts that appear to have been last renovated during the War of the Castes. The latter category—popular with backpackers—reflects the town's origins as a pit stop for traders en route to or from Central America.

Of the all-inclusive resorts along the coast, some are better than others. Many are in remote areas with little to do; to get to the sights, or to get some decent food, you may find yourself at the mercy of the hotel shuttle service (if there is one) or waiting for long stretches of time for the bus or spending large sums of money for taxis. The rule seems to be that the larger the hotel, the more bland the food. To avoid *turista* (traveler's diarrhea), be especially wary of creamed dishes or mayonnaise-based foods that have been sitting for hours in an all-inclusive buffet.

Hotel rates can drop as much as 50% in the low season (September to approximately mid-December). In the high season, it's virtually impossible to find hotels in the $ price range, especially in Playa del Carmen, unless you opt to camp. During Christmas week, prices rise as much as $100 a room. More and more hotels include breakfast in their rates. Hotel addresses listed below are the street addresses. Mailing addresses are not generally used, and hotels do not rely on the mail for reservations, as service is slow or nonexistent. You are much safer making your reservation over the phone or via fax or e-mail. All hotels have air-conditioning and in-room phones unless otherwise noted.

CATEGORY	COST*
$$$$	over $100
$$$	$70–$100
$$	$40–$70
$	under $40

All prices are for a high season standard double room excluding tax (12%) and service charge.

Nature

The wildlife on the Caribbean coast is unsurpassed in Mexico, except perhaps in Baja California. The reefs, lagoons, cenotes, and caves along the Caribbean and down the Río Hondo (Hondo River, along the border between Mexico, Belize, and Guatemala) that have been left untouched by development are filled with alligators, giant turtles, sharks, and tropical fish. The forests are home to wild pigs, foxes, turkeys, iguanas, lizards, and snakes that can be spotted in the clearings. Jaguars, monkeys, white-tail deer, armadillos, tapir, wild boars, peccaries, ocelots, raccoons, and badgers all inhabit the tropical jungle's most isolated retreats. Birders come to stare into the jungle and the seaside marshes for glimpses of parrots, toucans, terns, herons, and ibis. Casual onlookers easily stumble across yellow, blue, and scarlet butterflies; singing cicadas and orioles; sparkling dragonflies; kitelike frigates; and night owls nesting in the trees.

At dusk, colorless crabs scuttle sideways toward the coconut groves over pale white limestone sand while tiny persistent mosquitoes and gnats bore through the smallest rips in window screens, tents, and mosquito nets. The seasons are marked here by the wildlife: northern songbirds return in winter, newborn jellyfish invade beaches in spring, clouds of butterflies are born in the early summer heat, and sea turtles crowd the beaches throughout summer to lay thousands of eggs. It all unfolds before your eyes.

Scuba Diving and Snorkeling

Scuba divers and snorkelers flock to Quintana Roo for its transparent turquoise-and-emerald waters strewn with rose, black, and red coral reefs and sunken pirate ships. Schools of black, gray, and gold angelfish; luminous green-and-purple parrot fish; earth-color manta rays; and scores of other jewel-tone tropical species seem oblivious to the curious humans and their underwater cameras. The visibility in these waters reaches 100 ft, so you can actually see the marine life and topography without getting wet. Akumal and Puerto Morelos have particularly good diving. If you want to get away from all nondiving distractions, except fishing, head for Banco Chinchorro.

A series of cenotes lies just off the highway between Playa del Carmen and Tulum. They're favorites with divers, snorkelers, and swimmers. Highway signs make them easy to find.

Exploring the Caribbean Coast

The coast is divided into two major areas. The stretch from Punta Tanchacté to Punta Allen, at the tip of the Sian Ka'an Biosphere, is called the Riviera Maya. It has the most sites and places to lodge. The more southern stretch, from Punta Allen to Chetumal, has been dubbed the Costa Maya. This is where civilization thins out and you can find the

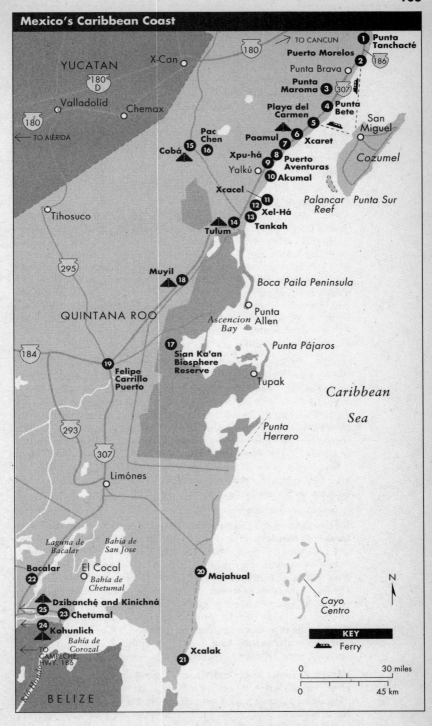

Mexico's Caribbean Coast

TO CANCUN

180

1 Punta
Tanchacté

186

Puerto Morelos

2

YUCATAN

X-Can

Punta Brava

**Punta
Maroma** **3**

307

180
D

**Playa del
Carmen**

4 Punta
Bete

Valladolid

Chemax

5

San
Miguel

180

TO MÉRIDA

**Pac
Chen**

6 Xcaret

Cozumel

Cobá **15**

16

Paamul **7**

Xpu-há **8** Puerto
Aventuras

Yalkú **9**

10 Akumal

Tihosuco

Palancar
Reef

Punta Sur

Xcacel

11

12 Xel-Há

13 Tankah

14

Tulum

295

Muyil **18**

Boca Paila Peninsula

QUINTANA ROO

Ascencion
Bay

Punta
Allen

184

17

Punta Pájaros

Sian Ka'an
Biosphere
Reserve

Tupak

Caribbean

293

19 Felipe
Carrillo
Puerto

Sea

307

Punta
Herrero

Limónes

Laguna de
Bacalar

Bahía de
San Jose

Bacalar

El Cocal

20 Majahual

Cayo
Centro

22

Bahía de
Chetumal

N

Dzibanché and Kinichná

25

23 Chetumal

24 Kohunlich

Bahía de
Corozal

KEY

TO
CAMPECHE,
HWY. 186

Ferry

Xcalak

21

0   30 miles

BELIZE

0   45 km

most alluringly beautiful tropical landscapes. The Río Bec Route starts
west of Chetumal and continues into Campeche.

*Numbers in the text correspond to numbers in the margin and on the
Mexico's Caribbean Coast map.*

Great Itineraries

Three to five days gives you enough time to visit most of the Riviera
Maya, from Punta Tanchacté to Tulum. With seven days you can cover
the entire coast; even longer visits allow you to see every attraction and
village. Playa del Carmen is a convenient base—it's closest to the
major ruins of Tulum and Cobá, and it has the best bus, taxi, and rental-
car services outside Cancún. You need a car to venture south of Tulum,
preferably a jeep or other vehicle that can efficiently negotiate ruts and
puddles the size of small Maya settlements.

IF YOU HAVE 3 DAYS

Get a room in ⊡ **Playa del Carmen** ⑤ and start out by visiting **Akumal** ⑩ for diving or deep-sea fishing, snorkeling, or swimming. Later
in the day cycle on a rented mountain bike or drive to the tiny lagoon
of Yalkú, which was around during the time of the Maya traders. On
Day 2, head out to the cenote at **Xel-Há** ⑫, where you can snorkel, swim,
sunbathe, and see some more-modest ruins. In the afternoon visit the
prehistoric underground caves at Aktun-Chen. On Day 3 head for **Tulum** ⑭ to take in the cliff-side Castillo temple. Afterward, climb down
to the small adjacent beach for a dip in the ocean. In the afternoon
head over to Tulum's hotel area, where you can enjoy a long walk along
the marvelous coastline and sample a lunch of fresh fish.

IF YOU HAVE 5 DAYS

Again, station yourself in ⊡ **Playa del Carmen** ⑤. Begin your travels
at **Xcaret** ⑥, a Disneylike ecological theme park where you can swim
with dolphins, snorkel in a cenote, and watch a flashy folkloric performance at night. Spend the morning of Day 2 at **Tulum** ⑭; you can
then spend the afternoon cooling off at **Xel-Há** ⑫ or at one of the numerous cenotes along Highway 307. On Day 3, explore the beaches
at **Paamul** ⑦ and **Xpu-há** ⑨ and continue on to **Akumal** ⑩ and Yalkú.
Spend Day 4 at the Maya village of **Pac Chen** ⑯ in the morning and,
after lunch, head for the ruins at **Cobá** ⑮. On Day 5, take a tour of the
Sian Ka'an Biosphere Reserve ⑰.

IF YOU HAVE 7 DAYS

Follow the five-day itinerary above; on Day 6 drive to the enormous
Laguna de Bacalar to marvel at its transparent layers of turquoise, green,
and blue waters—figure about three hours to drive straight through.
Visit the colonial San Felipe Fort in the village of **Bacalar** ㉒ and spend
the night in ⊡ **Chetumal** ㉓, visiting the Museo de la Cultura Maya.
On Day 7, head to **Kohunlich** ㉔, known for its huge stucco masks of
ancient Maya rulers and the surrounding jungle's ruins. Head into the
nearby farmlands to visit the majestic pyramids of **Dzibanché** and
Kinichná ㉕; then drive back up the coast to ⊡ **Playa del Carmen** ⑤,
stopping at the **Cenote Azul**, the largest sinkhole in Mexico, and at
Muyil ⑱, with its small Maya temple and remote lagoon.

When to Tour the Caribbean Coast

High season or not, if you are driving, start early in the day to beat
the tour buses; most come from nearby Cancún and Playa del Carmen,
Mexico's most popular resorts. Be sure to get to your overnight stop
before dark. September and October are hurricane months so expect
plenty of rain—and mosquitoes.

THE RIVIERA MAYA

The Caribbean coast in Mexico is in the state of Quintana Roo (keen-*tah*-nah *roh*-oh), bordered on the northwest by the state of Yucatán, on the west by Campeche, and on the south by Belize. Quintana Roo didn't exist until Mexican politicians decided to develop the area for tourism. It was officially recognized in 1974—the same year the first two hotels popped up in Cancún, where development was first focused.

It takes patience to discover the coast's treasures. Beaches and towns are not easily visible from the main highway—the road from Cancún to Tulum is 1–2 km (½–1 mi) from the coast. Thus there is little to see but dense vegetation, lots of billboards, a couple of roadside markets, and signs marking entrances to the businesses, ruins, resorts, beaches, and campgrounds hidden off the road.

The Mexican government under the old ruling PRI (Institutional Revolutionary Party) sold vast tracts of land and beaches to various corporations, and they have built huge resorts. The frenzy of building has affected the wildlife and coral reefs along the coast—as well as the beachside Maya communities, which have had to relocate to the jungle. Beach access has been limited to others, too, as the highway from Playa del Carmen to Tulum is lined with what seems like a giant barbed-wire fence punctuated with security gates. Many David-and-Goliath battles are taking place along the coast as environmentalists fight to preserve what land and wildlife are left against the onslaught of progress and keep the beaches open for everyone to enjoy. Fortunately, thanks to the federal government's foresight, 1.3 million acres of coastline and jungle have been set aside as the Sian Ka'an Biosphere Reserve. Whatever may happen along the coast, this protected area gives the wildlife, and the travelers who seek the Yucatán of old, someplace to go.

Apart from the decidedly U.S. influence—thanks to Cancún—in northern Quintana Roo, the music, food, and cultural traditions of the Caribbean coast are Yucatecan. Although the beach resorts' "international" restaurants and modern shopping malls flourish within 16 km (10 mi) of small Maya settlements, their culture remains intact.

Aside from Playa del Carmen, there isn't much in the way of nightlife on the coast unless you happen upon some entertainment in a fancy hotel bar. Nor is shopping sophisticated here. There is little in the way of high-quality crafts, except in Playa del Carmen and its vicinity, where the number of good folk-art and crafts shops has been increasing.

Punta Tanchacté

❶ *27½ km (17 mi) south of Cancún on Hwy. 307.*

The Riviera Maya experience starts at Punta Tanchacté, with small hotels on long stretches of beach caressed by turquoise waters. It's quieter here than in Cancún, and you can walk for miles with only the birds for company.

Lodging

$$$$ 🏨 **Escape Paraiso Maya Hotel.** On a secluded stretch of beach, this low-key, all-inclusive hotel offers ocean views, lush grounds, and palapa-covered walkways. Rooms have either two twin beds or one double and are decorated with Maya designs and colorful art. The pools are small but still pleasant, as is the outdoor Jacuzzi. Activities such as volleyball, snorkeling, diving, and evening shows are offered, and the food is excellent. A free shuttle transports guests to nearby Puerto Morelos, Cancún, or Playa del Carmen. ⌧ *Cancún–Puerto Morelos*

Hwy./Hwy. 307, Km 27.5, ☎ FAX *998/872–8088,* WEB *www.paraisomaya. com. 60 rooms. Restaurant, 2 pools, dive shop, snorkeling, bar, dance club, theater. MC, V.*

$$$ ⊞ **Sand Castle.** A spectacular atrium with a high, arched ceiling overlooks the beach at this Mediterranean-style property. You can rent the whole house (great for families), one floor, or one studio. The first-floor villa has a full-size kitchen, a living room, two bedrooms, and 2½ large bathrooms with a small patio facing the ocean. The upstairs studios have private baths, kitchenettes, large sundecks, and a balcony atrium. The entire house can sleep 10 people, making this a great bargain if you share. ✉ *Cancún–Puerto Morelos Hwy./Hwy. 307, Km 27.5,* ☎ *998/872–8093 or 998/872–8094,* FAX *998/872–8093. 1 villa, 2 studios. Pool, hot tub, massage, beach, snorkeling, shop. MC, V.*

Outdoor Activities and Sports

WATER SPORTS

Snorkeling Adventure (☎ 998/880–6559) offers great all-day snorkeling trips. This personable operation is on the Punta Tanchacté beach, with a palapa bar, hammocks, and a volleyball net. The trip includes three snorkel excursions to two different reefs, all you can drink (beer and tequila included), and a buffet lunch. It will even pick you up in Cancún.

Puerto Morelos

❷ *8 km (5 mi) south of Punta Tanchacté on Hwy. 307, 36 km (22 mi) south of Cancún.*

For years, Puerto Morelos was known as the small, relaxed coastal town where the car ferry left for Cozumel. This lack of regard actually helped it avoid the development that engulfed other communities, though now the construction of massive all-inclusive resorts nearby (640 rooms in total) may spoil the fishing-village atmosphere. Still, more and more people are discovering that Morelos, exactly halfway between Cancún and Playa del Carmen, makes a great base for exploring the region.

In ancient times this was a point of departure for pregnant Maya women making pilgrimages by canoe to Cozumel, the sacred isle of the fertility goddess, Ixchel. Remnants of Maya ruins exist along the coast here, but nothing has been restored. Foreigners increasingly have been buying up the land in town to build Mediterranean-style houses and condos, so most of the native population now lives across the highway in what is called the *cruceros* (crossroads). Unfortunately, the building boom isn't translating into inexpensive rooms—long-term accommodation is impossible to find, and there are few budget options.

The town itself is small but colorful, with a central plaza surrounded by shops and restaurants; its trademark is a leaning lighthouse. Puerto Morelos's greatest appeal lies out at sea: the superb coral reef only 1,800 ft offshore, which provides excellent grounds for snorkeling and scuba diving. Dive sites include an intact Spanish galleon with coral-crusted cannons and the Cave of the Sleeping Sharks (of documentary-movie fame), 8 km (5 mi) east of the town. The proximity of the reef creates an exceptionally calm and safe beach, though it isn't as pretty as others, as it isn't cleared of seaweed on a regular basis. Still, you can walk for miles here and see only a few people. In addition, the mangroves in back of town are home to 36 species of birds, making it a great place for birders.

Aside from a few decent restaurants, there is no nightlife in Puerto Morelos—which has prompted locals affectionately to name it Muerto Morelos ("dead Morelos"). But there is a strong community of environmentalists and artists here, and thanks to them the coral reef has been declared a national marine park. This status should provide some protection against the encroaching commercial development and help Morelos retain its fragile ecosystem and charming milieu.

Dining and Lodging

$–$$ ✕ **Che Carlito's.** Some of the best food in town is at this lovely restau-
★ rant run by Carlito and his family, in the Casita del Mar hotel. Choices include delicious empanadas, chicken fajitas, fresh salads, pastas, and incredible steaks that rival anything at the larger steak houses in Can-cún (and for half the price). The restaurant has an outdoor terrace with a palapa bar that leads down to the beach. ⊠ *Casita del Mar, Calle Heriberto Frias 6,* ☏ *998/871–0522. MC, V.*

$–$$ ✕ **Johnny Cairo's.** A former Ritz-Carlton chef brought many of his fa-vorite recipes to this colorful spot, decorated with colonial Mexican furniture and art. The chicken wings and fish with mango sauce are good choices, but expect some surprises, as the menu changes daily. On Sunday there's all-you-can-eat barbecue for $11 per person. Ask for a table on the large terrace overlooking the ocean, or enjoy the palapa bar on the beach, which is particularly lively during the hotel's monthly full-moon party. ⊠ *Hacienda Morelos, Av. Rafael Melgar,* ☏ *998/871–0449. No credit cards.*

$ ✕ **Twin Delphines Taquería & Restaurant.** You can watch the moon rise as you eat a delicious dinner at this open-air restaurant run by a local Mexican chef. The menu, which changes according to the season and what's available, offers specialties such as marinated shark with sautéed vegetables. When the weather is bad, this place is closed. ⊠ *Twin Delphines Aquarium, Av. Rafael Melgar,* ☏ *no phone. No credit cards.*

$$$$ ⌂ **Ceiba del Mar Hotel & Spa.** For peace and quiet, this resort on a se-
★ cluded beach may be just the ticket. Rooms are clustered in eight buildings and all have ocean-view terraces. The outstanding Mexican decor features beautiful furnishings from Guadalajara made of hard-wood, painted tiles, wrought iron, and bamboo. A first-class spa of-fers massage and beauty treatments. You can also experience the *temascal,* a traditional Aztec steam bath with aromatic herbs that's heated with volcanic rocks. The price includes a Continental breakfast, dis-creetly delivered to your room through a hidden closet chamber. ⊠ *Av. Niños Heroes s/n,* ☏ *998/871–0533; 800/235–5892 in the U.S.;* FAX *998/871–0458;* WEB *www.ceibadelmar.com. 120 rooms, 6 suites. 2 restaurants, cable TV with movies, in-room safes, tennis court, spa, pool, beach, dive shop, bar, shop, laundry service, meeting room, car rental, travel services. AE, MC, V.*

$$$ ⌂ **Casita del Mar.** This hotel has an incredible beach, lovely pool, and a great restaurant—Che Carlito. Rooms are average size, with either twin beds or one king-size bed. The bathrooms are exceptionally clean and well done. Ask for the ocean-facing suites; they have fantastic beach views and are perfect for watching the sunrise. The price of a room in-cludes full breakfast. ⊠ *Calle Heriberto Frias 6, 4 blocks north of town,* ☏ FAX *998/871–0301,* WEB *www.hotelcasitadelmar.8m.com. 17 rooms. Restaurant, some rooms with cable TV, pool, beach, snorkeling, fish-ing, laundry service; no room phones. MC, V.*

$$ ⌂ **Casa Caribe.** This small, pretty hotel sits a few blocks from the town
★ center and five minutes from the beach. The breezy rooms have king-size beds and roomy tile baths. Terraces have hammocks and views of the ocean or the mangroves. A large kitchen, huge terrace, and lounge area are available for guests' use. The grounds include a walled court-yard and a fragrant tropical garden. Children under 10 stay free. ⊠ *Av. Javier Rojo Gómez and Ejercito Mexicano, 3 blocks north of town,* ☏ *998/871–0049; 763/441–7630 in the U.S.;* WEB *www.us-webmasters.*

com/Casa-Caribe/. 6 rooms. Refrigerators; no air-conditioning, no room phones, no room TVs. No credit cards.

$$ 🖭 **Hotel Inglaterra.** The pluses at the Inglaterra, the only budget hotel in town, are that it's clean, secure, and close to the beach. It also offers free tea and coffee and a large, sunny upstairs deck. However, the staff can be cranky and there isn't much atmosphere. The hotel is sparse, with basic rooms: one double, one single bed, a functional bathroom, ceiling fans, and absolutely no view (or air) from the windows. Four minisuites offer air-conditioning, kitchenettes, small fridges, and hot plates. ⊠ *Av. Niños Héroes 29,* ☎ ℻ *998/871–0418. 14 rooms, 4 minisuites. Fans, some kitchenettes, some refrigerators, cable TV in dining room; no air-conditioning in some rooms. No credit cards.*

$$ 🖭 **Hotel Ojo de Agua.** Travelers looking for a peaceful atmosphere on the beach are likely to be pleased by this family-run hotel. Half of the guest rooms have kitchenettes, and all are decorated in cheerful colors with ceiling fans and views of the sea and courtyard gardens. An open-air restaurant serves good regional Mexican dishes along with American food. The beach offers superb snorkeling directly out front, including *ojo de agua,* an underwater cenote shaped like an eye. This is the best bargain around. ⊠ *Av. Javier Rojo Gómez and Calle Lazaro Cardenas, 2 blocks north of town,* ☎ *998/871–0027,* ℻ *998/871–0202,* 🕸 *www.ojo-de-agua.com. 36 rooms. Restaurant, some kitchenettes, pool, beach, dive shop, snorkeling, laundry service; no room phones. MC, V.*

Outdoor Activities and Sports

WATER SPORTS

Enrique at **Almost Heaven Adventures** (☎ 998/871–0230), in the main square by the currency exchange, can set up snorkeling and fishing trips. **Brecko's** (⊠ Casita del Mar, Calle Heriberto Frias 6, ☎ 998/871–0301) offers snorkeling and deep-sea fishing in a 25-ft boat. Owner Shade Haseman also takes people out on sailing excursions aboard his Hobie Cat. Snorkeling trips start at $15–$20 and fishing trips at $200. On a day trip with **H.E.A.D. South** (High Energy Adventure Day; ☎ 998/871–0483, headsouthmx@yahoo.com), Billy Alexander takes you out to snorkel at beaches littered with treasure from Spanish shipwrecks or to explore nearby cenotes. Trips start at $65. **David Sanchez** (☎ 998/871–0006), an accredited dive master, is also a good bet for scuba-diving day trips. **Sub-Aqua Explorers** (☎ 998/871–0018) can set up scuba-diving excursions.

Shopping

Alma Libre Libros (⊠ Av. Tulum, on main plaza, ☎ 998/871–0264) is the only English-language bookstore on the coast, with more than 20,000 books in stock. You can trade in your books for 25% of their cover prices and replenish your holiday reading. It's open October–April, Tuesday–Saturday 9–noon and 6–9.

The **Collectivo de Artesanos de Puerto Morelos** (Puerto Morelos Artists' Cooperative; ⊠ Avs. Javier Rojo Gómez and Isla Mujeres, ☎ no phone) is a series of palapa-style buildings where local artisans display their jewelry, hand-embroidered clothes, hammocks, and other items that make good souvenirs. You might find some real bargains here. It's open daily from 8 AM until dusk.

Rosario & Marco's Art Shoppe (⊠ Av. Javier Rojo Gómez 14, ☎ no phone), close to the ferry docks, is run by the eponymous couple from their living room. They paint regional scenes such as markets, colonial homes, and flora and fauna as well as portraits. Marco also creates replicas of Spanish galleons.

En Route   The biologists running the **Croco-Cun** (⊠ Hwy. 307, Km 30, ☎ 998/ 884–4782) crocodile farm and miniature zoo just north of Puerto

Morelos have collected specimens of many of the reptiles and some of the mammals indigenous to the area. They offer immensely informative tours—you may even get to handle a baby crocodile or feed the deer. Be sure to wave hello to the 500-pound crocodile secure in his deep pit. The farm is open daily 8:30–5:30; admission is $6.

South of Puerto Morelos, the 150-acre **Jardin Botanico del Dr. Alfredo Barrera Marin** (Dr. Alfredo Barrera Marín Botanical Garden) (⊠ Hwy. 307, Km 36, ☎ no phone) is one of the largest tropical gardens in Mexico. Named for a local botanist, it exhibits the plants and flowers of the peninsula labeled in English, Spanish, and Latin. There's also a tree nursery, a remarkable orchid and epiphyte garden, a reproduction of a *chiclero* (gum arabic collector), an authentic Maya house, and an archaeological site. A nature walk goes directly through the mangroves for some great bird-watching (bring that bug spray). A tree-house lookout offers a spectacular view—but the climb is not for those afraid of heights. The garden is open daily 9–5, and admission is $5.

Punta Brava

7 km (4½ mi) south of Puerto Morelos on Hwy. 307.

Punta Brava is also known as South Beach in Puerto Morelos. It's a long, winding beach strewn with seashells. On windy days, its shallow waters are whipped up into waves large enough for bodysurfing.

Lodging

$$$$ ⊞ **El Dorado Royale.** This luxurious adults-only, all-inclusive resort is surrounded by 500 acres of tropical jungle and 1½ mi of unspoiled beach. It offers junior suites with Mexican furnishings, small sitting rooms, king-size beds, indoor hot tubs, and ocean-facing terraces. The casitas have domed roofs, king-size beds, and oceanfront palapa terraces. Three restaurants offer à la carte menus with exceptional food. Despite the posh surroundings, the staff is friendly, warm, and down to earth. ⊠ *Hwy. 307, Km 25, Kantenah Bay,* ☎ *998/884–8341; 800/ 290–6679 in the U.S.;* FAX *998/884–8342;* WEB *www.eldorado-resort.com. 200 rooms, 70 suites. 3 restaurants, some in-room hot tubs, tennis court, spa, 7 pools, beach, snorkeling, shop, 3 bars, laundry service, travel services, car rental, free airport shuttle; no kids. AE, MC, V.*

Punta Maroma

❸ *2 km (1 mi) south of Punta Brava on Hwy. 307.*

Nestled in a bay where the winds don't reach the waters, this gorgeous beach remains calm even on blustery days. To the north you can see the land curve out to another beach, **Playa del Secreto;** to the south the curve that leads eventually to Punta Bete is visible.

Dining and Lodging

$$$$ ✕⊞ **Maroma.** Peacocks wander through the jungle walkways and flow-
★ ers scent the air at this romantic adults-only hotel, a favorite for honeymooners. Rooms are decorated with whimsical artifacts and original artwork and have king-size beds draped in mosquito nets and small sitting areas. A full breakfast (included in the room rate) is served every morning on each room's private terrace. The restaurant excels in gourmet fare such as lobster bisque and honeyed rack of lamb. ⊠ *Hwy. 307, Km 51,* ☎ *998/872–8200,* FAX *998/872–8220,* WEB *www.maromahotel. com. 31 rooms, 3 suites, 2 villas. Restaurant, pool, spa, beach, snorkeling, horseback riding, bar, theater, laundry service, airport shuttle; no air-conditioning, no room phones, no room TVs, no kids. AE, MC, V.*

Punta Bete

❹ *13 km (8 mi) south of Punta Maroma on Hwy. 307, then about 2 km (1 mi) off the main road.*

The one concession to "progress" here has been a slight improvement in the road. Take this bumpy 2⅓-km (1½-mi) ride through the jungle to arrive at a 6½-km-long (4-mi-long) isolated beach dotted with bargain bungalow-style hotels and thatch-roof restaurants. A few more-comfortable accommodations are available if you want to spare yourself some grit in your personal belongings.

Lodging

$$$$ ☒ **Kai Luum II.** The lazy man's answer to camping out, this much-loved
★ vacation spot offers "tentalapas"—large canvas tents under palapa roofs with ocean-view porches and hammocks—for adults only (over age 16). Inside are double beds with fluffy pillows; bathrooms are shared and there is no electricity. The outdoor restaurant, serving Yucatecan specialties, is under a giant palapa roof lit by oil lamps. Breakfast and dinner are included in the rate. Many guests are repeat visitors. ☒ *Hwy. 307, Km 62, beyond Posada del Capitán Lafitte (reservations: Turquoise Reef Group, Box 2664, Evergreen, CO 80439),* ☎ *998/850–4826 or 800/538–6802; 303/674–8735 in the U.S.;* ℻ *303/674–8735 in the U.S.;* 𝗪𝗘𝗕 *www.mexicoholiday.com. 29 tents. Restaurant, beach, snorkeling, fishing, bar, car rental, airport shuttle; no air-conditioning, no room phones, no room TVs, no kids. AE, MC, V.*

$$$$ ☒ **Posada del Capitán Lafitte.** This warm, family-friendly resort was named after a famous pirate known to frequent local waters. Guests stay in duplexes and three-unit cabanas—opt for the newer cabanas on the tranquil north end of the beach. One of the first resorts on the Riviera Maya, the hotel has aged gracefully, despite the tacky cement "fortress" marking the highway turnoff. Breakfast and dinner are included. ☒ *Hwy. 307, Km 62 (reservations: Turquoise Reef Group, Box 2664, Evergreen, CO 80439,* ℻ *303/674–8735 in U.S.),* ☎ ℻ *984/ 873–0212;* ☎ *800/538–6802 in the U.S.;* 𝗪𝗘𝗕 *www.mexicoholiday.com. 62 rooms. Restaurant, pool, beach, dive shop, fishing, horseback riding, bar, car rental, airport shuttle. AE, MC, V.*

$$ ☒ **Cocos Cabañas.** Enjoy tranquillity and seclusion at these cozy palapa bungalows set back 30 yards from the beach. The cabanas are colorful and bright and have a queen- or king-size bed, bath, hammocks, and a terrace that leads to a tropical garden. Breakfast, lunch, and dinner are served at the Grill Bar, which serves fresh fish and Italian food. ☒ *Playa Xcalacoco, follow signs and take dirt road off Hwy. 307, Km 42, for about 3 km [2 mi],* ☎ *998/874–7056,* ℻ *9/887–9964. 5 cabanas. Restaurant, beach; no room phones, no room TVs. No credit cards.*

$ ☒ **Cabañas Xcalacoco.** Roughing it on the beach is romantic in one of these seven white cabanas. All have double beds, hammocks, and small porches, but there's no electricity—kerosene lamps light the nights. There are also camping facilities with showers and a place to park recreational vehicles, which by no means interfere with cabana views. ☒ *Playa Xcalacoco, follow signs and take dirt road off Hwy. 307, Km 42, for about 3 km [2 mi],* ☎ *no phone. 7 cabanas. Beach, camping;no air-conditioning, no room phones, no room TVs. No credit cards.*

Playa del Carmen

❺ *10 km (6 mi) south of Punta Bete, 68 km (42 mi) south of Cancún.*

Once upon a time, Playa del Carmen was a fishing village with a ravishing, deserted beach. The villagers fished and raised coconut palms to produce copra, and the only foreigners who ventured here were society dropouts and beach bums. These days, however, it's the fastest-growing city in Mexico, with a population of more than 30,000 and a pace almost as hectic as Cancún's. The beach is still delightful—alabaster-white sand, turquoise-blue waters—it's just not deserted.

The most consistent sound you hear throughout Playa del Carmen is that of jackhammers. For the past few years a construction boom has been continually transforming the city every few months. Hotels, restaurants, and shops multiply faster than you can say "Kukulcán," and many new businesses are branches of Cancún establishments whose owners have taken up permanent residence in Playa or commute daily between the two. Some of the changes have been for the better. Avenida 5, the first street parallel to the beach, has been turned into a pedestrian walkway with quaint cafés and street art and entertainment. Unfortunately, these changes have made driving to the beachfront hotels difficult, unless you know exactly where you're going, and parking has become a nightmare.

Avenida Juárez, running east–west from the highway to the beach, is the main commercial zone for the Riviera Maya corridor. Here, locals visit the food shops, pharmacies, auto-parts and hardware stores, and banks that line the curbs. People traveling the coast by car usually stop here to stock up on supplies—it's the last bank, grocery store, and gas station until Tulum. A bus station marks the end of Avenida Juárez.

The ferry pier, where boats arrive from and depart for Cozumel (on the hour), is another bustling part of town. Take a stroll north from the pier along the beach to find the serious sun worshipers. On the south side of the pier is the edge of the sprawling Playacar complex. The development is a labyrinth of residential homes and all-inclusive resorts bordered by an 18-hole championship golf course. The excellent 32-acre **Xaman Ha Aviary** (⊠ Paseo Xaman-Ha, Playacar, ☎ 984/873–0593), in the middle of the Playacar development, is home to more than 30 species of native birds. It's open daily 9–5, and admission is about $8.

Playa del Carmen is no longer the budget haven it once was, as prices, particularly in hotels, have been rising steadily. It's one of the most expensive stops along the coast. Things change fast here, and while peace and quiet may no longer describe the town, Playa does make a fun introduction to the Caribbean coast.

Dining and Lodging

Playa has scores of hotels, and more are opening. Playa's most luxurious rooms are at the 880-acre Playacar development; the more modest rooms are farther north. Competition among the smaller hotels is fierce, so most ask for a deposit (usually the price of one night) before taking your reservation. As for the dining scene, mediocrity reigns supreme, though most restaurants have great decor.

$–$$$$ ✕ **Palapa Hemingway.** A mural of Che Guevara sporting a knife and fork looms larger than life in this palapa seafood restaurant focused on Cuba and its revolution. The grilled shrimp, fish, and steaks are good choices, as are the fresh salads, pastas, and chicken dishes. ⊠ *Av. 5 between Avs. 12 and 14,* ☎ *984/873–0004. MC, V.*

$–$$$$ ✕ **Yaxche.** This is the best restaurant along the Riviera Maya. The decor
★ includes hand-carved stelae from famous ruins and ceiling and wall murals of Maya gods and kings, but the real knockout is the food. Dishes such as *halach winic* (chicken in a spicy four-pepper sauce) and *tikinchic* (fish in a sour orange-onion sauce with annatto-seed spice) bring Maya cuisine to gourmet levels. Finish your meal with a "Maya Kiss" (Kahlúa and Xtabentun, a local liqueur flavored with anise and honey). ⊠ *Calle 8 at Avs. 5 and 10,* ☎ *984/873–2502. AE, MC, V.*

$–$$$ ✗ **Captain Dave's.** Self-styled local character Dave Baker, originally from Memphis, serves up southern cooking at this joint just a block off Avenida 5. The slow-cooked (five hours) barbecue is ready at 2 PM each afternoon; other headliners include fried chicken, navy beans, and "real" corn bread. At night, the restaurant turns into more of a honky-tonk when Dave's country-singer friends from Memphis entertain. ⊠ *Av. 10 and Calle 6,* ☎ *no phone. MC, V.*

$–$$$ ✗ **La Parrilla.** Excellent Mexican fare is the draw at this boisterous, touristy restaurant. The smell of sizzling *parrilla mixta* (a grilled, marinated mixture of lobster, shrimp, chicken, and steak) can make it difficult to resist grabbing one of the few available tables. It offers live music, friendly service, and strong margaritas until well after the witching hour. ⊠ *Av. 5 at Calle 8,* ☎ *984/873–0687. AE, MC, V. No lunch.*

$–$$ ✗ **Casa del Agua.** You can dine and shop at the same time in this em-
★   porium of European cuisine on the top floor of a handicrafts store, created by the Spath family. Gunther, the Swiss patriarch, was former general manager of the nearby Las Palapas hotel, where he created much of the menu. Here he offers German, Italian, and Swiss dishes like sliced chicken Zurich with spaetzle (homemade Swiss pasta) and fresh mushroom gravy, and the ever-popular steak Roquefort. Finish up with mama Spath's "Hot Love" ice cream-and-hot blueberries dessert. ⊠ *Av. 5 at the corner of Calle 2,* ☎ *984/803–0232. MC, V.*

$–$$ ✗ **Media Luna.** The Canadian couple that runs this stylish restaurant, formerly called Zas, has combined vegetarian dishes with the best of Toronto's cuisine, then spiced them both with Mexican flavors. Owner-chef Carla creates dishes such as curried root-vegetable puree with cilantro cream and black-crusted fish with steamed rice. A fixed-price lunch for $5 and dinner for $8 are featured daily. ⊠ *Av. 5 at Calles 12 and 14,* ☎ *no phone. No credit cards.*

$–$$ ✗ **Milano.** Locals in the know dine at this little hole-in-the-wall, which fancies music by Italian tenors. There are tasty salads, seven different spaghettis, and daily specials like spaghetti in baby clam sauce. Everything is fresh and authentic, and the service is fast. ⊠ *Calle 6 Nte. between Avs. 5 and 10,* ☎ *no phone. MC, V.*

$ ✗ **Café Sasta.** This sweet little café offers a variety of fantastic coffee drinks (cappuccino, espresso, mocha blends), teas, light sandwiches, and excellent baked goods. The staff is very pleasant—something that is becoming rare in Playa. ⊠ *Av. 5 between Calles 8 and 10,* ☎ *984/873–3030. No credit cards.*

$ ✗ **Hot.** Open at 6 AM, this is the place to stop for breakfast. The egg dishes are very good, especially the chili-cheese omelet, as are the baked goods and the hot coffee. Salads and sandwiches are lunch options. ⊠ *Calle 10 between Avs. 5 and 10,* ☎ *984/876–4370. No credit cards.*

$ ✗ **Sabor.** The prices have gone up and beer and wine are now on the menu, but the savory salads, sandwiches, and baked goods are still tasty and the location is great. Seats at breakfast and lunch are hard to find; avoid breakfasting here if you don't like rap music. ⊠ *Av. 5, between Calles 2 and 3,* ☎ *no phone. No credit cards.*

PLAYACAR RESORT

$$$$ 🏨 **Iberostar Tucan and Quetzal.** This unique, luxurious, all-inclusive resort has worked hard at preserving its natural surroundings—among the resident animals are flamingos, ducks, hens, turtles, fish, toucans, even a family of monkeys. Spacious rooms are decorated in cheerful Caribbean colors. The four restaurants serve decent Mexican and international fare. Playa del Carmen is a 30-minute walk or a $4 cab ride north. ⊠ *Fracc. Playacar, Playacar,* ☎ *984/873–0200; 888/923–2722 in the U.S.;* FAX *984/873–0424;* WEB *www.iberostar.com. 700 rooms. 4 restaurants, cable TV, 2 tennis courts, 4 pools, health club, spa, dive* shop, 2 bars, nightclub, recreation room, baby-sitting, children's programs (ages 4–12), laundry service, free parking. AE, MC, V.

$$$$ ★ ⚄ **Royal Hideaway.** On a breathtaking stretch of beach, this 13-acre, ultra-luxurious adults-only resort offers exceptional amenities and superior service. The two- and three-story villas are a fusion of Spanish-Mexican colonial architecture and are surrounded by winding rivers, waterfalls, and fountains. Each villa has its own concierge to take care of your needs. Deluxe rooms have two queen beds, sitting areas, and ocean-view terraces. The lobby area features a medley of art and artifacts from around the world. Meals are à la carte, and the resort is wheelchair accessible. ⊠ *Fracc. Playacar, Lote 6, Playacar,* ☎ *984/873–4500; 877/284–0935 in the U.S.;* FAX *984/873–4506;* WEB *www.allegroresorts.com. 192 rooms, 8 suites. 5 restaurants, in-room data ports, cable TV, 2 tennis courts, 2 pools, exercise equipment, spa, beach, windsurfing, snorkeling, bicycles, 3 bars, library, recreation room, theater, shops, laundry service, concierge, meeting rooms, travel services, free parking; no kids. AE, MC, V.*

HOTELS IN TOWN

$$$$ ★ ⚄ **Lunata.** This small but classy inn has Spanish tile floors, hand-tooled furniture, and an elegant, high-ceilinged entrance. Rooms are decorated with dark hardwood furnishings and high-quality crafts and have sitting areas and terraces, some with hammocks. Phones are in the process of being installed. A Continental breakfast is laid out in the lush tropical garden each morning for guests. Service is personal and gracious. ⊠ *Av. 5 between Calles 6 and 8,* ☎ *984/873–0884,* FAX *984/873–1240,* WEB *www.lunata.com. 10 rooms. Cable TV, laundry service. AE, MC, V.*

$$$$ ⚄ **Shangri-La Caribe.** Shangri-La used to be on the outskirts of Playa, but now it's considered part of northern downtown. Still, it remains a tranquil beachside resort with attractive whitewashed bungalows. Comfortable beds, tile floors, baths, and balconies or patios with hammocks decorate the rooms. A large, circular palapa serving light American and Mexican fare is a gathering spot for guests. Breakfast and dinner are included in the rate. ⊠ *Calle 38 between Av. 5 and Zona Playa (reservations: Turquoise Reef Group, Box 2664, Evergreen, CO 80439),* ☎ *984/ 873–0611; 800/538–6802 in the U.S.;* FAX *984/873–0500;* WEB *www. mexicoholiday.com. 70 bungalows. Restaurant, coffee shop, pool, beach, dive shop, snorkeling, fishing, bar, laundry service, car rental, airport shuttle; no air-conditioning, no room phones, no room TVs. AE, MC, V.*

$$$–$$$$ ⚄ **Deseo Hotel & Lounge.** A high-concept, high design boutique hotel, Deseo brings the stark, modernist aesthetic to downtown Playa del Carmen. Rooms have sand-colored marble floors, white walls, and billowing curtains. You can either get a room with a balcony or one that overlooks the lounge area downstairs. The suites have freestanding baths separated from the rest of the room by a curtain. All rooms open out onto the pool area where you can relax on large daybeds. This is not the place for those looking for a tranquil vacation: the trendy bar has its own DJ and stays crowded late into the night. ⊠ *Av. 5 and Calle 12,* ☎ *984/879–3620,* FAX *984/879–3621,* WEB *www.hoteldeseo.com. 15 rooms, 3 suites. Room service, in-room data ports, in-room safes, minibars, pool, bar, lounge; no room TVs. AE, MC, V.*

$$$ ⚄ **Hotel Molcas.** Steps from the ferry docks, this colonial-style hotel has been in business since the early 1980s and has aged gracefully. The rooms have dark-wood furniture and face the pool, the sea, or the street. The second-floor pool area is quite glamorous, with white tables, umbrellas, and uniformed waiters. Although it's in the heart of all the bustle, the hotel is well insulated from the noise and is rather serene. ⊠ *Av. 5 at Calle 1 Sur,* ☎ *984/873–0070,* FAX *984/873–0138,* WEB *www.molcas.com. 25 rooms. Restaurant, pool, beach, bar; no room phones. AE, MC, V.*

$$$ ⊡ **Itzaes.** This modern, colonial-style hotel is business-traveler friendly,
★   with modem hookups in rooms, concierge, car rental, and minibars. Huge
guest rooms have two double beds, dark wood furniture, a desk area,
tiled floors, and full bathroom amenities including a hair dryer. Divers
like to stay here, as it's two blocks from the beach. Rates include Con-
tinental breakfast. ⊠ *Av. 10 and Calle 6,* ☎ *984/873–2397,* FAX *984/873–
2373,* WEB *www.itzaes.com. 16 rooms. Cable TV, in-room data ports, mini-
bars, pool, concierge, car rental. MC, V.*

$$$ ⊡ **Mosquito Blue.** At once casual, exotic, and elegant, the rooms and
lobby of this beautiful adults-only hotel have lovely mahogany furni-
ture, Indonesian decor, and soft lighting. King-size beds and great views
round out the rooms. A cloistered courtyard has a garden, pool, and
open-air bar. Children under age 16 are not allowed. ⊠ *Calle 12 between Avs. 5 and 10,* ☎ FAX *984/873–1335,* WEB *www.mosquitoblue.com.
46 rooms, 1 suite. Restaurant, cable TV, 2 pools, gym, massage, 2 bars,
laundry service; no kids under 16. AE, MC, V.*

$$$ ⊡ **Tukan Condotel Villas and Beach Club.** The look is exclusive and
expensive, but the rates aren't as high as you might expect. Rooms and
suites are well separated from one another and offer private terraces,
tiny kitchenettes, tile floors, and painted wood furniture. The large,
tranquil jungle garden has a pool and a natural cenote. Included in the
room rate is a buffet breakfast at the Tucan Maya restaurant across
the street. ⊠ *Av. 5, between Calles 14 and 16,* ☎ *984/873–0417,* FAX
*984/873–0668. 56 rooms, 39 suites. Grocery, cable TV, kitchenettes,
pool, bicycles, bar; no room phones, no air-conditioning in some
rooms. MC, V.*

$$–$$$ ⊡ **Baal Nah Kah.** True to its name, which means "home hidden among
★   the gum trees" in Maya, this small hotel is quite homey. Guests have
the use of a large kitchen, common sitting room, and barbecue pit. The
five bedrooms and one studio are on different levels, affording com-
plete privacy. Two rooms have spacious balconies with panoramic
views of the ocean; all have tile baths, fans, double or king-size beds,
and Mexican decor. A small café next door serves breakfast, snacks,
and light meals. The beach is a block away. ⊠ *Calle 12 near Av. 5,* ☎
984/873–0110, FAX *984/873–0050,* WEB *www.cancunsouth.com/
baalnahkah. 5 rooms, 1 studio. Fans; no air-conditioning. No credit cards.*

$$ ⊡ **Delfin.** One of the older hotels in town, the Delfín retains the laid-
back charm of old Playa. In the heart of town, although not on the
beach, the hotel is a good choice for its bright, airy rooms cooled by
sea breezes and decorated with colorful mosaics. Some rooms also have
wonderful ocean views. Restaurants and other amenities are within close
walking distance. The management is exceptionally helpful. ⊠ *Av. 5
at Calle 6,* ☎ FAX *984/873–0176,* WEB *www.hoteldelfin.com. 14 rooms.
No air-conditioning, no room phones. MC, V.*

$$ ⊡ **Hotel Casa Tucan.** The owners have worked hard at creating a cozy
community a short distance from the main drag. The peaceful gardens
here are home to a small menagerie of rabbits, ducks, birds, and tur-
tles, and the hotel has a variety of clean and cheerful rooms geared to
different budgets. The property also includes a restaurant, a game
room with billiards, a meditation palapa, a TV bar, a language school,
and a specially designed dive pool that is used by the on-site dive cen-
ter. Families are welcome. ⊠ *Calle 4 between Avs. 10 and 15,* ☎ *984/
873–0283. 20 rooms. Restaurant, pool, dive shop, billiards, bar, recre-
ation room; no air-conditioning, no room phones. MC, V.*

$$ ⊡ **Maya Brick.** The best thing about this hotel is that it's in the middle of Avenida 5 but—because it is set back from the street and is sur-
rounded by a tropical garden—still surprisingly quiet. Rooms are small
but clean, with double beds and private baths, and open onto the garden and small pool. The staff is a bit cool, however. ⊠ *Av. 5 between*

Calles 8 and 10, ☎ *984/873–0011,* FAX *984/873–2041. 29 rooms. Restaurant, pool; no room phones. MC, V.*

$$ 🏠 **Paraiso Azul's (Casa de Gopala).** For years this small hotel has been a favorite destination for travelers seeking clean, comfortable, and reasonably priced accommodations. Once you pass through the wooden doors, you enter a private jungle that is cool and tranquil. Rooms are spacious, bright, and airy, with large windows, two double beds, and Mexican accents. Guests can use the pool at the Hotel Casa Tucan. This is a great place to experience the laid-back rhythm of the old Playa. ✉ *Calle 2 between Avs. 10 and 15,* ☎ FAX *984/873–0054. 16 rooms. Fans; no air-conditioning, no room phones. No credit cards.*

$–$$ 🏠 **Posada Freud.** This quirky little hotel on the main strip has a European flavor. Each room is decorated differently, with Mexican textiles and wall murals. The bigger rooms have refrigerators and coffeemakers. The inner courtyard and garden do a remarkable job of keeping out the Avenida 5 noise. Guests get a discount on food at a local restaurant. ✉ *Av. 5 between Calles 8 and 10,* ☎ FAX *984/873–0601. 12 rooms. Some refrigerators; no air-conditioning in some rooms. No credit cards.*

$$ 🏠 **Posada Mariposa.** One of the best hotels in Playa, this impeccable
★ Italian-style property in the quiet north section of town is comfortable and well priced. Rooms center on a tropical garden filled with plants, flowers, trees, and a small fountain. All have ocean views, luxurious bathrooms, and shared patios and are furnished with queen-size beds and wall murals. Suites have full kitchens. Sunset on the rooftop is quite spectacular, and the beach is five minutes away down a private road. ✉ *Av. 5 No. 314, between Calles 24 and 26,* ☎ *984/873–3886,* FAX *984/ 873–1054,* WEB *www.posadamariposa.com. 18 rooms, 6 apartments. Car rental, free parking; no air-conditioning, no room phones. No credit cards.*

$–$$ 🏠 **La Ruinas Camp Grounds.** The cheapest place in Playa is near the beach, and it's also the only authorized campground in town. Lodging options include cabanas (with baths), palapas and tent spaces (with communal baths), and RV spaces. ✉ *Calle 2 and Av. 5 Nte.,* ☎ FAX *984/873–0405. 5 cabanas. No air-conditioning in some rooms. No credit cards.*

Nightlife and the Arts

Most of Playa closes down around 11 PM, but a growing number of bars and discos stay open until the wee hours. Unfortunately, Playa's drug culture sometimes surfaces in the clubs. Resist the temptation to indulge, not only because it can land you in jail but because you may get robbed during drug transactions.

Babaloo (✉ Av. 5 between Calles 8 and 10, ☎ 980/0444–0186) has a popular terraced bar, which gets extra lively at night til 3 AM. The **Blue Parrot** (✉ Calle 12 at Av. 1, ☎ 984/873–0083) has live music every night until midnight; the bar sometimes stays open until 3 AM. **Capitán Tutix** (✉ Calle 4 Nte., ☎ no phone) is a beach bar designed to resemble a ship. Good drink prices and live jazz keep the crowd dancing until dawn. To party off the beach check out **House** (✉ Calle 6 between Avs. 5 and 10, ☎ 984/973–3189), a dance club that plays the latest in techno music.

Outdoor Activities and Sports

DIVING

Playa del Carmen's scuba scene has grown considerably in the past few years. Most dive shops offer similar services, but the quality of the equipment and dive instructors varies; it's best to shop around. The **Abyss** (☎ 984/873–2164) offers training courses in addition to dive trips. The oldest shop in town, **Tank-Ha Dive Shop** (☎ FAX 984/873–5037) has PADI-certified teachers and runs diving and snorkeling trips to the reefs and caverns. **Yucatek Divers** (☎ 984/873–0283) specializes in cenote dives and diving packages and works with divers who have disabilities.

GOLF

The golf course in Playa is an 18-hole, par-72 championship course designed by Robert Von Hagge. Greens fees range from $110 to $165 with a special twilight rate. Information is available from the **Casa Club de Golf** (☎ 984/873–0624).

HORSEBACK RIDING

Rancho Dos Amigos (☎ 984/883–1138) offers horseback expeditions on the beach and in the jungle. The two-hour trips start at $35 and include food, drinks, and bilingual guides. Two-hour trips run by **Rancho Loma Bonita** (☎ 984/887–5465) start at $45.

MOUNTAIN BIKING

You can rent bicycles from **Universal Rent** (✉ Av. 10 between Calles 12 and 14, ☎ 984/879–3358). The best (and safest) bike path is through Playacar.

SKYDIVING

Thrill seekers can take the plunge high above Playa in a tandem sky dive (you're hooked up to the instructor the whole time). **SkyDive** (✉ Plaza Marina 32, ☎ 984/873–0192) even videotapes your trip so you have proof that you did it.

Shopping

Avenida 5 between Calles 4 and 10 is the best place to shop along the coast. Unique shops and boutiques sell folk art and textiles from around Mexico, and clothing stores carry original designs created from hand-painted Indonesian batiks. Shops usually are open from about 10 in the morning to 9 or 10 at night.

Amber Museum Shop (✉ Av. 5 between Calles 4 and 6, ☎ FAX 984/873–0446) has elegantly crafted amber jewelry by a local designer who imports the amber from Chiapas; there is also a small jewelry-making workshop for children. **La Calaca** (✉ Av. 5 between Calles 6 and 8; ✉ Av. 5 and Calle 4; ☎ 984/873–0177 for both) has an eclectic collection of wooden masks and other carvings. The playful devils and angels are of note. **Mayan Arts Gallery** (✉ Av. 5 between Calles 6 and 8, ☎ 984/879–3389) has an extensive collection of hand-carved Maya masks and *huipiles* (the white sack-like dresses traditionally worn by Mayan women) from Mexico and Guatemala. **Selva y Mar** (✉ Av. 5 between Calles 4 and 6, ☎ 984/873–0525) showcases beaded masks made by Mexico's Huichol Indians. **Telart** (✉ Av. Juárez 10, ☎ 984/873–0066) carries textiles from all over Mexico.

Xcaret

 6 *11 km (6½ mi) south of Playa del Carmen, 72 km (45 mi) south of Cancún.*

South of Playa del Carmen is Xcaret, once a sacred Maya city and port, now a 250-acre ecological theme park on a gorgeous stretch of coastline. You can't escape Xcaret—it's the most heavily advertised park on the coast, with its own buses, magazines, and stores. Though billed as "nature's sacred paradise," it's expensive, contrived, and crowded.

Highlights of the park include an aviary, a butterfly pavilion, botanical gardens, riding stables, a tropical aquarium with a sea-turtle nursery (where thousands of turtle eggs are incubated and thus saved from predators), a nursery for abandoned flamingo eggs, an artificially created beach for snorkeling and swimming, a dive center with myriad sporting activities, a replica of a Maya village, a small zoo, some Maya ruins, and an underground river ride where you snorkel through a series of caves. There is even a Dolphinarium, where you can attend a dolphin workshop and touch swimming dolphins (although not swim with them) for $80 a person (book early; only 36 people a day are allowed).

Evenings, there are folkloric extravaganzas that begin with a reenactment of the Maya ball game and end with a performance by the famed Voladores de Papantla (Fliers of Papantla) from Veracruz. A new program, done in partnership with the Carnival Corporation, calls for the construction of a home port for cruise ships that will be able to berth four at a time by 2006.Plan to spend the day and plenty of money. The $45 (per adult) entrance fee covers only access to the grounds and the exhibits; all other expenses, from lockers to snorkel and swim gear to horseback riding, are extra. You can buy tickets from any travel agency or major hotel along the coast. ☎ *998/880–6618 in Cancún.* ⚏ *$45 (including show).* ⊙ *Daily 8:30 AM–9 PM.*

Paamul

❼ *10 km (6 mi) south of Xcaret.*

Beachcombers and snorkelers are fond of Paamul, a crescent-shape lagoon with clear, placid waters sheltered by a coral reef at the lagoon's mouth. Shells, sand dollars, and even glass beads—some from the sunken pirate ship at Akumal—wash onto the sandy parts of the beach. In June and July you can see one of Paamul's chief attractions: sea-turtle hatchlings on the beach.

Lodging

$$$ ⊡ **Cabañas Paamul.** On a perfect white-sand beach, this rustic hostelry is the place for seclusion. Ten bungalows face the sea, each with two double beds, ceiling fans, and hammocks. A large palapa houses the restaurant. Farther along the beach are 10 no-frills cabanas, which offer more privacy. The property includes 140 full-service hookups (gas, water, and drainage) for motor homes and tents and a full-service dive shop offering PADI and NAUI certification courses. ⊠ *Hwy. 307, Km 85,* ☎ *984/875–1051. 10 bungalows, 10 cabanas. Restaurant, beach, dive shop, bar, laundry service; no air-conditioning in some rooms, no room phones, no room TVs,. No credit cards.*

Puerto Aventuras

❽ *5 km (3 mi) south of Paamul.*

While the rest of the coast has been caught up in development fever, Puerto Aventuras has been quietly doing its own thing. It's emerged as a popular vacation spot, particularly for families, though it's not the place to experience Yucatecan culture, as it's really much like any planned community in the United States. The 900-acre self-contained resort is built around its 95-ship marina. It also offers a beach club, an 18-hole golf course, restaurants, shops, a great dive center, tennis courts, doctors, a school, and an excellent museum. The **Museo CEDAM** displays artifacts—coins, sewing needles, nautical devices, clay dishes—recovered from sunken ships by members of the Mexican Underwater Expeditions Club (CEDAM), founded in the 1960s. Entrance fee is by donation. Even if you don't stay at the complex, the museum is worth a visit.

Dining and Lodging

$–$$$ ✕ **Café Olé International.** With fresh food and a varied menu, this café is the laid-back hub of Aventuras. Chicken satay and coconut shrimp are good lunch or dinner choices; rib-eye cuts are also popular. During the high season, musicians from around the world play until the wee hours. ⊠ *Across from Omni Puerto Aventuras hotel,* ☎ *984/873–5125. MC, V.*

$$$$ 🏨 **Casa del Agua.** This small, discreet, and romantic hotel, lovingly
★ designed by a Mexican painter, has one of the most sumptuous beaches on the coast and four very large air-conditioned suites, all strikingly different from one another. The Arroyo suite has a stream of water running above a round king-size bed; the Caleta has a double shower in a secluded garden; the Cenote offers a meditation room and a to-die-for ocean view; and the Cascada commands a stunning view of Puerto Adventuras from its L-shape balcony. Rates include full breakfast; dinner is by reservation only. ⊠ *East of marina,* ☎ *984/873–5184,* 🌐 *www.casadelagua.com. 4 suites. Internet access, spa, massage, beach, airport shuttle. No credit cards.*

$$$$ 🏨 **Omni Puerto Aventuras.** Low key and elegant, this all-inclusive resort is a good place for some serious pampering. Each room has a king-size bed, sitting area, ocean-view balcony or terrace, and hot tub. The beach is steps away, and the pool seems to flow right into the sea. A complimentary Continental breakfast and newspaper arrive at your room every morning by way of a cubbyhole to avoid disturbing your slumber. You are within walking distance of a golf course and marina. Ask about the all-inclusive plan for $69 extra per person. ⊠ *Carretera Chetumal–Puerto Juárez (on beach near marina),* ☎ *984/873–5101,* 🆋 *984/873–5102,* 🌐 *www.omnihotels.com. 30 rooms. 2 restaurants, Internet café, 2 tennis courts, 2 pools, gym, beach, dive shop, 2 bars, shop, baby-sitting, laundry service, meeting room, free parking. AE, MC, V.*

Outdoor Activities and Sports

DIVING
Aquanuts (⊠ Center Complex, by marina, ☎ 🆋 984/873–5280) is a full-service dive shop that specializes in cave and cenote diving and offers certification courses.

En Route The Maya-owned and -operated eco-park called **Cenotes Kantún Chi** has a series of cenotes and underground caverns that are great for snorkeling and diving. The site includes some small Maya ruins and a botanical garden. The place is not at all slick, so it offers a nice break from the more commercial attractions along the coast. ⊠ *Hwy. 307, 3 km (2 mi) south of Puerto Aventuras,* ☎ 🆋 *984/873–0021.* 🎟 *$2.* ☉ *Daily 8:30–5.*

Xpu-há

🟤 *3 km (2 mi) south of Puerto Aventuras.*

This used to be a tranquil little beach until developers turned it into an overpriced eco-park, which subsequently closed. Since then, two megaresorts have invaded the beach, one of which hijacked a popular cenote that happened to lie on its property and is no longer open to the public.

Lodging

$$$$ 🏨 **Copacabana.** This lavish, all-inclusive resort was designed around the surrounding jungle, cenotes, and beach, leaving them virtually untouched. The lobby has bamboo furniture and a central waterfall underneath a giant palapa roof. The rooms have beautiful wood furniture, king-size beds, and private terraces with jungle views. Three large pools, separated from the outdoor hot tubs by an island of palm trees, look out onto the exceptional beach. The food is exceptional and served à la carte. ⊠ *Carretera Chetumal/Hwy. 307, Km 264.5,* ☎ *984/875–1800; 800/562–0197 in the U.S.,* 🆋 *984/875–1818,* 🌐 *www.hotelcopacabana.com. 224 rooms. 4 restaurants, cable TV, 3 pools, gym, spa, beach,* *snorkeling, windsurfing, 4 bars, dance club, recreation rooms, shops, baby-sitting, children's program (ages 4–12), laundry service, business services, meeting rooms, travel services. MC, V.*

$$ 🖭 **Hotel Villas del Caribe.** Leon, the laid-back manager, makes sure you are well looked after at this throwback to simpler days. The rooms are basic, with double beds, simple furniture, and hot water. You can have great, inexpensive food (especially the fish) at Café del Mar on the beach morning, noon, and night. ⊠ *Hwy. 307, Xpu-há X-4 (look for sun sign),* ☎ *984/876–9945. 14 rooms. Restaurant, beach, bar; no room phones. No credit cards.*

Akumal

🔟 *37 km (23 mi) south of Playa del Carmen, 102 km (63 mi) south of Cancún.*

The Maya name means "place of the turtle," and for hundreds of years this beach has been a nesting ground for turtles (the season is June–August and the best place to see them is on Half Moon Bay). The place first attracted international attention in 1926, when explorers discovered the *Mantanceros,* a Spanish galleon that sank in 1741. In 1958, Pablo Bush Romero, a wealthy businessman who loved diving these pristine waters, created the first resort, which became the headquarters for the club he formed—the Mexican Underwater Expeditions Club (CEDAM). Akumal soon became a gathering spot for wealthy underwater adventurers who flew in on private planes and searched the waters for sunken treasures, some of which you can see at the Museo CEDAM in Puerto Aventuras.

These days Akumal, where little Spanish is heard and the 4th of July is a bigger holiday than Mexican Independence Day, is probably the most Americanized community on the coast. Hotels, private homes, and condos line the streets, which can become very crowded. Akumal doesn't have a center but consists of three distinct areas: Half Moon Bay, with some pretty beaches, the best snorkeling around, and the greatest concentration of rentals; Akumal proper, a large resort with a market, grocery stores, laundry facilities, and a pharmacy; and, farther up across the highway, the original Maya community. The large community of ex-patriots and repeat visitors is really the heart and soul of Akumal. They are responsible for starting up some important ecological movements along the Quintana Roo coast, such as recycling, animal rescue, and reef protection. Be sure to visit the **Ecological Center,** on the main road, which offers programs like turtle watching.

Akumal is famous for its underwater scenery. The reef, which is about 425 ft offshore, shelters the bay and its exceptional coral formations and sunken galleon; the sandy bottom allows snorkelers to wade out at the rocky north end, where they can view the diverse underwater topography. Fishing for giant marlin, bonito, and sailfish is also popular.

Area dive shops sponsor resort courses and certification courses, and luxury hotels and condominiums have year-round packages that cover accommodations and diving. Hotel rooms are at a premium during the high season, mid-December–April, when reservations should be made well in advance.

Devoted snorkelers may want to walk to **Yalkú,** a couple of miles north of Akumal in Half Moon Bay, along an unmarked dirt road. A series of small lagoons that gradually reach the ocean, Yalkú is home to schools of parrot fish in superbly clear water with visibility to 160 ft. It's now an eco-park, which means it has a toilet, a small parking lot, and an entrance fee of about $6.

Dining and Lodging

$–$$ ✕ **Que Onda.** A Swiss Italian couple created this northern Italian restaurant at the end of Half Moon Bay. Served under a charming open-air palapa, dishes include great homemade pastas, shrimp flambéed in cognac with a touch of saffron, and vegetarian lasagna made with spinach. Que Onda also has an intimate six-room hotel next to the restaurant, which is creatively furnished with native Mexican and Guatemalan handicrafts. ✉ *Caleta Yalkú lots 97–99, enter through Club Akumal Caribe and turn left, or go north to very end of road at Half Moon Bay,* ☎ *984/875–9101. MC, V. Closed Tues.*

$ ✕ **Restaurante Oscar y Lalo.** A couple of miles outside of Akumal, at Bahías de Punta Soliman, is this wonderful restaurant run by a local Maya couple. The seafood is excellent and the pizza divine. If you're inspired to sleep on the beach, campgrounds and RV hookups are available. ✉ *Hwy. 307 north of Akumal (look for faded white sign),* ☎ *no phone. No credit cards.*

$ ✕ **Turtle Bay Café & Bakery.** This funky café offers delicious (and healthful) breakfasts and lunches. The real specialties are great smoothies and fresh baked goods. It has a pretty garden to sit and drink coffee in, and its location by the Ecological Center makes it the closest thing to a downtown Akumal has. ✉ *Plaza Ukana I, Loc. 15 (beginning of Half Moon Bay road),* ☎ *no phone. No credit cards. No dinner.*

$$$$ ▦ **Club Akumal Caribe & Villas Maya.** This beachfront resort was founded
★ by Pablo Bush Romero in the 1960s to host his diving buddies and still offers congenial accommodations and staff. Rooms have rattan furniture; large, comfortable beds; lovely tile work; and ocean views. The quaint but rustic bungalows are surrounded by a tropical garden and have lots of beautiful Mexican tile. More secluded options are the one-, two-, and three-bedroom condominiums called Villas Flamingo, on Half Moon Bay, with kitchenettes and a separate beach and pools. Dive and meal-plan packages available. ✉ *Hwy. 307, Km 104,* ☎ *984/875–9012; 800/ 351–1622 in the U.S. and Canada; 800/343–1440 in Canada;* ▨ *www.hotelakumalcaribe.com. 21 rooms, 40 bungalows, 4 villas, 1 condo. Restaurant, some kitchenettes, pool, beach, 2 dive shops, bar, children's programs (ages 5–14), baby-sitting; no room phones. AE, MC, V.*

$$$$ ▦ **Club Oasis Akumal.** One of the all-inclusive pioneers, this hotel remains intimate, sophisticated, and understated, with gorgeous mahogany railings, doors, furniture, and floors amid tropical plants and flowers. Rooms are spacious, with terraces, king-size beds, and sitting areas. The bathrooms are exceptional: sunken tile showers with Moorish arches and windows with beach views. The food is good, and the beach is a beacon for water-sports activities. ✉ *South of Akumal off Hwy. 307,* ☎ *984/875–7300,* 𝔽𝔸𝕏 *984/875–7302,* ▨ *www.oasishotels. com.mx. 182 rooms. 2 restaurants, cable TV, tennis court, 4 pools, beach, dive shop, bicycles, snorkeling, 2 bars, baby-sitting, laundry service, car rental, travel services. AE, MC, V.*

$$$ ▦ **Vista Del Mar.** Each smallish room has an ocean view, king-size bed, small refrigerator, and colorful decor with Guatemalan-Mexican accents. Next door are more expensive condos with Spanish colonial decor. The spacious one-, two-, and three-bedroom units have full kitchens, living and dining rooms, and oceanfront balconies. They are a great bargain off-season. ✉ *South end of Half Moon Bay,* ☎ *984/875– 9060; 877/425–8625 in the U.S.,* ▨ *www.akumalinfo.com. 15 rooms, 8 condos. Restaurant, grocery, cable TV with movies, some kitchenettes, pool, beach, dive shop; no air-conditioning in some rooms. AE, MC, V.*

Outdoor Activities and Sports

SCUBA DIVING

Akumal Dive Center (⊠ about 10 mins north of Club Akumal Caribe, ☎ 984/875–9025) is the oldest and most experienced dive operation, offering reef or cenote diving, fishing, and snorkeling.

En Route **Aktun-Chen** is Maya for "the cave with cenote inside." These amazing underground caves, estimated to be about 5 million years old, are the largest in the area. You walk through the underground passages, past stalactites and stalagmites, until you reach the underground cenote with its various shades of deep green. You don't want to miss this one. ⊠ *Hwy. 307 between Akumal and Xel-Há, Km 107,* ☎ *984/884–0444,* WEB *www.aktunchen.com.* ✎ *$7 (including 1-hr tour).* ☉ *Daily 8:30–4.*

Xcacel

⑪ *7 km (4½ mi) south of Akumal.*

Xcacel is a symbol of what has gone wrong along the coast. It's one of the few remaining nesting grounds for the endangered Atlantic green and loggerhead turtles. For years it was a federally protected zone, until it was sold—illegally—in 1998 to a Spanish conglomerate. The group immediately tried to push through an elaborate development plan that would have destroyed the nesting grounds. This prompted Greenpeace, in cooperation with biologists, scientists, and other locals, to fight an international campaign, which they won, to save the turtles. You can visit the turtle center or offer to volunteer. The Friends of Xcacel Web site (www.turtles.org/xcacel.htm) has more information.

Xel-Há

⑫ *3 km (2 mi) south of Laguna de Xcacel.*

Brought to you by the people who manage Xcaret, Xel-Há (pronounced shel-*hah*) is a natural aquarium made from coves, inlets, and lagoons cut out of the limestone shoreline. The name means "where the water is born," and the river here forms a natural spring that flows out to meet the saltwater, creating a perfect habitat for tropical marine life. Scattered throughout the park are small Maya ruins, including **Na Balaam,** known for a yellow jaguar painted on one of its walls. Low wooden bridges over the lagoons allow for leisurely walks around the park, and there are spots to rest or swim. While there seem to be fewer and fewer fish each year, and the mixture of fresh- and saltwater can cloud visibility, there is still enough here to impress novice snorkelers.

The place gets overwhelmingly crowded, so come early, before the tour buses. The grounds are well equipped with bathrooms, restaurants, and a shop. At the entrance you will receive specially prepared sunscreen that won't kill the fish; other sunscreens are prohibited. For an extra charge, you can "interact" (not swim) with dolphins. ☎ *984/875–4070 or 984/875–4071.* ✎ *$25.* ☉ *Daily 8–8.*

If you're sick of tour buses, head across the road to the compact, little-visited **Xel-Há Archaeological Site.** Its squat structures are thought to have been inhabited from the Late Preclassic until the Late Postclassic period. The most interesting sights are on the north end of the ruins, where remains of a Maya *sacbé* (road) and mural paintings in the **Jaguar House** sit near a tranquil, deep cenote. The site takes about 45 minutes to visit. ☎ *No phone.* ✎ *$3, free Sun.* ☉ *Daily 8–5.*

Tankah

⑬   *9½ km (6 mi) south of Xel-Há on the dirt road off Hwy. 307.*

In ancient Maya times, Tankah, located between Xel-Há and Tulum, was a more important trading city than Tulum. Many centuries later, it evolved into a beach without too much development. Since electricity was brought in in 2001, all this has changed. The growing number of very small hotels offers rooms and cabanas at reasonable prices. None of them have phones in the rooms.

Dining and Lodging

$ ✕🏠 **Casa Cenote.** Mostly known as a restaurant (and still the only place to eat on the beach), Casa Cenote stands beside a large fresh- and salt-water cenote full of tropical fish. You can go for a snorkeling trip and then rest in the shade while you wait for your meal. The simple menu includes burgers, chicken, fish, beer, and margaritas. On Sunday, folks can lunch on an all-you-can-eat Texas barbecue for $12, including coleslaw and beans. Diners can now lodge here ($$$$), in seven rooms with attractive equipal furniture (leather furniture originally from the state of Jalisco) and small patios facing the beach. The rate includes breakfast and dinner. ⊠ *Turn left at end of dirt road from Hwy. 307 into Tankah (look for Casa Cenote sign),* ☎ *998/874–5170,* WEB *www.casacenote.com. 7 rooms. Restaurant, beach, dive shop, snorkeling; no air-conditioning. MC, V.*

$$$ 🏠 **Blue Sky.** The prettiest lodge on Tankah, this small, luxury boutique hotel offers suites with one-of-a-kind pieces like Cuban oil paintings, hand-made Guatemalan bedspreads, handblown vases, silver inlaid mirrors, and hand-tooled chairs made from native chichén wood. A few suites have fold-out sofas for sleeping more people. The open-air dining room is swept of mosquitoes by a special carbon dioxide machine developed by the U.S. military. A tropical breakfast is included in the rate. ⊠ *Bahía Tankah, past Casa Cenote,* ☎ *998/801–4004,* FAX *984/873–5225,* WEB *www.blueskymexico.com. 6 suites. Restaurant, no air-conditioning, Internet access, beach, snorkeling, library, shop. No credit cards.*

$$$ 🏠 **Tankah Dive Inn.** A friendly East Texas family runs this guest house on a windswept stretch of beach. There is great diving off the shore, so the inn is geared toward and popular with divers. Rooms are large and bright, comfortable though not luxurious. The view from the up-stairs restaurant–living room is spectacular. The casual kitchen turns out great meals on request or lets the guests cook. The rate includes Continental breakfast; other meals are extra. Family members offer cave diving and teach scuba certification courses. ⊠ *Bahía Tankah 16,* ☎ *998/874–2188,* WEB *ww.tankahdiveinn.com. 5 rooms. Restaurant, beach, dive shop; no air-conditioning. No credit cards.*

Tulum

♦ ⑭   *2 km (1 mi) south of Tankah, 130 km (81 mi) south of Cancún.*

One of the Caribbean coast's biggest attractions, Tulum is the Yucatán Peninsula's most-visited Maya ruin, attracting more than 2 million people annually. Unfortunately, this means you have to share the site with roughly half of the tourist population of Quintana Roo on any given day, even if you arrive early. Though most of the architecture here is of unremarkable Postclassic (AD 900–1541) style, the amount of attention that Tulum receives is not entirely undeserved. Its location by the blue-green waters of the Caribbean is indeed breathtaking.

The Tulum parking lot, just off the highway, has separate areas for cars ($1) and buses. There's an enormous cement slab building filled with burger joints and tacky shops selling junky souvenirs manned by aggressive salespeople. An electric shuttle car hustles visitors from the parking lot to the temples ($1 each way); otherwise it's a ½-km (¼-mi) walk. Another small open market selling souvenirs is at the shuttle stop.

At the entrance to the ruins you can hire a guide, but keep in mind that some of their information is more entertaining than historically accurate. (Disregard that stuff about virgin sacrifices atop the altars.) Because you are not allowed to climb or enter the fragile structures—only three really merit close inspection anyway—you can take in the ruins in two hours. You might, however, want to allow extra time for a swim or a stroll on the beach, where ancient Maya beached their canoes.

Tulum is one of the few Maya cities known to have been inhabited when the conquistadors arrived in 1518. In the 16th century, Tulum functioned as a safe harbor for trade goods from rival Maya factions; it was considered neutral territory where merchandise could be stored and traded in peace. The city reached its height when traders, made wealthy through the exchange of goods, for the first time outranked Maya priests in authority and power. When the Spaniards arrived, they forbade the Maya traders to sail the seas, and commerce among the Maya died.

Tulum's pre-Columbian name, Zama, from the word *zamul* (dawn), suggests "city of the dawn"; Tulum means "wall." When the Spaniards arrived, Juan de Grijalva and his men, who spotted Zama from their ships, were so intimidated by the enormity of its vivid 25-ft-high blue, white, and red walls that they were reluctant to land. What they had seen was four towns so close to one another that they appeared to be one continuous metropolis.

Tulum has long held special significance for the Maya. A key city in the League of Mayapán (AD 987–1194), it was never conquered by the Spaniards, although it was abandoned about 75 years after the Conquest. For 300 years thereafter, it symbolized the defiance of an otherwise subjugated people; it was one of the last outposts of the Maya during their insurrection against Mexican rule in the War of the Castes, which began in 1846. Uprisings continued intermittently until 1935, when the Maya ceded Tulum to the government.

The Postclassic architecture at Tulum reflects strong Toltec influences, the result of contact by Maya traders with Tula, seat of the Toltec government in central Mexico. Although artistic refinements found elsewhere in the Maya world are missing here, the site is well preserved. Frederick Catherwood sketched its magnificent ruins during his 1842 explorations with John L. Stephens. Those sketches eventually illustrated a book by Stephens, *Incidents of Travel in Central America, Chiapas and Yucatan,* which became the archaeological bible of its time.

You enter the archaeological site through a low limestone gateway in a crumbling wall. Low-lying structures dot the site's 60-acre grassy field, wrapped on three sides by a 3,600-ft-long wall, formerly a double wall. The first significant structure is the two-story **Temple of the Frescoes,** to the left of the entryway. The temple's vault roof and corbel arch are examples of Classic Maya architecture. Faint traces of blue-green frescoes outlined in black on the inner and outer walls refer to ancient Maya beliefs (the clearest frescoes are hidden from sight now that you can't walk into the temple). Reminiscent of the Mixtec style, the frescoes depict the three worlds of the Maya and their major deities and are decorated with stellar and serpentine patterns, rosettes, and ears of maize and other offerings to the gods. One scene portrays the rain god seated on a four-legged animal—probably a reference to the Spaniards on their horses.

124

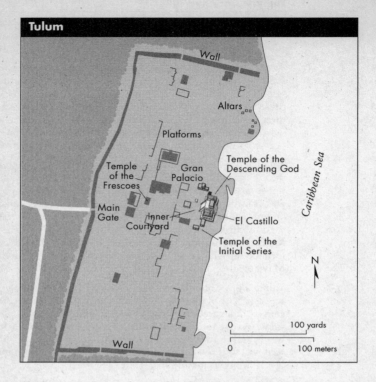

Tulum

The largest and most famous building, the **Castillo** (castle), looms at the edge of a 40-ft limestone cliff just past the Temple of the Frescoes. Atop the castle, at the end of a broad stairway, sits a temple with stucco ornamentation on the outside and traces of fine frescoes inside the two chambers. (The stairway has been roped off, so the top temple is inaccessible.) The front wall of the Castillo has faint carvings of the Descending God and columns depicting the plumed serpent god, Kukulcán, who was introduced to the Maya by the Toltecs. The regal structure overlooks the rest of Tulum and an expanse of dense jungle to the west; the blue Caribbean blocks access from the east.

To the left of the Castillo is the **Temple of the Descending God**—so called for the carving of a winged god plummeting to earth over the doorway. The same deity is seen in stucco masks in the corners and is thought either to be Ab Muzen Cab, the bee god, or to be associated with the planet Venus, guardian of the coast and of commerce.

The other buildings at the site typically have flat roofs resting on wood beams and columns with few distinguishing features. Buildings were laid out along straight streets running the length of the site with a slight dip, or culvert, between two gentle slopes. The tiny cove to the left of the Castillo and Temple of the Descending God is a good spot for a cooling swim, but there are no changing rooms. A few small altars sit atop a hill at the north side of the cove and have a good view of the Castillo and the sea. It's believed that they were lit by torches to serve as lighthouses for canoes being beached at night. ▧ *$8, free Sun.; use of video camera extra.* ⊙ *Daily 8–5.*

At the old turnoff on Highway 307 to the ruins, which is called the *crucero,* is a Pemex gas station. A few feet south is the current entrance to the ruins, clearly marked with overhead signs. Still farther south is a turnoff for the road leading to the coast and eventually the Sian Ka'an reserve. The majority of hotels, cabañas, campgrounds, beaches, and restaurants are along this route.

Back on the highway about 4 km (2½ mi) south of the ruins is the present-day village of Tulum. As Tulum's importance as a commercial center increases, markets, restaurants, shops, services, and auto-repair shops continue to spring up along the road. Growth has not been kind to the pueblo, however, and it has become rather unsightly, with a wide four-lane highway running down the middle. Despite this blight, its restaurants offer good food, especially vegetarian dishes.

Dining and Lodging

Tulum's official Web page for hotels and cabanas is www.hotelstulum.com.

$$$$ ✕🏠 **Las Ranitas.** Both stylish and ecologically correct, Las Ranitas ("the
★   little frogs") creates its own power through wind-generated electricity, solar energy, and recycled water. Each chic room is decorated with gorgeous tile and fabric from Oaxaca. Terraces overlook the gardens and ocean, and jungle walkways lead down to the breathtaking beach. The pièce de résistance is the French chef, who creates incredible food that matches the hotel's magic (in the $$ price range). ✉ *Carretera Tulum–Boca Paila, Km 9 (last hotel before Sian Ka'an Biosphere Reserve),* ☎ FAX *984/877–8554,* WEB *www.lasranitas.com. 17 rooms. Restaurant, tennis court, pool, pool, beach, snorkeling. No credit cards. Closed mid-Sept.–mid-Nov.*

$$$ ✕🏠 **Zamas.** Set on the wild and isolated Punta de Piedra (Rock Point), with ocean views as far as the eye can see, this spectacular, kick-back-and-groove hotel draws a lot of the U.S. business-suit crowd. The romantically rustic cabanas—with bare-bulb lighting, mosquito nets over the spartan beds, big tile bathrooms, and gay Mexican colors—and are nicely distanced from one another, offering privacy and space. The restaurant ($–$$) is one of the best on the coast, with an eclectic Italian-Mexican-Yucatecan menu and fresh fish that comes from the first catch of the day. ✉ *Carretera Tulum–Boca Paila, Km 5,* ☎ *984/ 871–2067; 415/387–9806 in the U.S.;* WEB *www.zamas.com. 15 cabañas. Restaurant, beach, bar; no air-conditioning, no room phones. No credit cards.*

$$ ✕🏠 **Don Armando Cabañas.** Come here to get primitive. Accommodations are your basic Maya hut made out of cut wood with screened windows, cement floors, double beds, and hammock; guests use a communal bathhouse. The beach location makes it all worthwhile. You won't find anything cheaper in the area. ✉ *Carretera Tulum–Boca Paila, Km 0.47,* ☎ *984/871–2417. 46 rooms. Beach; no air-conditioning, no room phones. No credit cards.*

$$$ 🏠 **Cabañas La Conchita.** This bed-and-breakfast has simple cabanas done in all natural woods, with exposed beams and wooden windows and floors. The comfortable bathrooms have plenty of hot water. All cabanas are on the water's edge. hidden in a lovely inlet. The full tropical breakfast is the perfect complement to roughing it mildly on the beach. ✉ *Carretera Tulum–Boca Paila, Km 4.5,* ☎ *984/871–2092,* WEB *www.different world.com. 8 rooms. Restaurant, beach, bicycles; no air-conditioning, no room phones. No credit cards.*

Cobá

⛰ ⑮ *49 km (30 mi) northwest of Tulum, 167 km (104 mi) southwest of Cancún.*

Cobá, Maya for "water stirred by the wind," flourished from AD 800 to AD 1100, with a population of as many as 55,000. Now it stands in solitude, with the jungle having taken many of its buildings. Cobá exudes a certain stillness, the silence broken by the occasional shriek of a spider monkey or the call of a bird. Processions of huge army ants cross the footpaths as the sun slips through openings between the tall hardwood trees, ferns, and giant palms.

Situated on five lakes between coastal watchtowers and inland cities, Cobá exercised economic control over the region through a network of at least 16 *sacbéob* (white stone roads), one of which measures 100 km (62 mi) and is the longest in the Maya world. The city once covered 70 square km (27 square mi), making it a noteworthy sister state to Tikal in northern Guatemala, with which it had close cultural and commercial ties. It is noted for its massive temple-pyramids, one of which is 138 ft tall, the largest and highest in northern Yucatán.

Archaeologists estimate that some 6,500 structures are present in the Cobá area, but only 5% have been uncovered, and it will take decades before the work is completed. Discovered by Teobert Maler in 1891, Cobá was subsequently explored in 1926 by the Carnegie Institute but not excavated until 1974, by the National Geographic Society.

The main groupings of ruins are separated by several miles of dense tropical vegetation, so the best way to get a sense of the immensity of the city is to scale one of the pyramids. It's easy to get lost here, so stay on the main road and don't be tempted by the narrow paths that lead into the jungle unless you have a qualified guide with you.

The first major cluster of structures, off the main path to your right as you enter the ruins, is the **Cobá Group,** whose pyramids are built around a sunken patio. At the near end of the group, facing a large plaza, is the 79-ft-high Iglesia (church), where some Maya people still place offerings and light candles in hopes of improving their harvests. Around the rear to the left is a newly restored ball court, where a sacred ball game was once played to petition the gods for rain, fertility, and other boons. According to ancient beliefs, the playing field represented the sky and the ball was the sun.

Farther along the main path to your left is the **Chumuc Mul Group,** little of which has been excavated. The principal pyramid here is covered with the remains of vibrantly painted stucco motifs (*chumuc mul* means "stucco pyramid").

A kilometer (½ mile) past this site is the **Nohoch Mul Group** (Large Hill Group), the highlight of which is the pyramid of the same name, the tallest at Cobá. The pyramid, which has 120 steps—equivalent to 12 stories—shares a plaza with **Temple 10.** The Descending God (also seen at Tulum) is depicted on a facade of the temple atop Nohoch Mul, from which the view is excellent. The temple seems to have been erected much later than the pyramid itself. It was from the base of this pyramid that the longest sacbé started. It extended all the way to Yaxuná, 20 km (12 mi) southwest of Chichén Itzá. Because of their great width (up to 33 ft), there is considerable speculation about the function of the sacbéob. The Maya had no beasts of burden, so they carried all cargo on their own backs. Thus the roads may have been designed to allow people to walk abreast in processions, suggesting that they played a role in religion as well as in trade. The roads' white limestone may have helped illuminate them for travelers at night. The unrestored **Crossroad Pyramid,** opposite Nohoch Mul, was where three sacbéob met.

Beyond the Nohoch Mul Group is the **Castillo,** with nine chambers that are reached by a stairway. To the south are the remains of a ball court, including the stone ring through which the ball was hurled. From the main route follow the sign to **Las Pinturas Group,** named for the still-discernible polychrome friezes on the inner and outer walls of its large, patioed pyramid. An enormous stela here depicts a man standing with his feet on two prone captives. Take the minor path for 1 km (½ mi) to the **Macanxoc Group,** not far from the lake of the same name. The main pyramid at Macanxoc is accessible by a stairway. The portal of the temple at its summit is divided by a column; there is also a molded lintel and the remains of a stucco painting. Many of the stelae here are intricately carved with dates and other symbols of the history of Cobá.

If you're keen to see more buildings, venture farther to the small **Kukulcán Group,** one of the larger satellites of Cobá, 5½ km (3½ mi) south of the Cobá group. Only five structures remain, and they are among the more puzzling ruins in the Maya world; their design and use have yet to be explained by archaeologists. The three-story temple is particularly intriguing because it is the only Maya structure in which the top story does not rest on filled-in lower stories.

Cobá is a 35-minute drive northwest of Tulum along a pothole-filled road that leads straight through the jungle. A number of freshwater cenotes along the way are worth stopping at for a swim. Don't even think of swimming at any of the lakes around Cobá—unless you want to become dinner for a member of the area's large and hungry crocodile population. Maps and books about the ruins are sold at the makeshift restaurants and shops that line the parking lot. None of the maps are particularly accurate. Several men with guide licenses congregate by the entrance and offer their services, most charging about $30 for a half-day tour. Bring plenty of bug repellent and water. You can buy sodas and snacks at the entrance. You can rent a bicycle at Cobá. It's a bumpy ride but still a fun way to check out the ruins.

You can comfortably make your way around Cobá in a half day, but spending the night in town is highly advised, as doing so will allow you to visit the ruins in solitude when they open at 8 AM. Even on a day trip, consider taking time out for lunch to escape the intense heat and mosquito-heavy humidity of the ruins. Buses depart from Cobá for Playa del Carmen and Tulum at least twice daily. Taxis to Tulum are still reasonable (about $14). ⊠ *$4, free Sun.; use of video camera $6.* ☉ *Daily 8–5.*

Lodging

$$ ⊞ **El Bocadito.** The warmth of the family who owns and operates this hotel makes up for the lack of luxury. Each of the extremely basic rooms has two double beds, a ceiling fan, toilet, and, if you are lucky, hot water. The ruins are a 10-minute walk away. Rooms fill up quickly—if you're thinking of spending the night, stop here before visiting the ruins. The restaurant next door serves simple but tasty meals. ⊠ *On road to ruins,* ☎ *988/874–2087. 10 rooms. No air-conditioning, no room phones. AE, V.*

$$ ⊞ **Uolis Nah.** This small thatch-roof complex has extra-large, quiet rooms with kitchenettes and basics such as high ceilings, two beds, fans, and tile floors. You're less than a mile from the Tulum highway but away from the noise. An extra person in a double room costs $11 more. ⊠ *Km 2 on road to Cobá,* ☎ *984/879–5013. 6 rooms. Fans, kitchenettes; no air-conditioning, no room phones. No credit cards.*

Pac Chen

⛰ ⑯ *20 km (13 mi) southeast of Cobá.*

Pac Chen can be visited only with Alltournative, an eco-tour company based in Playa (☎ 984/873–2036, 𝖶𝖤𝖡 www.alltournative.com). The unusual soft-adventure experience is definitely worth your while. Pac

Chen is a Maya jungle settlement of 125 people who still live in traditional rounded thatch huts; have no electricity, paved roads, indoor plumbing, or televisions; and still pray to the gods for good crops. The inhabitants make their living farming pineapple, beans, and plantains—and, of course, welcoming tourists. Alltournative pays them by the number of tourists it brings in, though no more than 80 are allowed per day. The money from the tours has made the village self-sustaining and has given them an alternative to logging and hunting, which were their main means of livelihood before.

The half-day tour starts with a trek through the jungle to a cenote where people grab on to a harness and Z-line to cross to the other side. Next is the Jaguar cenote, set deeper into the forest, where visitors rappel down the cavelike sides into a cool underground lagoon. Lunch is taken under an open-air palapa overlooking another lagoon, where canoes wait to be boarded after the meal. The food includes typical Maya dishes like *achiote* (annatto seed) chicken prepared over a wood-fed grill, fresh tortillas, beans, and watermelon.

Sian Ka'an Biosphere Reserve

⑰ *15 km (9 mi) south of Tulum to the Punta Allen turnoff, located within Sian Ka'an; 137 km (85 mi) south of Cancún.*

Sian Ka'an ("where the sky is born") was first settled by the Maya in the 5th century AD. In 1986 the Mexican government established the 1.3-million-acre **Sian Ka'an Biosphere Reserve** as an internationally protected area. The next year, it was named a World Heritage Site by the United Nations Educational, Scientific, and Cultural Organization (UNESCO); later, it was extended by 200,000 acres. The Riviera Maya and Costa Maya split the Biosphere Reserve; Punta Allen and north belong to the Riviera Maya, while everything south of Punta Allen is part of the Costa Maya.

Sian Ka'an participates in the UNESCO program "Man and the Biosphere," whose mandate is to maintain and preserve the ecological diversity in biologically rich areas while educating the locals to do likewise. Such reserves are particularly important in developing countries, where encroaching on dwindling resources is the only way large segments of the population know how to survive.

Under the program the land is divided for various purposes, including research, preservation, and economic activities in conjunction with conservation. Assisted by scientists, the local population in Sian Ka'an makes a living through fishing, lobster harvesting, and small farming and receives support from low-impact tourism, biological research, and sustainable development programs.

The Sian Ka'an reserve constitutes 10% of the land in Quintana Roo and covers 100 km (62 mi) of coast. Freshwater and coastal lagoons, mangrove swamps, watery cays, savannas, tropical forests, a barrier reef, hundreds of species of local and migratory birds, fish, other animals and plants, and fewer than 1,000 local residents (primarily Maya) share this area. There are approximately 27 ruins (none excavated) linked by a unique canal system—one of the few of its kind in the Maya world in Mexico. This is one of the last undeveloped stretches of coastline in North America.

Many species of the once-flourishing wildlife have fallen into the endangered category, but the waters here still teem with rooster fish, bonefish, mojarra, snapper, shad, permit, sea bass, and crocodiles. Fishing the flats for wily bonefish is especially popular, and the peninsula's few lodges also run deep-sea fishing trips. The beaches are wide and white, and although many of the palms have succumbed to the yellowing palm disease imported from Florida, the vegetation is growing back.

In order to see the sites you must take a guided tour offered by one of the private, nonprofit organizations, such as **Amigos de Sian Ka'an** (✉ Crepúsculo 18, at Amanecer, Sm 44, Mz 13, Cancún, Quintana Roo 77506, ☎ 998/848–1618, 998/848–2136, or 998/880–6024, FAX 998/887–3080). The four-hour boat tour includes bird-watching, a visit to the Maya ruins of Xlapak (where you can jump into one of the channels and float downstream), and a tour of the mangroves. Tour groups depart from Cabañas Ana y José in Tulum every Wednesday and Saturday morning; the fee includes a bilingual guide and binoculars.

To explore on your own, follow the road past Boca Paila to the secluded 35-km (22-mi) coastal strip of land that is part of the reserve. You'll be limited to swimming, snorkeling, and camping on the beaches, as there are no trails into the surrounding jungle. The narrow, extremely rough dirt road down the peninsula is filled with monstrous potholes and after a rainfall is completely impassable. Don't attempt it unless you have four-wheel drive. Most fishing lodges along the way close for the rainy season in August and September, and accommodations are hard to come by. The road ends at Punta Allen, a fishing village whose main catch is spiny lobster, which was becoming scarce until ecologists taught the local fishing cooperative how to build and lay special traps to conserve the species. There are several small, expensive guest houses. If you haven't booked ahead, start out early in the morning so you can get back to civilization before dark.

Lodging

$$$$
★ ✕▥ **Boca Paila Fishing Lodge.** Home of the "grand slam" (fishing lingo for catching three different kinds of fish at once), this charming lodge has nine spacious cottages, each with two double beds, couches, large bathrooms, and screened-in sitting areas. Boats and guides for fly-fishing and bonefishing are provided; tackle is for rent at the lodge. Meals, included in the room rate, are excellent, ranging from fresh fish to Maya specialties. During the high season, a 50% prepayment is required and the minimum stay is one week (three nights the rest of the year). ✉ *Boca Paila Peninsula (reservations: Frontiers, Box 959, Wexford, PA 15090, ☎ 724/935–1577 or 800/245–1950). 9 cottages. Restaurant, beach, snorkeling, fishing, bar, laundry service, airport shuttle; no air-conditioning in some rooms, no room phones. No credit cards unless arranged with Frontiers.*

$$$$
★ ✕▥ **Casa Blanca Lodge.** This American-managed, all-inclusive lodge is set on a rocky outcrop on remote Punta Pájaros island—reputed to be one of the best places in the world for light-tackle saltwater fishing. Ten large, modern guest rooms have tile and mahogany bathrooms and provide a pleasant tropical respite at dusk. An open-air thatch-roof bar welcomes anglers with drinks, fresh fish dishes, fruit, and vegetables at the start and end of the day. Only weeklong packages can be booked March–June. Rates include charter flight from Cancún, all meals, a boat, and a guide; nonfishing packages are cheaper. ✉ *Punta Pájaros (reservations: Frontiers, Box 959, Wexford, PA 15090, ☎ 724/935–1577; 800/245–1950 for Frontiers; ☎ 800/533–7299 for Outdoor Travel). 10 rooms. Restaurant, bar; no air-conditioning, no room phones. MC, V.*

Muyil

❽ *24 km (15 mi) south of Tulum on Hwy. 307.*

This photogenic archaeological site at the northern end of the Sian Ka'an Biosphere is definitely underrated. Once known as Chunyaxché, it is now called by its ancient name, Muyil. Dating from the Late Preclassic era (300 BC–AD 200), it was connected by road to the sea and served as a port between Cobá and the Maya centers in Belize and Guatemala. A 15-ft-wide sacbé, built during the Late Postclassic period (AD 1200–1541), extended from the city to the mangrove swamp and was still in use when the Spaniards arrived.

Structures were erected at 400-ft intervals along the white limestone road, almost all of them facing west, but there are only three still standing. At the beginning of the 20th century, the ancient stones were used to build a chicle (gum arabic) plantation, which was managed by one of the leaders of the War of the Castes. The most notable site at Muyil today is the remains of the 56-ft **El Castillo**—one of the tallest on the Quintana Roo coast—at the center of a large acropolis. During excavations of the Castillo, jade figurines representing the moon goddess Ixchel were found. Recent excavations at Muyil have uncovered some smaller structures, but these excavations were halted by the death of the archaeologist in charge.

The ruins stand near the edge of a deep-blue lagoon and are surrounded by nearly impenetrable jungle—bring bug repellent. You can drive down a dirt road on the side of the ruins to swim or fish in the lagoon. The bird-watching is also exceptional here. ✉ *$3, free Sun.* ☉ *Daily 8–5.*

THE COSTA MAYA

The coastal area south of Punta Allen is more purely Maya than the tourist stretch between Cancún and Punta Allen. Here, seaside fishing collectives and close-knit communities carry on ancient traditions while the close proximity to Belize lends a Caribbean flavor, particularly in Chetumal, where you'll hear both Spanish and the local Caribbean patois. The Costa Maya also encompasses the southern part of the Sian Ka'an Biosphere.

Felipe Carrillo Puerto

⑲ *99 km (61 mi) south of Tulum.*

Formerly known as Chan Santa Cruz, Felipe Carrillo Puerto—the Costa Maya's first major town—is named after the man who became governor of Yucatán in 1920. He was hailed as a local hero after instituting a series of reforms to help the impoverished *campesinos* (farmers or peasants). Assassinated by the alleged henchman of the presidential candidate of an opposing party in 1923, he remained a popular figure long after his death.

The town was a political, military, and religious asylum during the 1846 War of the Castes; rebels fled here after being defeated at Mérida. It was also in this town that the famous cult of the Talking Cross took hold. The Talking Cross was a sacred symbol of the Maya; it was believed that a holy voice emanated from it, offering guidance and instruction. In this case the cross appeared emblazoned on the trunk of a cedar tree, and the voice urged the Indians to keep fighting. (The voice was actually an Indian priest and ventriloquist, Manual Nahuat, prompted by the Maya rebel José Maria Barrera.) Symbolic crosses were subsequently placed in neighboring villages, including Tulum, inspiring the Maya. They continued fighting until 1915, when the Mexican army finally gave up. The Cruzob Indians ruled Quintana Roo as an independent state, much to the embarrassment of the Mexican government, until 1935, when the Cruzob handed Tulum over and agreed to Mexican rule.

Felipe Carrillo remains very much a Maya city, with even a few old-timers who cling to the belief that one day the Maya will once again rule the region. It exists primarily as the hub of three highways, and the only vestige of the momentous events of the 19th century is the small, uncompleted temple—on the edge of town in an inconspicuous, poorly marked park—begun by the Indians in the 1860s and now a monument to the War of the Castes. The church where the Talking Cross was originally housed also stands. Several humble hotels, some good restaurants, and a gas station may be incentives for stopping here on your southbound trek.

Dining and Lodging

$ ✕ ⊞ **El Faisán y El Venado.** The price is right at this clean and comfortable hotel. The restaurant does a brisk business with the locals because it is centrally located and has good Yucatecan specialties such as *poc chuc* (pork marinated in sour-orange sauce), *bistec a la yucateca* (Yucatecan-style steak), and *pollo pibíl* (chicken baked in banana leaves). ⊠ *Av. Benito Juárez 781,* ☎ *983/834–0702 hotel; 983/834–0043 restaurant. 35 rooms. Restaurant, cable TV; no air-conditioning. No credit cards.*

Majahual

20 *71 km (44 mi) southeast of Felipe Carrillo Puerto on Hwy. 307 to the Majahual exit south of Limones; turn left and continue 56 km (35 mi).*

The road to Majahual is long, but once here you have a chance to see one of the last authentic fishing villages on the coast. It's very laid-back, with simple, inexpensive accommodations and lots of small restaurants serving fresh fish. Activities include lounging, fishing, snorkeling, and diving. With the airport already built but lying abandoned in a northern field, and a new cruise dock and shopping plaza, this village is slated to become the next Cozumel. Come and enjoy it while it remains a simple and quaint village—a dying breed along this coast.

Lodging

$$$ ⊞ **Maya Ha Resort.** This modern resort rising disconcertingly out of the jungle is a glimpse of things to come in Majahual. The property's architecture is based on the Maya sites of Chichén-Itzá and Kabah. In the restaurant-pool area is a giant pyramid decorated with reproductions of stelae found at famous ruins; it offers a spectacular view. The 16 suites have double beds, refrigerators, and color TV. There's a state-of-the-art dive shop, and the resort offers special dive packages. Rates are per couple for a weeklong stay. ⊠ *Follow dirt road from Majahual village about 10 km (6 mi),* ☎ 🆏 *983/831–0065;* ☎ *800/346–6116 in the U.S.;* 🆆 *www.mayaharesort.com. 16 suites. Restaurant, refrigerators, pool, dive shop, boating, bar, airport shuttle. AE, MC, V.*

$–$$ ⊞ **Las Cabañas del Doctor.** Each of these basic but quaint cabañas along the beach has a double bed; bathrooms are private or shared. There's electricity until 10 PM and fishing just outside the door. The hotel can arrange for a boat and captain but you must bring your own gear. ⊠ *Av. Majahual 6, between Calles 2 and 4 Sur,* ☎ 🆏 *983/832–2102. 7 cabanas. Restaurant, beach; no air-conditioning, no room phones. No credit cards.*

Xcalak

21 *Hwy. 307 to the Majahual exit south of Limones; turn left, go 56 km (35 mi) to the checkpoint, and turn south (left) onto the highway for 60 km (37 mi).*

It's quite a journey to get to Xcalak, but it's worth the effort. This peninsula is a combination of savannas, marsh, streams, and lagoons dotted with islands that act as a refuge for local wildlife. It's lush with tropical flowers, birds, and butterflies and has fabulously deserted beaches. Xcalak is on the tip of the peninsula that divides Chetumal Bay from the Caribbean. There are no tourist amenities and the hotels along the peninsula cater mostly to rugged types who come to bird-watch on **Bird Island** or to dive at **Banco Chinchorro,** a 42-km (26-mi) coral atoll and national park some two hours northeast by boat.

Dining and Lodging

$$$ ✕🏨 **Costa de Cocos.** For the ultimate in privacy, relaxation, and gor-
 ★   geous scenery, you can't beat Costa de Cocos, 2 km (1 mi) from Xcalak. Twelve cabanas with double beds and private bathrooms offer 24-hour wind-powered electricity. The proprietor, Dave Randall, is immensely knowledgeable about the peninsula and the reef offshore and can help you plan special fly-fishing trips along the coast, sea-kayak outings, or bird-watching excursions to Bird Island. Rates include two meals. Reserve well in advance. ✉ *Xcalak Peninsula, follow Hwy. 307 to sign for Mahuahual, turn right at road to Xcalak,* ☎ *983/831–0110,* WEB *www.costadecocos.com. 14 cabanas. Restaurant, beach, dive shop, snorkeling, boating; no air-conditioning, no room phones. No credit cards.*

$$$–$$$$ 🏨 **Playa Sonrisa.** This American-owned property, formerly called Villa Caracol, offers little beachfront bungalows, ocean-view cabanas, or veranda rooms, all bright and clean and decorated with dried-flower arrangements, single beds, and flowered curtains. You can snorkel off the dock, and fishing trips can be arranged. The room rate includes a Continental breakfast. ✉ *Xcalak Peninsula, 54 km (33 mi) south of Majahual, 5 km (3 mi) past Costa de Cocos,* ☎ FAX *983/838–1872,* WEB *www.playasonrisa.com. 2 rooms, 2 cabanas, 2 bungalows. Beach, dock; no air-conditioning in some rooms, no room phones. MC, V.*

$$–$$$ 🏨 **Sin Duda.** Margo and Robert offer five luscious rooms, one stylish studio, and two apartments on a lovely, wild stretch of beach. Smaller rooms come with single or double beds, trundle beds, and plenty of closet space. Guests share a fully equipped kitchen and a dining and balcony area. For more privacy, opt for Studio 6, a self-contained studio in a separate building, or Suite 7 or 8, with their own kitchens and living rooms. All have been decorated with collectibles such as Mexican pottery and furniture created by Robert. ✉ *Xcalak Peninsula, 54 km (33 mi) south of Majahual, 15 km (10 mi) past Costa de Cocos (reservations: 34 North Ferndale, Mill Valley, CA 85712),* ☎ FAX *983/ 831–0006,* ☎ *415/380–9031 in the U.S.,* WEB *www.sindudavillas.com. 5 rooms, 1 studio, 2 apartments. Some kitchens, beach, snorkeling, fishing; no air-conditioning, no room phones. No credit cards.*

Bacalar

 ㉒   *112 km (69 mi) south of Felipe Carrillo Puerto, 320 km (198 mi) south of Cancún, 40 km (25 mi) northwest of Chetumal.*

Founded in AD 435, Bacalar is one of the oldest settlements in Quintana Roo. Of some historical interest is the **Fuerte de San Felipe** (San Felipe Fort), an 18th-century stone fort built by the Spaniards, using stones from the nearby Maya pyramids, as a haven against marauding pirates and Indians. It was later reclaimed by the Maya for use during the War of the Castes. The monolithic structure is right on the plaza and overlooks the lake. These days it houses government offices and a museum with exhibits on local history (ask for someone to bring a key if museum doors are locked). ☎ *No phone.* 🎟 *$2.* ⊙ *Tues.–Sun. 10–6.*

The spectacularly vast **Laguna de Bacalar,** also known as the Lake of the Seven Colors, is the second-largest lake in Mexico (56 km [35 mi] long) and is frequented by scuba divers and other lovers of water sports. Seawater and freshwater mix in the lake, intensifying the aquamarine hues, and the water contrasts starkly with the green jungle. Drive along the lake's southern shores to enter the affluent section of the town of Bacalar, with elegant waterfront homes. Also in the vicinity are a few hotels and campgrounds.

Just beyond Bacalar is the largest sinkhole in Mexico, **Cenote Azul,** 607 ft in diameter, with clear blue waters that afford unusual visibility even at 200 ft below the surface. With lush vegetation all around and underwater caves, the cenote (open daily 8–8) attracts divers who specialize in this somewhat tricky type of dive. At **Restaurant Cenote Azul** you can linger over fresh fish and a beer while gazing out over the deep blue waters or enjoy a swim off its docks. A giant all-inclusive resort that opened in 2001 may be the harbinger of more to come, disturbing the tranquillity of this area.

Dining and Lodging

$$$$ ✕🏨 **Rancho Encantado.** On the shores of Laguna Bacalar, 30 minutes north of Chetumal, the Rancho comprises 12 Maya-theme *casitas* (cottages), each with Oaxacan furnishings, a patio and hammock, a refrigerator, a sitting area, and a bathroom. Breakfast and dinner are included in the room rate (no red meat is served). You can swim and snorkel off the private dock leading into the lagoon, and excellent tours to the ruins in southern Yucatán, Campeche, and Belize are available. Pick a room close to the lagoon or you will hear trucks zooming by at night. ✉ *South on Hwy. 307, look for sign (reservations: Box 1256, Taos, NM 87571,* FAX *505/751–0972 in the U.S.),* ☎ *983/831–0037; 800/505–6292 in the U.S.;* WEB *www.ranchoencantado.com. 12 casitas. Restaurant, refrigerators, hot tub, massage, bar, laundry service, travel services; no air-conditioning, no room phones. MC, V.*

$$$ 🏨 **Laguna.** Outside Bacalar and before the final military checkpoint, ★ this brightly colored and eclectically designed hotel has the feel of a summer lodge. The small cabins are staggered on a hill overlooking the lagoon. A garden path leads down to a lovely dock-restaurant area where you can swim or use the canoes. The rooms are simple, clean, and comfortably equipped with overhead fans, and the staff is hospitable. ✉ *Hwy. 307, Km 40,* ☎ FAX *983/834–2206. 15 cabins. Restaurant; no air-conditioning, no room phones. No credit cards.*

Chetumal

㉓ *58 km (36 mi) south of Bacalar, 382 km (237 mi) south of Cancún.*

Chetumal is the final-stop town on the Costa Maya. Originally called Payo Obis, it was founded by the Mexican government in 1898 in a partially successful attempt to gain control of the lucrative trade of precious hardwoods, arms, and ammunition and as a military base against the rebellious Indians. The city, which overlooks the Bay of Chetumal at the mouth of the Río Hondo, was devastated by a hurricane in 1955 and rebuilt as the capital of Quintana Roo and the state's major port. Though Chetumal remains the state capital, it attracts few visitors other than those en route to Central America or those traveling to the city on government business.

At times, Chetumal feels more Caribbean than Mexican; this is not surprising, given its proximity to Belize. The mixed population includes some black Caribbeans and Middle Eastern immigrants, resulting in an eclectic blend of music (reggae, salsa, calypso) and cuisines (Yucatecan, Mexican, and Lebanese). Although Chetumal's provisions are modest, the town has a number of parks along a pleasant, extended waterfront—the Bay of Chetumal surrounds the city on three sides. There is an excellent museum and a gorgeous university.

Paseo Bahía is the main thoroughfare and runs along the water for several miles. A walkway runs parallel to this road and is a popular gathering spot at night. If you follow the road it turns into the Chetumal–Calderitas highway and after 16 km (10½ mi) leads to the ruins of **Oxtankah.** Archaeologists believe this may be the city where the Chaktemal Kingdom was started by Gonzalo Guerrero, father of the Mestizo race (later known as Mexicans). It's open daily 8–5; admission is $4, except Sunday, when it's free.

Downtown Chetumal has been spruced up to attract tourists. Mid-range hotels and tourist-friendly restaurants have been popping up along Boulevard Bahía and on nearby Avenida Héroes. Tours are run to the fascinating nearby ruins of Kohunlich, Dzibanché, and Kinichná, a trio dubbed the "Valley of the Masks."

The sure standout in Chetumal is the **Museo de la Cultura Maya,** a sophisticated, interactive museum dedicated to the complex world of the Maya. Exhibits explain Maya social classes, politics, and customs; Maya architecture; their use of plants for medicinal and domestic purposes; and the Maya calendar. The most impressive display is the three-story Sacred Ceiba Tree. The Maya use this symbol to explain the relationship between the cosmos and earth. The first floor represents the roots of the tree where the Maya underworld, Xibalba, reigns. The middle floor is the tree trunk, known as Earth, or Middle World, home to humans and all their trappings. The top floor is the leaves and branches and the 13 heavens of the cosmic Otherworld. It's a fascinating introduction to the Maya world. ⊠ *Av. Héroes and Calle Mahatma Gandhi,* ☎ *983/832–6838.* ⊡ *$3.* ☉ *Tues.–Thurs. 9–7, Fri. and Sat. 9–8, Sun. 9–2.*

Dining and Lodging

Restaurants come and go quickly in Chetumal, but you can always find simple neighborhood eateries offering tacos, enchiladas, and other Mexican specialties.

$–$$ ✕ **Sergio's Pizzas.** Locals rave about this pizzeria's grilled steaks, barbecued chicken (made with the owner's own sauce), and garlic shrimp, along with smoked-oyster and seafood pizzas. (Pasta is not the thing to order here.) ⊠ *Av. Alvaro Obregón 182, at Av. 5 de Mayo,* ☎ *983/832–0882. MC, V.*

$ ✕ **Expresso Cafe.** At this bright, modern café, you get an appealing view of the huge, placid Bay of Chetumal. Choose from more than 15 kinds of coffee as well as fresh salads, sandwiches, and chicken dishes. ⊠ *Blvd. Bahía 12,* ☎ *983/832–2654. No credit cards.*

$$$ ⊞ **Holiday Inn Puerta Maya.** This may be a small Holiday Inn, but it's working hard to provide luxury accommodations in Chetumal. The lobby resembles a nicely decorated living room with rattan furniture. Room also have rattan furniture, as well as soft sunset colors and small terraces. A tropical garden with Maya sculptures surrounds the moderate-size pool. The hotel location, directly across from the museum, is a bonus. ⊠ *Av. Héroes 171, Col. Centro,* ☎ *983/835–0400,* FAX *983/832–1676. 108 rooms, 7 suites. Restaurant, pool, bar, travel services, no-smoking rooms. MC, V.*

$$ ⊞ **Los Cocos.** The lush, jungle-theme decor of this hotel's outdoor restaurant and lobby ends when you enter the rooms. However, the rooms are comfortable, with air-conditioning, in-room phones, and TVs, and there is a pleasant garden area with a large swimming pool. The waterfront is within easy walking distance; the restaurant is popular with both locals and travelers. ⊠ *Av. Héroes 134, at Calle Chapulte-pec,* ☎ *983/832–0544,* ℻ *983/832–0920. 80 rooms. Restaurant, cable TV, pool, bar, shop, meeting room, car rental. AE, MC, V.*

$$ 🖭 **Hotel Marlon.** This clean, comfortable hotel decorated in pastel colors is one of the best deals in town. It offers plenty of hot water, air-conditioning, a nice outdoor pool, a great little restaurant, and a small but sweet piano bar. The staff exemplifies traditional Mexican hospitality. ⊠ *Av. Juárez 87,* ☎ *983/832–9411 or 983/832–9522,* ☎ ℻ *983/832–6555. 36 rooms. Restaurant, pool, meeting room, car rental, travel services. AE, MC, V.*

THE RÍO BEC ROUTE

The area known as the Río Bec Route enjoyed little attention for years, but the Mexican government opened it up by building a highway, pre-serving previously excavated sites, and uncovering more ruins. Visit-ing here has no less of a decidedly pioneer feel, however, because of the rustic conditions and continuing discoveries taking place.

Río Bec is one of the principle Maya architectural styles, recognizable by the stone roof combs that stand atop temples like latticework. Río Bec doorways were often carved like open mouths, and steep pyramids have narrow staircases leading up to cone-shape tops. The Río Bec Route con-tinues beyond Quintana Roo's **Valley of the Masks** into Campeche. Xpu-jil, the first major site in Campeche, is 115 km (72 mi) west of Chetumal.

Hotels and restaurants in the area are scarce, so it's best to make Chetumal your base for exploring.

Kohunlich

⛰ ㉔ *42 km (26 mi) west of Chetumal on Rte. 186, 75 km (47 mi) east of Xpujil.*

Kohunlich is renowned for the giant stucco masks on its principal pyra-mid, the **Edificio de los Mascarones** (Mask Building). It also has one of the oldest ball courts in Quintana Roo, and the remains of a great drainage system at the **Plaza de las Estelas** (Plaza of the Stelae). The masks—about 6 ft tall—are set vertically into the wide staircases at the main pyramid, called **Edificio de las Estelas** (Building of the Ste-lae). First thought to represent the Maya sun god, they are now con-sidered to be composites of the rulers of Kohunlich. Another giant mask was discovered in 2001 in the building's upper staircase. Archaeolo-gists believe that Kohunlich was built and occupied during the Early and Late Classic periods by various Maya groups, which accounts for the different styles of architecture. It is thought that there are at least 500 mounds on the site waiting to be explored. Excavations have turned up 29 individual and multiple burial sites inside a residence build-ing called **Temple de Los Viente-Siete Escalones** (Temple of the Twenty-Seven Steps). This site does not have a great deal of tourist traffic, so there is thriving flora and fauna. ☎ *No phone.* 🎟 *$3.* ☼ *Daily 8–5.*

Lodging

$$$$ ✕🖭 **Explorean Kohunlich.** Amid the remains of the Kohunlich ceremo-nial grounds, this all-inclusive, adults-only ecological resort offers ad-venture without giving up amenities. Daily excursions include trips to nearby ruins, lagoons, and forests for kayaking, rock climbing, and hik-ing. You return in the evening to luxurious quarters decorated in natu-ral textiles, wood, and rattan. Showers open onto a small backyard garden. The outdoor pool and hot tub have views of the ruins in the distance. ⊠ *Chetumal–Escarega Hwy., Km 5.65 (same road as the ruins),* ☎ *55/*

5201–8350; 877/397–5672 in the U.S.; WEB *www.theexplorean.com. 38 suites. Restaurant, pool, bicycles, bar, meeting room; no room phones, no kids. No credit cards.*

Dzibanché and Kinichná

⚡ ㉕ *1 km (½ mi) east of turnoff for Kohunlich on Rte. 186; follow signs for 24 km (15 mi) north to fork for Dzibanché (1½ km [1 mi] from fork) and Kinichná (3 km [2 mi] from fork).*

Sister cities Dzibanché and Kinichná are thought to have been the most powerful alliance ruling southern Quintana Roo during the Maya Classic period (AD 300–AD 900). The fertile farmlands surrounding the ruins are still used today as they were hundreds of years ago, and the winding drive deep into the fields makes you feel like you're coming upon something undiscovered.

Despite the absence of visitors, the few ruins that have been excavated in the area are well restored and very accessible. At Dzibanché ("place where they write on wood"), several carved wooden lintels have been discovered; the most perfectly preserved sample can be found in a supporting arch at the **Plaza of Xibalba.** Also at the plaza is the **Temple of the Owl,** where a recessed tomb was found atop the temple, the second discovery of its kind in Mexico (the first was at Palenque in Chiapas). In the tomb were magnificent clay vessels painted with white owls—messengers of the underworld gods. Two more buildings have been restored as excavation continues. Several other plazas are surrounded by temples, palaces, and pyramids, all in the Río Bec style. The carved stone steps at **Edificio 13** and **Edificio 2** still bear traces of stone masks. The famed lintel of **Temple IV,** with eight glyphs dating to AD 618, is housed in the Museo de la Cultura Maya in Chetumal. ☎ *No phone.* 🎟 *$4.* ☉ *Daily 8–5.*

After you see Dzibanché, make your way back to the fork in the road and head to **Kinichná** ("house of the sun"). The site consists of a two-level pyramidal mound split into Acropolis B and Acropolis C, apparently dedicated to the sun god. Two mounds at the foot of the pyramid suggest that the temple was a ceremonial site. Here a giant Olmec-style jade figure was found. At its summit, Kinichná affords one of the finest views of any archaeological site in the area. ☎ *No phone.* 🎟 *$4.* ☉ *Daily 8–5.*

THE CARIBBEAN COAST A TO Z

To research prices, get advice from other travelers, and book travel arrangements, visit www.fodors.com.

AIR TRAVEL

Almost everyone who arrives by air into this region flies into Cancún. In Chetumal, however, there is an airport on the southwestern edge of town, along Avenida Alvaro Obregón where it turns into Route 186. In Playa del Carmen, there's an air strip across from Plaza Antigua.

➤ AIRPORT INFORMATION: **Chetumal airport** (⊠ Rte. 186, Chetumal, ☎ 983/832–0664).

BOAT AND FERRY TRAVEL

Passenger-only ferries and two large speedboats depart from the dock at Playa del Carmen for the 45-minute trip to the main pier in Cozumel. They leave approximately every hour on the hour 5 AM–11 PM, with no ferries at noon, 2, 8, or 10. Return service to Playa runs every hour on the hour 4 AM–10 PM, with no ferries at 5, 11 AM, 1, 7, or 9 PM. Call ahead, as the schedule changes often.

➤ BOAT AND FERRY INFORMATION: **Playa del Carmen passenger ferry** (☎ 984/872–1508, 984/872–0588, or 984/872–0477).

BUS TRAVEL

The bus station in Chetumal (Avenida Salvador Novo 179) is served by ADO, Caribe Express, and other lines. Buses run regularly from Chetumal to Cancún, Villahermosa, Mexico City, Mérida, Campeche City, and Veracruz, as well as Guatemala and Belize.

Playa del Carmen has two bus stops. Buses arriving from south of Playa and continuing north to Cancún drop people off at the terminal on the highway. All other buses leave from downtown. All the major bus lines run express, first-class, and second-class buses to major destination points. Service to Cancún is every 10–20 minutes, and buses to Chetumal leave twice daily. It's always best to check the times at the main bus terminal (Avenida Juárez at Avenida 5). The scheduled times change frequently.

➤ BUS INFORMATION: **ADO** (☎ 984/832–9877). **Caribe Express** (☎ 984/832–7889).

CAR RENTAL

Most first-class hotels in Puerto Aventuras, Akumal, and Chetumal also rent cars. In Puerto Morelos you are better off renting from Cancún, as there aren't many bargains in town. In Playa del Carmen, it's best to stick with the bigger rental agencies: Hertz, Budget, and Thrifty. If you want air-conditioning or automatic transmission, reserve your car at least one day in advance.

➤ MAJOR AGENCIES: **Budget** (✉ Continental Plaza, Playa del Carmen, ☎ 984/873–0100). **Hertz** (✉ Plaza Marina, Loc. 40, Playa del Carmen, ☎ 984/873–0702). **Thrifty** (✉ Calle 8 between Avs. 5 and 10, Playa del Carmen, ☎ 984/873–0119).

CAR TRAVEL

The entire coast from Punta Sam near Cancún to the main border crossing to Belize at Chetumal is traversable on Highway 307. This straight road is entirely paved and has been widened into four lanes south to Xcaret. Drive with caution—there are lots of speed demons on this highway. Puerto Morelos, Playa del Carmen, Tulum, and Felipe Carrillo Puerto have gas stations. Beyond this point, there are no gas stations per se, but small stores sell gas in Bacalar and Xcalak.

Highway 307, also known as Route 186, parallels the coastline for the 382 km (237 mi) between Cancún and Chetumal. Although buses do travel regularly along the coast and are suitable for day trips, a rental car or four-wheel-drive vehicle allows you to explore more thoroughly and creatively.

Good roads that run into Highway 307 from the west are Route 180 (from Mérida and Valladolid), Route 295 (from Valladolid), Route 184 (from central Yucatán), and Route 186 (from Villahermosa and, via Route 261, from Mérida and Campeche). There is an entrance to the *autopista* toll highway between Cancún and Mérida off Highway 307 just south of Cancún. Approximate driving times are as follows: Cancún to Felipe Carrillo Puerto, 4 hours; Cancún to Mérida, 4½ hours (3½ hours on the *autopista* toll road, $27); Carrillo Puerto to Chetumal, 2 hours; Carrillo Puerto to Mérida, about 4½ hours; Chetumal to Campeche, 6½ hours.

The road from Cancún to Xcaret is a well-lit, four-lane highway with traffic lights but it is often filled with seemingly crazed drivers commuting between Cancún and Playa del Carmen. Defensive driving is a must. Past Xcaret, the road converts to a two-lane coastal highway with reflectors but no lights. Nonetheless, most drivers continue to travel at breakneck speeds until Tulum. Past Tulum, things slow down and the road is in good shape, although it's deserted at night and exceptionally dark. Follow proper road etiquette—vehicles in front of you that have their left turn signal on are saying "pass me," not "I'm going to turn."

If you drive south of Tulum, keep an eye out for military and immigration checkpoints. Have your passport handy, be friendly and cooperative, and don't carry any items, such as firearms or drugs, that might land you in jail.

ECOTOURISM

You can visit the ruins of Cobá and the Maya village of Pac-Chen, located deep in the jungle, with Alltournative Expeditions. The group offers a variety of other ecotours as well. ATV Explorer offers two-hour rides through the jungle on all-terrain vehicles; explore caves, see ruins, and snorkel in a cenote. Tours start at $38.50.

➤ CONTACTS: **Alltournative Expeditions** (⊠ Av. 10 No. 1, Plaza Antigua, Playa del Carmen, ☎ 984/873–2036, WEB www.alltournative.com). **ATV Explorer** (⊠ Hwy. 307, 1 km [½ mi] north of Xcaret, ☎ 984/ 873–1626).

E-MAIL

Many of the more remote places on the Caribbean coast rely on e-mail and the Internet as their major forms of communication. In Playa del Carmen, Internet service is cheap and readily available. The best places charge $3 per half hour and include Cyberia Internet Café and Atomic Internet Café. In Tulum, try the Internet Club.

➤ SERVICES: **Atomic Internet Café** (⊠ Av. 5 at Calle 8, Playa del Carmen). **Cyberia Internet Café** (⊠ Calle 4 at Av. 15, Playa del Carmen). **Internet Club** (⊠ Av. Ote. 89, Tulum).

EMERGENCIES

In Puerto Morelos, there are two drugstores in town on either side of the gas station on Highway 307.

In Playa del Carmen, there's a pharmacy at the Plaza Marina shopping mall; several others are on Avenida 5 between Calles 4 and 8. There are two pharmacies on Avenida Juárez between Avenidas 20 and 25.

➤ CHETUMAL: **Chetumal Hospital General** (⊠ Av. Andres Quintana Roo, ☎ 983/832–1932). **Farmacia Social Mechaca** (⊠ Av. Independencia 134-C, ☎ 983/832–0044). **Police** (⊠ Av. Insurgentes and Av. Belice, ☎ 983/832–1500). **Red Cross** (⊠ Av. Héroes 279, ☎ 983/832–0571).

➤ PLAYA DEL CARMEN: **Centro de Salud** (⊠ Av. Juárez at Av. 15, ☎ 984/ 872–1230 ext. 147). **Police** (⊠ Av. Juárez between Avs. 15 and 20, ☎ 984/873–0291). **Red Cross** (⊠ Av. Juárez at Av. 25, ☎ 984/873– 1233).

LODGING

The Internet is a great tool for finding rentals. Akumal has a good Web presence, and with a bit of surfing you can find some bargains. For information about Akumal condo rentals try www.akumal-villas.com or www.lascasitas.com.

Puerto Aventuras has a large community of condo owners who rent out their properties. Caribbean Realty has price lists and availability information.

Mary Lowers of Mayansites Bookings can help you arrange house and apartment rentals in other areas along the coast.

➤ CONTACTS: **Caribbean Realty** (Sally Wood Evans; ⊠ Centro Comercial Marina, Puerto Aventuras, ☎ 984/873–5098, FAX 984/873–5158,

WEB www.caribbean-realty.com). **Mayansites Bookings** (☎ 877/620–8715 in the U.S., WEB www.mayansites.com).

MAIL AND SHIPPING

The Chetumal post office is open weekdays 8–7 and Saturday 8–noon. The Playa del Carmen post office is open weekdays 8–7.
➤ POST OFFICES: **Chetumal** (✉ Calle Plutarco Elias 2, ☎ 983/832–2578). **Playa del Carmen** (✉ Av. Juárez, next to the police station, ☎ 983/873–0300).

MONEY MATTERS

Local banks in Playa del Carmen include Bital, Bancomer, Banamex, Inverlat, and Bancrecer. In Chetumal, Bital and Bancomer offer banking services, including currency exchange.
➤ BANKS: **Banamex** (✉ Av. Juárez between Avs. 20 and 25, Playa del Carmen, ☎ 984/873–0825). **Bancomer** (✉ Av. Juárez between Calles 25 and 30, Playa del Carmen, ☎ 984/873–0356; ✉ Av. Alvaro Obregón 222, at Av. Juárez, Chetumal, ☎ 983/832–5300). **Bancrecer** (✉ Av. 5 by the bus station, Playa del Carmen, ☎ 984/873–1561). **Bital** (✉ Av. Juárez between Avs. 10 and 15, Playa del Carmen, ☎ 984/873–0272; ✉ Av. 30 between Avs. 4 and 6, Playa del Carmen, ☎ 984/873–0238; ✉ Av. Héroes 37, Chetumal, ☎ 984/832–2776). **Scotiabank Inverlat** (✉ Av. 5 between Av. Juárez and Av. 2, Playa del Carmen, ☎ 984/873–1488).

TELEPHONES

In Chetumal the government-run telephone office, TELMEX, is at Avenida Juárez and Calle Lázaro Cárdenas. For long-distance and international calls, you might also try the booths on Avenida Héroes: one is on the corner of Ignacio Zaragoza, and the other is just opposite Avenida Efraín Aguilar, next to the tourist information booth.

You can find TELMEX phones that use phone cards in every town up and down the coast (buy the cards in gift shops and grocery stores). There are several long-distance calling stations in Playa del Carmen on Avenida 5 as well as in front of the post office on Avenida Juárez and at the corner of Avenidas Juárez and 5. Luxury hotels charge $1 a minute for calls made from your room, so many visitors buy phone cards and use phones outside their hotels.

Note that area codes for telephone numbers throughout Mexico were changed in November 2001, although the process is expected to take several years to complete. In many Caribbean coast towns, changes have been made, and area codes are three digits, with seven digit telephone numbers. Note that some older printed material might not reflect the changes. The area code for Playa del Carmen is 984; for Puerto Morelos it is 998.

TOURS

Although some guided tours are available in this area, the roads are quite good for the most part, so renting a car is an efficient and enjoyable alternative. Most of the sights you see along this stretch are natural, and you can hire a guide at the ruins. If you would like someone else to do the planning and driving for you, contact Maya Sites Travel Services, which offers inexpensive tours and the chance to create your own travel itinerary.

AIR TOURS

From Playa del Carmen, AeroFerinco has daily flights to Cancún, Chetumal, Belize, Tikal, Veracruz, and Villahermosa.

MAYA RUINS

Based in Playa del Carmen, Tierra Maya Tours runs trips to the ruins of Chichén Itzá, Uxmal, Palenque, and Tikal. It can also help you with transfers, tickets, and hotel reservations. Many first-class hotels in Playa del Carmen and Puerto Aventuras can arrange day tours to Tulum, Chichén Itzá, and Cobá.

In Chetumal, Turistica Maya de Quintana Roo offers tours to Kohunlich, Dzibanché, the Laguna de Bacalar, and Fuerte de San Felipe.

➤ TOUR-OPERATOR RECOMMENDATIONS: **AeroFerinco** (☎ 983/873–0636, WEB www.aeroferinco.com). **Maya Sites Travel Services** (☎ 719/256–5186; 877/620–8715 in the U.S.; WEB www.mayasites.com). **Tierra Maya Tours** (✉ Av. 5 at Calle 6, Playa del Carmen, ☎ 984/873–1385, FAX 984/873–1386). **Turistica Maya de Quintana Roo** (✉ Av. Héroes 165-A, Chetumal, ☎ 983/832–0555, FAX 983/832–9711).

TRANSPORTATION AROUND THE CARIBBEAN COAST

You can hire taxis in Cancún to go as far as Playa del Carmen, Tulum, or Akumal, but the price is steep unless you have many passengers. Fares run about $65 or more to Playa alone; between Playa and Tulum or Akumal, expect to pay at least another $25. It's much cheaper from Playa to Cancún, with taxi fare running about $30; negotiate before you hop into the cab. Getting a taxi along Highway 307 can take a while. Ask your hotel to call one for you.

TRAVEL AGENCIES

There are more major travel agencies and tour operators along the coast than ever, and first-class hotels in Playa del Carmen, Puerto Aventuras, and Akumal usually have their own in-house travel services.

➤ LOCAL AGENT REFERRALS: **Alltournative Expeditions** (✉ Av. 10 No. 1, Plaza Antigua, Playa del Carmen, ☎ 984/873–2036). **IMC** (✉ Plaza Antigua, Playa del Carmen, ☎ 984/873–1439, FAX 984/873–1439, WEB www.imcplay.com). **Turistica Maya de Quintana Roo** (✉ Holiday Inn Puerta Maya, Chetumal, ☎ 984/832–0555 or 983/832–2058, FAX 984/832–9711).

VISITOR INFORMATION

The Tourist Information Booth in Chetumal is open weekdays 8:30–2:30 and 6–9. In Playa del Carmen it's open Monday–Saturday 8 AM–9 PM.

➤ TOURIST INFORMATION: **Chetumal** (✉ Av. Héroes opposite Av. Efraín Aguilar, ☎ 983/832–3663). **Playa del Carmen** (✉ Av. Juárez by the police station, ☎ 983/873–2804).

6 MÉRIDA AND THE STATE OF YUCATÁN

Ancient Maya ruins—the spectacular Chichén Itzá and Uxmal foremost among more than a dozen sites—have long been the main appeal of the State of Yucatán. But the less-traveled city of Mérida, with its superb restaurants, markets, cultural offerings, and unique mix of Spanish and French architectural styles, is also well worth exploring. The peninsula's north coast is the kind of often-ignored place that allows you to discover your own Mexico, along with flocks of flamingos at the Celestún and Río Lagartos estuaries.

Updated by
Jane Onstott

C ULTURALLY, the Yucatán is one of the richest parts of Mexico. It is the heart of a fascinating juxtaposition of two powerful civilizations—that of the Maya and that of transplanted Europeans. Vestiges of the past are evident in this land of oval thatch-roof huts and stately old mission churches, and in its people—particularly the women who still dress in traditional garb. Mysterious "lost cities" lie hidden in the forests. Small fishing villages dot beaches that are so far unjaded by the tourist industry. In the midst of this exotic landscape stands the elegant city of Mérida, for centuries the main stronghold of Spanish colonialism in the land of the Maya.

There is a marvelous eccentricity about Mérida. Fully urban, with maddeningly slow-moving traffic, it has a friendly, self-contented air that would suggest a small town more than a state capital. Unfortunately, many colonial buildings were lost to reckless "renovation" in the 20th century, and the city, although sprawling, is hardly imposing. Tucked among the newer and less-beautiful facades, however, are some grandiose colonial structures adorned with iron grillwork, carved wooden doors, and archways concealing lush gardens that hark back to the city's heyday as the wealthiest capital in Mexico.

Mérida is a city of obvious contrasts, from its varied facades to its residents, who—although increasingly aware and proud of Maya accomplishments—a century ago looked to Europe for their cultural identity. The Maya Indian presence is unmistakable: people are short, with square faces and almond eyes, and many women wear *huipiles* (hand-embroidered, tuniclike white dresses). Craftspeople and vendors from the outlying villages come to town in their huaraches (woven leather sandals) and hats woven from the supple *jipi* fibers. The Maya—long portrayed (falsely) as docile and peace-loving—provided the Spaniards and the mainland Mexicans with one of their greatest challenges. Nearly five hundred years after the Spanish conquest, the Maya are Mexico's largest indigenous population, and many remain in the Yucatán, the land of their ancestors. To this day the Maya in the most remote or isolated villages may speak no Spanish, or just enough to get by.

Yucatán tried to secede from the rest of Mexico in the 1840s and, as late as the 1920s and 1930s, rebellious pockets of Maya communities held out against the *dzulobs* (outsiders). Yucatecans speak of themselves as *peninsulares* first, Mexicans second. Don't be surprised to see locals wearing T-shirts that say, "Republic of Yucatán." It could well have been this independent attitude that induced Governor Salvador Alvarado, in 1915, to convene the first feminist congress in the country (and Latin America as well) here, with the idea of liberating women "from being social wards and from the traditions that have suppressed them for years." This congress, which Alvarado described as "brilliant," was so successful that it was followed by the second congress in Mexico City in 1921, when women asked for the right to vote. They were finally granted that right in 1953.

One of the world's great ancient cultures, Maya civilization thrived for about 1,500 years, although it was in a state of decline when the conquistadors arrived in AD 1527. To discourage resistance to Catholic conversion and virtual slavery, the invaders burned defiant Maya warriors at the stake and drowned and hanged local women. Huge agricultural estates brought riches to the Spaniards, and Mérida soon became a strategic administrative and military center, the gateway to Cuba and to Spain. Francisco de Montejo's conquest of Yucatán took three gruesome wars, a total of 24 years. "Nowhere in all America was resistance to

Spanish conquest more obstinate or more nearly successful," wrote the historian Henry Parkes. By the 18th century, huge maize and cattle plantations flourished throughout the peninsula, and the wealthy *hacendados* (plantation owners), left largely to their own devices by the viceroys in faraway Mexico City, accumulated fortunes under a flagrantly feudal system. The social structure—based on Indian peonage—barely changed as the economic base shifted to the export of dyewood; henequen, or sisal, a natural fiber used to make rope; and chicle, or gum arabic, a chewing-gum staple.

Insurrection came during the War of the Castes in the mid-1800s, when the enslaved indigenous people rose up with long-repressed furor and massacred thousands of whites. The United States, Cuba, and Mexico City finally came to the aid of the ruling elite, and between 1846 and 1850 the Indian population of Yucatán was effectively halved. Those Maya who did not escape into the remote jungles of neighboring Quintana Roo or Chiapas or get sold into slavery in Cuba found themselves, if possible, worse off than before under the dictatorship of Porfirio Díaz. During his regime, thousands of Yaquis and other natives of northern Mexico were snatched from their homes and sent to the peninsula to work as slave labor for the hacendados. The fruits of their labor can be seen today in the pretentious French-style mansions that stretch along Mérida's Paseo Montejo.

Yucatán was then and still is a largely agricultural state, although the economic importance of tourism and the *maquiladoras* (assembly plants or factories, usually foreign-owned) has grown steadily in the last quarter century. These factories cut and assemble goods for such U.S. brand names as Gap and Liz Claiborne. More than 65 maquiladoras employ more than 25,000 workers (up from 6,200 in 1995) around Mérida, and additional plants are expected to open.

With some 725,000 inhabitants, the capital accounts for more than a third of the state's population, but many still live in villages, maintaining conservative traditions and lifestyles. Apart from the goods produced by the maquiladoras for overseas markets, the state also exports honey, textiles, henequen, orange-juice concentrate, fresh fish, hammocks, and wood products.

Physically, too, Yucatán differs from the rest of the country. Its geography and wildlife have more in common with Florida and Cuba—with which it was probably once connected—than with the central Mexican plateau and mountains. A flat limestone slab possessing no significant rivers or lakes, it is rife with cenotes (sinkholes) both above the ground and below, caves with stalactites, and thick (but short and relatively dry) jungle. Wild ginger and spider lilies grow in profusion. Vast flamingo colonies nest at estuaries on the northern and western coasts, where undeveloped sandy beaches extend some 370 km (230 mi). Deer, turkeys, boars, ocelots, tapirs, and armadillos once flourished in this tropical climate (the average temperature is 82°F, or 28°C)—they now survive in a few protected areas.

But it is, of course, the celebrated Maya ruins—including Chichén Itzá, Uxmal, and a spate of smaller sites—that bring most people to the State of Yucatán. Indeed, the Puuc hills south of Mérida have more archaeological sites per square mile than any other place in the hemisphere. Most of the roads in this region are paved and two-lane, and the government is accelerating the pace at which it is fixing up the rest. Local travel agencies are adept at running tours.

Pleasures and Pastimes

Beaches

Yucatán's beaches are no match for those of Cancún and the Caribbean. That said, the north coast of the peninsula has long stretches of wide, soft white-sand beaches—shared mainly by local children, fishermen, and the odd sunbather. Progreso, where Mérida residents go to beat the heat, is unpretentious and affordable, and on summer weekends it can be nearly as lively as the Mexican Caribbean. Empty beaches stretch for about 64 km (40 mi) to the east, punctuated by small fishing villages that are catching the eye of developers as tourism very slowly takes off. Independent travelers, bird-watchers, and nature lovers head for the more remote and less service-oriented beaches of Celestún, Sisal, and Telchac Puerto.

Bird-Watching

More than 500 bird species have been sighted in the Yucatán, both along the coast and inland. The most famous are the flamingos, which can be seen in the natural parks at Celestún and Río Lagartos at any time of year. The largest flocks of both flamingos and birding enthusiasts can be found during the spring months, when thousands of the birds— 90% of the entire flamingo population of the Western Hemisphere— come to Río Lagartos to nest.

Dining

Dining out is a pleasure in Mérida. The city's 50-odd restaurants dish out a superb variety of cuisines—primarily Yucatecan, of course, but also Lebanese, Italian, French, Chinese, and Mexican—at very reasonable prices. And tony cafés have been sprouting up in atmospheric colonial edifices that lend a European air to casual dining. Generally, reservations are advised for $$$ restaurants, but only in high season. Casual but neat dress is acceptable at all Mérida restaurants. Avoid wearing shorts in the more expensive places.

Beach towns north of Mérida such as Progreso, Sisal, and Telchac Puerto, as well as Río Lagartos to the east and Celestún to the west, serve fresh-caught seafood, although the dishes are prepared quite simply. A real gourmet dish is the blue crab at Celestún. However, you can't go wrong with most restaurants, whether they are thatch-roof affairs along the beach or in-town eateries.

If you enjoy eating with local people, stop at one of the many *loncherías* (diners) in the small towns and downtown districts of cities for *panuchos* (small, thick tortillas stuffed with beans and topped with shredded meat or fish), empanadas (turnovers filled with meat, fish, potatoes, or, occasionally, beans), tacos, or *salbutes* (fried tortillas smothered with diced turkey, pickled onion, and sliced avocado). However, take care with the habañero chilies, which can have smoke coming out of your ears even when eaten in moderation.

All restaurants are open for breakfast, lunch, and dinner unless otherwise noted.

CATEGORY	COST*
$$$$	over $15
$$$	$11–$15
$$	$6–$10
$	under $6

*per person, for a main course at dinner

Fishing

Those interested in sportfishing for such catch as grouper, red snapper, and sea bass, among others, are likely to get their fill in Yucalpetén, west of Progreso. Río Lagartos also has good fishing in its murky waters. In the Parque Natural del Flamenco Mexicano in Celestún, you have your choice of river or gulf fishing. Fly-fishing is beginning to catch on on Isla Holbox, the tiny island that straddles the Quintana Roo–Yucatán state line.

Lodging

The state of Yucatán has 7,000 hotel rooms, about a third the number of rooms in Cancún. Accommodations outside Mérida fit the low-key, simple pace of the region, where internationally affiliated properties are the exception rather than the rule. Instead, charming former haciendas such as the Hacienda Katanchel work as elegant yet expensive bases from which to explore the countryside. If you don't want to blow your budget on luxury accommodations, there are plenty of simple, small hotels looked after by friendly proprietors.

Mérida has many and varied choices, among them top-end chain establishments, classic older hotels housed in charming colonial or early 20th century-mansions, and basic lodgings geared toward budget travelers less concerned with creature comforts. As in the rest of Mexico, the facade rarely reveals the character of the hotel behind it, so check out the interior before turning away.

Location is very important: if you plan to spend most of your time enjoying Mérida, stay in the vicinity of the main square or along Calle 60. If you're a light sleeper, however, you may be better off staying in one of the places along or near Paseo Montejo, about a 20-minute stroll (but an easy cab ride) from the main square—or choose a room with double-pane windows to cut out traffic noise. In general the public spaces in Mérida's hotels are prettier than the sleeping rooms. Most hotels have air-conditioning, and even budget hotels have been installing air-conditioning in at least a few rooms, to keep up with the competition.

CATEGORY	COST*
$$$$	over $100
$$$	$70–$100
$$	$40–$70
$	under $40

All prices are for a standard double room, excluding 12% tax.

Ruins

Maya ruins from the Classic period, about AD 200–AD 900, are Yucatán's greatest claim to fame and world-renowned. The Maya city of Chichén Itzá, midway between Cancún and Mérida, was the first Yucatán ruin to be excavated and extensively restored for public viewing, in the late 1930s. Its main pyramid is one of the most familiar images of Mexico. Uxmal, south of Mérida, is almost as spectacular. Since the early 1990s, a combination of government interest in these ruins as a matter of national pride and Mexico's participation in the Mundo Maya program with four Central American nations has been fueling a restoration boom. (In addition, increased government funding has spurred a surge in excavations during the past few years.) Each of the archaeological sites along the Ruta Puuc (Puuc Route) south of Uxmal, though not large, has something striking to offer amateur archaeologists, and more-recently discovered sites such as Aké and Ek Balam invite adventuresome travelers to explore where few people have set foot in the past few centuries.

Glyphs heralding royal births, deaths, and marriages as well as successful battles and celestial events were recorded on stelae, lintels, and murals; these are of crucial importance to scientists attempting to date the rise and fall of the Maya cities. Unfortunately, many other historical records were lost with the near total destruction of the Maya codices (or books) by early Catholic priests and bishops, such as Bishop Diego de Landa, who considered the writings heretical and even works of the devil.

But Maya temples are not the only ruins that tug at the imagination in Yucatán. Grandiose Spanish colonial churches, often built on the same site of stones scavenged from dismantled pyramids, dominate rural towns throughout the state. The opulence of a more recent era can be seen at haciendas where wealthy plantation owners grew henequen. Originally, there were 500 haciendas. Some plantations still operate on a small scale, and some of the lavish mansions have been turned into museums or allowed to crumble, but a few are being restored as inns and restaurants.

Shopping

Although Yucatecan artisans don't produce many different crafts, what items they do create are among the finest in the country. For the most part, Mérida is the best place in Yucatán to buy local handicrafts at reasonable prices. The main products include *hamacas* (hammocks), *guayaberas* (pleated dress shirts for men), leather sandals, huipiles, baskets, *jipis* ("Panama" hats made of huano palm fibers), leather goods, gold- and silver-filigree jewelry, masks, and piñatas.

Hammocks are one of the most popular craft items sold here. They are available in cotton or nylon (and, very rarely, silk), as well as in the very rough and scratchy henequen fiber. Nylon hammocks dry quickly and may be best for humid or wet climates. Cotton is comfortable, but the colors fade fastest. Double-threaded hammocks are sturdier and stretch less than single-threaded ones, a difference that can be identified by studying the density of the weave. Hammocks come in different sizes: *sencillo,* for one person (a rather tight fit); *doble,* very comfortable for one but crowded for two; *matrimonial* (also called king-size), which decently accommodates two; and *familiares* or *matrimoniales especiales,* which can theoretically sleep an entire family. (When more than one person shares a hammock, they should lie sideways in the hammock, not lengthwise.) For a good-quality matrimonial nylon or cotton hammock, expect to pay about $25. Sencillos go for about $15. Unless you are an expert, it's best to buy a hammock at one of the specialty shops in Mérida, many of which let you climb in to try the size.

Exploring the State of Yucatán

Mérida is the hub of Yucatán and the best base for exploring the rest of the state. From there, highways radiate in every direction. To the east, along Route 180 to Cancún, are the famous Chichén Itzá ruins and the low-key colonial city of Valladolid. Heading south on Route 261, you come to Uxmal and the Ruta Puuc, a series of the most outstanding small ruins in Yucatán. Route 261 north from Mérida takes you to the seaport and beach resort of Progreso. To the west, separate secondary highways go to Celestún and Sisal, two fishing villages with white-sand beaches, the former on the edge of the Parque Natural Celestún wildlife preserve.

Most roads in the state are narrow, paved two-lane affairs that pass through small towns and villages, although there is one toll road from Mérida to Cancún. Rarely is traffic heavy on them, and they are in good shape, usually devoid of potholes and unexpected bumps. Highway 176, which runs parallel to the north coast from Mérida, was widened to four lanes in 2000, improving access to a series of small inland towns.

Numbers in the text correspond to numbers in the margin and on the State of Yucatán and Mérida maps.

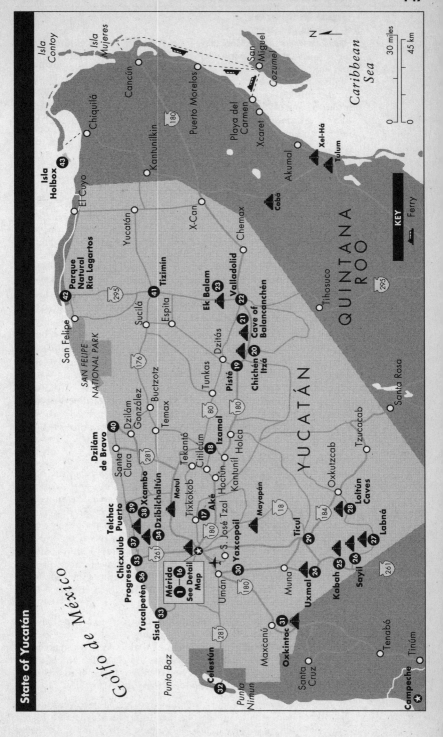

State of Yucatán

Golfo de México

Caribbean Sea

QUINTANA ROO

YUCATÁN

SAN FELIPE NATIONAL PARK

Parque Natural Ría Lagartos

KEY

Ferry

30 miles
45 km

Isla Contoy
Isla Mujeres
Cancún
San Miguel
Cozumel
Puerto Morelos
Chiquilá
Playa del Carmen
Xcaret
Kantunilkin
Xel-Há
Tulum
Akumal
Isla Holbox
Cobá
El Cuyo
Yucatán
X-Can
Chemax
San Felipe
Tizimín
Ek Balam
Valladolid
Cave of Balancanchén
Sucilá
Espita
Dzitás
Chichén Itzá
Tihosuco
Santa Rosa
Pisté
Tunkas
Buctzotz
Temax
Citilcún
Izamal
Holca
Kantunil
Oxkutzcab
Tzucacab
Dzilám González
Dzilám de Bravo
Santa Clara
Xcambo
Dzibilchaltún
Motul
Tixkokob
Aké
S. José Tzal
Hoctún
Mayapán
Loltúm Caves
Labná
Telchac Puerto
Chicxulub Puerto
Progreso
Yucalpetén
Sisal
Mérida
See Detail Map
Umán
Yaxcopoil
Muna
Ticul
Kabah
Sayil
Uxmal
Oxkintoc
Maxcanú
Santa Cruz
Tenabó
Tinúm
Celestún
Punta Baz
Punta Nimun
Campeche

1–16
17 Aké
18
19 Pisté
20
21
22
23 Ek Balam
24
25 Kabah
26
27
28
29
30
31 Oxkintoc
32 Celestún
33 Sisal
34 Dzibilchaltún
35
36 Progreso
37
38 Xcambo
39
40
41 Tizimín
42
43 Isla Holbox

180
295
176
80
184
18
261
281

Great Itineraries

IF YOU HAVE 3 DAYS

Spend two days in ⌂ **Mérida** ①–⑯, savoring the city's unique character as you make your way among the historic churches and mansions and enjoy the parks and restaurants. (If you can plan around a Sunday, so much the better, as the city center is closed to traffic and cultural events are scheduled throughout the day.) On Day 3, drive or take a tour to one of Yucatán's most famous Maya ruins—either **Chichén Itzá** ⑳ or **Uxmal** ㉔. Each is within about two hours of Mérida, making for an ideal day trip.

IF YOU HAVE 7 DAYS

First explore the sights of **Mérida** ①–⑯, and then take two separate overnight excursions from the city. Spend the night at one of the archaeological hotels near ⌂ **Uxmal** ㉔, and the next day explore the Ruta Puuc, the series of lost cities south of Uxmal that includes **Kabah** ㉕, **Sayil** ㉖, and **Labná** ㉗, as well as the fascinating **Loltún Caves** ㉘, returning to Mérida through **Ticul** ㉙. On the second excursion, to ⌂ **Chichén Itzá** ⑳, allow as much as a full day en route to explore the small ruins at **Aké** ⑰ or the more lively modern-day towns in the area, such as ⌂ **Izamal** ⑱ and **Valladolid** ㉒. After visiting Chichén Itzá, you may wish to beat the afternoon heat by exploring the **Cave of Balancanchén** ㉑ or swimming in one of the cool subterranean cenotes nearby. You might also head north from Valladolid to see the flamingo nesting grounds at **Parque Natural Río Lagartos** ㊷.

IF YOU HAVE 10 DAYS

In addition to visiting the sights noted above, you may want to add one or more beach days to your itinerary. An obvious choice is **Progreso** ㉟, with a stop en route from **Mérida** ①–⑯ to see the ruins of **Dzibilchaltún** ㉞, and perhaps side trips to explore some of the small north-coast beach towns such as **Yucalpetén** ㊱, **Telchac Puerto** ㊴, **Dzilám de Bravo** ㊵, or **Sisal** ㉝. In **Celestún** ㉜, guided boat trips are available into **Parque Natural del Flamenco Mexicano,** a protected habitat for flocks of pink flamingos and other aquatic birds.

When to Tour Mérida and the Yucatán

Sunday is special in Yucatán. Mérida blocks off traffic in the downtown area as what seems to be the entire population of the city mingles in the zócalo and other parks and plazas to socialize and watch live entertainment. Sidewalk cafés along this route are perfect vantage points from which to watch the passing parade of people as well as the folk dancers and singers. Sunday is also the day when admission to museums and archaeological sites is free, an important consideration given that entrance fees at the various ruins have been on the rise. This is something to keep in mind if you plan to explore the Ruta Puuc, where you can visit seven Maya sites, each of which charges a separate admission on other days of the week.

Thousands of people, from international sightseers to Maya shamans, swarm to Chichén Itzá for the vernal equinox (the first day of spring), when the afternoon light creates a shadow that looks like a snake moving slowly down the side of the main pyramid. The phenomenon also occurs on the autumnal equinox, but the rain clouds at that time of year sometimes block the sun, spoiling the effect.

Another good time to come is the end of October. Mexico's traditional Day of the Dead—which, in Mérida, is called by its Maya name, Hanal Pixan, or "food for departed souls"—begins with the Feast of All Saints, November 1. On the eve of this celebration, the families of deceased children typically clean and decorate their child's grave or erect altars in the home. Mérida dresses up its main square with dozens of "huts" representing different villages around the state. Inside are small altars filled with the time-honored offerings to the departed souls of children and adults. Coinciding with this celebration is Mérida's Otoño Cultural, the Autumn Cultural Festival, usually held the last week of October or early November. During this two-week event, free or inexpensive classical-music concerts, dance performances, and art exhibits take place almost nightly at theaters and open-air venues around the city.

High season here generally corresponds to high season in the rest of Mexico: Christmastime, Easter week, and the months of July and August. Rainfall is heaviest between June and October, bringing with it an uncomfortable humidity. The coolest months are November–January; April and May are usually the hottest.

MÉRIDA

Travelers to Mérida are a loyal bunch, content to return again and again to favorite restaurants, neighborhoods, and museums. The city's traffic, complete with diesel fumes and noise, is frustrating, particularly after a peaceful stay on the coast or at one of the archaeological sites, but the city's merits far outweigh its flaws. Mérida is the cultural and intellectual center of the peninsula, with museums and attractions that can greatly enhance your insights into the history and character of Yucatán. Indeed, the quality and number of its offerings make it one of Mexico's leading cultural centers. Consider making it one of the first stops in your travels, and make sure your visit includes a Sunday, when traffic is light and the city seems to revert to a more gracious era.

Most streets in Mérida are numbered, not named, and most run one way. North–south streets have even numbers, which ascend from east to west; east–west streets have odd numbers, which ascend from north to south. Street addresses are confusing because they don't progress in even increments by blocks; for example, the 600s may occupy two or more blocks. A particular location is therefore usually identified by indicating the street number and the nearest cross street, as in "Calle 64 at Calle 61," or "Calle 64 between Calles 61 and 63," which is written "Calle 64 x 61 y 63." Although it looks confusing at first glance, this system is actually extremely helpful.

Zócalo and Surroundings

The zócalo, the oldest part of town, has been dubbed the Centro Histórico (Historic Center) by city officials. The city has been restoring all the colonial buildings in the area to their original splendor, and it's not uncommon to see work proceeding on facades on several streets at once.

A Good Walk

Start at the **zócalo** ①: see the **Casa de Montejo** ② (now a Banamex bank), on the south side; the **Palacio Municipal** ③ and the **Centro Cultural de Mérida Olimpo** ④, on the west side; the **Palacio del Gobierno** ⑤, on the northeast corner, and, catercorner, the **Catedral de San Ildefonso** ⑥; and the **Museo de Arte Contemporáneo** ⑦ on the east side. Step out on Calle 60 from the cathedral and walk north to **Parque Hidalgo** ⑧ and the **Iglesia de la Tercera Orden de Jesús** ⑨, which is across Calle 59. Continue north along Calle 60 for a short block to the **Teatro Peón Contreras** ⑩, which lies on the east side of the street; the entrance to the **Universidad Autónoma de Yucatán** ⑪ is on the west side of Calle 60 at Calle 57. A block farther north on the west side of Calle 60 is the **Parque de Santa Lucía** ⑫. From the park, walk north four blocks and turn right on Calle 47 for two blocks to **Paseo Montejo** ⑬. Once on this street, continue north for two long blocks to the **Palacio Can-**

150

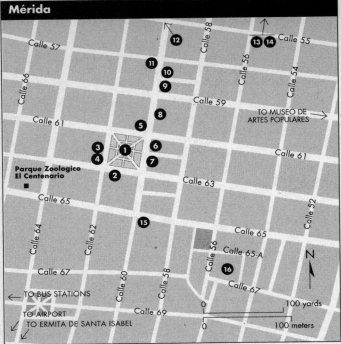

Mérida

tón ⑭. From here look either for a *calesa* (horse-drawn carriage) or cabs parked outside the museum to take you back past the zócalo to the **Mercado de Artesanías "García Rejón"** ⑮ and the **Mercado Municipal** ⑯—or walk if you're up to it.

Sights to See

② **Casa de Montejo.** This stately palace sits on the south side of the plaza, on Calle 63. Francisco de Montejo—father and son—conquered the peninsula and founded Mérida in 1542; they built their "casa" 10 years later. The property remained with the family until the late 1970s, when it was restored by banker Agustín Legorreta and converted to a bank. Built in the French style, it represents the city's finest—and oldest—example of colonial Plateresque architecture, which typically has elaborate ornamentation. A bas-relief on the doorway—the facade is all that remains of the original house—depicts Francisco de Montejo the younger, his wife, and daughter as well as Spanish soldiers standing on the heads of the vanquished Maya. Even if you have no banking to do, step into the building weekdays between 9 and 5 to glimpse the leafy inner patio.

⑥ **Catedral de San Ildefonso** (St. Ildefonse Cathedral). Begun in 1561, this is the oldest cathedral in Mexico and the second-oldest on the North American mainland. It sits on the east side of the plaza. It took several hundred Maya laborers, working with stones from the pyramids of the ravaged Maya city, 36 years to complete it. Designed in the somber Renaissance style by an architect who had worked on the Escorial in Madrid, its facade is stark and unadorned, with gunnery slits instead of windows, and faintly Moorish spires. Inside, the black **Cristo de las Ampollas** (Christ of the Blisters) occupies a side altar to the left of the main one. The statue is a replica of the original, which was destroyed during the Revolution (this was also when most of the gold that typically burnished Mexican cathedrals was carried off). According to one of many legends, the Christ figure burned all night yet appeared the next morning unscathed—except that it was covered with the blisters for which it is named. The crucifix above the side altar is reputedly the second largest in the world. ✉ *Calle 60 at Calle 61, centro,* ☎ *no phone.* ⊙ *Daily 7–11:30 and 4:30–8.*

❹ Centro Cultural de Mérida Olimpo (Mérida Olimpo Cultural Center). Referred to as just Olimpo, this is the best venue for free cultural events in the city. The beautiful, porticoed cultural center was built adjacent to City Hall in late 1999, occupying what used to be a parking lot. The marble interior is a showcase for top international art exhibits, classical-music concerts, conferences, and theater and dance presentations. Next door, a movie house renovated to its 1950s look shows art films most nights: classics by such directors as Buñuel, Fellini, and Kazan. The complex also includes a Librería Dante bookstore and cybercafé. ✉ *Calle 62 between Calles 61 and 63, centro,* ☎ *999/928–2020.* ▨ *Free.* ⊙ *Tues.–Sun. 10–10.*

Ermita de Santa Isabel (Hermitage of St. Isabel). At the far south of the city stands the hermitage (circa 1748), part of a Jesuit monastery also known as the Hermitage of the Good Trip, which was restored in 1966. A resting place in colonial days for travelers heading to Campeche, and the most peaceful place in the city, the restored chapel is an enchanting spot to visit at sunset (when it is open) and perhaps a good destination for a ride in a calesa. Next door is a huge garden with many botanical species, a waterfall, and footpaths bordered with bricks and colored stones. ✉ *Calles 66 and 77, La Ermita,* ☎ *no phone.* ▨ *Free.* ⊙ *Church and garden open only during Mass; check with tourism department for current schedule.*

❾ Iglesia de la Tercera Orden de Jesús (Church of the Third Order of Jesus or Church of the Jesuits). To the north of Parque Hidalgo is one of Mérida's oldest buildings and the first Jesuit church in the Yucatán. The church was built in 1618 of limestone from a Maya temple that had stood on the site, and faint outlines of ancient carvings are still visible on the stonework of the west wall. Although it is a favorite place for society weddings because of its antiquity, the church interior is not very ornate.

The former convent rooms in the rear of the building now host the small **Pinoteca Juan Gamboa Guzmán** (State Repository of Paintings). The first room is dedicated to temporary exhibits; the second displays striking bronze sculptures of the Yucatán's indigenous people by its most celebrated 20th-century sculptor, Enrique Gottdiener. On the second floor are about 20 forgettable oil paintings—mostly of past governors and a few saints. ✉ *Calle 59 between Calles 58 and 60, centro,* ☎ *no phone.* ▨ *$1, free Sun.* ⊙ *Tues.–Sat. 8–8, Sun. 8–2.*

⓯ Mercado de Artesanías "García Rejón" (García Rejón Crafts Market). Two long rows of stalls near the municipal market sell regional crafts at reasonable prices: these include straw hats, hammocks, locally made liqueurs such as Ixtabentún and mescal, leather sandals, and jewelry. Postcards and other souvenirs can also be found. ✉ *Calle 60 at Calle 65, centro,* ☎ *no phone.* ⊙ *Weekdays 9–6, Sat. 9–4, Sun. 9–1.*

★ ⓰ Mercado Municipal (Municipal Market). At this pungent, labyrinthine market, sellers of chilies, herbs, trinkets, and fruit occupy almost every patch of ground. In the early morning hours, the place is jammed with housewives and restaurateurs who come to pick the freshest of the fresh to serve that day. On the second floor of the main building is the **Bazar de Artesanías Municipales** (Municipal Handicrafts Bazaar), the principal handicrafts market, where you can buy pottery, embroidered clothes, men's guayabera dress shirts, hammocks, and straw bags.

Jewelry sellers occupy the row at the foot of the stairs leading up to the Bazar de Artesanías. ⊠ *Calle 56 at Calle 67, centro,* ☎ *no phone.* ⊘ *Mon.–Sat. dawn–dusk, Sun. 8–3.*

❼ Museo de Arte Contemporáneo (Museum of Contemporary Art). Originally designed as an art school but used until 1915 as a seminary, this enormous two-story building is full of light, just perfect for an art museum. It showcases the works of Yucatecan artists such as Gabriel Ramírez Aznar and Fernando García Ponce and has excellent international art exhibits in the second-floor galleries. These make up for the halfhearted reproductions of some of the world's masterpieces in the World History of Art room. There's also a bookstore (closed Sunday). ⊠ *Pasaje de la Revolución 1907, between Calles 58 and 60 (on main square), centro,* ☎ *999/928–3258 or 999/928–3236.* ⊠ *$2.20, free Sun.* ⊘ *Wed.–Mon. 10–6.*

Museo de Artes Populares (Museum of Folk Art). If you love Mexican crafts, trek several blocks east of the main square to this museum, housed in a fine old mansion. The ground floor is devoted to Yucatecan arts and crafts, such as weaving, straw baskets, filigree jewelry, carved wood, and beautifully carved conch shells, as well as exhibits on huipil products and the like. The second floor focuses on the popular arts of the rest of Mexico. ⊠ *Calle 59 No. 441, at Calle 50, La Mejorada,* ☎ *no phone.* ⊠ *Free.* ⊘ *Tues.–Sat. 9–8, Sun. 8–2.*

⓮ Palacio Cantón. The most compelling of the mansions on ☞ **Paseo Montejo**, the pale-peach palacio presently houses the air-conditioned **Museo de Antropología e Historia** (Museum of Anthropology and History). Designed by Enrique Deserti, who also did the blueprints for the Teatro Peón Contreras, the building has grandiose airs that seem more characteristic of a mausoleum than a home, but in fact it was built for a general between 1909 and 1911. There is marble everywhere, likewise Doric and Ionic columns and other Italianate Beaux Arts flourishes. From 1958 to 1967 the mansion served as the residence of the state governor. In 1977 it became a museum dedicated to the culture and history of the Maya. Although it's not as impressive as its counterparts in other Mexican cities, it can serve as an introduction to ancient Maya culture before you visit nearby Maya sites. Exhibits explain the Maya practice of dental mutilation and incrustation. A case of "sick bones" shows how the Maya suffered from osteoarthritis, nutritional maladies, and congenital syphilis. The museum also has conch shells, stones, and quetzal feathers that were used for trading. There is a bookstore on the premises; it's not open on Sunday. ⊠ *Calle 43 and Paseo Montejo, Paseo Montejo,* ☎ *999/923–0557.* ⊠ *$3.50, free Sun.* ⊘ *Tues.–Sat. 8–8, Sun. 8–2.*

❺ Palacio del Gobierno (State House). Occupying the northeast corner of the main square is this structure, built in 1885 on the site of the Casa Real (Royal House). The upper floor of the State House contains Fernando Castro Pacheco's vivid murals of the bloody history of the conquest of the Yucatán, painted in 1978. On the main balcony (visible from outside on the plaza) stands a reproduction of the **Bell of Dolores Hidalgo**, on which Mexican independence rang out on the night of September 15, 1810, in the town of Dolores Hidalgo in Guanajuato. On the anniversary of the event, the state governor tolls the bell to commemorate the occasion. ⊠ *Calle 61 between Calles 60 and 62, centro.* ⊠ *Free.* ⊘ *Daily 8 AM or 9 AM–9 PM.*

❸ Palacio Municipal (City Hall). The west side of the main square is occupied by this 17th-century building, which is painted pale yellow and trimmed with white arcades, balustrades, and the national coat of arms. Originally erected on the ruins of the last surviving Maya structure, it was rebuilt in 1735 and then completely reconstructed along colonial lines in 1928. It remains the headquarters of the local government. ⊠ *Calle 62 between Calles 61 and 63, centro.* ⊙ *Daily 9–8.*

⑫ **Parque de Santa Lucía.** The rather plain park at Calles 60 and 55 draws crowds to its Thursday-night performances by local musicians and folk dancers; shows start at 9. The small church opposite the park dates from 1575 and was built as a place of worship for the African and Caribbean slaves who lived here. The churchyard functioned as the cemetery until 1821.

⑧ **Parque Hidalgo.** A half block north of the main plaza, at Calles 60 and 59, is this small, cozy park, officially known as Plaza Cepeda Peraza. Renovated mansions turned hotels and sidewalk cafés line the south side of the park, which comes alive at night with marimba bands and street vendors.

⌡ **Parque Zoológico El Centenario.** Mérida's great children's attraction, this is a large, somewhat tacky amusement complex consisting of playgrounds; rides (including ponies and a small train); a roller-skating rink; snack bars; and cages with more than 300 marvelous native monkeys, birds, reptiles, and other animals. It also has picnic areas, pleasant wooded paths, and a small lake where you can rent rowboats. The French Renaissance–style arch (1921) commemorates the 100th anniversary of Mexican independence. ⊠ *Av. Itzaes between Calles 59 and 65 (entrances on Calles 59 and 65), centro,* ☏ *no phone.* 🎫 *Free.* ⊙ *Daily 8–5.*

⑬ **Paseo Montejo.** North of downtown, this 10-block-long street was *the* place to reside in the late 19th century, when wealthy plantation owners sought to outdo each other in the opulence of their elegant mansions. Inside, the owners typically displayed imported Carrara marble and antiques, opting for the decorative and social standards of New Orleans, Cuba, and Paris over styles that were popular in Mexico City. (At the time there was more traffic by sea via the Gulf of Mexico and the Caribbean than there was overland across the lawless interior.) The broad boulevard, although still lined with tamarinds and laurels, has lost most of its former panache, however, and many of the once-stunning mansions have fallen into disrepair. Others are being restored as part of a citywide beautification program bolstered by private investment.

⑩ **Teatro Peón Contreras.** This 1908 Italianate theater was built along the lines of the grand turn-of-the-20th-century European theaters and opera houses. In the early 1980s the marble staircase and the dome and frescoes were restored. Today, in addition to performing arts, the theater also houses the main **Centro de Información Turística,** to the right of the lobby, as well as the occasional art exhibit. The information center distributes maps and brochures and can provide details about attractions in the city and state. A café serving cappuccino and other coffees, plus light snacks and some meals, spills out to a patio from inside the theater to the right of the information center. ⊠ *Calle 60 between Calles 57 and 59, centro,* ☏ *999/923–7354; 999/924–9290 tourist-information center.* ⊙ *Theater daily 7 AM–1 AM, tourist-information center daily 8 AM–9 PM.*

⑪ **Universidad Autónoma de Yucatán.** The arabesque university plays a major role in the city's cultural and intellectual life. The folkloric ballet performs on the patio of the main building Friday at 9 PM ($4). A Jesuit college built in 1618 previously occupied the site; the present building, which dates from 1711, has crenellated Moorish ramparts and archways. Bulletin boards just inside the entrance announce upcoming cultural events. ⊠ *Calle 60 between Calles 57 and 59, centro,* ☏ *999/924–8000.*

① **Zócalo** (main square). Meridanos also traditionally call this the Plaza Principal and Plaza de la Independencia, and it's a good spot from which to begin any tour of the city. Ancient, geometrically pruned laurel trees and *confidenciales* (S-shape benches designed for tête-à-têtes) invite lingering. The plaza was laid out in 1542 on the ruins of T'hó, the Maya city demolished to make way for Mérida, and is still the focal point around which the most important public buildings cluster. Lampposts keep the park beautifully illuminated at night. ⊠ *Bordered by Calles 60, 62, 61, and 63, centro.*

Dining and Lodging

$$$–$$$$ ✕ **Habichuela.** Both the food and service at this quietly elegant spot
★ are excellent. Custom-made hardwood furniture, marble floors, and lots of leaded-glass accents lead local businessmen here for power lunches; at night, it's filled with families and couples. For starters, sample seafood crepes or salmon pâté. Meat, fish, and fowl are prepared with flair; try the chicken Veronica stuffed with serrano ham; also delicious are butterflied shrimp with ginger, tamarind, or fruit sauce. The chocolate-mousse cake is the star of the dessert menu. ⊠ *Calle 21 No. 416, at Calle 8 (about 20 mins by car from main square), Col. México Oriente,* ☎ *999/926–3626. AE, MC, V. No breakfast.*

$$$–$$$$ ✕ **Pancho's.** This pleasant restaurant fills a narrow patio framing a small bar popular with the locals. The food, expensive by local standards, is Mexican but familiar to foreigners raised on fajitas and other fare found in Mexican restaurants outside Mexico. Waiters—dressed in white muslin shirts and pants of the Revolution era—recommend the shrimp in tequila, and the tequila in general. On the walls are sepiatone posters of Pancho Villa and friends, along with manicured shrubs dressed in tiny white lights, and candles in sconces. Drinks are two for one between 6 PM and 8 PM. ⊠ *Calle 59 No. 509, between Calles 60 and 62, centro,* ☎ *999/923–0942. MC, V.*

$$–$$$$ ✕ **Alberto's Continental Patio.** This romantic restaurant in a 1727 building is adorned with mosaic floors from Cuba. The two dining rooms are fitted with handsome antiques and stone sculptures, and candles glow in glass lanterns. A lovely courtyard surrounded by rubber trees is ideal for starlit dining. There's lots of Lebanese food: shish kebab, fried *kibi* (meatballs of ground beef, wheat germ, and spices), cabbage rolls, hummus, eggplant dip, and tabbouleh; don't forget the pita bread, almond pie, and Turkish coffee. There are Mexican dishes and meatless options for vegetarians. ⊠ *Calle 64 No. 482, at Calle 57, centro,* ☎ *999/928–5367. AE, MC, V.*

$$–$$$$ ✕ **La Bella Epoca.** You'll pay for the ambience at this somewhat pretentious yet elegantly restored mansion, where crystal chandeliers sparkle and tiny balcony tables overlook Parque Hidalgo. Arrive for dinner before 8 PM to claim one of the balcony tables overlooking the street. An ambitious but almost unreadable handwritten menu includes French, Mexican, Middle Eastern, Yucatecan, vegetarian, and Maya dishes. Consider the *sikil-pak* (a dip with ground pumpkin seeds, charbroiled tomatoes, and onions) or the succulent *pollo pibíl* (chicken baked in banana leaves). ⊠ *Hotel del Parque, Calle 60 No. 497, between Calles 57 and 59, centro,* ☎ *999/928–1928. AE, MC, V.*

$$ ✕ **Hong Kong.** If you tire of regional food, head to this sparkling eatery for some of Mérida's most authentic Chinese food. The wontons and egg rolls are served hot and crispy. There's a preponderance of chicken and shrimp dishes, and only a few for vegetarians. During weekend lunch (when only the $9 buffet is served) the place is jammed—and the loud clink of silverware and the sight of running waiters is not conducive to lingering. It's a long walk down Paseo Montejo, and best reached by taxi. ⊠ *Calle 31 No. 113, between Calles 22 and 24, Col. México Oriente,* ☎ *999/926–1441 or 999/926–7439. AE, MC, V.*

$$ ✕ **Pizza Bella.** Under an arcade surrounding the main square, this restaurant serves espresso, cappuccino, and Mexican and American breakfasts as well as pizza. Checkered tablecloths atop wooden tables and an eclectic collection of wall decorations, from maps to beer advertisements, add atmosphere to an otherwise standard pizza joint. ⊠ *Calle 61 No. 500, centro,* ☎ *999/923–6401. No credit cards.*

$–$$ ✕ **Via Olimpo.** Linger over a coffee and a book at this main-square café, or spend an afternoon people-watching. On Sunday, this is a coveted spot from which to view the performances on the square. A student minstrel group sings Wednesday–Saturday in the colonial dining room while clients feast on light dishes, *poc chuc* (pork marinated in sour-orange juice and spices), *papadzules* (corn tortillas with hard-cooked egg and pumpkin-seed sauce), smoked-turkey sandwiches, or hamburgers and fries. Crepes are popular, as is the $8 breakfast buffet. The local intelligentsia keeps the place, open 24 hours, hopping. Spirits are also served. ⊠ *Calle 62 between Calles 63 and 61, centro,* ☎ *999/923–5843. AE, MC, V.*

$ ✕ **Alameda.** You really get a good deal for your money here (the most expensive main dish is about $4). Middle Eastern and vegetarian specialties share the menu with standard Yucatecan fare at this nondescript side-street restaurant. Businessmen linger over grilled beef shish kebab, pita bread, and coffee; some old couples have been coming in once a week for years. Everything is served without side dishes—if you want beans or potatoes with your eggs, you must ask for them. Meat-free dishes include tabbouleh and spongy, lemon-flavor spinach turnovers. Alameda closes at 7:30 PM. ⊠ *Calle 58 No. 474, near Calle 57, centro,* ☎ *999/928–3635. No credit cards. No dinner.*

$ ✕ **Los Almendros.** This Mérida classic takes credit for the invention of the regional specialty poc chuc. The food can be greasy, and local spices can overwhelm the main ingredients. Still, Los Almendros is a good introduction to Yucatecan cuisine: *cochinita pibíl* (pork baked in banana leaves), pork sausage, papadzules. Sangria—with or without alcohol—washes it all down. The English-language menu has pictures and descriptions. There is live music nightly 2–5 and 7:30–11 and a regional show Friday at 8. ⊠ *Calle 50 No. 493, between Calles 57 and 59, La Mejorada,* ☎ *999/928–5459. AE, MC, V.*

$ ✕ **Amaro.** Statesman Andrés Quintana Roo was born in 1787 in this historic home, which takes on a romantic glow at night with candlelit tables in the open patio—bring a sweater. The menu is heavy on health drinks and vegetarian food like eggplant curry and soup made with *chaya,* a vegetable similar to spinach. If you're missing your favorite comfort foods, order a side of mashed potatoes or french fries, or a salad made with fresh local veggies. ⊠ *Calle 59 No. 507, between Calles 60 and 62, centro,* ☎ *999/928–2451. No credit cards. Closed Sun. in Apr.–Nov.*

$ ✕ **Anfitrion.** The classic Lebanese-Yucatecan cuisine at this unpretentious local favorite screams "fresh." For starters, there's mounds of soft pita bread, chili-spiked olive oil for dipping, wonderful Lebanese dry yogurt, and hummus. The daily luncheon dish is often Yucatecan food: breaded pork in fresh tomato sauce with chopped ham and peas, or a succulent tripe casserole with bacon, chickpeas, and ham. These inexpensive specials include rice, beans, coffee, and dessert. For dessert try *caballero pobre* (literally, "poor gentleman"), made of stale bread in a light raisin-and-cinnamon syrup. ⊠ *Calle 15 No. 109, between Calles 20 and 22, Col. Yucatán,* ☎ *999/920–0326. MC, V. Closed Tues. No dinner.*

$ ✕ **Café La Habana.** Old-fashioned ceiling fans and a gleaming wood
★ bar contribute to the Old Havana nostalgia at this overwhelmingly popular café. The aroma of fresh-ground coffee fills the air at this busy 24-hour place with a no-smoking section sometimes closed due to lack of interest. Sixteen javas are offered, including Irish, frappé, espresso, and Arab. The menu has light snacks such as lime soup, as

well as some entrées, including spaghetti, fajitas, and breaded shrimp. The waiters are friendly and service is brisk. ⊠ *Corner of Calles 59 and 62, centro,* ☎ *999/928–6502. No credit cards.*

$ ✕ **La Casona.** This pretty mansion turned restaurant near Parque Santa Ana has an inner patio, arcade, and swirling ceiling fans. The bar has live romantic music on weekends. The accent is Yucatecan, with poc chuc, pollo pibíl, and *huachinango* (red snapper baked in banana leaves) among the recommended dishes. There are some Italian offerings, including homemade ravioli, manicotti, and linguine. Vegetables or pasta accompany most orders. ⊠ *Calle 60 No. 434, between Calles 47 and 49, centro,* ☎ *999/923–9996. MC, V. Closed Sun.*

$ ✕ **Dante's.** Lovers and families crowd this modern, bustling coffeehouse on the second floor of one of Mérida's largest bookshops. The house specialty is crepes, 18 varieties with either sweet or savory fillings; light entrées such as tacos and pizzas also are served. You can order cappuccino and specialty coffees as well as beer and wine. A small theater in back of the bookstore puts on evening comic sketches and live music from time to time, and puppet shows on Sunday at 10 AM. ⊠ *Prolongación Paseo Montejo 138-B, Paseo Montejo,* ☎ *999/927–7441. No credit cards.*

$$$$ ✕🏨 **Hacienda Katanchel.** This romantic, rambling 17th-century
★ henequen hacienda was brought back to its original splendor by Anibal Gonzalez and his wife, Monica Hernandez. Rooms and suites in spacious pavilions line a winding garden walkway; they have overhead fans, hammocks, huge tile bathrooms, and plunge pools. The double beds look like pieces of modern sculpture. Everything at this member of the Small Luxury Hotels of the World has been carefully restored, even the 19th-century red Marseille tile roofs. The gorgeous restaurant serves contemporary Yucatecan cuisine, making liberal use of the hacienda's organically grown fruits and vegetables. Offerings include cream of beet soup, chicken in pumpkin seed and pistachio sauce, and desserts such as vanilla ice cream with tangy sour-orange sauce. Massages using herbs and floral essences bring pampering to a new level. Expensive excursions by plane or private car can be arranged. ⊠ *25 km (15 mi) east of Mérida on Hwy. 180 (toward Cancún),* ☎ *999/923–4020 or 800/223–6510;* FAX *888/882–9470 from the U.S; 999/923–4000;* WEB *www.hacienda-katanchel.com. 25 rooms, 13 suites. Restaurant, pool, massage, bar, car rental, travel services. AE, MC, V.*

$$$$ ✕🏨 **Hacienda Teya.** The draw at this beautiful henequen-era hacienda
★ 13 km (8 mi) from the city is the fabulous regional food; reservations for Sunday lunch or dinner are essential. After a typical lunch of cochinita pibíl or baked chicken, you can stroll in the orchard or surrounding gardens, or swim in the huge rectangular pool. The 10 guest rooms have handmade rustic furniture, TV, and a whirlpool bath; rates include Continental breakfast. ⊠ *13 km (8 mi) east of Mérida on Hwy. 180, Kanasín,* ☎ *999/924–3800; 999/924–3880 in Mérida;* FAX *999/924–5853;* WEB *www.haciendateya.com. 10 rooms. Restaurant, in-room hot tubs, pool, bar, free parking. AE, MC, V.*

$$$$ 🏨 **Fiesta Americana Mérida.** This posh hotel and shopping-business
★ center caters to business travelers, conventions, and high-end travelers, its lovely facade echoing Paseo Montejo mansions on an epic scale. The colonial accents carry into the spacious lobby, with gleaming marble and a 300-ft-high stained-glass atrium. Floral prints and slightly larger-than-life proportions maintain the theme of bygone elegance in the guest rooms, which nonetheless have all the modern conveniences, including remote-control TV and three phones. Guests on the business floor have access to the Fiesta Club for morning breakfast or afternoon appetizers. ⊠ *Av. Colón 451, at Paseo Montejo, Paseo Montejo,* ☎ *999/942–1111 or 800/343–7821,* FAX *999/942–1122,* WEB *www.fiestaamericana.com. 323 rooms, 27 suites. 2 restaurants, in-room*

data ports, pool, health club, 2 bars, shops, business services, car rental, travel services, free parking, no-smoking rooms. AE, MC, V.

$$$$ ☷ **Villa Mercedes.** Luxury, comfort, and style describe this Art Nouveau home converted into an elegant hotel. Built for and owned by a wealthy Meridian family since 1903, the hotel has gleaming marble floors, period furnishings, pretty gardens and grounds, and a wonderful although quite formal restaurant. ⊠ *Av. Colón 500, between Calles 60 and 62, Paseo Montejo,* ☎ 999/942–9000, 𝖥𝖠𝖷 999/942–9001, 𝖶𝖤𝖡 *www.hotelvillamercedes.com.mx. 79 rooms, 3 suites. Restaurant, room service, pool, bar, business services, meeting rooms, free parking. MC, V.*

$$$–$$$$ ☷ **Holiday Inn.** This is probably the most light-filled hotel in Mérida, with floor-to-ceiling windows throughout the lobby area and tiled dining room that are set off with bright yellows and pinks. Rooms and suites face an open courtyard and have comfy armchairs, minibars, marble bathrooms, and color TVs with U.S. channels. Amenities include irons and ironing boards, hair dryers, alarm clocks, data ports, and more. ⊠ *Av. Colón 468, at Calle 60, Paseo Montejo, 97000,* ☎ 999/925–6877 or 800/465–4329, 𝖥𝖠𝖷 999/925–7755, 𝖶𝖤𝖡 *www.basshotels.com. 209 rooms, 5 suites. 2 restaurants, room service, minibars, tennis court, pool, gym, bar, car rental, travel services, free parking, no-smoking rooms. AE, DC, MC, V.*

$$$–$$$$ ☷ **Hyatt Regency Mérida.** The city's first deluxe hotel is still among its most elegant. Rooms are regally decorated with russet-hue quilts and rugs set off by blond-wood furniture and cream-color walls. Amenities include a top-notch business center, bathtubs, and hair dryers. The beautiful marble lobby comes alive with piano music at night and guests at the popular Peregrina restaurant. ⊠ *Av. Colón 344, at Calle 60, Paseo Montejo, 97000,* ☎ 999/942–0202, 999/942–1234; 800/233–1234 in the U.S.; 𝖥𝖠𝖷 999/925–7002; 𝖶𝖤𝖡 *www.hyatt.com. 296 rooms, 4 suites. 2 restaurants, room service, minibars, 2 tennis courts, pool, gym, bar, business services, car rental, shop, travel services, free parking, no-smoking rooms. AE, DC, MC, V.*

$$$ ☷ **El Conquistador.** Views of the city from El Conquistador's rooftop solarium and pool area (accessed by an ancient elevator) are superlative, the dining room is renowned for its daily breakfast buffet, and the staff is helpful. Still, the prices at this hotel, which caters to German tour groups, are relatively high considering that the amenities here aren't as extensive as at some of the other area hotels. The contemporary-style rooms include satellite TV; half have tile floors, the others carpeting. ⊠ *Paseo Montejo 458, at Calle 45, Paseo Montejo,* ☎ 999/926–2155; 800/823–1331 in the U.S.; 𝖥𝖠𝖷 999/926–8829. *157 rooms, 4 suites. Restaurant, coffee shop, room service, pool, 2 bars, travel services, free parking. AE, MC, V.*

$$$ ☷ **Casa del Balam.** This pleasant hotel two blocks from the zócalo is
★   still owned by the Barbachanos, pioneers of Yucatán tourism. Rocking chairs in the hallways impart a colonial feeling, as do the carved cedar doors and other lovely touches. The rooms are well maintained, with painted sinks, refrigerators, hair dryers, and double-pane windows. Meals are served around the splashing fountain on the open courtyard or inside the restaurant. Guests have access to a golf and tennis club about 15 minutes (by car) from the hotel. ⊠ *Calle 60 No. 488, centro,* ☎ 999/924–8844; 800/624–8451 in the U.S.; 𝖥𝖠𝖷 999/924–5011. *51 rooms, 3 suites. Restaurant, room service, minibars, pool, bars, car rental, travel services, free parking, no-smoking rooms. AE, DC, MC, V.*

$$$ ☷ **Casa Mexilio.** Four block from the main square is this eclectic bed-and-breakfast run by partners Jorge and Roger. Middle Eastern wall hangings, French tapestries, and colorful tile floors crowd the public spaces; individually decorated rooms have tile sinks and folk-art furniture. Casa Mexilio lacks the amenities of the larger hotels; some find

it private and romantic, although for others it's a bit too intimate. ✉ *Calle 68 No. 495, between Calles 57 and 59, centro, 97000,* ☎ FAX *999/ 928–2505;* ☎ *800/538–6802 in the U.S.;* WEB *www.mexicoholiday.com. 8 rooms. Restaurant, pool. MC, V.*

$$$ ⌹ **Mérida Misión Park Inn Plaza.** The Misión has two major assets: an excellent location in the heart of downtown and its colonial charm. There are patios and fountains in public areas, along with a pool and a bar with romantic music nightly. The rooms have wicker furniture, cable TV, hair dryers, minibars, and safes. Rooms in the colonial section surround a pretty courtyard; those in the modern 11-story annex don't have as much character, but the ones on the upper floors have good city views. ✉ *Calle 60 No. 491, centro,* ☎ *999/923–9500 or 888/ 224–8837,* FAX *999/923–7665. 137 rooms, 8 suites. Restaurant, snack bar, room service, minibars, pool, bar, car rental, travel services, free parking, no-smoking rooms. AE, DC, MC, V.*

$$ ⌹ **Casa San Juan.** This B&B is housed in a restored colonial mansion, although the furniture is mismatched and not terribly antique or elegant. Guest rooms vary in size and decoration, but most have double beds, firm mattresses, and ceiling fans; a few have air-conditioning. Affable host Pablo da Costa, a former hotelier from Cuba, can give you tips on visiting the city—in five languages. ✉ *Calle 62 No. 545-A, between Calles 69 and 71, centro,* ☎ *999/986–2937,* FAX *999/986–2937,* WEB *www.casasanjuan.com. 10 rooms. Fans, travel services. MC, V(when booked from the U.S).*

$$ ⌹ **Dolores Alba.** This comfortable, friendly star at the low end of the
★ $$ range is sister to the equally engaging hotel-restaurant in Pisté, near Chichén Itzá. The newer wing has spiffy rooms with quiet yet strong air-conditioning, fans, and telephones, TVs, and comfortable beds; rooms in the older section, with no air-conditioning or TV, are less expensive. The big, rectangular pool is surrounded by lounge chairs and shaded by giant trees, and there's a comfortable restaurant and bar at the front of the property. ✉ *Calle 63 No. 464, between Calles 52 and 54, centro,* ☎ *999/928–5650,* FAX *999/928–3163,* WEB *www.doloresalba.com. 95 rooms. Restaurant, fans, pool, bar, free parking; no air-conditioning in some rooms. No credit cards.*

$$ ⌹ **Gran Hotel.** Cozily situated on Parque Hidalgo, this legendary 1901 hotel is the oldest in the city and retains an aura of history. Guest rooms have cedar furniture and high ceilings. Some rooms have small double beds, so check before you reserve. Request one of the rooms with tiny balconies, if you don't mind noise from the park. Most of the others have no windows at all; those on the second floor in the back are the quietest. Fidel Castro chose one of these when he stayed here; Porfirio Díaz stayed in one of the sumptuous corner suites, which have small living and dining areas. ✉ *Calle 60 No. 496, centro,* ☎ *999/923–6963 or 999/924–7632,* FAX *999/924–7622,* WEB *www.mayanroutes.com/ hotels/merida/ghfactsheet.html. 25 rooms, 7 suites. Restaurant, pizzeria, room service, fans, bar, travel services, free parking. MC, V.*

$$ ⌹ **Best Western María del Carmen.** This modern hotel with a striking, salmon-color tile entrance caters to business travelers, tour groups, and those who desire secure parking. The main square, the market, and other major sights are within easy walking distance. Rooms have lacquered furniture and ornate Chinese lamps. ✉ *Calle 63 No. 550, between Calles 68 and 70, centro;* ☎ *999/923–9133; 800/528–1234 in the U.S.;* FAX *999/923–9290;* WEB *www.bestwestern.com. 86 rooms, 4 suites. Restaurant, room service, pool, bar, meeting room, travel services, free parking. AE, MC, V.*

$$ ⌹ **Posada Toledo.** The beautiful old colonial house evokes its former elegance with high ceilings, floors of Moorish pattern tile, and old-fashioned carved furniture. The breakfast room is particularly fine, with antique stained glass. Antiques also clutter the halls, along with faded portraits of 19th-century family life. Guest-room quality varies more than the rates would reflect, so inspect your room before checking in. No. 5 is an elegant two-room suite that was originally the mansion's master bedroom. If you're a light sleeper, ask for a room away from the courtyard. ⊠ *Calle 58 No. 487, at Calle 57, centro,* ☎ *999/923–1690,* FAX *999/923–2266. 21 rooms, 2 suites. Fans, free parking. MC, V.*

$$ ⌑ **Residencial.** Location is the major draw at this classy bright-pink hotel, a replica of a 19th-century French colonial mansion. It sits on Calle 59, the main entrance to town, and has gated parking. Its elegant dining room is more recommended for its silk drapes and fine linen tablecloths than for the food itself. Rooms have powerful showers, comfortable beds, remote-control cable TV, and spacious closets. The small swimming pool in the central courtyard is pleasant for reconnoitering but far from private. ⊠ *Calle 59 No. 589, at Calle 76, centro,* ☎ *999/924–3899 or 999/ 924–3099,* FAX *999/924–0266,* WEB *hotelresidencial.com.mx. 64 rooms, 2 suites. Restaurant, room service, pool, bar, free parking. AE, MC, V.*

Nightlife and the Arts

Mérida has an unusually active and diverse cultural life, including free government-sponsored music and dance performances many evenings, as well as sidewalk art shows in local parks. On Saturday check out the **Noche Mexicana,** a free, outdoor spectacle of music, dance, comedy, and regional handicrafts that draws more locals than tourists. It happens 8 PM–11 PM at the foot of Paseo Montejo at Calle 47. On Sunday, when six blocks around the zócalo are closed off to traffic, you can hear live music at Plaza Santa Lucía and Parque Hidalgo: mariachis, marimbas, folkloric dance, and other treats at the main plaza. Check with the tourism office for specific times and locations of performances.

For more information on these and other performances, consult the tourist office, the local newspapers, or the billboards and posters at the **Teatro Peón Contreras,** Calle 60 at Calle 57; the **Universidad Autónoma de Yucatán,** Calle 57 at Calle 60; the **Teatro Mérida,** Calle 60 at Calle between Calles 59 and 61; or **Centro Cultural Olimpo,** on the northwest corner of the main plaza.

Bars
Pancho's (⊠ Calle 59 No. 509, between Calles 60 and 62, centro, ☎ 999/923–0942), open daily 6 PM– 2:30 AM; has a lively bar as well as a restaurant and dance floor. Dancing sometimes erupts spontaneously at **La Planta Alta** (⊠ Paseo Montejo 444, at Calle 56-A, ☎ 999/927– 9847), open daily from 5:30 PM until about 1 AM, but most people are content to converse (i.e., shout), listen to music, sip drinks, and watch large-screen music videos.

Dancing
Ay Caray (⊠ Calle 60 No. 482, between Calles 55 and 57, centro, ☎ 999/924–1090) is a lively video bar, with salsa and rock shows until 1 AM, after which there are two hours of dancing. It's open Tuesday– Sunday 9 PM–3 AM. **Pancho's** (⊠ Calle 59 No. 509, between Calles 60 and 62, centro, ☎ 999/923–0942) attracts locals and foreigners for a mix of live salsa and Western music.

Film
Cine Colón (⊠ Av. Reforma 363-A, Colón, ☎ 999/925–4500) shows English action films with Spanish subtitles. International art films are shown (for about $2.50) most days at noon, 5 and 8 PM at **Teatro de Mérida** (⊠ Calle 60 between Calles 59 and 61, centro, ☎ 999/924– 7687 or 999/924–9990). Standard box-office hits are shown at **Cine**

Fantasio (✉ Calle 59 No. 492, at Calle 60, centro, ☎ 999/923–5431), which has one screen only. **Cine Internacional** (✉ Plaza Internacional, Calle 58 between Calle 59 and Callejón del Congreso, centro, ☎ 999/923–0250) has mainly American films with Spanish subtitles.

Folkloric Shows

Paseo Montejo hotels such as the Fiesta Americana, Hyatt Regency, and Holiday Inn stage dinner shows with folkloric dances; check with concierges for schedules. The **Folkloric Ballet of the University of Yucatán** presents a combination of music, dance, and theater, every Friday at 9 PM (every other Friday in off-seasons) at the Universidad Autónoma de Yucatán (✉ Calle 57 at Calle 60, centro, ☎ 999/924–7260); tickets are $3. This includes the "University Serenade," with music, folkloric dance, and poetry. (There are no shows from August 1 to September 22 and during the last two weeks of December.) **100% Yuca** (✉ Calle 25 No. 251, between Calles 38 and 38-A, Col. García Ginerés, ☎ 999/920–3104) is a regional restaurant that has live music beginning at 1 PM and dance shows starting at 3:30 PM. It's popular with both tourists and local families. **Tianos** (✉ Calle 60 No. 461, between Calles 51 and 53, centro, ☎ 999/923–7118) hosts a colorful show of regional dancing nightly at 8 PM (with dinner only). The service is slow and the mock sacrifice of a bare-midriffed damsel hokey, but the show is still fun.

Outdoor Activities and Sports

Baseball

Baseball is played with enthusiasm February–July at the **Kukulcán Sports Center** (✉ Calle 14 No. 17), next to the Santa Clara brewery.

Bullfights

Bullfights are held sporadically December–May and during holiday periods at the **Plaza de Toros** (✉ Paseo de la Reforma near Calle 25, Col. García Ginerés, ☎ 999/925–7996). Contact your hotel travel desk or one of the tourist information centers for scheduling information and tickets; seats in the sun go for $5 to $20 and seats in the shade for $8 to $50, depending on the fame of the bullfighter.

Golf

The 18-hole championship golf course at **Club de Golf La Ceiba** (✉ Carretera Mérida–Progreso, Km 14.5, ☎ 999/922–0053) is open to the public. It is about 16 km (10 mi) north of Mérida on the road to Progreso; greens fees are about $50, and it's closed Monday.

Tennis

At the **Fiesta Americana Mérida** (✉ Av. Colón 451, Paseo Montejo, ☎ 999/920–2194), guests have access to two lighted outdoor courts. The one tennis court at **Holiday Inn** (✉ Av. Colón 498, at Calle 60, Colón, ☎ 999/925–6877) is lighted at night. The **Hyatt Regency Mérida** (✉ Calle 60 No. 344, Colón, ☎ 999/942–0202) has two lighted outdoor courts.

Shopping

A Shopping Tour

Mérida is the best place on the Yucatán to shop, and making a round of the shops is worthwhile for local color even if you don't buy a thing. Start in the market district, catercorner from the post office. You can pick up some sun protection for your head at **El Becaleño** (✉ Calle 65 No. 483, between Calles 56 and 58, centro, ☎ 999/985–0581), which produces Yucatán's fine Panama-style hats, often referred to as *jipis*. To the west of El Becaleño is the huge **Mercado Municipal Lucas de Galvez,** as you turn right just past the post office onto Calle 56. Nip into the market under the EL PUERTO DE VERACRUZ sign; you can find lots of typical jewelry in this area. There isn't as much filigree being made as there once was, but the designs here are interesting and the quality is mostly good (usually 8- to 10-karat gold or gold-dipped).

Look for the stairway; the second floor has hammocks, guayaberas, and huipiles, cotton dresses, and blouses—some eyelet, others richly embroidered or decorated with silk ribbons. Leave the market the way you entered, and then plunge back in directly under the MERCADO MUNICI-PAL LUCAS DE GALVEZ sign. Ask around for *los huaraches*; dozens of stalls sell the fabulous native leather footwear, some with tire-tread bottoms. Many of these shoe and sandal styles have been used for hundreds of years. They are sturdy and, once you break them in, quite comfortable.

Return to Calle 65, turn right, and walk the length of the block between Calles 56 and 54. Here is piñata heaven: every imaginable shape and color, as well as the candy that goes inside.

By now you are likely to want to escape the frenzy of the marketplace for the relative calm of the central district. Turn left (north) on Calle 54 and walk three blocks to Calle 59. Go left again and walk 3½ blocks. **Guayaberas Jack** (✉ Calle 59 No. 507, between Calles 60 and 62, centro, ☎ 999/928–6002) has an excellent selection of guayaberas and typical women's cotton *filipinas* (house dresses) and blouses. Continue up the block and turn left onto Calle 62. For a great selection of hammocks, go to **El Aguacate** (✉ Calle 62 No. 492, ☎ 999/923–1838). Now you can cool your hot heels under the arcade: walk south to the square and turn left to buy some refreshing sherbet from **Dulcería y Sorbetería Colón,** next door to the Nicte-Ha restaurant.

Malls

Mérida has several shopping malls, but the largest is **Gran Plaza** (✉ Calle 50 Diagonal 460, Fracc. Gonzalo Guerrero, ☎ 999/944–7657), with more than 90 shops. It's just outside town, on the highway to Progreso (called Carretera a Progreso beyond the Mérida city limits). **Pasaje Picheta** is a very pleasant, though tiny, mall on the north side of the zócalo, next to the Nicte-Ha restaurant. It has a travel agency, art gallery, Internet facility, newspaper stands, a music/CD store, some nice souvenir shops, and a food court.

Markets

The **Mercado Municipal** (✉ Calle 56 at Calle 67, centro) has crafts, food, flowers, and live birds, among other items. Guides often approach tourists by this market. They expect a tip and won't necessarily show you to the best deals. You're better off visiting some specialty stores first to learn about the quality and types of hammocks, hats, and other crafts; then you'll have an idea of what you're buying—and what it's worth—if you want to bargain in the market.

If you are interested strictly in handicrafts, visit the government-run **Casa de Artesanías** (✉ Calle 63 No. 503, between Calles 64 and 66, La Mejorada, ☎ 999/923–5392). It sells folk art from throughout Mexico, including hand-painted wooden mythical animals from Oaxaca, handmade beeswax candles and leather bags from Mérida, and hand-embroidered vests, shawls, blouses, and place mats from Chiapas. Look for good-quality hammocks here, too. The quality and variety of merchandise are always improving. There's also a showcase full of hard-to-find traditional filigree jewelry in silver, gold, and gold-dipped versions. The **Bazar García Rejón** (✉ Calle 65 at Calle 62, centro) has rather sterile rows of indoor stalls with leather items, palm hats, and handmade guitars, among other things. Still, it's worth a look.

Sunday brings an array of wares into Mérida. Starting at 9 AM on Sunday, the **Bazar de Artesanías** (Handicrafts Bazaar; ⊠ in front of Palacio Municipal, across from main square, centro) sells lots of huipiles and women's dresses as well as hats and costume jewelry. The **Bazar de Artes Populares** (Popular Art Bazaar; ⊠ Parque de Santa Lucía, corner of Calles 60 and 55, centro), which starts at 9 AM on Sunday, sometimes has work by local artists. It also has locally produced crafts.

Specialty Stores

BOOKS

Librería Dante (⊠ Calle 58 at Calle 60, Parque Hidalgo, ☎ 999/923–9060; ⊠ Calle 17 No. 138-B, at Prolongación Paseo Montejo, Col. Itzimná, ☎ 999/927–7676; ⊠ Calle 62 and 61, on main plaza, centro, ☎ 999/928–2611) has art and travel books, and all branches carry at least a small selection of English-language books and a Mexico City daily newspaper. They are open Monday–Saturday 8 AM–9:30 PM and Sunday 10–6.

CLOTHING

Mexicanísimo (⊠ Calle 60 No. 496, at Calle 61, Parque Hidalgo, ☎ 999/923–8132) sells expensive designer cotton clothing inspired by regional dress. You might not wear a guayabera to a business meeting as some men in Mexico do, but the shirts are cool, comfortable, and attractive; for a good selection, try **Camisería Canul** (⊠ Calle 62 No. 484, between Calles 57 and 59, centro, ☎ 999/923–0158). Pick up a jipi (or order one custom made) at **El Becaleño** (⊠ Calle 65 No. 483, between Calles 56 and 58, centro, ☎ 999/985–0581); the famous hats are made at Becal in Campeche by the González family.

GALLERIES

The **Casa de Cera** (⊠ Calle 74-A No. 430-E, between Calles 41 and 43, ☎ 999/920–0219) sells signed series of collectible indigenous figures made of wax. The **Galería Ateneo Peninsular** (⊠ Calle 60 between Calle 61 and Pasaje Revolución, centro, ☎ no phone) sponsors shows by international artists. The **Galería Georgia Charuha** (⊠ Calle 60 between Calles 59 and 61, centro, ☎ 999/923–0495) shows mainly the owner's work, modern themes of Yucatán life in aguafuerte, pencil, and occasionally oil paint. The **Galería Casa Colón** (⊠ Av. Colón 507, Col. García Ginerés, ☎ 999/925–7952) highlights modern-day Mexican painters in the setting of a colonial home. Contemporary paintings and photographs are shown in the lobby of the **Teatro Peón Contreras** (⊠ Calle 60 between Calles 59 and 57, centro, ☎ 999/923–7354).

HAMMOCKS

A great place to purchase hammocks is **El Aguacate** (⊠ Calle 58 No. 604, at Calle 73, centro, ☎ 999/928–6429; ⊠ Calle 62 between Calles 61 and 59, centro, ☎ no phone), a family-run outfit with many sizes and designs and two locations. **El Hamaquero** (⊠ Calle 58 No. 572, between Calles 69 and 71, centro, ☎ 999/923–2117) has knowledgeable personnel who let you try out the hammocks before you buy. "Pancho Loco Maya," of **La Poblana** (⊠ Calle 65 between Calles 58 and 60, centro, ☎ no phone), will not only sell you one of the store's thousands of hammocks, he'll tell you how to store, hang, wash, and get in and out of it. **Tejidos y Cordeles Nacionales** (⊠ Calle 56 No. 516-B, between Calles 65 and 63, centro, ☎ 999/928–5561), the oldest hammock store in Mérida, is a family-run, no-frills shop.

JEWELRY

La Canasta (⊠ Calle 60 No. 500, at Calle 61, centro, ☎ 999/928–1978) has a good selection of filigree jewelry, both sterling silver and gold-dipped. It also has lots of cotton blouses for women, and local liqueurs. **La Perla Maya** (⊠ Calle 60 Nos. 485–487, between Calles 59 and 61, centro, ☎

999/928–5886) sells old-fashioned, silver Yucatecan filigree earrings and pins, although the selection isn't as good as it once was. **Tane** (⊠ Hyatt Regency, Calle 60 No. 344, at Av. Colón, Paseo Montejo, ☎ 999/ 942–0202) is an outlet for exquisite (and expensive) silver earrings, necklaces, and bracelets, some that incorporate ancient Maya designs.

CHICHÉN ITZÁ AND VALLADOLID

Although you can get to Chichén Itzá (120 km [74 mi] east of Mérida) along the shorter Route 180, it's far more scenic to follow Route 80 until it ends at Tekanto, then head south to Citilcúm, east past Izamal to Dzitás, and south again to Pisté. These roads have no signs but are the only paved roads going in these directions. Among the several villages you pass along Route 80 is Tixkokob, a Maya community famous for its hammock weavers. A short detour southeast from Tixkokob are the ruins of Aké.

Aké

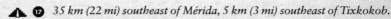 *35 km (22 mi) southeast of Mérida, 5 km (3 mi) southeast of Tixkokob.*

This tiny site, opened to the public at the end of 1996, is a convenient stop along the Mérida–Izamal course, on Route 80. The bizarre sight of the remains of a hacienda built next to a Maya temple is the most striking feature here. In fact, the site is named after the Hacienda of San Lorenzo Aké; both the hacienda and the local church are constructed of stones taken from the Maya temple. Estimates put occupation of the site around 200 BC to AD 900. A wall surrounding the city along with several temples and roads—one of which measured 33 km (20 mi) long and leads directly to Izamal—have been discovered so far, indicating this was an important city in its day. All that's excavated is a pyramid with rows of columns (35 total) at the top, very reminiscent of the Toltec columns at Tula, outside Mexico City. You can climb to the top of the ruins to see farmers cultivating the surrounding fields. You need a vehicle with high ground clearance to navigate the rutted dirt road that leads to the ruins. ⊠ *$2.* ⊙ *Daily 9–5.*

Izamal

⑱ *68 km (42 mi) southeast of Mérida.*

One of the best examples of a Spanish colonial town in the Yucatán, Izamal is nicknamed Ciudad Amarillo ("yellow city") because its most important buildings are painted earth-tone yellow by city ordinance. In the center of town stands the enormous 16th-century **Convento de San Antonio de Padua** (Monastery of St. Anthony of Padua), perched on—and built from—the remains of a Maya pyramid devoted to Itzamná, god of the heavens. The monastery's church, where Pope John Paul II led prayers in 1993, has a gigantic atrium, a colonnaded facade (supposedly second only to that of the Vatican in size), frescoes of saints (discovered in 1996), and rows of 75 yellow arches. The Virgin of the Immaculate Conception, to whom the church is dedicated, is the patron saint of the Yucatán. A statue of the Virgin was brought here from Guatemala in 1562 by Bishop de Landa. Miracles are ascribed to her, and a yearly pilgrimage takes place in her honor.

Pony traps surround the town's large main square, which fronts the cathedral. There are far worse ways to spend an afternoon than to trot around this pleasant town and then lounge in the square enjoying the local action.

Kinich Kakmó pyramid is all that remains of the royal Maya city that flourished here thousands of years ago, during the Early Classic period (AD 300–600). The enormous structure stands a few blocks from the Monastery of St. Anthony de Padua. It's under excavation, but it's worth walking over for a look.

On Sunday a special air-conditioned car attached to the regular train makes a round-trip excursion between Mérida and Izamal. The fare ($23) includes lunch, a folkloric show, and a city tour in a horse-drawn carriage. Tickets can be purchased through any travel agent. The train leaves the Mérida train station (☎ 999/926–1722 or 999/926–2057), on Calle 55 at Calle 48, Sunday at 8:15 AM and leaves Izamal for the 20-minute return trip at 3 PM.

Coming to Izamal on Route 80 from Mérida, cut south at Tekanto and east again at Citilcúm (the road has no number, and there are few signs).

Pisté

⑲ *116 km (72 mi) southeast of Mérida.*

The town of Pisté serves mainly as a base camp for travelers to Chichén Itzá. Hotels, campgrounds, restaurants, and handicrafts shops tend to be less expensive here than those at the ruins. At the west end of town is a Pemex gas station, but the town has no bank, so bring all the cash you'll need. On the outskirts of Pisté and a short walk from Chichén Itzá is **Pueblo Maya,** a pseudo-Maya village with a shopping and dining center for tour groups. The restaurant serves a bountiful buffet at lunch ($12).

Across from the Dolores Alba hotel, in town, is the **Parque Ik Kil** ("place of the winds"). The park is built around a lovely cenote where you can swim between 8 AM and 6 PM for $3. The park includes the Restaurant el Jardín, which serves Mexican and international fare; a swimming pool; bungalows inspired by Maya dwellings; and a row of shops where artisans demonstrate their crafts. ⊠ *Carretera Mérida–Puerto Juárez, Km 112,* ☎ *985/851–0000.*

Dining and Lodging

$$ ✕🏨 **Pirámide Inn Resort.** All the rooms in this two-story, American-owned '50s-style motel are clean and comfortable, with tile floors, air-conditioning, and large square desks; some have TVs. The garden contains a small Maya pyramid and an enormous rectangular swimming pool, and the restaurant is one of the best in Pisté. Some good vegetarian dishes are available, in addition to regional cuisine. ⊠ *Calle 15-A No. 28, at Calle 20, 97751,* ☎ *985/851–0115,* FAX *985/851–0114,* WEB *www.piramideinn.com. 50 rooms. Restaurant, pool, free parking. MC, V.*

$$ 🏨 **Dolores Alba.** The best low-budget choice near the ruins is this family-run hotel, a longtime favorite in the area south of Pisté. Rooms have colonial-style furniture and air-conditioning. Hammocks hang by one of the two pools, and breakfast and dinner are served family-style in the main building. Free transportation to Chichén Itzá is provided, and there is a covered, guarded parking lot. ⊠ *Carretera Mérida–Cancún, Km 122, 3 km (2 mi) south of Chichén Itzá,* ☎ *999/928–5650,* FAX *999/928–3163,* WEB *www.doloresalba.com. 40 rooms. Restaurant, 2 pools, free parking. No credit cards.*

Chichén Itzá

🔺 **⑳** *About 1 km (½ mi) east of Pisté.*

One of the four most magnificent Maya ruins—along with Palenque in Chiapas in Mexico, Tikal in Guatemala, and Cobá in Honduras—Chichén Itzá was the most important city in Yucatán from the 10th through the 12th century. Its architectural mélange covers pre-Hispanic Mesoamerican history and shows the influence of several different Maya groups.

Because epigraphers have been able to read 85% of the Chichén inscriptions, the site's history has become clearer to archaeologists. At one time it was believed that Chichén Itzá was dominated by the Toltecs from present-day central Mexico; now historians believe that the city was indeed influenced by trade with the north, not, however, by conquest. Chichén *was* altered by successive waves of inhabitants, and archaeologists are able to date the arrival of these waves by the changes in the architecture and information contained in inscriptions. That said, they have yet to explain the long gaps of time when the buildings seem to have been uninhabited. The site is believed to have been first settled in AD 432, abandoned for an unknown period of time, then rediscovered in 868 by the Maya-speaking Itzás, who migrated north from the region of the Petén rain forest around Tikal (in what is now northern Guatemala). The latest data point to the city's having been refounded by not only the Itzás but also by two other foreign groups—one from the Valley of Mexico (near present-day Mexico City) and another from Ek Balam. The trio formed a ruling triumvirate.

Chichén Itzá means "the mouth of the well of the Itzás." The Itzás may have also abandoned the site, but they were the dominant group until 1224, when the city appears to have been abandoned for all time. Francisco de Montejo established a short-lived colony here in the course of his conquest of Yucatán in the mid-1500s. At the turn of the 20th century, U.S. Consul General Edward Thompson, an engineer by training with a sharp eye for finding hidden pyramids, purchased Chichén Itzá and carried out some of the earliest excavations at the site, basing himself at a hacienda on the grounds (now the Hacienda Chichén) and, as was the custom of the day, carting many treasures away to the Peabody Museum at Harvard University. Years later, when the Mexican government began to realize what it had lost, many of the pieces were returned.

The enormity and gracefulness of this site are unforgettable. Chichén Itzá incarnates much of the fascinating and bloody history of the Maya, from the steep temple stairways down which sacrificial victims were undoubtedly hurled to the relentlessly ornate beauty of the smaller structures. The site's audacity and vitality are almost palpable. Chichén Itzá encompasses approximately 6 square km (2½ square mi), though only 30 to 40 structures and buildings of the several hundred at the site have been fully explored. These buildings include possibly the largest ball court in Mesoamerica; a sacrificial well once filled with precious offerings (it was dredged by Mexican diver Pablo Bush Romero, and many of its treasures are now found in the INAH archaeology museum in Mexico City); and a round building—one of the only ones in the Maya lands—that was possibly the most elegant and sophisticated of the Maya observatories. The site also has stone sculptures of Kukulcán, the plumed serpent god (the Aztecs' name was Quetzalcóatl), reclining Chacmools (intermediaries or messengers between gods and humans), steam baths for ritual purification, ruined murals, astronomical symbols, and broad *sacbés* (literally "white ways," used for ceremonial purposes and as trade arteries), leading to other ancient centers.

Chichén Itzá is divided into two parts, called Old and New, although architectural motifs from the Classic period are found in both sections. A more convenient distinction is topographical, since there are two major complexes of buildings separated by a dirt path. The martial, imperial architecture of the Itzás and the more cerebral architecture and astronomical expertise of the earlier Maya are married in the 98-ft-tall pyramid called **El Castillo** (the Castle), which dominates the site and rises above all the other buildings.

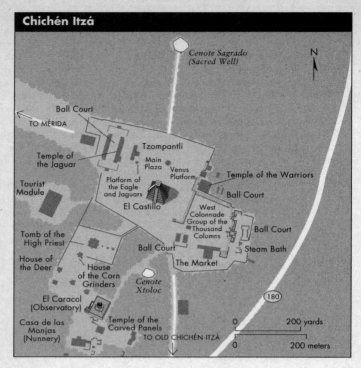

Chichén Itzá

Cenote Sagrado (Sacred Well)

N

Ball Court

TO MÉRIDA

Tzompantli

Temple of the Jaguar

Main Plaza

Venus Platform

Temple of the Warriors

Tourist Module

Platform of the Eagle and Jaguars

El Castillo

West Colonnade

Group of the Thousand Columns

Ball Court

Tomb of the High Priest

Ball Court

Steam Bath

House of the Deer

House of the Corn Grinders

The Market

Cenote Xtoloc

180

El Caracol (Observatory)

Casa de las Monjas (Nunnery)

Temple of the Carved Panels

TO OLD CHICHÉN ITZÁ

0   200 yards

0   200 meters

Atop the Castillo is a temple dedicated to Kukulcán/Quetzalcoatl, the legendary Toltec priest-king from Tula in the Valley of Mexico who was held to be an incarnation of the mystical plumed serpent. According to ancient lore, Quetzalcoatl went into exile, disappearing to the east but promising to return one day. The Aztecs, who inherited the cult of Quetzalcóatl from the Toltecs, later initially mistook the Spanish conquistador Hernán Cortés for this god, transforming the prophecy into a nightmarish reality.

Four stairways, each facing one of the four cardinal points, provided access to the temple; two are used today. If you're afraid of heights, hold on to the chain running down the center. Each access way consists of 91 very steep and narrow steps, which, when you count the temple platform itself, makes a total of 365 (one for each day of the Mayas' extraordinarily accurate solar calendar). Fifty-two panels on the sides stand for the years of a sacred cycle, while the 18 terraces symbolize the months of the year. An open-jawed plumed serpent rests on the balustrade of each stairway, and serpents reappear at the top of the temple as sculptured columns. This is one of the rare examples in the Maya world of a temple with four stairways, which represents the symbolic partitioning of the world into four parts, according to mythic lore.

At the spring and fall equinoxes, the afternoon light strikes one of these balustrades in such a way as to form a shadow representation of Kukulcán undulating out of his temple and down the pyramid to bless the fertile earth. Then as now, this phenomenon is viewed from the broad plaza on the northern side of the pyramid, a space reserved for ritual ceremonies by the Maya. Tens of thousands of people travel to Chichén Itzá to see this phenomenon, particularly in the spring, when there is little likelihood of rain. Hotel reservations for the event should be made well in advance; a year ahead is not unreasonable.

In 1937 archaeologists discovered a more ancient temple inside El Castillo. A humid, slippery stairway leads up to an altar that once held two statues: a Chacmool and a bejeweled red tiger. The tiger, which had jade-encrusted discs embedded into its body and a turquoise disc laid on top of it, probably as an offering, is now in the National Anthropology Museum (Museo Nacional de Antropología) in Mexico City. The inner temple is open to the public for only a few hours in the morning and again in the afternoon. Claustrophobes should think twice before entering: the stairs are narrow, dark, and winding, and there is often a line of tourists going both ways, making the trip somewhat frightening.

Each evening there's a sound-and-light show that highlights the architectural details in El Castillo and other buildings with a clarity the eye doesn't see in daylight. The accompanying narration is drawn rather loosely from the works of Bishop Landa and from the few surviving Maya texts, including the Books of Chilam Balam and Popul Vuh. Some of the data are incorrect, showing a lack of respect for historical detail. Landa initially burned all the Maya manuscripts he collected but later, overcome with remorse and admiration for the Maya, wrote their history. Regardless of the flaws of the show, the narration and setting seem particularly powerful on nights of a full moon.

The temple rests on a massive trapezoidal square, on the west side of which is Chichén Itzá's largest **ball court,** one of seven on the site. Its two parallel walls are each 272 ft long, with two stone rings on each side, and 99 ft apart. The game played here was something like soccer (no hands were used), but it had a strictly religious significance. Bas-relief carvings at the court depict a player being decapitated, the blood spurting from his neck fertilizing the earth. Other bas-reliefs show two teams of opposing players pitted against each other during the ball game. Originally it was thought one team represented the invader Toltecs, but evidence points out the fact that the wardrobe design of the "Toltecs" has very Maya elements and that there never was a ball game between the two. The acoustics are so good that someone standing at one end of the court can in theory clearly hear the whispers of another person at the other end.

Between the ball court and El Castillo stands a **Tzompantli,** or stone platform, carved with rows of human skulls. In ancient times such walls were made of real skulls: the heads of enemies impaled on stakes. This concept was most likely imported from Tenochtitlán, the onetime Aztec capital at the site of present-day Mexico City.

The predilection for human sacrifice was once believed to have been unknown to the Maya, but research has verified that they indulged in their own forms of the ritual for hundreds of years. Legend has it that the **Sacred Well,** a cenote 65 yards in diameter that sits 1 km (½ mi) north of El Castillo at the end of a sacbé, was used for human sacrifices; another cenote at the site supplied drinking water. Skeletons of about 50 people were found in the first well. The sacrificial victims, many of them children of both sexes, were drugged before being dropped into the well. It is said that if any of the victims survived until noon, they were fished out of the well in the hopes that they would recount the psychic visions they had experienced. Hunac Ceel, the notorious ruler of Mayapán in the 1250s, hurled himself into its depths to prove his divinity and survived.

Many archaeologists believe that nonhuman sacrifices were carried out by local chiefs hundreds of years after Chichén Itzá was abandoned. Thousands of artifacts made of gold, jade, and other precious materials, most of them not of local provenance, have been recovered from the brackish depths of the cenote. Long on display at Harvard's Peabody Museum, many of the finds were returned to the Mexican government. Trees and shrubs have washed into the well over the centuries, and their remains have prevented divers from getting to the bottom; because the cenote is fed by a network of underground rivers, it cannot be drained. More treasure undoubtedly remains. The well's excavation (by Pablo Bush Romero) launched the field of underwater archaeology later honed by the late Jacques Cousteau.

East of El Castillo is the **Group of the Thousand Columns** with the famous **Temple of the Warriors,** a masterful example of the Itzá influence at Chichén Itzá. The temple was used as a meeting place for the high lords of the council that ruled Chichén Itzá. The temple-top sculpture of the reclining Chacmool—its head turned to the side, the offertory dish carved into its middle—is probably the most photographed symbol of the Maya. This temple also resembles Pyramid B at Tula (sans Chacmool), the Toltecs' homeland, north of Mexico City. The resemblance is what originally led scholars to believe that there was a Toltec connection to the site. However, the carvings of the lords found here are equivalent to carvings discovered at Copán in Honduras.

Masonry walls carved with feathered serpents and frescoes of eagles and jaguars consuming human hearts are among the unmistakably Itzá details. (The Itzá were great traders and in turn undoubtedly influenced by Toltec motifs they had seen on their journeys.) Note the columns inscribed with impressive feathered serpent with open jaws. They symbolize the ancient War Serpents of the Itzá, mythical creatures that were thought to serve as vehicles for communicating with the underworld. Using columns and wood beams instead of the Maya arches and walls to divide space enabled the architects to expand the interior and exterior spaces dramatically. These spaces were also used for ritual dancing and processions associated with the council meetings. Murals of everyday village life and scenes of war can be viewed here, and an artistic representation of the defeat of one of the Itzás' Maya enemies can be found on the interior murals of the **Temple of the Jaguar,** west of the Temple of the Warriors at the Ball Court.

To get to the less visited cluster of structures at **New Chichén Itzá**—often confused with Old Chichén Itzá—take the main path south from the Temple of the Jaguar past El Castillo and turn right onto a small path opposite the ball court on your left. Archaeologists have been restoring several buildings in this area, including the Tomb of the High Priest, where several tombs with skeletons and jade offerings were found, and the northern part of the site, which was used for military training and barracks for the army. Some smaller abodes not yet reconstructed are believed to have been guest houses or sleeping quarters for nobles who lived in the center of the city. The work of the Maya epigraphers is helping to identify the function of each of the structures. As work continues, certain ruins will be roped off and closed to visitors.

The most impressive structure within this area is the astronomical observatory called El Caracol. The name, meaning "snail," refers to the spiral staircase at the building's core. Built in several stages, El Caracol is one of the few round buildings constructed by the Maya. Judging by the tiny windows oriented toward the four cardinal points, and the structure's alignment with the planet Venus, it was used for observing the heavens. Since astronomy was the province of priests and used to determine rituals and predict the future, the building undoubtedly served a religious function as well.

After leaving El Caracol, continue south several hundred yards to the beautiful La Casa de las Monjas ("the nunnery") and its annex, which have long panels carved with flowers and animals, latticework, hieroglyph-covered lintels, and Chaac masks (as does the nunnery at Uxmal). It was the Spaniards who gave the structure this sobriquet; no one knows exactly how it was used by the Maya.

At so-called **Old Chichén Itzá,** south of the remains of Thompson's hacienda, the architecture shows less outside influence: a combination of Puuc and Chenes Maya styles—with playful latticework, Chaac masks, and gargoylelike serpents on the cornices—dominates. (This style also crops up at Uxmal, Kabah, Labná, and Sayil.) Highlights include the Date Group, so named because of its complete series of hieroglyphic dates; the House of the Phalli; and the Temple of the Three Lintels. Maya guides will lead you down the path by an old narrow-gauge railroad track to even more ruins, barely unearthed, if you ask. A fairly good restaurant and a great ice cream stand are in the entrance building, as is a gift shop where you can purchase film, bus tickets, postcards, and books. A small museum includes information on the migration patterns of the ancient Maya inhabitants and some small sculptures recovered from the site. ☎ *$8.50 (includes museum and sound-and-light show), free Sun.; parking $2; use of video camera $7.* ☉ *Daily 8–5; sound-and-light show Apr.–Oct., daily at 8 PM, Nov.–Mar., daily at 7 PM.*

Lodging

$$$$ 🏨 **Mayaland.** The hotel closest to the ruins, this charming 1920s lodg-
★ ing is set in a large garden on the 100-acre site. You can actually see part of Old Chichén from the grounds, and the hotel has its own entrance to the ruins. Colonial-style guest rooms have decorative tiles, air-conditioning, and cable TV. The 24 bungalows at the rear of the hotel are the quietest and prettiest accommodations, with hammocks on the wide verandas, bathtubs, and thatch roofs. Snacks served poolside are a better choice than the expensive meals in the dining room. ✉ *Carretera Mérida–Puerto Juárez, Km 120,* ☎ *999/924–2099; 800/ 235–4079 in the U.S.;* FAX *999/924–6290,* ☎ FAX *985/851–0129;* WEB *www.mayaland.com. 24 bungalows, 67 rooms, 10 suites. 4 restaurants, room service, minibars, tennis court, 3 pools, volleyball, 2 bars, travel services, free parking. AE, DC, MC, V.*

$$$ 🏨 **Hacienda Chichén.** A converted 16th-century hacienda with its own
★ entrance to the ruins, this hotel once served as the headquarters for the Carnegie expedition to Chichén Itzá. The rustic-chic cottages have handwoven bedspreads, dehumidifiers, and air-conditioning. All rooms, which are simply but beautifully furnished in colonial Yucatecan style, have verandas but no phone or TV. There's a satellite TV in the library. An enormous old pool as well as a chapel now used for weddings grace the landscaped gardens. Meals are served on the patio overlooking the grounds or in the air-conditioned restaurant. ✉ *Carretera Mérida–Puerto Juárez, Km 120,* ☎ *985/851–0045, 999/924–2150; 800/624–8451 in the U.S.;* ☎ FAX *999/924–5011. 24 rooms, 4 suites. Restaurant, pool, bar, free parking; no room phones. AE, DC, MC, V.*

Cave of Balancanchén

 21 *6 km (4 mi) east of Chichén Itzá.*

The Cave of Balancanchén, a shrine whose Maya name translates as "throne of the jaguar," remained virtually undisturbed from the time of the conquest until its discovery in 1959. Inside are some of the artifacts—mostly vases, jars, and incense burners—once used in sacred rituals. Although there are seven chambers, only three are open. You walk past tiers of stalactites and stalagmites; one group (according to the guides) forms the image of a sacred ceiba tree. Visit the underground cenote, filled with blind fish, where Maya priests worshiped at an altar the gods of rain and water. In order to explore the shrine you must take one of the guided tours, which depart almost hourly. You need to be in fairly good shape for the tour and wear comfortable shoes. Also at the site is a sound-and-light show that fancifully recounts Maya history. A small museum at the entrance is very informative. The caves are just 6 km (4 mi) from Chichén Itzá; you can catch a bus or taxi or arrange a tour at Mayaland hotel. ✉ *$4.50 (including tour), free Sun.; sound-and-light show $4; parking $2 extra.* ⊘ *Daily 9–5; tours leave daily at 11, 1, and 3 (English); 9, noon, 2, and 4 (Spanish); and 10 (French).*

Valladolid

㉒ *44½ km (28 mi) east of Chichén Itzá.*

The second-largest city in the State of Yucatán, Valladolid is a picturesque provincial town, much smaller than Mérida. It has been enjoying growing popularity among travelers en route to or from Chichén Itzá or Río Lagartos who want a change from the more touristy places. Montejo founded Valladolid in 1543 on the site of the Maya town of Sisal. The city suffered during the War of the Castes—when the Maya in revolt killed nearly all Spanish residents—and again during the Mexican Revolution.

Today, however, placidity reigns in this agricultural market town. The center is mostly colonial, although it has many 19th-century structures. The main sights are the colonial churches, principally the large **Catedral de San Servacio** (San Servace Cathedral) on the central square and the 16th-century **Convento y Iglesia de San Bernadino** (San Bernardino Church and Monastery) three blocks southwest. Both were pillaged during the War of the Castes. A briny but pretty cenote in the center of town draws lots of local boys busily showing off for each other; if you're not up for a dip, visit the adjacent **ethnographic museum.** West of the main square and on the old highway to Chichén Itzá, you can swim with the catfish in lovely, mysterious **Cenote Dzitnup,** in a cave lit by a small natural skylight; admission is $2.50.

Valladolid is renowned for its cuisine, particularly its sausages; try one of the restaurants within a block of the central square. You can find good buys on sandals, baskets, and the local liqueur, Xtabentún, flavored with honey and anise.

Dining and Lodging

$$ ✕🏨 **El Mesón del Marqués.** On the north side of the main square is this well-preserved, very old hacienda, which was built around a lovely courtyard. All rooms have air-conditioning, phones, and cable TV and are attractively furnished with rustic and colonial touches. The 25 junior suites have large bathrooms with bathtubs. The charming restaurant, set under porticos surrounding the courtyard, serves Yucatecan specialties such as pollo pibíl and local sausage served in different ways. It's open 7 AM–11 PM. ✉ *Calle 39 No. 203, 97780,* ☎ *985/856–2073 or 985/856–3042,* 𝖥𝖠𝖷 *985/856–2280. 58 rooms, 25 suites. Restaurant, pool, bar. AE.*

$$ 🏨 **Ecotel Quinta Real.** This attractive salmon-color hotel is a mix of colonial Mexican and modern. Near a leafy park five blocks from downtown, the pretty rooms have cool tile floors, cable TV, air-conditioning, and spacious balconies. Wander the tree-filled garden; visit the pool, palapa bar, tennis court, or duck pond; or head to the game room for Ping-Pong or billiards. Continental breakfast is included in the room rate. ✉ *Calle 40 No. 160-A, at Calle 27, 97780,* ☎ *985/856–3472 or 985/856–3473,* 𝖥𝖠𝖷 *985/856–2422,* 𝖶𝖤𝖡 *www.ecotelquintareal.com.mx. 48 rooms. Restaurant, tennis court, pool, bar, car rental, travel services, free parking. MC, V.*

$ 🖼 **María de la Luz.** This main-plaza hotel is built around a shallow, kid-ney-shape swimming pool surrounded by banana trees. The plain rooms have tile bathrooms, air-conditioning, firm beds, and color cable TV. The street-side restaurant is attractively furnished with high-backed rattan chairs and linen cloths; Mexican dishes are predictable and inexpensive, but tasty. Pollo pibíl is a house specialty. ⊠ *Calle 42 No. 193-C, between Calles 39 and 41, 97780,* ☎ ⅎAX *985/856–2071 or 985/856–1181. 68 rooms, 2 suites. Restaurant, pool, bar, free parking. MC, V.*

Ek Balam

⛰ ㉓ *20 km (12 mi) north of Valladolid, off Rte. 295.*

The site of Ek Balam ("black jaguar"), a powerful city that was driven by a marine economy, opened to the public in 2000. It contains two concentric walls surrounding a main area, a rare configuration in Maya sites, plus 45 structures in the main excavation field. Prominent among them is the stunning **Tower** pyramid, set off by two small tem-ples with staircases; a giant monster mask crowns its summit, which is embedded with marvelous glyphs and friezes. Archaeologists have learned that the Tower was a mausoleum for King Ukit IV. Priceless funerary objects have been uncovered and are under study. Buried with the king were pearls, thousands of perforated seashells, gold, jade, mother-of-pearl pendants, and small bone masks with moveable jaws. Another Ek Balam ruler, Hun-Pik-Tok, was part of a ruling triumvi-rate of Chichén Itzá in the second phase of development. 🎟 *$2, free Sun.* ⏰ *Daily 8–5.*

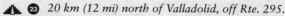

UXMAL AND THE RUTA PUUC

After passing the large Maya town of Umán on Mérida's southern out-skirts, you'll enter one of the less-populated areas of the Yucatán. From the highest point on the peninsula, the 500-ft crest between the present village of Muna and the ruins of ancient Uxmal, an unbroken expanse of low tropical forest reaches all the way to the southern horizon. The highway to Uxmal and Kabah is a fairly traffic-free route through uncultivated woodlands, punctuated here and there by oval thatch-roof huts and roadside stands.

The forest seems to thicken beyond Uxmal, which was in ancient times the largest and most important Puuc city. Raised and cobbled ceremonial roads connected it to a number of smaller ceremonial centers that, de-spite their apparent subservience to the lords of Uxmal, boasted lofty pyramids and ornate palaces of their own. Several of these satellite sites, including Kabah, Sayil, and Labná, are open to the public; they stand along a side road known as the "Ruta Puuc," which winds eastward and eventually joins Route 184, a highway linking Mérida with Felipe Carrillo Puerto, Quintana Roo, on the Caribbean coast, and serving the largest concentration of present-day Maya agricultural towns on the peninsula. From the east end of the Ruta Puuc near Loltún Caves, it takes motorists less than an hour either to retrace their route back to Uxmal or to return to Mérida on Route 184.

If you don't have your own wheels, a great option for seeing the ruins of the Ruta Puuc is the **ATS** tour (⊠ Calle 69 No. 544, between Calles 68 and 70, ☎ 999/923–2287) that leaves Mérida at 8 AM from the sec-ond-class bus station. The tour stops for half an hour each at the ruins of Labná, Xlapac, Sayil, and Kabah, giving you just enough time to scan the plaques, climb a few crumbling steps, and poke your nose into a crevice or two. You get almost two hours at Uxmal before heading back to Mérida at 2:30 PM. The trip costs $9 per person, is unguided,

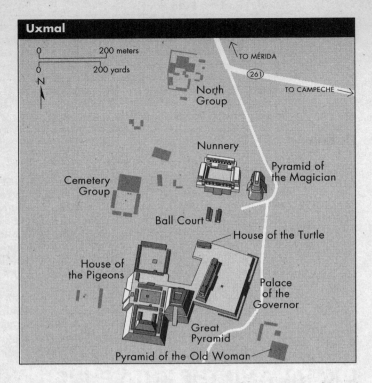

and does not include entrance to the ruins. If you go on Sunday, entrance to all archaeological sites is free.

Uxmal

★ ◭ ㉔ *78 km (48 mi) south of Mérida on Rte. 261.*

If Chichén Itzá is the most impressive Maya ruin in Yucatán, Uxmal is arguably the most beautiful. Where the former has a Maya Itzá grandeur, the latter seems more understated and elegant—pure Maya. The architecture reflects the Late Classic renaissance of the 7th–9th centuries that arose after the decline of the Classic cities such as Palenque and Tikal. Although the name translates as "thrice built" (referring to the three levels of the Governor's Palace, in which older temples were buried), the site was actually rebuilt, abandoned, and reoccupied in several stages, for reasons still unknown. Itzá invaders briefly occupied Uxmal in the 10th century. The site reemerged as a Maya ceremonial center in the Postclassic era and was deserted for the last time some 90 years before the conquest. When American explorer John Lloyd Stephens came upon Uxmal in 1840, it was owned by a descendant of the Montejo family, whose predecessors had conquered Yucatán three centuries earlier.

The site is considered the finest and largest example of Puuc architecture, which embraces such details as ornate stone mosaics and friezes on the upper walls, rows of columns, and soaring vaulted arches. Lines are clean and uncluttered, with the horizontal—especially the parallelogram—preferred to the vertical. Many of the flat, low, elongated buildings were built on artificial platforms and laid out in quadrangles. The cult of the rain god, Chaac, who is depicted here with a long curled nose and whose image appears throughout Yucatán, was of supreme importance in this region of heavy but irregular rainfall. The area lacks surface water, but the problem was solved by ingenious Maya engineers who dug cisterns, called *chultunes,* for collecting rainwater. Drought may be the reason that Uxmal was periodically abandoned.

While most of Uxmal hasn't been restored, three buildings in particular merit attention:

At 140 ft high, the **Pyramid of the Magician** is the tallest and most prominent structure at the site. Unlike most other Maya pyramids, which are stepped and angular, it has a strangely round-corner design. Built five times at 52-year sequences to coincide with the ceremony of the new fire, each time over the previous structure, the pyramid has a stairway on its western side that leads through a giant open-mouthed mask of Chaac to two temples at the summit. The mask motif is repeated on one side of the stairs. You get a magnificent panoramic view of Uxmal and the hills by climbing to the top. The pyramid's name is based on a legend concerning a dwarf magician hatched from an egg, who built the structure. It is especially lovely at night, when its pale beige slope glows in the moonlight.

West of the pyramid lies the **Quadrangle of the Nuns,** considered by some to be the finest part of Uxmal. The name was given to it by the Spanish conquistadors because it reminded them of a convent building in Old Spain. According to research, what is called the **Nunnery** was actually the palace and living quarters of a high lord of Uxmal by the name of Chaan Chak, which means "abundance of rain." You can see his carved figure on Stela No. 14, now on exhibit at the museum at the entrance to the site. Chaan Chak also inaugurated the ball court at Uxmal on January 15 and 16, AD 901, inscriptions say. You may enter the four buildings; each comprises a series of low, gracefully repetitive chambers that look onto a central patio. The building on the southern side is broken by a tall corbeled arch that is formed by placing ceiling stones increasingly close to and on top of one another until they meet at a central supporting capstone. Elaborate decoration—stone latticework, masks, geometric patterns reminiscent of ancient Greek ornamentation, representations of the classic Maya thatch hut (*na*), coiling snakes, and some phallic figures—blankets the upper facades, in contrast with the smooth, sheer blocks that face the lower walls. The mosaics that thrust into the upper facade are huge, sometimes surpassing several feet in size.

Continue walking south; you pass the ball court before reaching the **Palace of the Governor,** which archaeologist Victor von Hagen considered the most magnificent building ever erected in the Americas. Interestingly, the palace faces east while the rest of Uxmal faces west. Archaeologists believe this is because the palace was used to sight the planet Venus. Covering 5 acres and rising over an immense acropolis, the palace lies at the heart of what must have been Uxmal's administrative center. Its 320-ft length is divided by three corbeled arches, which create narrow passageways or sanctuaries. Decorating the facade are intricate friezes (along the uppermost section), geometrically patterned carvings overlaid with plumed serpents, stylized Chaac masks, and human faces. These mosaics required more than 20,000 individually cut stones.

First excavated in 1929 by the Danish explorer Franz Blom, Uxmal served in 1841 as home to American explorer John Lloyd Stephens, who wrote of it: "The whole wears an air of architectural symmetry and grandeur. If it stood at this day on its grand artificial terrace in Hyde Park or the Garden of the Tuileries, it would form a new order . . . not unworthy to sit side by side with the remains of Egyptian, Grecian, and Roman art."

Today a sound-and-light show recounts Maya legends, including the kidnaping of an Uxmal princess by a king of Chichén Itzá, and focuses on the people's dependence on rain—thus the cult of Chaac. The artificial colored light brings out details of carvings and mosaics that are easy to miss when the sun is shining—for example, the stone replicas of *nas* (thatch-roof huts), which bear a remarkable resemblance to contemporary huts, on one facade of the nunnery. The show is performed nightly in Spanish; earphones provide an English translation. ⊠ *Site, museum, and sound-and-light show $8.50; free Sun. (English-translation of sound-and-light show, $3); parking $2; use of video camera $8. ☉ Daily 8–5; sound-and-light show Apr.–Oct., nightly at 8 PM; Nov.–Mar., nightly at 7 PM.*

Dining and Lodging

$ ✕ **Las Palapas.** A great alternative to the area's hotel dining rooms, this family-run restaurant specializes in delicious Yucatecan dishes served with homemade tortillas. When tour groups request it in advance, the owners prepare a traditional feast, roasting the chicken or pork pibíl-style, in a pit in the ground. If you see a tour bus in the parking lot, stop in—you may chance upon a memorable fiesta. ⊠ *Hwy. 261, 5 km (3 mi) north of the Uxmal ruins,* ☎ *no phone. No credit cards.*

$$$$ ⊡ **Hacienda Uxmal.** Just across the road from the ruins, and the oldest hotel at the site, this pleasant colonial-style building has lovely floor tiles, ceramics, and iron grillwork. The rooms—all with ceiling fans, satellite TV, and air-conditioning—are fronted with wide, furnished verandas; the courtyard contains two pools surrounded by gardens. Ask about packages that include free or low-cost car rentals, or comfortable minivans traveling to Mérida, Chichén, or Cancún. ⊠ *Carretera Merida-Campeche, Km. 78,* ☎ *997/976–2012; 998/884–4510 in Cancún; 800/235–4079 in the U.S.;* ℻ *997/976–2011; 998/884–4510 in Cancún;* WEB *www.mayaland.com. 80 rooms, 2 suites. 2 restaurants, room service, 2 pools, billiards, Ping-Pong, bar, free parking. AE, MC, V.*

$$$$ ⊡ **Lodge at Uxmal.** Classy materials (glossy red-tile floors, carved and polished hardwood doors and rocking chairs, and local weavings) are combined with luxury amenities in a sprinkling of rustic-looking, two-story thatch-roof buildings. All have bathtubs, cable TV, and minibars, as well as fans, screened windows, plus air-conditioning. Suites have king-size beds and jet baths. The effect is suitably comfortable yet luxuriant. ⊠ *Carretera Uxmal, Km 78,* ☎ *998/884–4510 in Cancún; 800/235–4079 in the U.S.;* ℻ *998/884–4510 in Cancún;* WEB *www.mayaland.com. 30 rooms, 10 suites. 2 restaurants, minibars, some in-room hot tubs, 2 pools, bar, free parking. AE, MC, V.*

$$ ⊡ **Villas Arqueológicas Uxmal.** Rooms in this pretty two-story Club Med property are small and functional, with wooden furniture that fits the niches nicely, and quiet air conditioners. Half of the rooms have garden views. The French and Continental food served in the restaurant—including niçoise salad, pâté, and filet mignon—can be a delightful change from regional fare. Meal plans are available and reasonable for Club Med guests. ⊠ *Carretera Uxmal, Km 76,* ☎ *997/976–2018 or 800/258–2633,* ℻ *997/976–2020. 40 rooms, 3 suites. Restaurant, pool, billiards, bar, library, free parking. AE, MC, V.*

Kabah

23 km (14 mi) south of Uxmal on Rte. 261.

Kabah, which experts estimate was first inhabited around 250 BC, was at one point the largest restoration project in the Yucatán. A ceremonial center of soft, almost Grecian beauty, it was once linked to Uxmal by a sacbé, at the end of which looms a great independent arch—now across the highway from the main ruins. The 151-ft-long **Kabah** (coiled mat)—also known as Palace of the Masks—is so called because of its 250 Chaac masks of inlaid stones. To some they resemble rolled-up straw mats. ⌨ *$2.50, free Sun.* ☉ *Daily 8–5.*

Sayil

 9 km (5½ mi) south of Kabah on Rte. 31 E.

Sayil, or "home of ants," is the oldest site of the Puuc group: experts believe the site flourished between AD 800 and AD 1000. It is renowned primarily for its majestic three-story **Gran Palacio,** built on a hill and containing more than 90 rooms and a figure of the goddess of fertility. The structure recalls Palenque in its use of multiple planes, its columned porticoes and sober cornices, and in the play of its long, graceful horizontal masses. ⌨ *$2.50, free Sun.* ☉ *Daily 8–5.*

Labná

 9 km (5½ mi) south of Sayil on Rte. 31 E.

The striking, monumental structure at Labná ("old house" or "abandoned house") is a fanciful corbeled arch rising high into a near peak, with elaborate latticework and a small chamber on each side. One theory says the arch was the entrance to an area where religious ceremonies were staged. The site was used mainly by the military elite and royalty. ⌨ *$2.50, free Sun.* ☉ *Daily 8–5.*

Loltún Caves

★ *18 km (11 mi) northeast of Labná.*

The Loltún ("stone flower" in Maya) is the largest known cave system in the Yucatán. This series of caverns contains wall paintings and stone artifacts from Maya and pre-Maya times (around 2500 BC), as well as stalactites and stalagmites. Some of the forms have been given descriptive names such as Corn Ear and Cathedral. Illuminated pathways wander a little over a kilometer (½ mile) through the caverns. You can enter the caves only on guided tours, which leave at 9:30, 11, 12:30, 2, 3, and 4. ⌨ *$4.50, free Sun.* ☉ *Daily 9–5.*

Ticul

 27 km (16½ mi) northwest of the Loltún Caves, 28 km (17 mi) east of Uxmal.

One of the larger towns in Yucatán, Ticul has a handsome 17th-century church and is a good base for exploring the Puuc region. Many descendants of the Xiu dynasty, which ruled Uxmal until the conquest, still live here. Industries include fabrication of huipiles and shoes, as well as much of the pottery you see around the Yucatán. **Arte Maya** (⌧ Calle 23 No. 301, between Calles 38 and 40, ☎ 997/972–1316) is a ceramics workshop that produces museum-quality replicas of archaeological pieces found throughout Mexico. The workshop's master craftsmen also produce smaller, souvenir-quality pieces that are both more affordable and more easily transported than their more ambitious pieces.

OFF THE
BEATEN PATH

MAYAPÁN – Those who are enamored of Yucatán and the ancient Maya may want to take a 49-km (30-mi) detour north of Ticul (via Mamá and Tekit) to Mayapán, the last of the major city-states on the peninsula, which flourished during the Postclassic era. It was demolished in AD

1450, presumably by war. It is thought that the city, with an architectural style reminiscent of Uxmal, was as big as Chichén Itzá, and there are more than 4,000 mounds to bear this out. At its height, the population could have been well over 12,000. A half dozen mounds are being vigorously excavated, including the palaces of Maya royalty and the temple of the benign god Kukulcán, where murals in vivid reds and oranges, plus stucco sculptures of Chaac, have been uncovered. The ceremonial structures that were faithfully described in Fray Diego de Landa's writings will look like they have jumped right out of his book when the work is completed. ⊠ *Off road to left before Telchaquillo; follow signs.* 🎫 *$2, free Sun.* ☉ *Daily 8–5.*

Dining and Lodging

$$ ✕ **Los Delfines.** Seafood is the strength of this friendly neighborhood restaurant, which has a high thatch roof and open sides. There's a full bar and a large seafood menu, including seafood cocktails, ceviche, many styles of shrimp, and seafood soup. Delfines also serves chicken, poc chuc, and other regional dishes. A selection of free appetizers is brought to your table soon after you're seated. Guests can use the small octagonal pool in the garden. The place is open daily 11–5. ⊠ *Calle 27 No. 216, between Calles 28 and 30,* ☎ *997/972–0401. No credit cards. No dinner.*

$ ✕ **Los Almendros.** This restaurant, one of the few in town open until 9 PM, is a good place to sample regional fare, including handmade tortillas. The *combinado yucateco* gives you a chance to try poc chuc and cochinita pibíl (two pork dishes) as well as *pavo relleno* (stuffed turkey) and sausage. Los Almendros looks rather run-down, but the staff is friendly and helpful, and the 30-year-old restaurant is popular with locals as well as tourists. ⊠ *Calle 23 No. 207-A,* ☎ *999/972–0021. AE.*

$ 🏨 **Plaza.** This very pleasant three-story hotel surrounds a large central patio and is just a block from the main plaza. It has clean bathrooms and firm mattresses, hammock hooks, telephones, fans, and TV. Choose a room with air-conditioning; the price difference is only about $5. ⊠ *Calle 23 No. 202, between Calles 26 and 26-A,* ☎ *997/972–0484,* FAX *997/972–0026. 25 rooms, 5 suites. Free parking; no air-conditioning in some rooms. AE, MC, V (with 6% surcharge).*

Yaxcopoil

30 *50 km (31 mi) north of Uxmal on Rte. 261.*

Yaxcopoil, a restored 17th-century hacienda, makes for a nice change of pace from the ruins. The building, with its distinctive Moorish double arch out front, has been used as a film set and is the best-known henequen plantation in the region. The museum's rooms are fitted with their original European furnishings; the machine room was used in the processing of henequen. The family chapel is in the garden. ⊠ *Rte. 261, Km 33,* ☎ *999/927–2606 or 999/950–1065.* 🎫 *$2.50.* ☉ *Tues.–Sat. 8 AM–sunset, Sun. 9–1.*

Oxkintoc

🔺 **31** *50 km (31 mi) south of Mérida on Rte. 180*

The archaeological site of Oxkintoc is 5 km (3 mi) east of Maxcanú, off Route 180, and contains the ruins of an important Maya capital that dominated the region from about AD 300 to 1100. Little was known about Oxkintoc until excavations began here in 1987. Bearing a pure Puuc architectural style, structures that have been excavated so far include two tall pyramids, a palace with stone statues of several ancient rulers, and a temple that serves as the entrance to Tzat Tun Tzat, a mysterious subterranean labyrinth. ⊠ *Off Rte. 184, 1½ km (1 mi) west of Rte. 180.* ☜ *$2, free Sun.* ☉ *Daily 8–5.*

PROGRESO AND THE NORTH COAST

Various routes lead from Mérida to towns along the coast, which spreads across a distance of 380 km (236 mi). Less-traveled roads dead-end at the forgotten former seaport of Sisal and the laid-back fishing village of Celestún, gateway to a flamingo reserve near the Campeche border. The busiest route, Highway 261, leads due north from Mérida to the modern shipping port and local beach playground of Progreso. To get to some of the small beach towns east of Progreso, head east on Highway 291 out of Mérida and then cut north on one of the many access roads. Wide, white, and generally shadeless beaches here are peppered with bathers from Mérida during Holy Week and in summer—but are nearly vacant the rest of the year.

The terrain in this part of the peninsula is absolutely flat. Tall trees are scarce, because the region was almost entirely cleared for coconut palms in the early 19th century and again for henequen in the early 20th century. Local Maya people still tend some of the old fields of henequen, a spike-leaf agave plant, even though there is little profit to be made from the rope fiber it produces. Other former plantation fields have run wild, overgrown with scrub and marked only by the low, white stone walls erected to mark their boundaries. Bird life is abundant in the area, and butterflies swarm in profusion throughout the dry season.

Celestún

 90 km (56 mi) west of Mérida.

This tranquil fishing village, with its air of unpretentiousness and gulf-coast flavor, sits at the end of a spit of land separating the Celestún estuary from the gulf on the western hump of the Yucatán. Celestún is the only point of entry to the **Parque Natural Ría Celestún,** a 100,000-acre wildlife reserve with extensive mangrove forests and salt flats and one of the largest colonies of flamingos in North America. Most of the flamingos took up residence here following Hurricane Gilbert in 1988, abandoning Ría Lagartos, which had been badly damaged by the high waters and wind. Clouds of pink wings soar over the pale blue backdrop of the estuary all year, but the best months for seeing them in abundance—as many as 500 flamingos at a time—are April through June. This is also the fourth-largest wintering ground for ducks of the gulf-coast region, with more than 300 other species of birds and a large sea-turtle population. Conservation programs sponsored by the United States and Mexico protect not only the birds and endangered hawksbill and loggerhead marine tortoises but species such as the blue crab and crocodiles as well.

The park is set among rocks, islets, and lovely white-sand beaches. There is good fishing in both the river and the gulf. Bring your bathing suit if you want to enjoy a swim in one of the cenotes. Most Mérida travel agencies run boat tours of the *ría* (estuary) in the early morning or late afternoon, or you can arrive in Celestún by car or bus and make arrangements there.

Popular with Mexican vacationers, the park's sandy beach is pleasant during the day but tends to get windy in the afternoon, with choppy water and blowing sand. To see the birds, hire a fishing boat at the dock outside town (the boats hang out under the bridge leading into

Celestún). A 75-minute tour for up to six people costs about $50, a two-hour tour around $75.

Celestún Expeditions (⊠ Calle 10 No. 97, between Calles 9 and 11, ☎ 988/916–2049) is a small company run by two natives of Celestún, David and Feliciano. They speak English well and are passionate about their work. In addition to the standard flamingo tours, they offer three-hour guided bike tours, jungle walks (day or night), crocodile tours at night, bird-watching excursions, and trips to the Maya ruins and haciendas. Tours range from $20 per person for the bike jaunt to $75 per person for the bird-watching outing. **Ecoturismo Yucatán** (⊠ Calle 3 No. 235, Col. Pensiones, ☎ 999/925–2187, 𝖥𝖠𝖷 999/925–9047) leads customized or more standard kayaking tours out of Mérida that begin in Celestún and enable you to explore the mangroves and estuaries of the western coast.

Dining and Lodging

$–$$ ✕ **La Palapa.** A conch-shell facade decorates the most popular seafood place in town, famous for its *camarones a la palapa* (fried shrimp smothered in a garlic and cream sauce). Unless it's windy or rainy, most guests dine on the beachfront terrace. Choose fresh fish (including sea bass and red snapper), plus crab, squid, or the most expensive plate: lobster tail and moro crab. Usually open 11 AM–7 PM, La Palapa sometimes closes early in low season. ⊠ *Calle 12 No. 105, between Calles 11 and 13,* ☎ *988/916–2063. MC, V.*

$$$$ 🛏 **Hotel Eco Paraíso Xixim.** On an old coconut plantation outside town, this hotel offers classy comfort in thatch-roof bungalows right on a long, seashell-strewn beach. Each suite has two comfortable queen beds, tile floors, and attractive wicker, cedar, and pine furniture. There's no air-conditioning, TVs, or phones, but the extra-large porch has twin hammocks and comfortable chairs. Bring strong insect repellent, as mosquitoes can be vicious. Room rates include ample breakfasts and dinners. Biking tours as well as those to old haciendas or archaeological sites can be arranged; kayaks are available for rent. Breakfast and dinner are included in the price. ⊠ *Camino Viejo a Sisal, Km 10,* ☎ *981/916–2100; 888/264–5792 in the U.S.;* 𝖥𝖠𝖷 *999/916–2111;* 𝖶𝖤𝖡 *www.ecoparaiso.com. 15 cabanas. Restaurant, fans, in-room safes, pool, beach, billiards, bar, library; no air-conditioning, no room phones, no room TVs. AE, MC, V.*

$ 🛏 **Hotel Sol y Mar.** Gerardo Vasquez, the friendly owner of this small hotel, also owns the local paint store next door and chose a tasteful combination of gray and rose for the walls and curtains of these cool, spacious units. Across the street from the town beach, this hotel has sparsely furnished rooms with two double beds, small table and chairs, and tile bathrooms. The more expensive rooms, downstairs, have air-conditioning, TV, and tiny refrigerators. There's no restaurant, but the recommended La Palapa restaurant is across the street. ⊠ *Calle 12 No. 104, at Calle 10,* ☎ *988/916–2166. 15 rooms. Air-conditioning in some rooms, fans, some refrigerators. No credit cards.*

Sisal

③ *50 km (31 mi) northwest of Mérida.*

Sisal got its name from the henequen, AKA sisal, that was shipped from this port in great quantity during the mid-19th century. With the rise of ports at Yucalpetén and Progreso, Sisal dwindled into little more than a fisherman's village and wharf. Sisal livens up in July and August when Meridanos come to swim and dine. Otherwise, it receives much less tourism than Celestún, which attracts birders and day-trippers. Nonetheless, Sisal has the requisite beachfront eateries selling fresh seafood, and a few attractions, including a **colonial customs house** and the private 1906 **lighthouse.** One of three offshore reefs, **Madagascar Reef** has excellent diving.

Lodging

$ **Hotel Felicidades.** A few minutes' walk up the beach east of the pier, this somewhat dingy hotel caters to tourists during the vacation months and can be fun when a crowd arrives. ⊠ *Calle 8 No. 1004, 97367,* ☎ *no phone. 10 rooms. No credit cards.*

Dzibilchaltún

🔺 ③④ *16 km (10 mi) north of Mérida.*

Dzibilchaltún ("the place with writing on flat stones") is a sizable archaeological site in the north Yucatán area, occupying more than 16 square km (10 square mi) of land cluttered with thousands of mounds, low platforms, piles of rubble, plazas, and stelae. It is also the longest continuously occupied city of this area, established around 500 BC in the Preclassic era and abandoned only when the conquistadors arrived in the 16th century. About equidistant between Mérida and Progreso (16 km [10 mi]), it had a marine and coastal economy and was more of an urban center than a ceremonial center.

For now Dzibilchaltún's significance lies in the stucco sculpture and ceramics, from all periods of Maya civilization, that have been unearthed here. The plain **Temple of the Seven Dolls** (circa AD 500) is one of a half dozen structures excavated on the site to date. Low and trapezoidal, the temple exemplifies the Late Preclassic style, which predates such Puuc sites as Uxmal. The remains of stucco masks adorn each side, and there are vestiges of sculptures of coiled serpents representing Kukulcán. During the spring and fall equinoxes, sunbeams fall at the exact center of two windows opposite each other inside one of the temple rooms, an example of the highly precise mathematical calculations for which the Maya are known. Studies have found that a similar phenomenon occurs at the full moon between March 20 and April 20. The stone cube atop the temple and the open chapel built by the Spaniards for the Indians are additional points of interest. Twelve sacbéob (or sacbé) lead to various groups of structures. Bones and ceremonial objects recovered by divers from the National Geographic Society between 1957 and 1959 suggest that the **Xlacah Cenote** was used for ceremonial offerings. These days, it's ideal for taking a dip if you're walking around the ruins in the heat.

An excellent museum called **Pueblo Maya** is at the entrance to the site. It's part of a national program dedicated to establishing museums devoted—and accessible—to the country's native peoples. It's fronted by a long, rectangular garden featuring a number of the huge sculptures found on the site plus botanical species common to the area. In the back, two *nas* (native huts) let you see how rural people still live today. The museum's collection (labeled in English as well as in Spanish) includes figurines, bones, jewelry, and potsherds found in the cenote as well as the seven crude dolls that gave the Temple of the Seven Dolls its name. It also traces the area's Hispanic history and highlights contemporary crafts from the region. An interactive touch-screen area covers the history and other details about the site, but it's only in Spanish. 🎟 *$5.50 (including museum), free Sun..* ☉ *Daily 8–5.*

Progreso

③⑤ *16 km (10 mi) north of Dzibilchaltún, 32 km (20 mi) north of Mérida.*

Progreso, the waterfront town closest to Mérida, is not particularly historic. It's also not terribly picturesque. On weekdays during most of the year the beaches are deserted, but when school is out (Easter week, July, and August) and on summer weekends it becomes a popular vacation spot for families from Mérida. And more and more retired Canadians are renting apartments here between December and April because of the low prices. Progreso has fine sand and shallow waters that extend quite far out, making for nice walks. Its water normally does not have the tantalizing clarity of the Caribbean off Quintana Roo, although sometimes it does acquire an aquamarine hue. Because it is so close to Mérida, many people come for the day only. It is, however, a perfectly pleasant overnight trip when skies are sunny, the sea is calm, and you have no expectations of a wild nightlife. The hotels are for the most part disappointing, but the small town does have a couple of attractions.

Progreso has been the chief port of entry for the peninsula since its founding in 1872, when the shallow port at Sisal, to the southwest, proved inadequate for handling the large ships that were carrying henequen cargo. Since 1989 the 2-km-long (1-mi-long) pier has been extended 9 km (5½ mi) out to sea to accommodate the hoped-for cruise-ship business and to siphon some of the lucrative tourist trade from Cozumel, but only a trickle of cruise ships are berthing here these days.

Progreso's attractions include its **malecón** (waterfront walkway), Calle 19, which is lined with seafood restaurants. Fishermen sell their catch on the beach east of the city between 6 and 8 AM.

Some 120 km (74 mi) offshore, the **Alacranes Reef** is where divers can explore sunken ships. **Pérez Island** is part of Alacranes Reef; it supports a large population of sea turtles and seabirds.

Dining and Lodging

$–$$ ✕ **Le Saint Bonnet.** This thatch-roof restaurant-bar with an open-air terrace on the malecón is *the* place for locals. It gets its pretentious French name from a French partner who has seen to it that all dishes have Gallic monikers, such as the popular shrimp St. Bonnet—jumbo shrimp stuffed with cheese, wrapped with bacon, breaded, fried, and served with crab sauce. You can complement these dishes with European or Chilean vintages. Try the caramel crepes or chocolate mousse for dessert. A live band plays tropical music daily 12:30–6:30 PM. ⊠ *Av. Malecón 150-D, at Calle 78,* ☎ *999/935–2299. AE, MC, V.*

$ ✕ **Pelícanos.** This restaurant facing the sea and malecón aims to please. It has the standard seafood lunches and Yucatecan breakfasts—fish grilled with garlic, *huevos motuleños,* but the waitstaff is helpful and friendly. ⊠ *Calle 19 No. 144, at Calle 20,* ☎ *969/935–0788. No credit cards.*

$$ 🏠 **Tropical Suites.** The location—on the north end of the malecón—of this clean but rather dilapidated Progreso standby is ideal, but the price is high for what you get. Rooms are nothing to write home about, with white plastic chairs and double beds on the soft side; most have cable TV. Those rooms touting kitchenettes have scuffed refrigerators but no stove. ⊠ *Calle 19 No. 143, at Calle 70,* ☎ *969/935–1263,* FAX *969/935–3093. 20 rooms. Fans, air-conditioning in some rooms, some kitchenettes, some refrigerators, free parking. No credit cards.*

Yucalpetén

③⑥   *3 km (2 mi) west of Progreso.*

Yucalpetén lies at the end of a narrow, marshy promontory. The harbor here dates only from 1968, when it was built to provide shelter for small fishing boats in hurricane season. Little goes on here other than some activity at the marina, where commercial fishermen in battered but picturesque and colorful vessels ply the sea for grouper, red snapper, dogfish, sea bass, and pompano. Just beyond Yucalpetén, the even tinier village of Chelem has a few beachfront bungalow hotels.

Chicxulub

③⑦ *6 km (4 mi) east of Progreso.*

One of the many small beaches strung along the highway east of Progreso, Chicxulub (chick-shoe-*loob*) is a small community where families from Mérida have beachfront weekend homes. A growing number of foreigners are getting wind of the once-inexpensive rentals in the nearby fishing village of Chicxulub Puerto, with its inviting beach and low winter rates. Chicxulub has also gotten press among scientists who theorize that debris raised by an asteroid that landed just offshore some 65 million years ago may have caused the extinction of the dinosaurs.

Dining and Lodging

$ ✕ **Moctezuma.** Those in the know who like really fresh seafood at reasonable prices recommend this unpretentious place. Moctezuma caters mainly to the locals who like to look over their fish before sending it into the kitchen. Dine on fresh-caught red snapper, grouper, sea bass, or lobster—grilled, baked, buttered, or breaded and nicely flavored with lime juice, annatto seed, cumin, and pepper. Appetizers are served with beer and mixed drinks before your meal. ⊠ *Carretera Chicxulub–Telchac,* ☎ *969/934–1271. No credit cards.*

$$ ✕▣ **Margarita's Ville.** Owner Margarita Gutiérrez has turned her childhood seaside getaway into a comfortable and very classy hotel. Additions to the wooden house include custom-made rattan furniture, orthopedic mattresses, quiet air-conditioning, fans, coffeemakers, and balconies shaded by high coconut palms. A Continental breakfast is included in the room rate. The property is for adults only. You can come just for a meal; call ahead if possible to make a lunch or dinner reservation for healthy, delicious salads and fresh seafood. ⊠ *Carretera Chicxulub–Telchac,* ☎ FAX *999/944–1434. 2 bungalows, 11 rooms. Restaurant, fans, pool, beach; no kids. No credit cards.*

Xcambo

10 km (6 mi) east of Chicxulub, off the Progreso hwy. at Xtampu.

Surrounded by a plantation where disease-resistant coconut trees are being developed, the site is a couple of miles inland following the turnoff for Xtampu. It's also in the hometown of former governor Victor Cervera Pacheco, who, it is rumored, had given priority to its excavation. Salt, which was a much-sought-after item of trade in the ancient Maya world, was produced in this area and made it prosperous. Indeed, the bones of 600 former residents discovered in burial plots showed they had been healthier than the average Maya. Two plazas have been restored so far, surrounded by rather plain structures. The tallest temple is the **Xcambo,** also known as the Pyramid of the Cross. Ceramics found at the site indicate that the city traded with other Maya groups as far afield as Guatemala, Teotihuácan, and Belize. The Catholic church on-site was built by dismantling these ancient structures, and until recently, locals hauled off the cut stones to build fences and foundations. ⊠ *Turn off the Progreso highway at Xtampu.* ▣ *$2.* ◎ *Daily 8–5.*

Telchac Puerto

③⑨ *15 km (9 mi) east of Xcambo, 43 km (27 mi) east of Progreso.*

This area is worth visiting for its proximity to Laguna Rosada, where flamingos come to nest, and for its lovely, empty beaches. This isolation may be short-lived, however, as several luxury hotels supposedly are in the planning stages; some 2,500 to 3,500 hotel rooms are slated to be built in the area between Dzilám de Bravo and Telchac Puerto. This coastline has been dubbed the Zona de Nuevo Yucatán (Zone of the New Yucatán), which suggests a rather sudden loss of innocence à la Cancún.

Dining and Lodging

$ ✕ **Bella Mar.** The view from the beach is a knockout, as are the daily specials. Owner-chef Veronica Crespo scouts the nearby fishing village for the freshest catch of the day and cooks it herself, adding sides of rice, beans, potatoes, or other veggies. Palapa-shaded tables line the beach for alfresco dining, and the ocean is inviting enough for a dip before or after lunch. You can even shower here. A fish plate costs a reasonable $5, while the most you'll pay is $9 for butterfly shrimp. ✉ *3 km (2 mi) west of Telchac Puerto on Telchac–San Crisanto highway,* ☎ *991/991–8274. No credit cards.*

$$$$ ▥ **Reef Yucatán.** This all-inclusive resort has changed hands several times and attempts to anchor other resorts for the "Nuevo Yucatán" concept. Rooms are pleasantly yet simply decorated and have direct-dial telephones, cable TV, and a balcony or terrace. Kayaks, snorkeling, a gym, and a long beach keep clients entertained in this region of few tourist attractions. The rate includes food and drink, nightly variety shows, and access to the disco. Spa services (massage, facial, etc.) and motorized water toys are extra. ✉ *Carretera a Progreso Telchac, Km 32,* ☎ *991/917–4100,* ℻ *991/917–4086,* ⟪WEB⟫ *www.reefyucatan.com. 150 rooms. 3 restaurants, room service, 2 pools, spa, gym, beach, bar, dance club, nightclub, children's programs (ages 4–12). AE, MC, V.*

Motul

32 km (20 mi) south of Telchac Puerto, 51 km (32 mi) northeast of Mérida.

Motul is the birthplace of the assassinated socialist governor of Yucatán, Felipe Carrillo Puerto, who is also known for his romance with U.S. journalist Alma Reed in the 1930s. His former house is a museum containing displays on his life and times. However, trying to gain admission may be a hassle because hours are sporadic and only in the evening, for cultural events. ▧ *Free.* ◷ *Daily about 5 PM–8 PM.*

Dzilám de Bravo

40 *40 km (25 mi) east of Telchac Puerto, 113 km (70 mi) northeast of Mérida.*

The pirate Jean Laffite supposedly lies buried just outside the village of Dzilám de Bravo. At least there's a grave so marked, and two of the 2,000 inhabitants claim to be his descendants. Stop here for a swim in the gentle waters, or hire a boat from a local fisherman to view the seabirds that congregate around the small strip of land offshore about 10 minutes away.

Tizimín

41 *108 km (67 mi) southeast of Dzilám de Bravo.*

Tizimín, renowned as the seat of an indigenous messianic movement during the 1840s Caste War, is at the junction of Highways 176 and 295. The town has a 17th-century church dedicated to the Three Wise Men, who are honored here during a festival that is held December 15–January 15.

If you are driving from Tizimín to Río Lagartos, before you leave town you can stop at the **Oficina del Reserva del Parque Natural Río Lagartos** (Flamingo Reserve Office; ✉ Calle 47 No. 415-A, between Calles 52 and 54, ☎ 986/863–4390), open weekdays 9–2 and 6–9, for park information. (Don't worry if you miss it; there's an information station near the Parque Natural Río Lagartos entrance.)

Parque Natural Río Lagartos

★ ㊷ *52 km (32 mi) north of Tizimín.*

If the thought of a phenomenal flamingo spectacle appeals, don't miss Parque Natural Río Lagartos. Flamingos can be seen year-round here but are particularly abundant from April through June. Actually encompassing a long estuary, the park was developed with ecotourism in mind, though most of the alligators for which it and the village were named have long since been hunted into extinction. In addition to seeing flamingos, birders also can spot snowy and red egrets, white ibis, great white herons, cormorants, pelicans, and even peregrine falcons flying over the murky waters. Fishing is good, too, and the protected hawksbill and green turtles lay their eggs on the beach at night.

Río Lagartos outdoes itself during the annual **Festival of Apostle Santiago** (July 20–26), with folk dances, bullfights, and processions. On the 1st of June, all the boats get decked out and parade in the lagoon in celebration of **Día de Marina** (Navy Day). To get here, you can drive or take a bus or a tour out of Mérida or Valladolid. Buses leave regularly from the second-class bus terminals of both cities to either Río Lagartos or, 10 km (6 mi) west of the park, San Felipe. A boat tour to see the flamingos is available from either point.

About ½ km (¼ mi) from the entrance to Río Lagartos is an information station (ESTACIÓN is written on it). This is the official reserve entrance. The helpful people who work here can contact a guide with a boat for you. The boat glides up the estuary east of the dock and in 10 minutes is deep into mangrove forests; another hour and the boat is at the flamingo feeding grounds.

Although there are some places around town you can walk to see birds, the best and most common way to see flamingos, egrets, herons, and other aquatic birds is by boat. Bilingual birding guides ($10–$15 an hour per group) can be arranged in advance with the reserve office in Tizimín (☎ 996/863–4390), or for about $45 for a group of four to six passengers through Diego Núñez at the Isla Contoy restaurant. Diego suggests arranging the 2½-hour tours at sunrise (6:30–7 AM) or ending at sunset to see the most activity.

You can make the 90-km 956 (56-mi) trip from Valladolid (1½ hours by car or 2 hours by bus) as a day trip (add another hour if you're coming from Mérida). Río Lagartos itself has just one hotel and few restaurants, but for a more relaxed trip, you can spend the night and get an early morning's start.

Dining and Lodging

$ ✕ **Isla Contoy.** Run by an amicable family, this seafood place two blocks from the estuary in Parque Natural Río Lagartos serves generous helpings of fish soup, fried fish fillets, shrimp, squid, and crab. There are also a few regional specialties and red-meat dishes. Signs at the entrance to the village point the way. Diego Núñez, whose family owns the restaurant, leads tours into the reserve. ✉ *Calle 19 No. 134,* ☎ *986/862–0000. No credit cards.*

$$ ✕⊡ **Hotel San Felipe.** This three-story white hotel in the beach town of San Felipe, 10 km (6 mi) west of Parque Natural Río Lagartos, is basic but adequate. White walls with red trim have either with two twin beds or a double bed, overhead fans, and reading lamps; the most expensive room has a private terrace with a hammock and sea view. The restaurant serves breakfast and lunch only, and it's mainly seafood. ⊠ *Calle 9 No. 13, between Calles 14 and 16 , San Felipe,* ☎ *986/862–2027. 18 rooms. Restaurant, fans, free parking. No credit cards.*

Isla Holbox

43 *141 km (87 mi) northeast of Valladolid.*

The tiny Isla Holbox (25 km [16 mi] long) sits at the eastern end of the Río Lagartos estuary and just across the Quintana Roo state line. A fishing fan's heaven because of the pompano, bass, barracuda, and shark thronging its waters, the island also pleases seekers of tranquillity who don't mind rudimentary accommodations (rooms and hammocks for rent) and simple palapa restaurants. Seabirds fill the air; the long, sandy beach is strewn with seashells; and the swimming is good on the gulf side.

To get here from Río Lagartos, take Route 176 to Kantunilkin and then head north on the unnumbered road for 44 km (27 mi) to Chiquilá. Continue by ferry to the island; schedules vary, but there are normally five crossings a day. The fare is $4 and the trip takes about 35 minutes. A car ferry makes the trip at 11 AM daily, returning at 5 PM. (You can also pay to leave your car in a lot in Chicquilá, in Quintana Roo.)

In addition to Villa Delfines, there are several clean, inexpensive lodgings in town. Right on the zócalo and a block from the beach is **Posada Amapola** (no phone), where you can get a private bath with hot water, air-conditioning, and a hammock (or double bed) for $20. There are several restaurants nearby, and the owners can help you set up a birding expedition.

Dining and Lodging

$$$$ ✕⊡ **Villas Delfines.** This fisherman's lodge is very expensive by island standards. Cabins are simple and have no TV or phone, but you can get your catch grilled in the restaurant, and if you get tired of fishing you can head to the zócalo to arrange for a birding trip. ⊠ *Domicilio Conocido,* ☎ *998/874–4014; 998/884–8606 reservations;* FAX *998/884–6342. 10 cabins. Restaurant, fans, bar. AE, MC, V.*

MÉRIDA AND THE STATE OF YUCATÁN A TO Z

To research prices, get advice from other travelers, and book travel arrangements, visit www.fodors.com.

AIR TRAVEL

Aerocaribe, a subsidiary of Mexicana, has flights from Cancún, Chetumal, Cozumel, Oaxaca City, Tuxtla Gutiérrez, Palenque, and Villahermosa, with additional service to Central America. It also flies from Cozumel and Cancún to Chichén Itzá. Aeroméxico flies direct to Mérida from Miami with a stop (but no plane change) in Cancún. Aviacsa flies nonstop from Mérida to Guadalajara, Mexico City, and Tijuana and makes connections to Cancún, Villahermosa, Tuxtla Gutiérrez, Tapachula, Oaxaca, Chetumal, and Mexico City. Mexicana has a connecting flight from Newark via Cancún and a number of other connecting flights from the United States via Mexico City.

➤ AIRLINES AND CONTACTS: **Aerocaribe** (☎ 999/928–6790). **Aeroméxico** (☎ 800/021–4000). **Aviacsa** (☎ 999/926–9087 or 999/925–6890). **Mexicana** (☎ 999/946–1332).

AIRPORTS

The Mérida airport, Aeropuerto Manuel Crescencio Rejón, is 7 km (4½ mi) west of the city on Avenida Itzaes, a 20- to 30-minute cab ride.

A private taxi from the airport costs $9 or $10. Bus 79 goes from the airport to downtown—very inexpensive, but a hassle if you've got more than a day pack or small suitcase. If you're driving into town, take the airport exit road, make a right at the four-lane Avenida Itzaes (the continuation of Route 180), and follow it to the one-way Calle 59, just past Parque Zoológico El Centenario. Turn right on Calle 59 and go straight until you reach Calle 62, where you turn right and drive a block to the main square. (Parking is difficult here.)

➤ AIRPORT INFORMATION: **Aeropuerto Manuel Crescencio Rejón** (☎ 999/946–1300).

BUS TRAVEL

Mérida's municipal buses run daily 5 AM–midnight, but service is somewhat confusing until you master the system. In the downtown area buses go east on Calle 59 and west on Calle 61, north on Calle 60 and south on Calle 62. You can catch a bus heading north to Progreso on Calle 56. There is no direct bus service from the hotels around the plaza to the long-distance bus station; however, taxis are reasonably priced.

There are several first-class bus stations offering deluxe buses with high-powered air-conditioning and spacious seats. The most frequently used is CAME (Camionera Mérida; Calle 70 No. 555, at Calle 71). From here you can take the major bus lines: ADO, UNO, and Clase Elite to Akumal, Cancún, Chichén Itzá, Playa del Carmen, Tulum, Uxmal, Valladolid, and other major Mexican cities. ADO, UNO, and Super Expresso have direct buses to Cancún from their terminal at the Fiesta Americana hotel, on Paseo Montejo.

Many second-class bus lines also have air-conditioning. Mérida has a handful of second-class bus stations serving different destinations. One of the most frequently used by travelers is El Terminal de Autobuses (Calle 69 No. 544, between Calles 68 and 70). It's right around the corner from the first-class CAME station, and from there you can reach Campeche, Ciudad del Carmen, Cancún, Ticul, Izamal, Valladolid, and Chichén Itzá, among other destinations.

As its name suggests, El Terminal de Autobuses a Progreso has departures for Progreso, every half hour 5:30 AM–7 PM. Transportation for Dzibilchaltún, midway between Mérida and Progreso, leaves regularly from Parque San Juan, at Calle 69 between Calles 62 and 64. You can also catch a comfortable air-conditioned van to Progreso, on Calle 60 between Calles 65 and 67, for the same price as the bus. Terminal de Autobuses del Noreste is the choice for Chicxulub Puerto, Telchac, and Río Lagartos.

There are other smaller lines in addition to these. If you're not sure which line to take, or are heading to a more out-of-the-way destination, look for the free magazine *Yucatán Today,* which often lists all of Mérida's bus stations and their locations and the destinations. Otherwise, check with the tourist office.

➤ BUS LINES AND STATIONS: **ADO/Super Expresso/UNO** (✉ Paseo Montejo at Av. Colón, ☎ 999/924–7868 or 999/924–8391; 999/925–0910 in Fiesta Americana). **Autotransportes del Sureste** (ATS; ☎ 999/923–2287). **Camionera Mérida** (CAME; ✉ Calle 70 No. 555, at Calle

71, ☎ 999/924–8391 or 999/924–4440). **Elite/Nuevos Horizontes** (☎ 999/923–9913). **Terminal de Autobuses del Noreste** (✉ Calle 50 No. 527-A, between Calles 65 and 67, ☎ 999/923–4602 or 999/324–6355). **Terminal de Autobuses (2da clase)** (✉ Calle 69 No. 544, between Calles 68 and 70, ☎ 999/923–2287 or 999/923–4440). **Terminal del Autobuses a Progreso** (Progreso station; ✉ Calle 62 No. 557, between Calles 65 and 67, ☎ 999/928–3965).

CAR RENTAL

Mérida has almost 20 car-rental agencies, including Budget, Hertz, National, and Thrifty outlets. Prices are sometimes lower if you arrange your rental in advance of your visit.

➤ MAJOR AGENCIES: ✉ **Advantage** (✉ Fiesta Americana, ☎ 999/920–1920). **Budget** (✉ Hotel Misión Mérida, Calle 60 No. 491, near Calle 57, ☎ 999/928–6759; ✉ Holiday Inn, Av. Colón 498 and Calle 60, ☎ 999/925–6877, ext. 516; ✉ airport, ☎ 999/946–1323). **Hertz** (✉ Fiesta Americana, ☎ 999/925–7595; ✉ Calle 60 between Calles 55 and 57, ☎ 999/924–2834 or 999/984–0028; ✉ airport, ☎ 999/946–1355). **National** (✉ Fiesta Americana, ☎ 999/925–7524; ✉ airport, ☎ 999/946–1394).

CAR TRAVEL

Driving in Mérida can be frustrating because of the one-way streets (many of which are in effect one-lane because of the parked cars) and because of dense traffic. But having your own wheels is the best way to take excursions from the city. For more relaxed sightseeing, consider hiring a cab for short excursions. Most charge approximately 120 pesos per hour.

Route 180, the main road along the gulf coast from the Texas border, passes through Mérida en route to Cancún. Mexico City lies 1,550 km (961 mi) west, Cancún 320 km (198 mi) due east.

The *autopista* is a four-lane toll highway between Mérida and Cancún. Beginning at the town of Kantuníl, 55 km (34 mi) southeast of Mérida, it runs somewhat parallel to Route 180. The toll road cuts driving time between Mérida and Cancún—around 4½ hours on Route 180—by about an hour and bypasses about four dozen villages. Access to the toll highway is off old Highway 180 and is clearly marked. The highway has exits for Valladolid and Pisté (Chichén Itzá), as well as rest stops and gas stations. Tolls between Mérida and Cancún total about $25. From Campeche it takes a little more than two hours to reach Mérida on Route 180, which is the fastest route. Another option is the three- to four-hour drive along Route 261 from Campeche, which passes the ruins of Uxmal and other ancient Maya sites as well as present-day Maya villages. From Chetumal, the most direct route to Mérida—it takes approximately nine hours—is Route 307 to Felipe Carrillo Puerto, then Route 184 to Muna, continuing north on Route 261. Although generally two lanes, these roads are in good condition.

CONSULATES

➤ CONTACTS: **United Kingdom** (✉ Calle 53 No. 498, at Calle 58, ☎ 999/928–6152). **United States** (✉ Paseo Montejo 453, at Av. Colón, ☎ 999/925–5011; 999/845–4364 after-hours emergencies).

CONSUMER PROTECTION

The bilingual Tourism Police give referrals for complaints and can direct you to government offices and the state police.

➤ CONTACT: **Tourism Police** (☎ 999/925–2555, ext. 260).

E-MAIL
Mérida's has sprouting places that offer Internet access (for a fee, of course), especially around the main square. Express Internet and Via Olimpo Café have air-conditioning, which can be a treat, and charge $2–$4 an hour.

➤ SERVICES: **Express Internet** (⊠ Café Express, Calle 60 No. 502, at Calle 59, ☎ 999/928–1691). **Via Olimpo Café** (⊠ Calle 62 at Calle 61, ☎ 999/923–5843).

EMERGENCIES
➤ DOCTORS AND HOSPITALS: **Centro Médico de las Américas** (⊠ Calle 54 No. 365 between Calle 33-A and Av. Pérez Ponce, ☎ 999/927–3199). **Red Cross Hospital** (⊠ Calle 68 No. 533, between Calles 65 and 67, ☎ 999/928–5391).

➤ EMERGENCY SERVICES: **Fire, police,Red Cross,** and **general emergency** (☎ 060).

➤ PHARMACIES: **Farmacia de Ahorros** (San Fernando branch: ⊠ Calle 60 at Av. Colón, ☎ 999/925–8126; Central branch: ⊠ Calle 60 at Calle 63, ☎ 999/928–5027). **Farmacia Yza** (☎ 999/926–6666 information and delivery).

ENGLISH-LANGUAGE MEDIA
Mérida has an English-language library, which is open weekdays 9–1 (plus 4–7 Thursday and Friday) and Saturday 10–1.

The newsstands under the portals in Plaza Picheta on the main square carry a limited supply of newspapers and magazines from Mexico City and the United States.

➤ LIBRARY: (⊠ Calle 53 No. 524, between Calles 66 and 68, Mérida, ☎ 999/924–8401).

MAIL AND SHIPPING
Mérida has only one post office, open weekdays 8–3 and Saturday 9–1. However, you can buy postage stamps at handicrafts shops in town. If you must send mail from Mexico, the Mex Post service can speed delivery a bit, even internationally, for a higher fee than regular mail.

➤ POST OFFICE: (⊠ Calle 65 at Calle 56, ☎ 999/928–5404 or 999/924–3590).

MONEY MATTERS
Most banks throughout Mérida are open weekdays 9–5. Banamex has its main offices, open weekdays 9–5 and Saturday 9–1:30, in the handsome Casa de Montejo, on the south side of the main square, with branches at the airport and the Fiesta Americana hotel. All have automatic teller machines that can be accessed with Cirrus, Plus, MasterCard, and Visa bank cards. Several other banks can be found on Calle 65, between Calles 62 and 60, and on Paseo Montejo, and most have the same automatic teller service.

CURRENCY EXCHANGE
There are several exchange houses in Mérida, including Casa de Cambio del Sureste, open weekdays 9–5 and Saturday 9–1; Centro Cambriano Canto, open weekdays 9–1 and 4–7; and two on the ground level of the Fiesta Americana hotel, open weekdays 9–5.

➤ EXCHANGE SERVICES: **Centro Cambriano Canto** (⊠ Calle 61 No. 468, between Calles 52 and 54, ☎ 999/928–0458).

TAXIS AND CARRIAGES
Taxis charge beach-resort prices, which makes them a little expensive for this region of Mexico. They don't normally cruise the streets for

passengers but are available at 13 taxi stands (*sitios*) around the city, or in front of the Hyatt Regency, Holiday Inn, Fiesta Americana, or other major hotels. The minimum fare is $3. Taxis operate around the clock.

You can hail horse-drawn *calesas* (pony traps) with sad-looking horses along Calle 60; it's hard to decide if it's more humane to let them stay where they are, or allow them to earn some feed by jogging through the traffic-filled streets. Their owners generally charge $11 an hour. Bargaining is acceptable.

➤ Taxi Companies: **Sitio Mejorada** (☎ 999/928–5589). **Sitio Parque de la Madre** (☎ 999/928–5322).

TELEPHONES

Towns and cities of all sizes in Yucatán state have three-digit area codes (LADAs) and seven-digit phone numbers. However, many of the numbers in brochures and other literature will undoubtedly be written in the old style. Mérida's area code is 999. To convert an older number into a current one for local dialing, just deduct 9s from the area code and add them to the beginning of the number until you have a seven-digit phone number. For example, 99/24–87–88 becomes the local number 924–8788; the new area code (999) need not be used unless you are dialing Mérida from outside the city, in which case you would dial 01–999/924–8788.

Mérida has many Ladatel phone booths: at the airport and bus stations, in the main plaza, at Avenidas Reforma and Colón, and throughout the city. You can make both local and international direct calls at these public phones. Coin-operated phones are history—these take only Ladatel cards, electronic phone cards you can buy at newsstands and pharmacies.

TOURS

Mérida has more than 50 tour operators, who generally go to the same places. What differs is the mode of transportation—and whether or not the vehicle is air-conditioned and insured. Beware the *piratas* (street vendors) who stand outside the offices of reputable tour operators and offer to sell you a cheaper trip. They have been known to take your money and not show up; they also do not carry liability insurance.

A two- to three-hour group tour of the city, including museums, parks, public buildings, and monuments, costs $20 to $55 per person. Or you can pick up an open-air sightseeing bus at Parque de Santa Lucía for $8 (departures are Monday–Saturday at 10, 1, 4, and 7 and Sunday at 10 and 1).

A day trip to Chichén Itzá, with guide, entrance fee, and lunch, costs approximately $53. For about the same price you can see the ruins of Uxmal and Kabah in the Puuc region; for a few more dollars you can add the neighboring sites of Sayil, Labná, and the Loltún Caves. Early afternoon departures to Uxmal allow you to take in the sound-and-light show at the ruins and return by 11 PM, for $56 (including dinner). Another option is a tour of Chichén Itzá followed by a drop-off in Cancún, for about $80. Most tour operators take credit cards.

Diego Núñez is an outstanding guide who conducts boat tours of Río Lagartos. He charges $42 for a 2½-hour tour, which accommodates five or six people. He usually can be found at the restaurant called Isla Contoy, which he runs.

Ecoturismo Yucatán is recommended for its kayaking trips along the northwest coast, as well as birding and biking adventures. Its specialty is arranging custom trips to suit the needs and abilities of its clients.

➤ TOUR OPERATORS: **American Express** (✉ Calle 56 No. 494, between Calles 41 and 43, ☎ 999/942–8200 or 999/924–4326, FAX 999/942–8270). **Amigo Travel** (✉ Av. Colón 508-C, Col. García Ginerés, ☎ 999/920–0101 or 999/920–0107). **Carmen Travel Service** (✉ Hotel María del Carmen, Calle 63 No. 550, at Calle 68, ☎ 999/924–1212, FAX 999/924–1288).**Diego Núñez** (c/o Restaurant Isla Contoy, ✉ Calle 19 No. 12, Tizimín, ☎ 998/862–0000). **Ecoturismo Yucatán** (✉ Calle 3 No. 235, between Calles 32-A and 34, Col. Pensiones, ☎ 999/920–2772 or 999/925–2187, FAX 999/925–9047). **Felgueres Tours** (✉ Holiday Inn, Av. Colón 498, at Calle 60, ☎ 999/920–4477 or 999/920–3444, FAX 999/925–6389).**Mayaland Tours** (✉ Calle 57 between Calles 58 and 61, ☎ 999/924–2099 or 800/235–4079; ✉ Fiesta Americana, Calles Colón and 60, ☎ FAX 999/924–6290); request a Mayaland guide rather than a guide subcontractor. **Yucatán Trails** (✉ Calle 62 No. 502, between Calles 57 and 59, ☎ 999/928–2582, FAX 999/924–1928).

TRANSPORTATION AROUND MÉRIDA AND THE STATE OF YUCATÁN

Getting around the state is fairly easy, either by public bus or car. There are many bus lines, and all have at least one round-trip run daily to the main archaeological sites and colonial cities. If you're visiting for the first time, a guided tour booked through one of the many Mérida travel agencies provides a good introduction to the city. If you're independent and adventurous, by all means hire a rental car and strike out on your own. Just take plenty of bottled water, fill up the tank whenever you see a station, and don't drive at night.

VISITOR INFORMATION

Mérida has an information kiosk at the airport that's open daily 8–8. The City Tourist Information Center and the kiosk at Calle 39 and Paso de Montejo are open weekdays 8–2 and 5–7. The state tourist center is open daily 8–8.

The tourist office in Progreso is open weekdays 9–1 and 3–7.

➤ MÉRIDA: **City Tourist Information Center** (✉ Calle 59 between Calles 62 and 64, ☎ 999/928–6547). **State Tourist Information Center** (✉ Teatro Peón Contreras, Calle 60 between Calles 57 and 59, ☎ 999/924–9290 or 999/924–9389).

➤ PROGRESO: **Tourist Office** (✉ Calle 30 No. 176, at Calle 37, ☎ 969/935–0104).

7 CAMPECHE

Ruins of fortifications and walls built to fend off pirates who ravaged Yucatán's gulf coast add old-world romance to Campeche City, the capital of this little-explored state. Among the remnants of Maya settlements that dot the rest of intriguing Campeche, Edzná is the best known and most accessible from the capital.

Updated by
Jane Onstott

CAMPECHE, THE LEAST-VISITED and most underrated corner of the Yucatán, is the perfect place for adventure. The people here are friendly and welcoming, the colonial cities and towns retain an air of innocence, and protected biospheres, farmland, and jungle traverse the remaining expanse. The forts of Campeche City have 300-year-old cannons pointing across the Gulf of Mexico, relics from pirate days that give the city an aura of romance and history. Beyond its walls, the pyramids and ornate temples of ancient Maya kingdoms—some of the most important discoveries in the Maya empire to date—lie waiting in tropical forests.

The terrain of the state of Campeche varies, from the northeastern flatlands to the rolling hills of the south. More than 60% of the territory is covered by jungle, which is filled with precious mahogany and cedar. The Gulf Stream keeps temperatures at about 26°C (78°F) year-round; the humid, tropical climate feels hotter, though it is eased by evening breezes. Campeche's economy is based on agriculture, fishing, logging, salt, tourism, and, since the 1970s, hydrocarbons—it is the largest producer of oil in Mexico. Currently there are 90 oil platforms dotting the Campeche coast, but most of the oil industry is concentrated at the western end of the state, near Ciudad del Carmen. There was talk of developing more offshore drills at Campeche City, but since it was named a UNESCO World Heritage site in 1999, this has been forestalled.

Campeche City's location on the gulf played a pivotal role in its history. Ah-Kin-Pech (Maya for "lord of the serpent tick")—from which the Spanish name of Campeche is derived—was the capital of an Indian chieftainship long before the Spaniards arrived in 1517. Earlier explorers had visited the area, but it was not until 1540 that the conquerors—led by Francisco de Montejo, and later his son—established a real foothold at Campeche (originally called San Francisco de Campeche), using it as a base for their conquest of the peninsula.

Because Campeche City was the only port and shipyard on the gulf, the Spanish ships, loaded with their rich cargoes of plunder from the Maya, Aztec, and other indigenous civilizations, dropped anchor here en route from Veracruz to Cuba, New Orleans, and Spain. News of this wealth spread, and soon the shores were overrun with pirates. From the mid-1500s to the early 1700s, such notorious corsairs as Diego the Mulatto, Lorenzillo, Peg Leg, Henry Morgan, and Barbillas swooped down repeatedly from their bases on Tris—or Isla de Términos, as Isla del Carmen was then known—pillaging and burning the city and massacring its people.

Finally, after years of appeals to the Spanish crown, the people received funds to build a protective wall around the city, with four gates and eight bastions. For some time thereafter, the city thrived on its exports, especially *palo de tinte*—a dyewood as valuable as gold that was used by the nascent European textile industry—but also hardwoods, chicle, salt, and henequen. However, when the port of Sisal on the northern Yucatán coast opened in 1811, Campeche's monopoly of the gulf traffic ended, and its economy fell into decline.

Modern-day Campeche City is still shaped by its history. Remnants of the sea and land gates and bastions divide it into two main districts: the historical center (where few people live) and the newer residential areas. Because the city was long preoccupied with defense, colonial architecture is less flamboyant here than elsewhere in Mexico. Churches are more subdued, flagstone streets are narrow because of the confines of the walls, and houses emphasize the practical over the decorative.

The face of the city has changed over the centuries: walls were torn down, bastions demolished, and landfill added to make room for expansion. Nonetheless, an aura of antiquity remains. By decree, no more colonial structures are allowed to be destroyed, and an ongoing beautification program keeps the city's largely two-story building facades in excellent condition.

Most of the state's 700,000 residents live in villages and small towns, where Maya traditions still hold sway. The countryside is dotted with fields of tobacco, sugarcane, rice, indigo, maize, and cocoa. There are citrus groves, and even the occasional windmill. The sea is rich with shrimp, barracuda, swordfish, and other catch; in the wilder regions, including the Calakmul Biosphere Reserve, jaguars, deer, tapir, and armadillos roam in their natural habitat.

The population of Campeche has changed in the last quarter century. Many refugees from Guatemala have returned home, and there has been an influx of Chol Maya homesteaders, who relocated from Chiapas after the Zapatista uprising. Many of the newcomers have settled on the southern edge of the Calakmul Biosphere Reserve, and even within the preserve itself.

Pleasures and Pastimes

Archaeological Sites
A thousand years ago, as today, the Maya were a diverse race. Of all the states in the peninsula, Campeche has the most Maya sites, with several styles completely different from anything found in the state of Yucatán or Quintana Roo. The Chenes style, found in central and southern Campeche, features facades with elaborate geometric patterns and giant zoomorphic masks. Doorways look like the open mouths of monsters or the creator god Itzamná. Passing through the jaws of the beast was a symbolic act of rejuvenation; Maya priests entered the doorway to travel through secret underground passageways and staircases that lead to the top of the pyramid. Spectators would watch the priest disappear into the underground and emerge atop the pyramids. The Río Bec style, found in the southern rain forest, incorporates many features of the Chenes style but has a signature characteristic—three towers of equal height. Roof combs and an architectural trick called false perspective make the towers seem larger than they actually are. The Río Bec style also borrowed its large platforms and plazas from the Petén style.

While most of the roads have been much improved, visiting the ruins—with the exception of Edzná, just outside Campeche City—requires driving hundreds of highway miles to the most remote part of the Yucatán Peninsula. While not for the faint-hearted, this is ideal for adventurers and those who shun the crowds of better known archaeological sites such as Palenque and Chichén Itzá. Archaeological sites are open daily; entrance is free Sunday and holidays.

Architecture
Nowhere in the Yucatán does Spanish colonial history feel more immediate than in the city of Campeche. An ongoing project under the direction of the Instituto Nacional de Antropología e Historia (INAH, the National Institute of Anthropology and History) and the municipal, state, and federal governments, has restored the facades of many of the city's 16th- to 19th-century houses and civic and religious buildings. To date, more than 1,600 facades have been rescued and repainted in subtle hues of butter yellow, dill and olive green, tan, peach, and blue-gray—usually trimmed in cream or white. Heritage blends easily with

pragmatism in the capital. Many historic buildings now house hotels, photocopy stores, boutiques, bakeries, and schools (though UNESCO guidelines prohibit the use of neon or unattractive signs, posters, and other modern trappings). The prevalence of well-preserved architecture from an earlier era makes this charming city more evocative of its colonial past and much less self-conscious than other historic districts.

Dining

There is nothing fancy about Campeche's restaurants, but the regional cuisine is renowned throughout Mexico—particularly the fish and shellfish stews, cream soups, shrimp cocktails, squid and octopus, crabs' legs, *panuchos* (chubby rounds of fried cornmeal covered with refried beans and topped with chopped onion and shredded turkey or chicken), and other specialties. Unusual seafood delicacies include the famous baby shrimp from the coastal town of Champotón; *pan de cazón* (baby shark cooked, shredded, and layered with tortillas, tomato sauce, and black beans); red snapper wrapped in banana leaves; *camarones al coco* (fried shrimp with a crispy layer of coconut, served with applesauce); *pulpo en su tinto* (octopus stewed and served in its own ink); and crayfish claws. Another popular dish is *pollo alcaparrado* (chicken with a sauce of capers, olives, saffron, and chilies). *Botanas* (appetizers) include *papadzules* (tortillas stuffed with hard-boiled eggs and covered with a pumpkin and tomato sauce), fruit conserves in syrup with chili peppers, and ceviche.

Fruits are served fresh, added to breads, made into juice and liqueurs, or marinated in rum or vinegar. Look for mango, papaya, *zapote* (sapodilla), *mamey sapote* (a sweet, fleshy fruit the size of a mango), *guanabana* (soursop), tamarind, melon, pineapple, and coconut, to name only a few. Because regional produce is plentiful, most restaurants fall into the $ to $$ price categories. Casual dress—though not always shorts—is fine in restaurants throughout Campeche, and reservations are not required. The ambience may be informal, but the service at restaurants is usually quite attentive.

CATEGORY	COST*
$$$	over $10
$$	$6–$10
$	under $6

*per person for a main course at dinner

Ecotourism

Although the infrastructure for ecotourism is still limited in Campeche, some of the state's wilderness is now protected in three ecological reserves. In the north is the Reserva Ecológica Peténes, which encompasses the coastline and the archaeological site of Isla Jaina. To the west is the Reserva Ecológica Laguna de Terminos, a large area covering the rivers, lagoons, mangroves, and forest just south of Laguna de Terminos. Southern Campeche contains one of the last primeval rain forests in Mexico, now legally protected under UNESCO's Man and the Biosphere program as the Calakmul Biosphere Reserve. It adjoins the much larger Maya Biosphere Reserve across the Guatemalan border, as well as a smaller reserve in Belize. The deep forest in the heart of the reserve is almost impossible to reach, but the outskirts afford plenty of opportunities to see a wide range of orchids and jungle wildlife, including spider monkeys, peccaries, boa constrictors, and hundreds of species of birds. In response to the destruction of certain parts in Campeche by the petroleum industry, the state has emerged as one of most environmentally aware regions of Mexico. Primarily an agricultural society, Campeche hasn't experienced urban sprawl or global commercialization—so it still has something left to preserve. For the most part, the people of Campeche, with cultural traditions of respect for the land still intact, are supportive of ecotourism. The conservation movement is still in its infancy, but already there has been rapid growth—all of the ruins have ecological bathrooms, and many members of the *ejidos* (land collectives) have participated in government-sponsored ecotourism workshops, seminars, and training courses.

Lodging

Hotels in Campeche City tend to be either moderate-to-expensive accommodations along the waterfront with only the most basic features of high-rise hotels (such as air-conditioning, restaurants, bars, and swimming pools) or small downtown lodgings offering mainly ceiling fans and a no-credit-card policy. The most worthy of those in the latter category are charming little hotels in refurbished early 20th-century buildings.

CATEGORY	COST*
$$$$	over $100
$$$	$70–$100
$$	$40–$70
$	under $40

All prices are for a standard double room, excluding service and 17% tax.

Exploring Campeche

Campeche City, the most accessible place in the state, makes a good hub for exploring other areas, many of which lack more than basic restaurants and primitive lodgings, if any. Bring your Spanish-English dictionary with you, since little English is spoken outside the capital, and you need to speak at least rudimentary Spanish. For purposes of exploration, the sights in the state of Campeche are arranged in three distinct regions. The northern interior, along Routes 261 and 180, contains the ruins of Edzná and other ancient cities as well as many modern Maya villages that can be visited easily en route between Campeche City and Mérida or Uxmal. The southwestern coast along Route 180—the only part of the Campeche coastline that is accessible by a continuous road—has several small towns and fishing villages that are all but eclipsed by oil-industry development. South of the capital, Route 186 stretches east toward Chetumal, the capital of Quintana Roo, passing numerous Maya ruins, some less than half a mile off the highway, others deep within the biosphere and unreachable in rainy season. Campeche's ruins are the subject of extensive research, thanks to a 1995 government grant, and a number of excavations at various ruins are under way. These ruins are more accessible than ever, as a two-lane highway now links Hopelchén, in the northeast, with the Chenes ruins of the south.

Numbers in the text correspond to numbers in the margin and on the State of Campeche and Campeche City maps.

Great Itineraries

While it may sound dauntingly ambitious to accomplish the Campeche City tour in one day, many of the sights described here can be seen in just a few minutes. For a more leisurely approach, schedule two days. Traveling throughout the state of Campeche could take from two to five days, depending on how much you want to explore on and off the beaten path.

IF YOU HAVE 1 DAY

Almost all interesting sights are within the compact historical district. You might want to begin or end your day in Campeche with a tram tour of the city's main sights. Another way to get a feel for the city's layout is to begin at the **Baluarte de San Carlos** ⑬ at the southern edge of the Ciudad Viejo, where a large model shows the original walls and gates, bastions, and forts. Then head into the heart of the old city along Calle 8 to take in its lovely colonial and Porfiriano buildings, ending up at the pretty **Parque Principal** ② for a stop at the **Catedral** ③. Take a lunch break at one of the small restaurants or cafés close to the main square; if you'd like to see a bustling city market, head for the **Mercado Público Pedro Sainz de Baranda.** Everything closes for at least two hours between 2 and 4 for siesta, so you may want to head back to your hotel and indulge in this fine Mexican tradition or visit the tranquil botanical gardens in the **Baluarte de Santiago** ⑥. After the siesta, when everything, including taxi service, comes to life again, hop in a cab for a late-afternoon visit to the **Fuerte de San Miguel** and its Museum of Maya Culture. On the way back, join the locals on the **malecón** ⑯ and enjoy the sunset or a breezy walk. At 8 o'clock (on weekends, or nightly during high season) head over to the **Puerta de Tierra** ⑧ and the Baluarte San Francisco to view the historical light-and-sound show called "Place of the Sun." Afterward stop for a drink or late dinner on the elegant second-floor balcony of Casa Vieja, a restaurant overlooking the main square.

IF YOU HAVE 3 DAYS

After a day in Campeche City, head inland the next morning to **Edzná** ㉓, a magnificently restored Maya ceremonial center an hour's ride from the city. On the way back, stop for a leisurely late afternoon lunch at the glamorous restored hacienda **Uayamon.** Return to your Campeche City hotel, and gather for dinner with the locals at the fun, informal **Cenaduría de San Francisco** for their jugs of delicious fresh fruit juices and well-known clove-spiked ham sandwiches. The next day, set out early for the **Hopelchén** ㉔ region, beyond Edzná, where you can explore the little-known Maya temples at **Hochob** ㉘, **Santa Rosa Xtampak** ㉖, and **Dzibilnocac** ㉗, as well as **Las Grutas de Xtacumbilxunaan** ㉕, one of the larger cave systems on the peninsula. From Hopelchén it is as easy to continue north toward Uxmal and Mérida as it is to return to Campeche City.

IF YOU HAVE 7 DAYS

With seven days, you can explore the southern part of the state in addition to the capital and the northern region. From Hopelchén—you can stay overnight in its very basic accommodations if you've spent a day in the area exploring—drive three hours south to **Xpuhil** ㉙ and the southern archaeological sites. To best appreciate the natural beauty of the rain forest and ruins, plan to spend two or three days in the area. **Becán** ㉞ and **Chicanná** ㉟ are within a couple of miles, and **Hormiguero** ㉜ and **Balamkú** ㊳ are not far off the highway, although in opposite directions. Local guides are recommended for these as well as for more remote sites such as **Río Bec** ㉝ and Calakmul, deep in the forests of the **Calakmul Biosphere Reserve** ㉟. From the Xpuhil area it is easy to return to Campeche City via the Escárcega–Champotón highway, with a stopover at **El Tigre** ㊲, a newly explored ruin two hours south of Escárcega. Or you can just as easily continue to the Caribbean coast, since you are right across the state line from Quintana Roo.

When to Tour Campeche

Both the capital and outlying villages of Campeche state, with their large Maya population, celebrate the Day of the Dead from October 31 to November 2 with special fervor because it corresponds to a similar ancient Maya observance. Colorfully embroidered regional dress, street celebrations, special meals, and altars of offerings to deceased

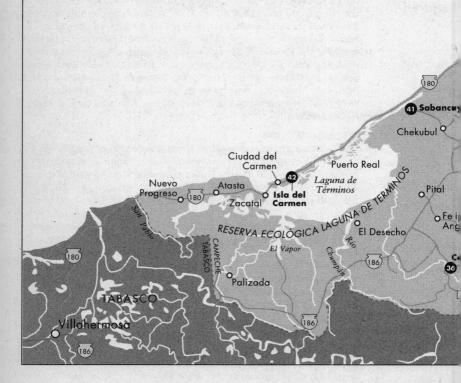

0   40 miles

0   60 km

*Golfo
de
México*

Sin

180

41 **Sabanc**

Chekubul

Ciudad del
Carmen   Puerto Real

Nuevo   *Laguna de
Progreso*   Atasta   42   *Términos*   Pital

180   Zacatal   **Isla del
Carmen**

RESERVA ECOLÓGICA LAGUNA DE TÉRMINOS

San Pablo   El Desecho

Fe i
Ang

CAMPECHE
TABASCO   *El Vapor*

180   186   C

Champán   36

Palizada   Río

TABASCO

186

Villahermosa

186

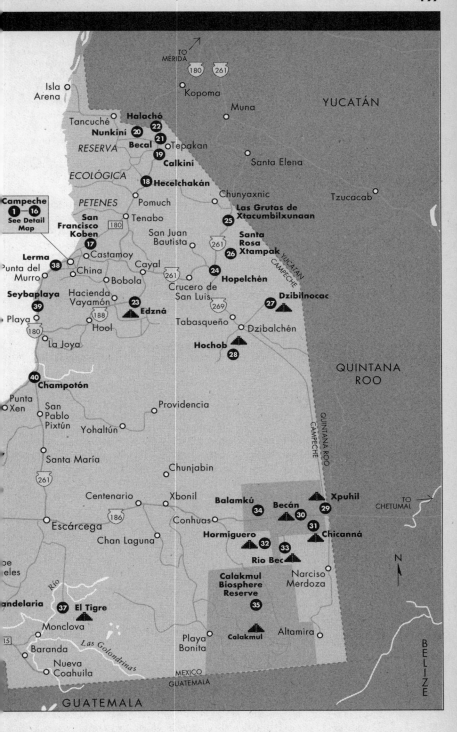

TO MÉRIDA

180 261

Isla Arena

Kopoma

Muna

YUCATÁN

Tancuché

Halachó

Nunkini 20 22

Becal 21

Tepakan

Santa Elena

RESERVA

19 **Calkiní**

Tzucacab

ECOLÓGICA

18 **Hecelchakán**

Pomuch

Chunyaxnic

Campeche
1 — 16
See Detail
Map

PETENES

**Las Grutas de
Xtacumbilxunaan**

25

**San
Francisco
Koben**

Tenabo

San Juan
Bautista

**Santa
Rosa
Xtampak**

261

17

Castamoy

26

Lerma

Cayal

YUCATÁN
CAMPECHE

38

China

261

Punta del
Murro

Bobola

Crucero de
San Luis

24 **Hopelchén**

Seybaplaya

Hacienda
Vayamón

269

39

23 **Edzná**

27 **Dzibilnocac**

Playa

180

Hool

Tabasqueño

Dzibalchén

La Joya

Hochob

28

**QUINTANA
ROO**

40 **Champotón**

Punta
Xen

Providencia

San
Pablo
Pixtún

Yohaltún

QUINTANA ROO
CAMPECHE

Santa María

Chunjabin

261

Centenario

Xbonil

Balamkú

Xpuhil

TO
CHETUMAL

Escárcega

186

Conhuas

34

Becán 29

Chicanná

Chan Laguna

30

31

Hormiguero

32

33

Río Bec

Río

**Calakmul
Biosphere
Reserve**

Narciso
Merdoza

andelaria

37 **El Tigre**

35

Monclova

Calakmul

Altamira

Las Golondrinas

15

Baranda

Playa
Bonita

N

Nueva
Coahuila

MEXICO
GUATEMALA

GUATEMALA

BELIZE

N

loved ones are typical. If you can't make it to one of the small towns for this celebration, stop in at the main plaza in Campeche City, where altars from different regions of the state are set up for the festival.

November also marks the end of the rainy season (the strongest rains fall July–September), when the risk of hurricanes is over and the rain forests of the interior, as well as the city foliage, are at their most luxuriant. Any time from November through March is good for traveling, but as elsewhere in Mexico, the Christmas and Holy Week holidays mean extremely crowded hotels and public transportation. The rainy season slows travel down and makes exploring the more remote ruins a bit treacherous.

CAMPECHE CITY

The city of Campeche has a time-weathered and lovely feel to it—no contrived, ultramodern tourist glitz here, just a friendly city by the sea (population 240,000) that is proud of its heritage and welcomes all to share in it. Residents are extremely appreciative of their hometown's transformation from a rather run-down state capital to a world-class historical site. The refurbishing of more than 1,600 houses and buildings has left Campeche looking much as it did 350 years ago. With little prompting, locals point out the beauty of the city and ask how you are enjoying your visit. This good-humored, open-minded attitude is described as *campechano,* an adjective that means "easygoing and cheerful." Mexicans still make up the majority of vacationers here. The city's biggest appeal is its history—you can easily imagine pirates attacking. The coastline is cluttered with commercial fishing operations, and there are few public beaches. Though it is easy to take in Campeche in a day or two, a longer stay allows you to absorb the traditional lifestyle—and maybe find a favorite café near the plaza.

Because it has been walled (though not successfully fortified) since 1686, most of the historic downtown is neatly contained in an area measuring just five blocks by nine blocks. Today, for the most part, streets running north–south are even-numbered, and those running east–west are odd-numbered. The city is easily navigable—on foot, that is. With its narrow cobblestone roads and lack of parking spaces, navigating a car can be a frustrating exercise, although drivers here are polite and mellow. Walking, on the other hand, is a pleasure, with historical monuments and evocative name plaques above street numbers serving as handy guideposts. While tourism is not as integral to the Campeche economy as it is in Cancún or even Mérida, the city attracts its share of business conventions, Mexican families on vacation, and enterprising *gringos* looking for less glitz and a bargain for their buck.

On strategic corners surrounding the old city, or Viejo Campeche, stand the seven remaining *baluartes* (bastions) in various stages of disrepair. These were once connected by a 3-km (2-mi) wall in a hexagonal fortification that was built to safeguard the city against the pirates who continually ransacked it. Only bits of the wall still stand, and two stone archways—one facing the sea, the other the land—are all that remain of the four gates that once provided the only means of access to Campeche. Although these walls helped protect the residents, it was not until 1771, when Fuerte de San Miguel was built on a hilltop on the outskirts of town, that pirates finally ceased their attacks.

Campeche was one of few walled cities in North or Central America and was built along the traditional lines of defensive Spanish settlements, such as Santo Domingo in the Dominican Republic, Cartagena in Colombia, and Portobello in Panama. The walls also served as a class

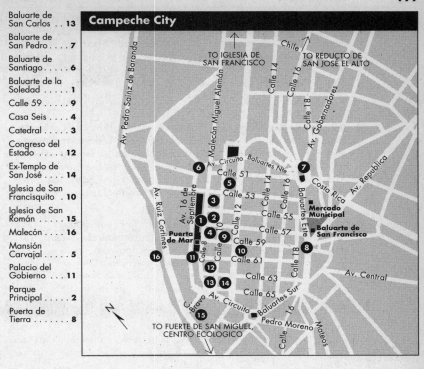

Campeche City

demarcation. Within them lived the ruling elite. Outside were the barrios of the Indians who aided the conquistadors and whose descendants continued to serve the upper class. The mulattoes brought as slaves from Cuba also lived outside the city walls.

A Good Walk

The Ciudad Viejo, the old city center, is the best place to start a walking tour, beginning with the **Baluarte de la Soledad** ①, which has a small Maya stelae museum. At the nearby **Parque Principal** ②, the city's central plaza, view some of the Yucatán Peninsula's most stately Spanish colonial architecture, including the **Catedral** ③ and, on the opposite side of the street, the **Casa Seis** ④. On Calle 10 between Calles 51 and 53 is the **Mansión Carvajal** ⑤, now home to government offices but worth a peek inside nonetheless. **Baluarte de Santiago** ⑥ is about one block to the north and one west, on Calle 8 at the corner of Calle 51. Head south on Calle 51 several blocks to the small, well-fortified **Baluarte de San Pedro** ⑦, at Circuito Baluartes Norte and Avenida Gobernadores. Walk west along Calle 18 to **Puerta de Tierra** ⑧ and the Baluarte San Francisco; then take **Calle 59** ⑨ past the beautiful **Iglesia de San Francisquito** ⑩. Continuing to Calle 8, turn west (left) and proceed for several blocks to get a look at the contrasting, modernistic designs of the **Palacio del Gobierno** ⑪ and the **Congreso del Estado** ⑫. A bit farther along Calle 8 past Calle 63 is **Baluarte de San Carlos** ⑬, the bastion that once was connected to the Puerta de Tierra. From there, head to the **Ex-Templo de San José** ⑭ and then the **Iglesia de San Román** ⑮. Both are considered masterpieces of colonial religious architecture. Finish the walk along the beachfront **malecón** ⑯.

Sights to See

⑬ **Baluarte de San Carlos.** Named for Charles II, King of Spain, this bastion, where Calle 8 curves around and becomes Circuito Baluartes, houses the **Sala de las Fortificaciones** (Chamber of the Fortifications), containing a scale model of the original defense system that is helpful for visualizing how the city was laid out. Also here is the **Museo de la Ciudad** (City Museum), with a rather paltry collection of photographs and maps of the city as it developed. Visit the basement dungeon, where captured pirates were jailed, and the rooftop for an ocean view, especially beautiful at sunset. ⊠ *Calle 8 at Calle 63, Circuito Baluartes, centro,* ☎ *no phone.* ▭ *50¢.* ☉ *Tues.–Sat. 8–8, Sun. 8–1.*

❼ **Baluarte de San Pedro.** Built in 1686 to protect the city from land attacks by pirates, this bastion's thick walls, flanked by watchtowers, now house a handicrafts and souvenir shop and a satellite office for the Secretary of Tourism, where you can book an English tour guide. Many of the tours to ruins such as Calakmul and Edzná leave from this point. ⊠ *Av. Gobernadores and Circuito Baluartes, centro,* ☎ *no phone.* ▭ *Free.* ☉ *Mon.–Sat. 9–9.*

❻ **Baluarte de Santiago.** The last of the bastions to be built (1704) has been transformed into the **X'much Haltún Botanical Gardens.** More than 200 plant species from the region are housed here, including the huge, beautiful *ceiba* tree, which had spiritual importance to the Maya, symbolizing a link between heaven, earth, and the underworld. Although the original bastion was demolished at the turn of the 20th century, and then rebuilt in the 1950s, architecturally the fort looks much the same as the others in Campeche—a stone fortress with thick walls, watchtowers, and gunnery slits. Extensive changes planned for 2002 include adding specimens of medicinal, botanical, and ornamental plants used by the Maya, and videos in English and Spanish explaining their use. ⊠ *Calles 8 and 59, Circuito Baluartes, centro,* ☎ *no phone.* ▭ *Free.* ☉ *Daily 9–6.*

★ ❶ **Baluarte de la Soledad.** Originally built to protect the **Puerta de Mar** (sea door), one of the four city gates through which all seafarers were forced to pass, this bastion is on the west side of Parque Principal. Because it stands alone, without any wall to shore it up, it resembles a Roman triumphal arch. The largest of the bastions, this one has comparatively complete parapets and embrasures that offer a sweeping view of the cathedral, municipal buildings, and the 16th- to 19th-century houses along Calle 8. Inside, the **Museo de las Estelas** (Stelae Museum) has artifacts that include a well-preserved sculpture of a man wearing an owl mask, columns from Edzná and Isla Jaina, and at least a dozen well-proportioned Maya stelae from ruins throughout Campeche. ⊠ *Calles 8 and 57, centro,* ☎ *no phone.* ▭ *$2.* ☉ *Mon. 8–noon, Tues.–Sun. 8–7:30.*

❾ **Calle 59.** On this city street, between Calles 8 and 18, once stood some of Campeche's finest homes, most of them two stories high, with the ground floors serving as warehouses and the upper floors as residences. The richest inhabitants built as close to the sea as possible; in case escape became necessary. (Legend has it that beneath the city a network of tunnels crisscrossed, linking the eight bastions and providing temporary refuge from pirates. The tunnel network has never been found, although rumors of its existence persist.) These days, behind the delicate grillwork and lace curtains, you can glimpse genteel scenes of Campeche life, with faded lithographs on the dun-color walls and plenty of antique furniture and gilded mirrors. To see the oldest houses in Campeche, walk south along Calle 10 past Circuito Baluartes to where it meets the malecón the San Román neighborhood.

★ ❹ **Casa Seis** (House No. 6). One of the first colonial homes built in Campeche, this is now the city's Cultural Center. It has been beautifully restored—the rooms are furnished with original antiques and a few reproductions to create a replica of a typical 19th-century colonial house. The original frescoes bordering the tops of the walls remain, some dating from 1500. The courtyard has Moorish architecture offset by lovely 18th-century stained-glass windows; it's used as an area for exhibits, lectures, and performances. The small restaurant off the original kitchen area serves excellent local specialities daily 9–2 and 6–10. ✉ *Calle 57, across from main plaza, centro,* ☎ *981/816–1782.* 🎫 *Free.* ☉ *Daily 9–9.*

★ ❸ **Catedral de la Inmaculada Concepción** (Cathedral of the Immaculate Conception). It took two centuries (from 1650 to 1850) to finish this grand temple, and as a result, it incorporates both neoclassical and Renaissance elements. The present cathedral occupies the site of Montejo's original church, which was built in 1540 on what is now Calle 55, between Calles 8 and 10. The simple exterior is capped with two bulbous towers rising on each side of the gracefully curved stone entrances, the fluted pilasters echoing those of the towers. Sculptures of saints in niches recall French Gothic cathedrals. The interior is no less impressive, with a single limestone nave, supported by Doric columns set with Corinthian capitals, arching toward the huge octagonal dome above a black-and-white marble floor. The pièce de résistance, however, is the magnificent Holy Sepulchre, carved from ebony and decorated with a multitude of stamped silver angels. ✉ *East side of the Plaza Principal, centro.* ☉ *Daily 6–noon and 5:30–7.*

☾ **Centro Ecológico de Campeche** (Campeche Ecological Center). High on a hill near the San Miguel Fort, this combination zoo, botanical gardens, and playground offers guided flora and fauna tours, games and activities for children, and educational lectures. ✉ *Av. Escénica s/n, colonia Fuerte San Miguel,* ☎ *981/811–2528.* 🎫 *10¢.* ☉ *Tues.–Fri. 9–1, Sat. 9–1 and 4–8, Sun. 9–4.*

⓬ **Congreso del Estado** (Congressional Building). A modernistic building resembling a flying saucer, the State Congress building contains the state legislative offices. The exterior is a strange example of 1960s architecture, although there's nothing much to see inside. ✉ *Calle 8, between Calles 61 and 63, across from Tourist Office, centro.*

⓮ **Ex-Templo de San José** (Former Church of Saint Joseph). The Jesuits built this fine Baroque structure in 1756, and today it is one of the most beautiful of the city's churches. It has a block-long facade and a portal that is completely covered with blue-and-yellow Talavera tiles and crowned with seven narrow stone finials that resemble both the roof combs on many Maya temples and the combs Spanish women used to wear as part of their elaborate hairdos. The former convent school next door is now the **Instituto Campechano** (Campeche Institute), used for cultural events and art exhibitions. Campeche's first lighthouse, built in 1864, now sits atop the right tower. Although it's currently not open to the public, the guard at the Instituto Campechano will let you in to see the church interior. Cultural events are held here Tuesday evening starting at 7. ✉ *Calle 10 at Calle 65, centro.*

☾ **Fuerte de San Miguel** (Saint Michael's Fort). The scenic Avenida Ruíz Cortínez near the west end of the city winds its way to a hilltop, where this fort commands one of the grandest views overlooking the city and the Gulf of Mexico. Built between 1686 and 1704, the fort was positioned to bombard enemy ships with its long-range cannons. But as soon as it was completed, pirates stopped attacking the city. Its impressive cannons were fired only once, in 1842, when General Santa Anna used Fuerte de San Miguel to put down a revolt by Yucatecan separatists seeking independence from Mexico. The fort houses the **Museo de la**

Cultura Maya (Museum of Mayan Culture), which has some world-class exhibits that include Maya mummies and funeral masks, as well as jewelry and pottery found at various tombs in the Calakmul ruins. Also noteworthy are funeral vessels, masks, many wonderfully expressive figurines from Isla Jaina, stelae and stucco masks from the Río Bec ruins, and an excellent pottery collection. The gift shop sells replicas of artifacts. The "El Guapo" tram ($2.20 round-trip) makes the trip daily at 10 AM, 6 PM, and 7 PM leaving from the east side of the main plaza, across from Los Portales; visitors are given about 10 minutes to see the fort before the tram returns them to the plaza. ⊠ *Av. Francisco Morazán s/n, west of town center, Fuerte de San Miguel,* ☎ *no phone.* 🎫 *$2.50.* ◷ *Tues.–Sun. 8:30–8.*

Iglesia de San Francisco (Church of Saint Frances). Away from the city center, in a residential neighborhood, stands this beautifully restored church, the oldest one in Campeche. It marks the spot where, some say, the first Mass on the North American continent was held in 1517—though the same claim has been made for Veracruz and Cozumel. One of Cortés's grandsons was baptized here, and the baptismal font still stands. ⊠ *Avs. Miguel Alemán and Mariano Escobedo, Barrio de San Francisco.* ◷ *Daily 8–noon and 5–7.*

🔟 **Iglesia de San Francisquito (Iglesia de San Roque)** (Church of Little Saint Frances). With its elaborately carved altars, Baroque columns adorned with gold leaf, and carved, wooden pews and creches with statues of San Francisco, this long, narrow church—built as a convent in 1565—adds to historic Calle 59's old-fashioned beauty. The church was originally called Iglesia de San Francisco, but now some know it only as Iglesia de San Roque—a name derived from the neighborhood in which it lies. ⊠ *Calle 12 at Calle 59, San Roque.* ◷ *Daily 8:30–noon and 5–7.*

⓯ **Iglesia de San Román** (Church of Saint Roman). Just outside the intramural boundary in the barrio of the same name, at Calles 10 and Bravo, San Román, with its bulbous bell tower typical of other Yucatán churches, was built to house the *naboríos* (Indians brought by the Spaniards to aid in the conquest and later used as household servants). The barrio, like other neighborhoods, grew up around the church. Built in the early part of the 16th century, the church became central to the lives of the Indians when an ebony image of Christ, the "Black Christ," was brought from Italy in about 1575. The Indians had been skeptical about Christianity, but this Christ figure came to be associated with miracles. The legend goes that a ship that refused to carry the tradesman and his precious statue was wrecked, while the ship that did take him on board reached Campeche in record time. To this day, the Feast of San Román—when the black-wood Christ mounted on a silver filigree cross is carried through the streets as part of a colorful and somber procession—is the biggest celebration of its kind in Campeche. ⊠ *Calles 10 y Bravo, San Román.* ◷ *Daily 7–1 and 3–7.*

⓰ **Malecón.** A broad sidewalk runs the length of Campeche's waterfront boulevard (the *malecón*), from east of the Hotel Debliz to the western outskirts of town, along Avenida Ruíz Cortínez. This popular landscaped boardwalk has sculptures, rest areas, and fountains that are lit up at night with neon colors, attracting joggers, strollers, and families enjoying the cool sea breezes and the view at sunset. On weekend nights, students turn the malecón into a party zone. Some of the best restaurants in the city can be found along this walkway.

❺ **Mansión Carvajal.** Built in the early 20th century by one of the wealthiest plantation owners in Yucatán, this eclectic mansion did time as the

Hotel Señorial before becoming an office for the state-run Delegacíon Integral de Familia (Family Institute), or DIF. The black-and-white tile floor, Art Nouveau staircase with Carrara marble steps and iron balustrade, and blue-and-white Moorish arcades are reminders of the city's heyday, when Campeche was the peninsula's only port. ⊠ *Calle 10 No. 584, between Calles 51 and 53, centro,* ☎ *981/816–7644.* ☒ *Free.* ☉ *Weekdays 8–2.*

Mercado Municipal (Municipal Market). To take in the heart of a true Mexican city, stroll through the market where locals shop for seafood, produce, and housewares. Beside the market is a small yellow bridge aptly named **Punte de Perro** (Dog Bridge)—four white plaster dogs guard the area. Try to arrive early, before it gets uncomfortably crowded. ⊠ *Av. Baluartes Este, between Calles 51 and 55, centro.* ☉ *Daily dawn–dusk.*

⓫ **Palacio del Gobierno** (Government Palace). One block inland from the malecón, on Avenida 16 de Septiembre, the flying saucer–shape Congreso del Estado (legislative building) shares a broad plaza with this much taller building, dubbed El Tocadiscos ("The Jukebox") by locals because of its outlandish facade. The eccentric architecture of these two capital buildings stands in odd contrast to the graceful colonial skyline of the adjacent Ciudad Viejo historic district. ⊠ *Av. 16 de Septiembre y Calle 61, centro.*

❷ **Parque Principal** (Main Square). The centerpiece of the old city, this park is also known as the Plaza de la Independencia. It is a focal point for many of the town's events, including concerts and dance performances held on weekends. There is a lovely café-bar under an old-fashioned gazebo in the center where you can watch the city's residents out for an evening stroll. ⊠ *Bounded by Calles 10, 8, 55, and 57, centro.*

★ ☕ ❽ **Puerta de Tierra** (Land Gate). Old Campeche ends here, at the only one of the four city gates with its basic structure intact. (The walls, arches, and gates were refurbished in 1987.) The stone arch intercepts a stretch of the partially crenulated wall, 26 ft high and 10 ft thick, that once encircled the city. You can walk along the full length of the wall to the **Baluarte San Juan,** where there are some excellent views of both the old and new cities. The staircase leads down to an old well, underground storage area, and dungeon. There is a two-hour light show (☒ $2.20) offered at Puerta de Tierra in Spanish (with French and English subtitles), Tuesday, Friday, and Saturday at 8:30 PM, daily during spring, summer, and Christmas vacation periods. The spectacle is performed by local musicians and dancers and gives an excellent historical overview of Campeche. ⊠ *Calles 18 and 59, centro.* ☉ *Daily 8–5.*

☕ **Reducto de San José el Alto.** This lofty redoubt, or stronghold, at the opposite end of town from Fuerte de San Miguel, is home to the **Museo de Armas y Barcos** (Museum of Arms and Boats). The displays focus on 18th-century weapons of siege and defense used in the many wars fought against the pirates. Also look for scale ships-in-a-bottle, manuscripts, and religious art. The view is terrific from the top of the ramparts, which were used to spot invading ships. The "El Guapo" tram ($2.20 round-trip) makes the trip daily at 9 AM, 11 AM, and 5 PM, leaving from the east side of the main plaza, across from Los Portales; visitors are given about 10 minutes to see the museum before the tram returns to the main plaza. ⊠ *Av. Escénica s/n, south of downtown, Reducto de San José,* ☎ *no phone.* ☒ *$2.50.* ☉ *Tues.–Sun. 8–8.*

Dining and Lodging

$$–$$$ ✕ **Hot Beach Pizza.** The two branches of this restaurant live up to their name: both are close to the beach, and the pizza is hot. The most popular pie is the *mexicana*, with ham and hot jalapeño peppers. Vegetarians have been tossed a bone: there's now a veggie pizza with fresh tomato, onion, and mild peppers. Open 7 AM to 11 PM, Hot Beach delivers to your hotel room. ⊠ *Av. Resurgimiento 57, between Calles 36 and 36a, Prado,* ☎ *981/816–6006. No credit cards;* ⊠ *Bajos Portales de San Francisco, San Francisco,* ☎ *981/811–3131. No credit cards.*

$$–$$$ ✕ **La Palapa del Balneario Popular.** One of the few seaside restaurants in Campeche, this place has live music after 3 PM and great ambience. Sit and watch the fishing boats on the gulf or enjoy a drink while the sun sets. Naturally, the fish and seafood cocktails are the freshest in town. ⊠ *Av. Resurgimientos, along the malecón, Col. Lazareto,* ☎ *981/ 816–5918. MC, V.*

$$–$$$ ✕ **La Pigua.** A favorite with local professionals lingering over long
★   lunches, La Pigua is arguably the best seafood restaurant in town, with the most pleasant ambience. The restaurant's two long glass walls form a terrarium of trees and plants. A truly ambitious lunch would start with a seafood cocktail, plate of cold crab claws, or *camarones al cocado* (coconut-encrusted shrimp), followed by fresh local fish in myriad presentations, and, for dessert, local peaches drenched in sweet liqueurs. ⊠ *Av. Miguel Alemán 179-A, Guadalupe,* ☎ *981/811–3365. MC, V. No breakfast or dinner.*

$–$$$ ✕ **El Guacamayo.** One of the oldest restaurants in Campeche (1947), this eatery is popular with locals and tourists. It serves regional specialties such as *cochinita pibíl* (pit-cooked pork) and excellent cream soups on the outdoor patio or indoors in the hacienda-style dining room. Be sure to visit the mascot, a colorful Guacamayo bird—but he goes to bed early, and the restaurant closes at 7 PM. ⊠ *Av. Miguel Alemán 143, centro,* ☎ *981/816–4636. AE, MC, V. No dinner.*

$–$$$ ✕ **Marganzo.** Traditional Campeche cuisine is served by a traditional-
★   ly attired waitstaff at this colorful and rustic restaurant a half block south of the plaza. Recommended is the *pompano en escabeche* (grilled fish with chilies and orange juice), as well as the fresh shrimp dishes ⊠ *Calle 8 No. 267, between Calles 57 and 59, centro,* ☎ *981/811– 3898. AE, MC, V.*

$–$$ ✕ **Casa Vieja.** Look for the hidden stairway on the east side of the plaza next to the Modatela store, and climb to this fabulous nightspot overlooking Campeche's main plaza. Dinner outside on the balcony is a perfect way to enjoy one of the city's savviest eateries. The Cuban owner has created an international menu of pastas, salads, and regional food, and even the music (occasionally live) is modern and international. Delicious desserts are prepared daily. ⊠ *Calle 10 No. 319 (altos), between Calles 57 and 55, centro,* ☎ *981/811–1311. No credit cards. No breakfast or lunch.*

$–$$ ✕ **Cenaduría los Portales.** Campechano families come here to enjoy a light supper, perhaps a *sandwich claveteado* (honey-flavored ham or turkey sandwich) or panuchos, along with a typical drink such as *horchata* (cold rice water flavored with cinnamon). The dining area is a colonial courtyard with tables decked out in checkered tablecloths. After eating you can stroll around Plaza San Francisco to walk off your meal. ⊠ *Calle 10 No. 86, at Portales San Francisco, 8 blocks northeast of Plaza Principal, San Francisco,* ☎ *981/816–5298. No credit cards. No breakfast or lunch.*

$–$$ ✕ **Chez Fernando.** This café-style eatery may have moved to a new lo-
★   cation, but it still offers Mediterranean, Italian, French, and Mexican food, including fresh pastas, salads, fish, chicken, and steak. The lasagna Florentine, pollo Dijon, and fettuccine gambetti are all excellent. The chocolate mousse is the best in the state. ⊠ *Av. Resurgimiento s/n, Jardín Coca Cola,* ☎ *981/816–2125. No credit cards. No lunch.*

$–$$ ✕ **La Parroquia.** The large entrance to La Parroquia, which faces Calle 55, is the best place in town for people-watching. Open 24 hours, this restaurant is a real locals' den—a comfortable family place with plastic tablecloths, a large menu, slow service, and televisions tuned to Mexican soccer. You can feast on inexpensive fried pompano, breaded shrimp, pan de cazón, or spaghetti, or just have a sandwich. Beer and tequila are also available. ⊠ *Calle 55 No. 8, between Calles 10 and 12, centro,* ☎ *981/816–8086. No credit cards.*

$ ✕ **La Malinches.** Tacos, tortillas, soups, and salads are served at this popular eatery along the malecón. The food is fresh and the prices low. ⊠ *Av. Justo Sierra Méndez and malecón, centro,* ☎ *981/811–3205. No credit cards. No lunch.*

$ ✕ **Restaurant Campeche.** This bright, clean eatery directly across from the central plaza offers hearty breakfasts, lunches, and dinners of Mexican and regional dishes. The only downside is the cranky waitstaff. ⊠ *Calle 57, across from main plaza, centro,* ☎ *no phone. No credit cards.*

$$$ 🏨 **Del Mar Hotel.** Formerly the Ramada Inn, this is the fanciest hotel
★ in town, even if by international standards it is quite average. Rooms are fairly large, with tasteful drapes and floor tiles, rattan furniture, color cable TV, and balconies that overlook the pool or the bay across the street. The lobby coffee shop, El Poquito, serves standard but tasty fare, and Lafitte's, the bar-restaurant, offers room service until 2 AM. ⊠ *Av. Ruíz Cortínez 51 (on the waterfront), 24000, centro,* ☎ *981/816–2233,* FAX *981/811–4124. 138 rooms, 11 suites. Restaurant, coffee shop, room service, pool, travel services, free parking. AE, MC, V.*

$$ 🏨 **Baluartes.** Sandwiched between the waterfront malecón and the Puerto del Mar (gateway to the old city), this big, square hotel is much prettier inside than out. Rooms are decorated in cool blue tones, and bathrooms have white tiles. All rooms have air-conditioning, double beds, phones, satellite TV, and ocean views. Baluartes has a huge pool facing the sea and is within walking distance of the historic district. ⊠ *Av. 16 de Septiembre 128, at Av. Ruíz Cortínez, 24000, centro,* ☎ *981/816–3911,* FAX *981/816–2410. 94 rooms, 8 suites. Restaurant, coffee shop, pool, bar, travel services, free parking. MC, V.*

$$ 🏨 **Debliz.** Northeast of the center, this large hotel caters to tour groups. Although the exterior and lobby look like an office building, the pool and deck areas are quite lovely. Rooms are decorated in soft pastels, with two double beds, cable TV, and balconies that look out onto the pool. There's also a decent restaurant and bar. You have to take a cab to the historical center—it's just a bit too far to walk. ⊠ *Av. Diá Ordaz 55, 24000, Col. La Ermita,* ☎ *981/815–2222,* FAX *981/815–2277. 137 rooms, 6 suites. Restaurant, snack bar, pool, bar, parking. AE, MC, V.*

$$ 🏨 **Del Paseo.** A block from the ocean, this pretty hotel lies in the quiet neighborhood of San Román, about a 15-minute walk from city center. Rooms are tasteful and comfortable, with modern rattan furniture, one double bed, a balcony, and cable TV. A pretty glass-roofed atrium with park benches and plants shelters the hotel complex. ⊠ *Calle 8 No. 215, 24000, San Román,* ☎ *981/811–0077 or 981/811–0100,* FAX *981/811–0097. 48 rooms, 2 suites. Restaurant, room service, hair salon, bar, car rental, free parking. AE, MC, V.*

$$ 🏨 **Hotel América.** A converted colonial home, this hotel has three levels of rooms that open onto large corridors with dramatic black-and-white checked floors, offsetting the white Moorish arches. The rooms all have two double beds, ceiling fans, local television, and bamboo furniture. Rooms facing the street have balconies but are noisier. This is one of the few hotels in the center with parking. ⊠ *Calle 10 No. 252, 24000, centro,* ☎ *981/816–4588,* FAX *981/816–4576. 52 rooms. Fans, parking (fee). AE, MC, V.*

$$ ☒ **El Regis.** This seven-room hotel is a good bargain and a mere two blocks from the plaza. Though a bit run-down, the Regis is a lovely old two-story colonial home with a huge wooden front door, high ceilings, and an airy inner atrium. All rooms are spic-and-span, with black-and-white tile floors, two double beds, and cupboard closets. The low points are an unfriendly staff, tiny bathrooms, poor lighting, and weak air-conditioning. The front doors are locked at 11 PM, but the night watchman will let you in. ☒ *Calle 12 No. 148, between Calles 55 and 57, 24000, centro,* ☎ *981/816–3175. 7 rooms. Fans; no room phones. No credit cards.*

$–$$ ☒ **Posada del Angel.** Directly across from the cathedral is this small hotel with clean, basic rooms that have one double bed. The staff is friendly, the lobby fridge is available for guests to use, and everything is within walking distance. ☒ *Calle 10 No. 307, between Calles 53 and 55, 24000, centro,* ☎ *981/816–7718. 14 rooms. Fans; no room phones, no room TVs. No credit cards.*

$ ☒ **Colonial.** This romantic building dates to 1812 but was converted
★ into a hotel in the 1940s, when its colorful tiles were added. All rooms are delightfully different, with cool cotton bedding, good mattresses, tile bathrooms, and window screens. Most rooms still have the original telephones and antique plumbing (which works quite well). Rooms 16, 18, 27, and 28 have wonderful views of the cathedral and city at night. Public areas include two leafy patios, a small sun roof, and a second-floor sitting room. ☒ *Calle 14 No. 122, between Calles 55 and 57, 24000, centro,* ☎ *981/816–2222. 30 rooms. Fans; no air-conditioning in some rooms, no room TVs. No credit cards.*

$ ☒ **Hotel López.** A pleasant place, and a good choice if you're on a budget, this little hotel has balconies in an undulating design and smallish standard rooms lit by fluorescent lights with tiny closets, armoires, luggage stands, and easy chairs. Rooms are cramped but clean. The narrow lobby feels a bit off-putting, with rooms rising up three stories on all sides. ☒ *Calle 12 No. 189, between Calles 61 and 63, 24000, centro,* ☎ FAX *981/816–3344 or 981/816–3021. 39 rooms. Fans; no air-conditioning in some rooms. No credit cards.*

Nightlife and the Arts

Each Saturday evening from 7 to 10:30 PM, the streets around the main square are closed to traffic and filled with folk and popular dance performances, singers, comics, handicrafts, and food and drink stands. If you're in town on a Saturday evening, don't miss these weekly festivities, called *Campechanísimo* (which roughly translates as "Really Really Campeche")—the entertainment is often first-rate and always free.

Discos
If you're in the mood to dance, try Campeche's discos. The high-tech **Jaxx** (☒ Av. Resurgimiento 112, Carretera a Lerma, ☎ 981/818–4555), formerly the Millennium club, offers laser shows and dance music on Friday and Saturday. **KY8** (☒ Calle 8 between Calles 59 and 61, centro, ☎ no phone), open Friday and Saturday only, plays dance music popular with locals. North of the city, **Plataforma 21** (☒ Privada Loma Azul 2 at Av. López Portillo, ☎ 981/812–6178 or 981/812–7193) is open Wednesday–Saturday. You need to take a taxi to get here.

Movies
Cinema Hollywood (☒ Lote 2, Manzana D, Zona Turística, centro, ☎ 981/816–1452) is close to the malecón and Plaza Comercial Ah Kim Pech and has six large screens showing the latest blockbuster movies.

Many movies are in English with Spanish subtitles; others are dubbed in Spanish.

Outdoor Sports and Activities

Hunting, fishing, and birding are popular throughout the state of Campeche. Contact **Don José Sansores** at the Snook Inn in Champotón (✉ Calle 30 No. 1, centro, ☎ FAX 981/828–0018) to arrange sportfishing or wildlife photo excursions in the Champotón area. **Francisco Javier Hernandez Romero** (✉ La Pigua restaurant, Av. Miguel Alemán 179–A, centro, ☎ 981/811–3365) can arrange boat or fishing trips to the Peténes Ecological Reserve. To enjoy a tour of Campeche Bay and the surrounding area, contact the **Marina Yacht Club** (✉ Av. Resurgimiento 120, Carretera a Lerma, ☎ FAX 981/816–1990). Times and duration of tours are set as per customer requests. Call ahead to make a reservation.

Shopping

Because Campeche is a seaport, ships-in-a-bottle, tacky statues made of seashells, and mother-of-pearl and black coral jewelry are everywhere. Note that buying black coral is environmentally incorrect, since the harvesting of the coral destroys reef that takes thousands of years to grow. In recognition of its endangered status, there are some restrictions regarding bringing black coral into the United States. You can find a good selection of basketry, straw hats, embroidered cloth, and clay trinkets.

Local Crafts

In a lovely old mansion, the government-run **Casa de Artesanía Tukulna** (✉ Calle 10 No. 333, between Calles 59 and 61, centro, ☎ 981/816–9088) sells well-made embroidered dresses, blouses, pillow coverings, regional dress for men and women, hammocks, Campeche's famous Panama hats, posters, books on Campeche ecology in Spanish, jewelry, baskets, and stucco reproductions of Maya motifs. The house is beautiful, with arched doorways, black-and-white tile floors, and chandeliers; it's worth a visit if only to admire the interior. The shop is open Monday–Saturday 9–8 and Sunday 10–2. The expensive **Veleros** (✉ Plaza Comercial Ah-Kin-Pech, centro, ☎ 981/981–2446), closed Sunday, is owned by craftsman David Pérez. It stocks his miniature ships, seashells, furniture with nautical motifs, and jewelry fashioned from sanded and polished bull's horns. The horns look much like tortoiseshell in thickness and color, though not as beautiful. But since it's no longer legal to hunt turtles or to import tortoiseshell to the United States, the horn is a good, legal alternative. Pérez's first shop, **Artesanía Típica Naval** (✉ Calle 8 No. 259, centro, ☎ 981/816–5708), is still thriving, but it's much smaller and more cramped than the mall store. Neither shop accepts credit cards.

Shopping Districts and Malls

Campeche City has two large, modern shopping malls within walking distance of each other. **Plaza Comercial Ah-Kin-Pech** (✉ Av. Pedro Sainz de Barnada, at Av. Ruíz Cortínez, centro), on the waterfront, has a variety of boutiques, clothing, and souvenir shops, as well as a grocery store. Across the street from Plaza Comercial Ah-Kin Pech is **Plaza del Mar** (✉ Av. Ruíz Cortínez, centro), home to a number of specialty stores. **Plaza Universidad** (✉ Av. Agustín Melgar, at Av. Universidad, Universidad) has a number of good boutiques. Visit the **Mercado Público Pedro Sainz de Baranda** (✉ Av. Circuito Baluartes Este, between Calles 51 and 55, centro) for food and craft items.

ROUTE 180: LA RUTA DE LOS ARTESANOS

The so-called short route to Mérida (192 km, or 119 mi) takes you past several picturesque villages, where many of the artisans in the state produce Campeche's famous handicrafts. For this reason it's been named the Artists' Route. It's also known as the Camino Real, or Royal Highway.

San Francisco Koben

🛈 *30 km (19 mi) north of Campeche, along Rte. 180 toward Mérida.*

You can find some real bargains in this small village, which has become a roadside market. Hammocks, textiles, hats, clothing, and bottled preserves are sold here. Twenty-nine kilometers (18 miles) north on Route 180 is the picturesque village of **Tenabo.** The town of **Pomuch,** famous for its breads, is north of Tenabo. Be sure to stop and try a cinnamon, anise, vanilla, or cheese loaf.

Hecelchakán

🛈 *60 km (37 mi) north of Campeche, along Rte. 180 toward Mérida.*

A beautiful 15th-century town with a magnificent church, former monastery, and school, Hecelchakán is the perfect spot to stop for lunch, watch a small colonial town in action, and stroll around to admire some of the lovely architecture. The area is noted for wonderful tamales as well as its sandals, hammocks, and textiles.

Hecelchakán's primary attraction is the **Museo Arqueológico del Camino Real.** In a 1660 house, the museum has an impressive collection of clay figurines from Isla Jaina and stelae of the Puuc style. It's worth the short detour off the highway to visit. ✉ *Rte. 180, north of Hecelchakán,* ☎ *no phone.* 🎟 *$1.70.* ☉ *Tues.–Fri. 9–1:30, Sat. 9–1 and 4–8, Sun. 9–noon.*

The only accessible road to **Isla Jaina** (Jaina Island) starts in Hecelchakán. Now part of the **Reserva Ecológica Peténes,** Isla Jaina is believed by some to be a giant cemetery for the Maya; others claim it is just an ancient city whose inhabitants buried their dead beneath their homes. The island is off-limits unless you have prior written permission from the National Institute of Anthropology and History (INAH) in Campeche. Another option is to tour the island with Hector Solis of **Espacios Naúticos** (☎ 981/816–1990). Mr. Solis's informal guided trips include a 1½-hour tour of the island and transport there and back by boat. Stops can be arranged for having breakfast or lunch, as well as for swimming at the beach.

On the outskirts of town are a number of old haciendas such as **Chunkanán,** and the village of **Dzitbalché,** where the Dzitbalché Verses (descriptions of Maya ceremonies and rituals) were written. Its church dates from 1768.

Calkiní

🛈 *24 km (17 mi) north of Hecelchakán.*

One of the most important towns along the Camino Real, Calkiní dates from the pre-Colombian Maya Ah-Canul dynasty. According to a local codex, the Ah-Canul chieftainship was founded here in 1443 after the destruction of the Post-Classic kingdom of Mayapán, in today's Yucatán state. The site chosen was beneath an enormous ceiba, a tree sacred to the Maya and frequently mentioned in their legends. The Ah-Canul was the most important dynasty at the time of the Conquest, during which the fighters who rebelled against the Spanish leader Montejo were put down in Mérida, dealing a great blow to the Maya spirit. The village of Calkiní is the jumping-off point for exploring the northeastern corner of Campeche.

Calkiní's major attraction is the **Parroquia de San Luis Obispo.** Franciscan friars built this church-fortress-convent between 1548 and 1776, and the Clarisas have used it as a cloistered convent since 1980. You can enter the church (even if the front gate is padlocked) by asking at the office around the right side of the building, but the convent itself is off-limits to tourists. Inside the church is an exquisite carved cedar altarpiece painted in rich gold, red, and black and a handsome pulpit carved with the symbols of the four Evangelists. The portal is Plateresque—a 16th-century Spanish style whose elaborate ornaments suggest silver plate—and the rest of the structure is Baroque. The facade has twin bell towers and a repeated shell motif. ⊠ *Off the town square.* 🎫 *Free.* ☉ *Wed. and Fri.–Mon. 7–noon and 3–9, Thurs. 7 AM–9 PM.*

North of town is the village of **Tepakán,** home of Cal-kin, a ceramics factory. **Cal-kin** (⊠ Carretera Calkiní–Tepakán, Km 1, ☎ 996/961-0232) produces the distinctive, hand-painted white, beige, and blue ceramics of Campeche. A four-piece setting starts at $40. The factory has a small store open weekdays 8–5, Saturday 8–4, and Sunday 9–1.

Nunkiní

㉑ *28 km (15 mi) west of Calkiní, look for the sign for Santa Cruz.*

In this small traditional Maya village, the women weave mats and rugs from the reeds of *huano* palm, incorporating traditional designs. The colorful church of **San Diego Apóstol** is found here.

If you continue going west to the village of Santa Cruz—there is only one road—to where the road curves north for another 15 km (9 mi), you pass the remains of the 18th-century **Santa Cruz** hacienda, and 13 km (8 mi) farther the **Tankuché** hacienda, which, despite efforts of preservation, is in decline. The original machines used to extract dye from Campeche wood are still on site. Fourteen kilometers (9 miles) away is **El Remote,** a wonderful water hole surrounded by sapodilla tress and mangroves. Continuing on the road, you enter the Peténes Ecological Reserve, where you can see flamingos, frigates, herons, and ibis in the mangroves. The final stop is the tiny fishing village of **Isla Arena,** where the birds outnumber humans.

Becal

㉑ *10 km (6 mi) north of Calkiní.*

The small town of Becal is noted for its famous *jipis,* known to most of the world as Panama hats. Local residents weave reeds of the huano palm in caves beneath their houses, where the humidity keeps the reeds flexible. As a result, the hats are so pliable that they can be rolled up in a suitcase with no harm done. First produced in the 19th century by the García family, the hats have become a village tradition. It's hard to resist photographing the statue of three giant hats in the center of the town plaza.

The workshop of Mario Farfán Herrera at **Artesanía Becaleña** (⊠ Calle 30 No. 210-A, ☎ 996/431-4046) sells the finest and most expensive hats in town. It also produces jewelry boxes, lamp shades, and other objects—all made from palm fibers. Buying jipis directly from the producers helps to sustain this faltering craft and keeps the tradition alive. The **Sociedad de Artesanas Becaleñas** (✉ Calle 34, between Calles 33 and 35, ☎ no phone), run by Rita Calán, sells fine hats and offers tours of an artisan's workshop.

Halachó

22 *6 km (4 mi) north of Becal.*

Just across the Yucatán state line from Becal is the village of Halachó. Although not an official part of the Artists' Route, this is a worthwhile stop for those in search of handcrafted baskets, rugs, and bags. Halachó, which means "reed rats," was so named because it was founded on the shores of a lake (long since dried up), where rats once lived in abundance in the reeds along the shore. The centerpiece of Halachó is a magnificent white, 18th-century mission church, **Iglesia Santiago Apóstol,** dedicated to the apostle James, patron saint of the conquistadors. Each year, standard-bearing pilgrims from surrounding towns and villages come to Halachó to pay homage at the equestrian statue of the saint, up a flight of stairs behind the altar. The church is open daily 8–noon and 3–8.

ROUTE 261: THE CHENES ROUTE

This is the longer way to reach the Yucatán capital of Mérida, passing by the Chenes ruins of eastern Campeche. Chenes-style temples are recognized by their elaborate stucco facades decorated with geometric designs, giant masks of jaguars, and birds. Also characteristic of the style are doorways shaped like the open mouth of a monster. It is a scenic route, leading through green hills with tall dark forests and valleys covered by low scrub, cornfields, and citrus orchards.

Edzná

 23 *55 km (34 mi) southeast of Campeche City.*

The Maya ruin of Edzná deserves more fame than it has. Archaeologists consider it one of the peninsula's most important ruins because of the crucial transitional role it played among several architectural styles. And as more people discover Campeche, its reputation is growing.

Occupied from around 300 BC to AD 1450, Edzná reached its pinnacle between AD 600 and AD 900. The 6-square-km (2-square-mi) expanse of savanna, broken up only by the occasional tall tree, is situated in a broad valley prone to flooding and flanked by low hills. Surrounding the site are vast networks of irrigation canals, the remnants of a highly sophisticated hydraulic system that channeled rainwater and water from the Champotón River into human-made *chultunes*, or cisterns. Over the course of several hundred years, Edzná grew from a humble agricultural settlement into a major political-religious center. The city served as a trading center of sorts, situated at a "crossroads" between the cities of the Petén region of Guatemala and the lowlands of northern Yucatán. The region's agricultural products were traded for hand-carved ritual objects and adornments from Guatemala.

Commanding center stage in the **Gran Acrópolis** (Great Acropolis) is the **Pirámide de los Cinco Pisos** (Five-Story Pyramid), which rises 102 ft. The structure consists of five levels, each narrower than the one below it, terminating in a tiny temple crowned by a roof comb. Hieroglyphs were carved into the vertical face of the 15 steps between each level, and numerous stelae depict the opulent attire and adornment of the ruling class—quetzal feathers, jade pectorals, and skirts of jaguar skin. Near the temple's base, the **Templo de la Luna** (Temple of the Moon), **Templo del Sureste** (Southwest Temple), **Templo del Norte** (North Temple), and **Temezcal** (steam bath) surround a small plaza. West of the acropolis, the Puuc-style **Plataforma de las Navajas** (Platform of the Knives) was so-named by a 1970 archaeological exploration that found a number of flint knives inside. The 264-ft-high edifice has 20 rooms with vaulted roofs; it was most likely a dwelling.

In 1992 Campeche archaeologist Antonio Benavides discovered that the Five-Story Pyramid was so constructed that, during certain dates of the year, the setting sun would illuminate the mask of the creator god, Itzamná, inside one of the pyramid's rooms. This happens annually on May 1, 2, and 3, the beginning of the planting season for the Maya—then and now—when they invoke the god to bring rain. It also occurs on August 7, 8, and 9, the days of harvesting and thanking the god for his help. A local anthropologist, Elvira del Carmen Tello, stages an ancient Maya production at Edzná each May. Check with the tourist office in Campeche City (☞ Visitor Information *in* Campeche A to Z, *below*) for information.

South of the Great Acropolis lies the **Small Acropolis,** whose four buildings each face a cardinal point in the compass. The heaviest looking is the **Temple of the Stairway with Reliefs,** which has a stairway decorated with crude reliefs showing seated figures, faces, and jaguars. The architectural style of this complex is derived from the Petén and Puuc schools; the structures were built between AD 800 and AD 1000.

Carved into the **Temple of the Masks (Building 414),** adjacent to the Small Acropolis, are some masks of the sun god with huge protruding eyes, filed teeth, and oversize tongues. If you look closely on the remaining masks you can see marks on the cheeks, which represent scarification such as that used by Maya nobles. Local lore holds that Edzná, which can be translated as "the house of the gestures (or grimaces)," might have been named for these images. More recent theories claim the name means "home of the echo" and refers to the acoustic effect between the main buildings of the site. Yet others say that it means "home of the Itzáes." Itzá is the name of a Maya group native to southwest Campeche, as well as a common Maya surname.

A variety of architectural styles have been discerned at this site. The Petén style of northern Guatemala and Chiapas is reflected in the use of acropoli as bases for pyramids; of low-lying structures that contrast handsomely with soaring temples; and of corbeled arch roofs, richly ornamented stucco facades, and roof combs. The Río Bec style, which dominated much of Campeche, can be seen in the slender columns, high towers, and exuberant stone mosaics. The multistory edifices, arched passageways, stone causeways, and hieroglyph-adorned stairways are representative of both the Chenes and Puuc styles.

If you're not driving, consider taking one of the inexpensive day trips offered by most travel agencies in Campeche; this is far easier than trying to get to Edzná by municipal buses. **Servicios Turísticos Picazh** (⊠ Calle 16 No. 348, between Calles 57 and 59, ☎ 981/816–4426) offers transportation only or guided service to Edzná at reasonable prices. ⊠ *Rte. 261 east from Campeche City for 44 km (27 mi) to Cayal, then Rte. 188 southeast for 18 km (11 mi),* ☎ *no phone.* ☒ *$3.30, free Sun.* ☉ *Daily 8–5.*

Lodging

$$$$ ⊞ **Hacienda Uayamón.** In the past, this elegant 1792 hacienda was, among other things, an ice factory. Abandoned in 1905, it was reborn in 1999 as a luxury hotel with an elegant restaurant. The original architecture and decor have been carefully preserved: in the library are exposed beam ceilings, cane chairs, sisal carpets, and dark wood bookshelves at least 12 ft high. Each casita has its own private garden, hot tub, and bathroom as well as a cozy bedroom. The remaining two walls of the machine house shelter the outdoor pool, and candles are still lit at the ruined chapel. ⊠ *9 km (5½ mi) north of Edzná,* ☎ *981/819–0335 or 981/819–0336,* ℻ *999/944–8484, Uayamon@ghm.com. 12 suites, 10 casitas. Restaurant, pool, bar, free parking. AE, MC, V.*

Hopelchén

㉔ *41 km (25 mi) north of the Edzná turnoff on Rte. 261, 153 km (95 mi) north of Xpuhil.*

Since 1985 Hopelchén has been home to an immigrant colony of blond-haired, blue-eyed Mennonites who came from northern Mexico looking for arable land. These people are very tradition-bound, and they still speak a Dutch-German dialect, although those who do business with outsiders learn Spanish. The Campeche group makes and sells Mennonite cheese, which can be purchased in shops and restaurants throughout the state.

Otherwise, Hopelchén—the name means "place of the five wells"—is a traditional Maya town noted for the lovely **Iglesia de San Francisco,** built in honor of St. Francis of Padua in 1667. Corn, beans, tobacco, fruit, squash, and *henequen* (sisal hemp) are cultivated in this rich agricultural center. If you want an ice cream cone, a magazine, or an old-fashioned treadle sewing machine, check out the **Escalante Heredia Hermanas** right on the town square—it's also the place to make long-distance phone calls.

Lodging

$　🏨 **Los Arcos.** Those who want to stay the night and explore the area can check into this hostelry. Named for the arches that span the front of the hotel, Los Arcos has basic rooms facing a traditional colonial-style courtyard. There is a small restaurant in the lobby. ⊠ *Calle 23 s/n, Col. Centro,* ☎ *996/822–0123. 32 rooms. Restaurant, fans, free parking. No credit cards.*

Las Grutas de Xtacumbilxunaan

㉕ *34 km (21 mi) north of Hopelchén.*

Just short of the state line between Campeche and Yucatán and a few miles before Bolonchén de Rejón are the Grutas de Xtacumbilxunaan ("shta-*cum*-bil-shu-nan"), the "caverns of the hidden women" in Spanish and Maya—where legend says a Maya girl disappeared after going for water. In ancient times, cenotes (sinkholes) deep in the extensive cave system provided an emergency water source during droughts. Only a few chambers are open to the public, because the rock surfaces are dangerously slippery and the depth of the caverns is 240 ft. In the upper part of the caves you can admire the delicate limestone formations, which have been given whimsical names such as "Witch's Ball" and "Devil's Bridge." You should book the two-hour tour through the tourist office in Campeche or in Hopelchén; there are sometimes guides at the site, but don't count on it. 🎫 *$2.* ☉ *Daily 8–5.*

Santa Rosa Xtampak

🔺 **㉖** *25 km (16 mi) east of Hopelchén, 10 km (6 mi) south of Las Grutas de Xtacumbilxunaan.*

Believed to have been the political center of the Chenes empire, this extensive site shows the influence of Puuc architecture as well. Although Xtampak was discovered in 1842, excavation didn't begin until 1995. It's believed that there are 100 structures in the area, although only 12 have been cleared. The most exciting find was the colossal **Palacio** (Palace), in the western plaza. Inside are two inner staircases running the length of the structure, each with openings that lead to different levels and ending in subterranean chambers. This combination is extremely rare in Maya temples. The **Casa de la Boca del Serpiente** (House of the Serpent's Mouth) is noteworthy for its perfectly preserved and integrated zoomorphic entrance. The mouth of the sacred earth monster, sometimes referred to as the god Itzamná, stretches wide to reveal a perfectly proportioned inner chamber. ⊠ *East of Hopelchén on Dzibalchén–Chencho road, watch for sign,* ☎ *no phone.* 🖃 *$2.50.* ⊙ *Daily 8–5.*

Dzibilnocac

 🕗 *18 km (11 mi) northeast of Dzibalchén, 69 km (43 mi) northeast of Hopelchén.*

To get to the rarely visited archaeological site of Dzibilnocac, you must first reach the village of Dzibalchén by traveling south on Route 261. From there, proceed north on a small side road to Vicente Guerrero, also known as Iturbide, a farming community 19 km (11½ mi) north—literally at the end of the road. Each corner of the town square has a small stone guardhouse built in 1850 during the War of the Castes, and the road around them eventually turns into a dirt path passing houses and ending at the ruins. Dzibilnocac was a fair-size ceremonial center between AD 250 and AD 900. Although there are at least seven temple pyramids here, the only one that has been partially excavated is the **Palacio Principal,** a Late Classic (AD 600–AD 800) palace that combines elements of the Puuc and Chenes architectural styles. Only one of the three towers remains intact; it contains a one-room square temple with beautifully executed carvings of Chaac on the outside walls. Under what remains of the middle tower, two small underground chambers can be accessed through a Maya arch. The farthest tower has a roof comb sticking up from a mound of grass, trees, and stones—an incongruous sight. ⊠ *South to Dzibalchén and then north to Vicente Guerrero,* ☎ *no phone.* 🖃 *Free.* ⊙ *Daily 8–5.*

Hochob

 🕗 *55 km (34 mi) southwest of Hopelchén, 15 km (9 mi) west of Dzibilnocac.*

The small Maya ruin of Hochob is an excellent example of the Chenes architectural style, which flowered in the Classic period from about AD 200 to AD 900. Most of the ruins in this area (central and southeastern Campeche) were built on the highest possible elevation to prevent flooding during the rainy season, and Hochob is no exception. It rests high on a hill overlooking the surrounding valleys. Another indication that these are Chenes ruins is the number of cisterns, or *chultunes,* found in the area. Since work began at Hochob in the early 1980s, four temples and palaces have been excavated at the site, including two that have been brought back to their original grandeur. **Structure III** has wonderfully preserved stucco carvings that are perfect examples of the intricate geometric designs of the Chenes style. Ask the guard to show you the series of natural and man-made chultunes that extend back into the forest. ⊠ *Southwest of Hopelchén on Dzibalchén–Chencho road,* ☎ *no phone.* 🖃 *Free.* ⊙ *Daily 8–5.*

ROUTE 186 TOWARD CHETUMAL

Campeche's archaeological sites, particularly those near the Quintana Roo border, are attracting more attention from scientists and travelers alike. Secluded yet accessible ruins are surrounded by tropical jungle—and for the most part are devoid of tourists. The vestiges of at least 10 little-known Maya cities lie hidden off Route 186 between Escárcega and Chetumal. Becán and the neighboring sites of Chicanná, Balamkú, and Xpuhil are just off Highway 186 near the Quintana Roo border; Hormiguero is 25 km southwest of Xpuhil. The road to Calakmul, near the Guatemala border south of Xpuhil, has been paved, making parts of the biosphere more accessible. Río Bec, on the other hand, is more difficult to reach.

You can see Xpuhil, Becán, Hormiguero, and Chicanná in a rather rushed day if you're en route between Escárcega and Chetumal. To see Balamkú and Calakmul as well, plan for another day and stay overnight at one of the hotels in the area. Add another full day to your itinerary if you want to include Río Bec; it requires a full-day guided tour through the jungle at the edge of the Calakmul Biosphere Reserve.

Southern Campeche is an area with genuine ecotourism. As late as 1950, the region was unoccupied. Then the Mexican government began colonizing the area with Maya settlers from Tabasco whose land had been seized by cattle barons. Later immigrants—also victims of the cattle industry—came from Veracruz, and when the Chicosen volcano erupted in Chiapas in the early 1980s, another wave of farmers appeared. The local people live a marginal existence in isolated communities, with only two schools serving them. About 25 communities of between 4,000 and 5,000 people live inside the Calakmul reserve, and another 2,500–3,000 people live just outside it. Their slash-and-burn technique of farming, which requires that sections of precious forests be burned down to make way for crops, is probably the most dangerous threat to the reserve. In an attempt to protect the land, alternative means of making a living, like beekeeping and pig farming, have been introduced to the farmers. They also have been taught organic farming methods that result in higher crop yields, so that more land need not be cleared for agriculture.

Another important alternative being offered is the Pronatura program, which trains local people to act as guides to the various ruins and for special excursions into the biosphere. As a result, the area offers excellent guides trained in environmental education, Maya culture, ecotourism, basic English, and local flora and fauna. Hiring a local guide not only enhances your visit to the ruins but gives economic support to the local community and helps preserve the area. Arrangements for English-speaking guides can be made through the tourist office in Campeche City. Guides can also be reserved through **Chicanná Ecovillage** in Xpuhil (⊠ Carretera Escárcega–Chetumal, Km 144, 9 km north of Xpuhil, ☎ 981/816–2233). **Rancho Encantado** (⊠ Bacalar, Quintana Roo, ☎ 800/505–6292 in the U.S., WEB www.encantado.com) offers guided trips to the area from its resort on the Mexican Caribbean.

The well-maintained Route 269 runs north from Xpuhil, connecting to Hopelchén, west of Campeche City. Travelers can now continue north from Xpuhil to visit several Chene-style ruins, from there returning to Campeche City or continuing north toward Yucatán state. Xpuhil's tiny bus station has at least one bus per day to Escárcega, Hopelchén, Chetumal, Campeche, and Cancún.

Xpuhil

 29 *300 km (186 mi) southeast of Campeche, 130 km (81 mi) south of Dz-ibilnocac, 125 km (78 mi) west of Chetumal.*

Xpuhil (literally "cat's tail," pronounced ish-*poo*-hil) comprises several buildings on the north side of the highway and one other, **Estructura V,** to the south. Other building groups have yet to be excavated. Buildings I–IV demonstrate architectural elements of both the Chenes and Río Bec styles. The elaborately carved facades and doorways fashioned like monsters' mouths reflect the Chenes style, while the Río Bec style is seen in the three adjacent pyramid-towers, which are connected by a long platform. In **Edificio I,** all three towers were once crowned by false temples, and at the front of each are the remains of 4 vaulted rooms (for a total of 12), each oriented toward one of the cardinal points and thought to have been used by priests and royalty. On the back side of the central tower is a huge mask of the rain god Chaac. ⊠ *$2.20.* ☉ *Daily 8–5.*

Lodging

$$$ ⊠ **Chicanná Ecovillage Resort.** Rooms in this comfortable jungle lodge are in two-story stucco duplexes with thatch roofs. Each unit has one king or two double beds, an overhead fan, screened windows, and a porch or balcony with a table and chairs. There's a library, a mediocre restaurant, and a small pool surrounded by flowering plants. There is no phone or fax at the hotel; both are available in nearby Xpuhil. For reservations, contact the Del Mar Hotel in Campeche City. ⊠ *Carretera Escárcega–Chetumal, Km 144, 9 km (5½ mi) north of village of Xpuhil,* ☎ *981/816–2233 for reservations. 32 rooms. Restaurant, fans, pool, bar, library. AE, MC, V.*

$$ ⊠ **Hotel Calakmul.** Señora María Cabrera is the owner of this charming hotel offering double or single rooms and small wooden cabanas. The rooms are comfortable and large but extremely basic, with bright coral-color walls, white tile floors, double beds, overhead fans, and bathrooms with hot water. The original wooden cabins are a bit cramped and have shared bathrooms. A restaurant offers delicious meals of meat or fish or *mole poblano* (turkey leg topped with rich, spicy chocolate sauce). ⊠ *Carretera Escárcega–Chetumal, Km 153, Xpuhil,* ☎ *983/ 871–6006. 13 rooms, 9 cabanas. Restaurant, fans; no air-conditioning, no room phones, no room TVs. No credit cards.*

Becán

 30 *7 km (4½ mi) west of Xpuhil.*

Becán ("road of the serpent") is thought to have been an important city within the Río Bec group, inhabited from around 600 BC. The city was unusual in that was surrounded by a moat, ½ km (¼ mi) long and ½ km (¼ mi) deep; entrance to the city was through one of seven gateways. Many archaeologists believe the moat served defensive purposes, and recent investigations have established that Becán was often under siege—more than likely from neighboring Calakmul. However, the constant skirmishes didn't seem to hinder the construction of more than 84 main buildings during its golden age, from AD 600 to AD 1000. The most exciting building is **Structure VIII,** whose underground passages lead to small subterranean rooms and to a concealed staircase leading to the top of the temple. Experts believe the building was used for rites of self-mutilation or other types of worship. Do hire a guide to explore these ruins; Miguel Perez Cortés, better known locally as "Zapata," is considered the best around. ⊠ *$3.50.* ☉ *Daily 8–5.*

Chicanná

 ③   *3 km (2 mi) east of Becán.*

Thought to have been an elite community related to the larger, more commercial city of Becán, Chicanná ("house of the serpent's mouth") was also in its prime during the Late Classic period. Of the four buildings surrounding the main plaza, **Structure II,** on the east side, is the most impressive. On the intricate facade are well-preserved sculpted reliefs and faces with long twisted noses, symbols of Chaac. In typical Chenes style, the doorway represents the mouth of the creator god Itzamná; surrounding the opening are large crossed eyes, fierce fangs, and earrings to complete the stone mask, which still bears traces of blue and red pigments. 💲 *$3.* ⊙ *Daily 8–5.*

Hormiguero

 ②   *19 km (12 mi) southeast of Xpuhil.*

Hormiguero is Spanish for "anthill," referring both to the looters' tunnels that honeycombed the ruins when archaeologists discovered them and to the number of large anthills in the area. The buildings here were constructed roughly between 400 BC and AD 1100 in the Río Bec style, with rounded lateral towers and ornamental stairways. The site has five temples, two of which have been excavated to reveal ornate facades covered with zoomorphic figures whose mouths are the doorways. **Structure II** was an important find because of its size (it is the largest structure on the site) as well as its beautifully preserved carved façade, rounded corners, and false staircases. **Structure V** has some admirable Chaac masks arranged in a cascade atop a pyramid. 💲 *$2.50.* ⊙ *Daily 8–5.*

Río Bec

 ③   *About 50 km (31 mi) south of Xpuhil.*

The sprawling Río Bec archaeological zone covers nearly 78 square km (30 square mi) in a region of uneven terrain and small hills. The zone includes five major ceremonial centers and 15 smaller temple groups, but although archaeologists have done extensive surveys of the area, little clearing or excavation has been done. The only structure that has been completely excavated and restored, known as **Río Bec B,** is a 55-ft-tall temple with two false-pyramid towers at opposite edges of a long, low building whose front entrance is the mouth of a serpent. Thoroughly exploring Río Bec requires an all-day trip with an experienced guide arranged through the tourist office in Campeche (☎ 981/816–5593). 💲 *Free.* ⊙ *Daily 8–5.*

Balamkú

 ③   *About 60 km (37 mi) west of Xpuhil, 80 km (50 mi) northwest of Río Bec.*

Located near the northeastern boundary of the Calakmul Biosphere Reserve, Balamkú (Temple of the Jaguar) is famous for the stunning molded stucco and polychrome frieze discovered here in 1995. Dated to the Classic period (between AD 550 and AD 650), this dazzling work is nearly 56 ft long and 13 ft high. It is composed of four adjacent carvings, two of a frog and two of a crocodile. On each rests the figure of the king wearing the mask of the sun god. Interspersed are carvings of jaguars and in the middle is a tomb. The original red and black paint can be seen in places. The fresco is enclosed to protect it from the elements, and flash cameras are prohibited. There are other structures here, but they're anticlimactic after the impressive fresco. 💲 *$2.* ⊙ *Daily 8–5.*

Calakmul Biosphere Reserve

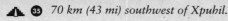 *70 km (43 mi) southwest of Xpuhil.*

Remote Calakmul ("twin towers") is in the isolated region near the Guatemala border. The area surrounding the ancient Maya city was declared a protected biosphere reserve in 1989; covering 1.8 million acres, Calakmul is the second-largest reserve of its kind on the continent, next to Sian Ka'an. Within its borders there are numerous species of flora and fauna, including some that are endangered. Among them are wildcats (jaguar, puma, ocelot), spider and howler monkeys, 329 different kinds of birds—Calakmul is perfect for birding—and 120 varieties of orchids, including a species of black orchid.

The Escárcega–Chetumal highway runs right through the reserve. Although structures will be excavated, the dense jungle surrounding them is being left in its natural state. Extensive information on the site's ecosystem is presented in tours conducted by local guides. Arrangements for an English-speaking tour guide must be made beforehand with the Campeche City tourist office.

Archaeologists and anthropologists estimate that the region may once have been inhabited by more than 50,000 Maya and have thus far mapped more than 6,250 structures of all sizes, including what may be the largest Maya building on the peninsula. More than 180 stelae have been found, as have twin pyramids that face each other across a plaza, similar to those at Tikal in Guatemala. However, Calakmul's towering, early Petén–style temples, with their long, sloping sides, are a bit bulky compared to Tikal's graceful pyramids.

Perhaps the most monumental discovery so far at Calakmul is a 1,000-year-old individual, found wrapped in animal skins (but not embalmed) and locked away in a royal tomb. The 1994 find is the first known example of this type of burial in the Maya world to date, and the remains are under study at the government's anthropology institute in Mexico City. Other items from the site—including a mummy and jade funeral masks—are on display at the Fuerte de San Miguel's Museum of the Maya in Campeche City.

Calakmul was a formidable military power in its time. It was first estimated to have been settled around 1500 BC, but now experts agree it was founded no earlier than 1000 BC. Historians believe it was probably the capital city of the mighty Serpent Head dynasty. The glyph with this symbol has been found on stelae in other cities of the ancient Maya empire, suggesting that Calakmul dominated a large number of tributary city-states. It reached the pinnacle of its power in the Late Classic period, when it held sway over Palenque in Chiapas and the superpowers Tikal in Guatemala and Caracol in Belize. Stelae under study also indicate that the new heads of tributary cities were obligated to journey to Calakmul to be formally consecrated in their duties by the leader of the Serpent Head lineage. Epigraphists also have discovered inscriptions relating the defeat of Calakmul's most famous ruler, Jaguar Paw, at the hands of arch rival Tikal in AD 695. After this the city's rulers decided to forge an alliance with groups to the north, most importantly with Río Bec.

From the entrance gate, it is a 60-km (37-mi) drive along a paved road to the parking area. The site is shrouded in thick rain forest, but paths with signposts lead to various temples. You can see only about a half dozen structures, including **Temple II** and **Temple VII**—twin pyramids separated by an immense plaza. Temple II, at 175 ft, is the tallest structure found here so far. Getting to the top involves climbing up a ragged rock incline, as the steps have not been completely restored yet. It's worth the effort, though, because the view from the top of the surrounding canopy of rain forest is spectacular. A stone mask uncovered on the facade of Temple II in 1997 is currently under study.

The facade and steps of slightly smaller **Temple I** have been restored, so it's easier to climb. A pair of royal tombs has been extracted from here, one of a female regent. There's a stela at the base of the pyramid overlooking the plaza. Parts of temples are scattered around one of the rain-forest paths—a state likely attributable to grave robbers who got away with the choice pieces. It's hard to thwart these criminals, since to do so would require a large corps of guards at the site, and there is no budget available for hiring them.

Upon entry to Calakmul, you must register yourself and your vehicle, paying an entrance fee for both at the gate. There is a module with rest rooms and a tiny bookstore on-site, but you have to bring your own food and water. *97 km (60 mi) east of Escárcega to the turnoff at Cohuas, then 65 km (40 mi) south to Calakmul. $11 per car (more for larger vehicles), plus $3.30 per person. ☉ Daily 8–5.*

Lodging

$$ Ⓗ **Puerta Calakmul.** Designed and built by a master woodworker and architect, these rustic cabanas are tucked away in the forest on the edge of the Calakmul biosphere and ruins. Built with natural wood and stone from the area, each has been decorated with jungle colors and has large showers, wooden tables, comfortable beds with overhead fans, and screened-in porches. Small ponds and sitting areas complete the Garden of Eden atmosphere, and nearby trails allow for hiking in the woods. A trailer park and campgrounds closer to the highway are under the same management. ✉ *Carretera Escárcega–Chetumal 186, Km 98.5, by entrance to Calakmul ruins,* ☎ ℻ *998/892–3403, 998/892–3406, or 998/884–1975. 15 cabanas, 8 trailer sites, 10 tents. Restaurant, pool; no air-conditioning, no room phones, no room TVs. No credit cards.*

Candelaria

⚓ ㊱ *95 km (59 mi) west of Calakmul Biosphere Reserve.*

Bird-watching, hunting, and fly-fishing in Lake Salsipuedes and Vieja Lagoon in the Candelaria River basin are what make this spot an increasingly popular destination. Primarily an agricultural hub producing wheat, corn, and sugarcane, Candelaria is also the starting-off point for a visit to the ruins of El Tigre.

Lodging

$$ Ⓗ **Autel Jardines.** Equipped with a number of amenities, offering the most comfortable lodgings in town, this hotel is an unexpected surprise. Rooms are spacious and have two double beds, large bathrooms, and cable TV, and each is decorated in the style of a different country. The owner, Manuel Valladares Hernández, can make arrangements (with advance notice) for a tour to El Tigre or for fly-fishing in the area. ✉ *Calle 27 No. 1, Col. Acalán,* ☎ *982/826–0064,* ℻ *981/816–0075, mvalladb@etzna.com. 28 rooms, 2 suites. Restaurant, pool, gym, bar, dance club, laundry service. AE.*

El Tigre

⚓ ㊲ *40 km (24 mi) south of Candelaria.*

With a new road from the village of Candelaria, El Tigre has become quite accessible. Right next to the Candelaria River, this port, inhabited since at least 300 BC, has the historic name of Itzankanac, capital of the province of Acalán and an important trading city that connected the Campeche coast with the Petén. Spanish conquistador Cortés passed through this area on his expedition to Honduras, and it was here that he supposedly hanged Cuauhtémoc, the last Aztec emperor. The archaeological site of El Tigre comprises a 656-ft-long ceremonial plaza surrounded by four structures, which, despite the obviously planned organization of the plaza, have no unifying style. Some of the stucco masks found have anthropomorphic features. Two large *sacbéob* (ceremonial roads) lead down to the river and a landing site. It's a long drive to reach the site, so you may need to stay overnight in the nearby village of Candelaria. ✆ *$2.* ✆ *Daily 8–5.*

ROUTE 180 TO VILLAHERMOSA

Heading southwest from Campeche, Route 180 hugs the coast, offering a wonderful view of the Gulf of Mexico. The deep-green sea is so shallow that the continental shelf is almost visible at low tide. Waves are rare and the current runs at a nearly imperceptible 0.3 knots.

Lerma

38 *13 km (8 mi) southwest of Campeche City.*

Playa Bonita, the first beach southwest of Campeche City, is in this rural village. Public buses to Lerma depart daily 6 AM–11 PM from the market in Campeche City (✉ Circuito Baluartes, between Calles 53 and 55). The unmarked beach has lockers, changing rooms, showers, and a snack bar. It is lovely during weekdays but crowded on weekends, and litter is a problem.

Seybaplaya

39 *About 7 km (4 mi) southwest of Lerma.*

Dozens of identical, turquoise-and-white fiberglass motor launches line the beach at the traditional fishing port of Seybaplaya. Its palm-fringed setting is the prettiest seascape on the Campeche coast. Snorkeling is good here, as a number of large coral heads are just offshore, along with an underwater cemetery for boats. The facade and bell tower of the gray stone church are painted in striking whitewash with cobalt-blue accents. Visitors looking for a challenge may want to climb the huge staircase that juts up the mountain, ending at the giant statue of Jesus with his arms outstretched. The view is incredible, but it is quite a hike. A couple of miles north along the beach road is **Payucán**—a beach with fine white sand and lots of herons, sandpipers, pelicans, and other seabirds—and **Punta del Morro** ("point of the nose"), a huge seaside cavern created by centuries of erosion. The sound of crashing waves echoes off the cavern's walls, adding to its drama.

About 9 km (5½ mi) southwest is **Siho Playa,** a rocky beach and the old home of the pirate Henry Morgan. Here the sea is quite calm and stays shallow for about 10 yards. Three kilometers (2 miles) southwest is the beautiful **Costa Blanca** beach, with lots of shells, birds, and smooth surf.

Champotón

40 *35 km (22 mi) southwest of Seybaplaya.*

The highway curves through a series of hills before reaching Champotón's immensely satisfying vista of open seas. Champotón is a charming little town with a bridge, *palapas* (thatch-roof huts) on the water, and plenty of swimmers and launches in sight. The Spaniards dubbed the outlying bay the Bahía de la Mala Pelea, or Bay of the Evil Battle, because it was here that the troops of the Spanish conqueror and explorer Hernández de Córdoba were trounced for the first time in Mexico, in 1517, by pugnacious Indians armed with arrows, slingshots, and darts. The famous battle is commemorated with a parade and fair on March 21.

The 17th-century church of **Nuestra Señora de las Mercedes** is the site for the large Virgin of Guadaloupe feast that begins on November 28 and ends on December 18. In the middle of town also stand the ruins of the **Fortín de San Antonio** (Small Fort of San Antonio). Champotón is ideal for bird-watching, fishing, and hunting. More than 37 kinds of fish, including shad, snook, and bass, live in Río Champotón; on land there are deer, wild boar, oscillated and Gould turkeys, doves, and quail. The mangroves and swamps are home to a variety of cranes and other waterfowl. The town is primarily an agricultural hub—its most important exports are lumber and chicle along with coconut, sugarcane, bananas, avocados, corn, and beans.

About a dozen small seafood restaurants make up **Los Cockteleros,** an area 5 km (3 mi) north of the center of Champotón. This is where *campechanos* head on weekends to munch fried fish or slurp down a variety of seafood cocktails, some with the famous sweet, spicy salsa. The open-air palapa eateries are near the beach and are open daily during daylight hours.

Approximately 15 km (9 mi) southwest of Champotón is another beautiful beach called **Punta Xen.** It's a long stretch of deserted sand interrupted only by birds and seashells. Across the highway are a few restaurants serving basic food.

Dining and Lodging

$–$$ ✕ **Las Brisas.** A favorite with locals, this is the best place in town for fresh fish, shrimp, and octopus. Open until 6 PM, Las Brisas is on the main street by the water and looks out onto the bay. ⊠ *Av. Eugenio Echeverría Castellot s/n, between 18 and 16 la Brisa,* ☎ *982/828–0515. No credit cards. No dinner.*

$ ▦ **Geminis.** On a hill overlooking the bay, this white hotel is the most modern in the village. Most rooms have air-conditioning, TV sets, and spacious double beds with colorful bedspreads. The restaurant, La Casona, serves delicious local specialties. ⊠ *Calle 30 No. 10,* ☎ *982/828–0008,* FAX *982/828–0094, hotel_geminis@hotmail.com. 24 rooms. Restaurant, fans, free parking; no room phones. No credit cards.*

$ ▦ **Snook Inn.** The walls that enclose this hotel give it an unassuming appearance. The extremely clean pool is surrounded by a garden, and the deck has comfortable chairs and tables. Rooms are simple, with tile floors, unadorned walls, so-so beds, and hammock hooks in the walls (bring your own hammock). The hotel is mainly the domain of serious anglers who come for fishing and hunting trips with hotel owner Don José Sansores and his son Fernando. ⊠ *Calle 30 No. 1,* ☎ FAX *982/828–0018. 20 rooms. Pool, free parking. No credit cards.*

Sabancuy

④1 *47 km (29 mi) west of Champotón.*

The launching point for exploring the **Laguna de Términos** and its many estuaries and mangroves, Sabancuy is the final village before high-tension lines start to follow the coastal highway and oil country starts.

The pretty beach here is not part of the village, which is actually off the main highway. Plan tours of this area ahead of time with the tourist office in Campeche City, since little English is spoken here. The secondary highway (pitted with potholes in various spots, which makes for slow going at times) leads to the ruins of El Tigre.

Dining and Lodging

$–$$$ ✗ **Viaductoplaya Restaurant Bar Turístico.** The catch of the day might include shrimp, squid, or fish at this beachside restaurant. Mexican favorites such as panuchos and grilled chicken are on the menu as well. Beer, wine, and liquor are available. ✉ *Carretera Carmen–Champotón, Km 77.50,* ☎ *982/825–0008. No credit cards.*

$$ 🏠 **Posada Bellavista.** This small, colonial-style hostelry has sparsely decorated but clean rooms equipped with the basics—two single beds, fans, and hot water. It's in front of the park adjacent to the municipal palace. ✉ *Calle Marina y J. Ortiz Avila,* ☎ *no phone. 10 rooms. No air-conditioning, no room phones, no room TVs. No credit cards.*

Isla del Carmen

42 *147 km (91 mi) south of Champotón.*

It was on this barrier island protecting the lagoon from the gulf that the pirates who raided Campeche hid from the mid-1550s to their expulsion in 1717. The island has served as a depot for everything from dyewoods and textiles to hardwoods, chicle, shrimp, and (for more than 20 years) oil.

If you're headed toward Tabasco, Veracruz, Chiapas, or other points west or south of Campeche, chances are you will pass through **Ciudad del Carmen.** A major hub and the second-largest city in Campeche, Ciudad is actually not on the island but on the adjoining peninsula's east end. The island is connected by east and west bridges to the mainland.

Ciudad del Carmen has some charming historic attractions that are worth a look, but the modern, commercialized sections of the city are a sad example of what happens when an oil company is given free rein. Parts of the bay are polluted, and the city is battling problems like prostitution and alcoholism, which is reflected in the cheap, ugly motels advertised as "men's clubs." Be prepared to pay higher prices for a safe hotel room than you would in Campeche City or other more tourist-oriented cities.

Isla del Carmen is not exactly a beach bum's paradise, but locals recommend two beaches north of town: **Bahamitas** and **Puerto Real,** at 15 km (9½ mi) and 30 km (18½ mi), respectively, along the Campeche highway. Both have bathrooms, showers, and restaurants and are popular with local people on weekends and holidays.

Sights to See

La Iglesia de la Virgen del Carmen. Two towers, each with a domed roof, grace this 1856 church. Inside is a gray-and-white marble altar dedicated to the Virgin of Carmen. During the two weeks preceding her important feast day (July 31), the city celebrates with fireworks, dances, fishing competitions, and livestock and agricultural expos. ✉ *Av. López Mateos and Calle 47,* ☎ *no phone.* ⊙ *Daily 8–2 and 5–7.*

Museo de la Ciudad (City Museum). In the building of the old hospital (Victoriano Nieves), this museum has displays about the pirates and the history of the city. ✉ *Calle 22,* ☎ *no phone.* ⊙ *Wed.–Sun. 10–8.*

Dining and Lodging

$$$ ╳ **El Cactus.** Meaty entrées welcome carnivorous appetites here, where dishes include succulent rib eye and a large filet mignon. The bone-marrow soup and the cheese pie are recommended. The restaurant's exterior resembles an adobe house with—you guessed it—cacti growing at the doorway. Inside are whitewashed stucco walls, wood furnishings, and quiet romantic background music. ⊠ *Calle 31 No. 132, Col. Cuauhtémoc (next to Hotel Lino), Ciudad del Carmen,* ☎ *938/382–4986. AE, MC, V.*

$$$$ ╳▥ **Holiday Inn.** All the amenities one has come to expect from a Holiday Inn can be found at this small hotel, including no-smoking rooms, airport shuttle, alarm clocks, and data ports. The lobby is intimate, with bamboo furniture and Mexican accents. Most rooms have king-size beds and small patios or terraces. The figure-8 pool, gymnasium, and restaurant are quite nice, and there is a golf course nearby. ⊠ *Calle 31 No. 273, Ciudad del Carmen,* ☎ *938/382–0890,* 𝖥𝖠𝖷 *938/382–0520,* 𝖶𝖤𝖡 *www.holiday-inn.com. 100 rooms, 6 suites. Restaurant, pool, gym, bar, free parking. AE, MC, V.*

$$$ ╳▥ **Eurohotel.** Geared toward Mexican business travelers, this contemporary, upscale hotel is close to the center of town. It provides lots of after-work relaxation options, including a gambling club. Modern rooms done in gray, blue, and cream colors have king-size beds, cable TV, room safes, and phones. Junior suites have a separate living area and bathtub; master suites have kitchenettes. The restaurant, Piamonte, serves some of Ciudad del Carmen's finest international fare. ⊠ *Calle 22 No. 208, Ciudad del Carmen,* ☎ *938/382–3044, 938/382–1031, or 938/382–3044; 888/562–0222 in the U.S.;* 𝖥𝖠𝖷 *938/382–3078;* 𝖶𝖤𝖡 *www.eurohotel.com.mx. 80 rooms, 12 suites. Restaurant, pool, bar, business services, meeting rooms. AE, DC, MC, V.*

CAMPECHE A TO Z

To research prices, get advice from other travelers, and book travel arrangements, visit www.fodors.com.

AIR TRAVEL

Aeroméxico has two flights daily from Mexico City to Campeche City. Aerocaribe flies to Veracruz, Villahermosa, Mérida, and Cancún.
➤ AIRLINES AND CONTACTS: **Aeroméxico** (☎ 800/021–4000). **Aerocaribe** (☎ 981/816–9074).

BUS TRAVEL

ADO, a first-class line, runs buses from Campeche City to Mérida, Villahermosa, and Ciudad del Carmen almost every hour, with less frequent departures for Cancún, Chetumal, Oaxaca, and other destinations. Adjacent to the ADO station, the second-class bus station has service on Unión de Camioneros to intermediate points throughout the Yucatán Peninsula, as well as less desirable service to Chetumal, Ciudad del Carmen, Escárcega, Mérida, Palenque, Tuxtla Gutiérrez, and Villahermosa. A half block from the ADO station is the office of the Elite Nuevos Horizontes bus company, which offers first-class service at least once a day to Mérida, Ciudad del Carmen, Mexico City, Veracruz, Cancún, Playa del Carmen, Jalapa, and Villahermosa.

Try to avoid an extended stopover in Escárcega, along Route 261. Though the government has beefed up security—Escárcega was an unsafe spot for tourists, with bus passengers the targets of robberies and assaults—and things have calmed down quite a bit, it is still not a place to linger, for safety as well as aesthetics.

Within Campeche City, buses run along Avenida Ruíz Cortínez and cost the equivalent of about 30¢.

➤ Bus Information: **ADO** (✉ Av. Gobernadores 289, at Calle 45, along Rte. 261 to Mérida, ☎ 981/816–3445). **Elite Nuevos Horizontes** (✉ Av. Gobernadores 575, between Calles 15 and 17, ☎ 981/811–0261). **Unión de Camioneros** (✉ Calle Chile, at Av. Gobernadores, ☎ no phone).

CAR RENTAL

Reliable rental agencies are AutoRent—which charges $45 a day including insurance and allows 200 km (120 mi) per day—and the slightly more expensive Maya Rent a Car, which rents small Chevys for $59 a day, including insurance and unlimited mileage.

➤ Major Agencies: **AutoRent** (✉ Hotel del Paseo, Calle 8 No. 215, ☎ 981/811–0100). **Maya Rent a Car** (✉ Del Mar Hotel, Av. Ruíz Cortínez, at Calle 59, ☎ 981/816–2233, ℻ 981/811–1618).

CAR TRAVEL

Campeche City is about two hours from Mérida along the 160-km (99-mi) *via corta* (short way), Route 180. The alternative route, the 250-km (155-mi) *via larga* (long way), Route 261, takes about three to four hours but passes the major Maya ruins of Uxmal, Kabah, and Sayil. From Chetumal, take Route 186 west to Escárcega, where you pick up Route 261 north; the drive takes about seven hours. Villahermosa is about six hours away if you drive inland via the town of Escárcega but longer if you hug the gulf and cross the bridge at Ciudad del Carmen. A toll road from Campeche City to Champotón costs $3 one-way and shaves 20 km (12 mi) off the 68-km (42-mi) road. Look for the 180 CUOTA sign when leaving the city for the coast. (The bridge toll is another $2.60 each way to Ciudad del Carmen.) A paved, two-lane highway south from Hopelchén to Xpuhil takes you to the Río Bec area and Calakmul from Mérida; there's no need to drive to Campeche City first unless you plan to visit there.

E-MAIL

In Campeche City, get on-line at En Red Cibercafé sucursal Universidad, open Monday–Saturday 10–10, or Cybercafé Campeche, open Monday–Saturday 9–9. Both places charge $1–$2 per hour.

➤ Services: **Cybercafé Campeche** (✉ Calle 61 No. 19-A, between Calles 10 and 12). **En Red Cibercafé sucursal Universidad** (✉ Av. Agustín Melgar 12).

EMERGENCIES

Las Ángeles Verdes (the Green Angels), an organization funded by the government, patrols the highways on a regular basis and offers emergency roadside assistance. Medical care is available at the government-funded Social Security Clinic or the Hospital General de Campeche.

➤ Doctors: **Hospital General de Campeche** (✉ Av. Central at Circuito Baluarte, ☎ 981/816–0920). **Social Security Clinic** (✉ Av. López Mateos and Av. Talamantes, ☎ 981/816–1855 or 981/816–5202).

➤ Emergency Services: **Emergencies** (☎ 060). **Police** (✉ Av. Resurgimiento 77, Col. Lazareto, ☎ 981/816–2309). **Red Cross** (✉ Av. Las Palmas, at Ah-Kim-Pech s/n, Campeche City, ☎ 981/815–2411).

➤ Hospital: **Hospital General** (✉ Av. Central at Circuito Baluartes, ☎ 981/816–0920).

➤ 24-Hour Pharmacy: **Clínica Campeche** (✉ Av. Central 65, near the Social Security Clinic, Campeche City, ☎ 981/816–5612).

MAIL AND SHIPPING

The post office (*correos*) in Campeche City is open weekdays 8–8, Saturday 9–1.

➤ SERVICES: **Post office** (✉ Av. 16 de Septiembre, between Calles 53 and 55, ☎ 981/816–2134).

MONEY MATTERS

Campeche City banks will change traveler's checks weekdays 9–4. Two large chains are Banamex and Bancomer.

➤ BANKS: **Banamex** (✉ Calle 53 No. 15, at Calle 10, ☎ 981/816–5251). **Bancomer** (✉ Av. 16 de Septiembre 120, ☎ 981/816–6622).

TAXIS

Taxis can be hailed on the street in Campeche City or from the stands by the bus stations, cathedral, and market. Because of the scarcity of taxis, it's quite common to share them with other people headed in the same direction—rarely will you have a cab to yourself, and drivers will not ask your permission to pick up another fare. To get picked up, just wait for one to slow down near you. A shared cab ride costs under $1. If you have one to yourself, it's $1.50–$3.

➤ TAXI COMPANY: **Radio Taxis** (☎ 981/816–1113 or 981/816–6666).

TELEPHONES

LONG-DISTANCE CALLS

TELMEX phones that take the electronic Ladatel cards are found throughout the city. Intertel also has long-distance phone and fax service. Another *larga distancia* (long-distance) store can be found at the corner of Calle 10 and Calle 59.

➤ SERVICE: **Intertel** (✉ Calle 57 No. 1, ☎ 981/816–6863, FAX 981/816–7334).

TOURS

Trolley tours of Campeche City leave from the Plaza Principal several times on the half hour in the morning, and generally in the evening at 6 and 8. The one-hour tour costs about $2. You can buy tickets on board the trolley, or ahead of time in the municipal tourist office right next to the cathedral, also on the plaza. It's a nice way to see the city, but although the tour is given in both English and Spanish, the horrid sound system makes the narrative nearly unintelligible.

Several tour operators have finally emerged to guide interested travelers to ruins throughout the state. Chito Tours and Servicios Turísticos S.A de C.V. are both recommended by the state tourism department and have offices in downtown Campeche City. Emerald Planet is an ecotourism outfitter that works closely with Pronatura, a nonprofit that helps administer the Calakmul Biosphere Reserve, and organizes tours to the area as well as to Belize and Guatemala. Pronatura sometimes organizes tours to the area as well.

➤ FEES AND SCHEDULES: **Chito Tours** (✉ Calle 51 No. 9, Int. C, between Calles 57 and 59, centro, ☎ 981/811–4700). **Emerald Planet** (✉ 2602 Timberwood Dr., No. 16, Fort Collins, CO 80528, ☎ 970/231–7751 in the U.S., FAX 303/447–0815, WEB www.emeraldplanet.com). **Servicios Turísticos S.A. de C.V.** (✉ Edificio San Marcos, Calle 57 No. 14, between Calles 10 and 12, Local 3, centro, ☎ 981/812–6485).

TRAVEL AGENCIES

➤ LOCAL AGENTS: **American Express/VIPs** (✉ Prolongación Calle 59, Edificio Belmar, Depto. 5, ☎ 981/811–1010 or 981/811–1000, FAX 981/816–8333, vips@campeche.sureste.com). **Destinos Maya** (✉ Av. Miguel Alemán 162 [altos], Loc.106, ☎ 981/811–0934; 713/440–0291 in the

U.S., FAX 981/811–0934). **Viajes Programados** (⊠ Calle 59 between Av. 16 de Septiembre and Av. Ruíz Cortínes, ☎ 981/811–1010).

VISITOR INFORMATION

The Secretaría de Turismo (Tourism Office) is open daily 9–3 and 6–9. The *oficina de turismo de municipio* (municipal tourism office) is open daily 8–2:30 and 4–8. The staff speaks very little English, but you can pick up a map. City trolley tours are booked here.

➤ TOURIST INFORMATION: **Oficina de turismo de municipio** (⊠ Calle 55, west of the cathedral, ☎ 981/811–3989 or 981/811–3990). **Secretaría de Turismo** (⊠ Av. Ruíz Cortínez s/n, Plaza Moch Couoh, across from Palacio del Gobierno, ☎ 981/816–9229, ☎ FAX 981/816–6767, turismo@campeche.gob.mx).

8 BACKGROUND AND ESSENTIALS

The Maya and Yucatán at a Glance

Spanish Vocabulary

THE MAYA AND YUCATÁN AT A GLANCE

11,000 BC Hunters and gatherers settle in Yucatán.

Preclassic Period: 2000 BC–AD 200

2,000 BC Maya ancestors in Guatemala begin to cultivate corn and build permanent dwellings.

1500–900 BC The powerful and sophisticated Olmec civilization develops along the Gulf of Mexico in the present-day states of Veracruz and Tabasco.

Primitive farming communities develop in Yucatán.

900–300 BC Olmec iconography and social institutions strongly influence the Maya populations in neighboring areas. The Maya adopt the Olmecs' concepts of tribal confederacies and small kingships as they move across the lowlands.

600 BC Edzná is settled. It will be inhabited for nearly 900 years before the construction of the large temples and palaces found there today.

400 BC– AD 100 Dzibilchaltún develops as an important center in Komchen, an ancient state north of present-day Mérida. Becán, in southern Campeche, is also settled.

300 BC Major construction begins in the Maya lowlands as the civilization begins to flourish.

300 BC– AD 200 New architectural elements, including the corbeled arch and roof comb, develop in neighboring Guatemala and gradually spread into the Yucatán.

300 BC– AD 900 Edzná becomes a city; increasingly large temple-pyramids are built.

Classic Period: 200–900

The calendar and the written word are among the achievements that mark the beginning of the Classic period. The architectural highlight of the period is large, stepped pyramids with frontal stairways topped by limestone and masonry temples, arranged around plazas and decorated with stelae (stone monuments), bas-reliefs, and frescoes. Each Maya city is painted a single bright color, often red or yellow.

200–600 Economy and trade flourish. Maya culture achieves new levels of scientific sophistication and some groups become warlike.

250–300 A defensive fortification ditch and earthworks are built at Becán.

300 The first structures are built at San Gervasio on Cozumel.

300–600 Kohunlich rises to dominate the forests of southern Quintana Roo.

400–1100 Cobá grows to be the largest city in the eastern Yucatán.

432 The first settlement is established at Chichén Itzá.

6th Century Influenced by the Toltec civilization of Teotihuacán in Central Mexico, larger and more elaborate palaces, temples, ball courts, roads, and fortifications are built in southern Maya cities, including Becán, Xpujil, and Chicanná in Campeche.

600–900 Northern Yucatán ceremonial centers become increasingly important as centers farther south reach and pass developmental climax; the influence of Teotihuacán wanes. Three new Maya architectural styles develop: Puuc (exemplified by Chichén Itzá and Edzná) is the dominant style; Chenes (in northern Campeche, between the Puuc hills and the Río Bec area) is characterized by ornamental facades with serpent masks; and Río Bec (at Río Bec and Becán) features small palaces with high towers exuberantly decorated with serpent masks.

850–950 The largest pyramids and palaces of Uxmal are built. By 975, however, Uxmal and most other Puuc sites are abandoned.

Postclassic Period: 900–1541

900–1050 The great Classic Maya centers of Guatemala, Honduras, and southern Yucatán are abandoned. The reason for their fall remains one of archaeology's greatest mysteries.

circa 920 The Itzá, a Maya tribe from the Petén rain forest in Guatemala, establish themselves at Champotón and then at Chichén Itzá.

987–1007 The Xiu, a Maya clan from the southwest, settle near ruins of Uxmal.

1224 An Itzá dynasty known as Cocomes emerges as a dominant group in northern Yucatán, building its capital at Mayapán.

1263–1440 Mayapán, under the rule of Cocomes aided by Canul mercenaries from Tabasco, becomes the most powerful city-state in Yucatán. The league of Mayapán—including the key cities of Uxmal, Chichén Itzá, and Mayapán—is formed in northern Yucatán. Peace reigns for almost two centuries. To guarantee the peace, the rulers of Mayapán hold members of other Maya royal families as lifelong hostages.

1441 Maya cities under Xiu rulers sack Mayapán, ending centralized rule of the peninsula. Yucatán henceforth is governed as 18 petty provinces, with constant internecine strife. The Itzá return to Lake Petén Itzá in Guatemala and establish their capital at Tayasal (modern-day Flores), one of the last un-Christianized Maya capitals, which will not be conquered by the Spanish until 1692.

15th Century The last ceremonial center on Cancún island is abandoned. Other Maya communities are developing along the Caribbean coast.

1502 A Maya canoe is spotted during Columbus's fourth voyage.

1511 Spanish sailors Jerónimo de Aguilar and Gonzalo Guerrero are shipwrecked off Yucatán's Caribbean coast and taken to a Maya village on Cozumel.

1517 Fernández de Córdoba discovers Isla Mujeres.

Trying to sail around Yucatán, which he believes to be an island, Córdoba lands at Campeche, marking first Spanish landfall on the mainland. He is defeated by the Maya at Champotón.

1518 Juan de Grijalva sights the island of Cozumel but does not land there.

1519 Hernán Cortés lands at Cozumel, where he rescues Aguilar. Guerrero chooses to remain on the island with his Maya family.

1527, 1531 Unsuccessful Spanish attempts to conquer Yucatán.

1540 Francisco de Montejo founds Campeche, the first Spanish settlement in Yucatán.

1541 Another unsuccessful attempt by the Spanish to defeat Yucatán.

Colonial Period: 1541–1821

1542 Maya chieftains surrender to Montejo at T'ho; 500,000 Indians are killed during the conquest of Yucatán. Indians are forced into labor under the *encomienda* system, by which conquistadors are charged with their subjugation and Christianization. The Franciscans contribute to this process.

Mérida is founded on the ruins of T'ho.

1543 Valladolid is founded on the ruins of Zací.

1546 A Maya group attacks Mérida, resulting in a five-month-long rebellion.

1562 Bishop Diego de Landa burns Maya codices at Maní.

1600 Cozumel is abandoned after smallpox decimates the population.

1686 Campeche's city walls are built for defense against pirates.

1700 182,500 Indians account for 98% of Yucatán's population.

1736 Indian population of Yucatán declines to 127,000.

1761 The Cocom uprising near Sotuta leads to the death of 600 Maya.

1771 The Fuerte (fort) de San Miguel is completed on a hill above Campeche, ending the pirates' reign of terror.

1810 Port of Sisal opens, ending Campeche's ancient monopoly on peninsular trade and its economic prosperity.

Postcolonial/Modern Period: 1821–Present

1821 Mexico wins independence from Spain by diplomatic means. Various juntas vie for control of the new nation, resulting in frequent military coups.

1823 Yucatán becomes a Mexican state encompassing the entire peninsula.

1839–42 American explorer John Lloyd Stephens visits Yucatán's Maya ruins and describes them in two best-selling books.

1840–42 Yucatecan separatists revolt in an attempt to secede from Mexico. The Mexican government quells the rebellion, reduces the state of Yucatán to one-third its previous size, creates the federal territories of Quintana Roo and Campeche, and recruits Maya soldiers into a militia to prevent further disturbance.

1846 Following years of oppression, violent clashes between Maya militiamen and residents of Valladolid launch the War of the Castes. The entire non-Indian population of Valladolid is massacred.

1848 Rebels from the Caste War settle in the forests of Quintana Roo, creating a secret city named Chan Santa Cruz. An additional 20 refugee families settle in Cozumel, which has been almost uninhabited for centuries. By 1890 Cozumel's population numbers 500, Santa Cruz's 10,000.

1850 Following the end of the Mexican War with the United States in 1849, the Mexican army moves into the Yucatán to end the Indian uprising. The Maya flee into the unexplored forests of Quintana Roo. Military attacks, disease, and starvation reduce the Maya population of the Yucatán Peninsula to fewer than 10,000.

1863 Campeche achieves statehood.

1872 The city of Progreso is founded.

1880–1914 Yucatán's monopoly on henequen, enhanced by plantation owners' exploitation of Maya peasants, leads to its golden age as one of the wealthiest states in Mexico. Prosperity will last until the beginning of World War II.

Waves of Middle Eastern immigrants arrive in Yucatán and become successful in commerce, restaurants, cattle ranching, and tourism.

Payo Obispo (present-day Chetumal) is founded on the site of a long-abandoned Spanish colonial outpost.

1901 The Cult of the Talking Cross reaches the height of its popularity in Chan Santa Cruz (later renamed Felipe Carrollo Puerto). The Cruzob Indians continue to resist the Mexican army.

U.S. consul Edward Thompson buys Chichén Itzá for $500 and spends the next three years dredging the Sacred Cenote for artifacts.

1902 Mexican president Porfirio Díaz asserts federal jurisdiction over the Territory of Quintana Roo to isolate rebellious pockets of Indians and increase his hold on regional resources.

1915 The War of the Castes reaches an uneasy truce after the Mexican Army leaves the Cruzob Indians to rule Quintana Roo as an independent territory.

1915–24 Felipe Carrillo Puerto, Socialist governor of Yucatán, institutes major reforms in land distribution, labor, women's rights, and education during Mexican Revolution.

1923–48 A Carnegie Institute team led by archaeologist Sylvanus Moreley restores the ruins of Chichén Itzá.

1934–40 President Lázaro Cárdenas implements significant agrarian reforms in Yucatán.

1935 Chan Santa Cruz rebels in Quintana Roo relinquish Tulum and sign a peace treaty.

1940–70 With collapse of the world henequen markets, Yucatán gradually becomes one of the poorest states in Mexico.

1968 The Mexican government selects Cancún as the site of the country's largest tourist resort.

1974 Quintana Roo achieves statehood. The first resort hotels at Cancún open for business.

1988 Hurricane Gilbert shuts down Cancún hotels and devastates the north coast of the Yucatán. The reconstruction is immediate. Within three years, the number of hotels on Isla Cancún triples.

1993 Under the guise of an environmentalist platform, Quintana Roo's newly elected governor Mario Villanueva begins systematically selling off state parks and federally owned land to developers.

1994 Mexico joins the United States and Canada in NAFTA (North American Free Trade Association), which will phase out tariffs over a 15-year period.

Popular Partido Revolucionario Institucional (PRI) presidential candidate Luis Donaldo Colosio is assassinated while campaigning in Tijuana. Ernesto Zedillo, generally thought to be more of a technocrat and "old boy"–style PRI politician, replaces him and wins the election.

Zedillo, blaming the economic policies of his predecessor, devalues the peso in December.

1995 Recession sets in as a result of the peso devaluation. The former administration is rocked by scandals surrounding the assassinations of Colosio and another high-ranking government official; ex-president Carlos Salinas de Gortari moves to the United States.

Quintana Roo governor Mario Villanueva is suspected of using his office to smuggle drugs into the state.

1996 Mexico's economy, bolstered by a $28 billion bailout led by the United States, turns around, but the recovery is fragile. The opposition National Action Party (PAN), which is committed to conservative economic policies, gains strength. New details emerge of scandals within the former administration.

1997 Mexico's top antidrug official is arrested on bribery charges. Nonetheless, the United States recertifies Mexico as a partner in the war on drugs. Party elections are scheduled for midyear. When Mexican environmentalists discover that Villanueva has sold the turtle sanctuary on Xcacel beach to a Spanish hotel chain, they begin an international campaign to save the site; Greenpeace stages a protest on the beach.

1998 Mexican author Octavio Paz dies.

U.S. Congress demands an investigation into the office of Mario Villanueva. Villanueva is refused entry into the United States when the DEA reveals that it has an open file on his activities.

1999 Raúl Salinas, brother of former Mexican president Carlos Salinas di Gortari (in exile in Ireland), is sentenced for the murder of a PRI leader.

Joaquin Hendricks, a retired military officer, is elected the new governor of Quintana Roo. Although he is thought to be an enemy of Mario Villanueva, the ex-governor sanctions Hendricks's rise to power. The Mexican government decides to arrest Villanueva on drug charges; Villanueva disappears.

2000 Spurning long-ruling PRI, Mexicans elect opposition candidate Vicente Fox president.

Fox government implements the "Financial Strengthening Program 2000–2001" as part of an economic reform and vows to clean up corruption.

2001 Ex-governor Mario Villanueva is captured, aided by DEA agents.

SPANISH VOCABULARY

Words and Phrases

	English	Spanish	Pronunciation
Basics			
	Yes/no	Sí/no	see/no
	Please	Por favor	pohr fah-**vohr**
	May I?	¿Me permite?	meh pehr-**mee**-teh
	Thank you (very much)	(Muchas) gracias	(**moo**-chas) **grah**-see-as
	You're welcome	De nada	deh **nah**-dah
	Excuse me	Con permiso/perdón	con pehr-**mee**-so/ pehr-**dohn**
	Pardon me/ what did you say?	¿Perdón?/Mande?	pehr-**dohn/mahn**-deh
	Could you tell me . . . ?	¿Podría decirme . . . ?	po-**dree**-ah deh-**seer**-meh
	I'm sorry	Lo siento	lo see-**en**-to
	Good morning!	¡Buenos días!	**bway**-nohs **dee**-ahs
	Good afternoon!	¡Buenas tardes!	**bway**-nahs **tar**-dess
	Good evening!	¡Buenas noches!	**bway**-nahs **no**-chess
	Goodbye!	¡Adiós!/ ¡Hasta luego!	ah-dee-**ohss/ ah**-stah-**lwe**-go
	Mr./Mrs.	Señor/Señora	sen-**yor**/sen-**yohr**-ah
	Miss	Señorita	sen-yo-**ree**-tah
	Pleased to meet you	Mucho gusto	**moo**-cho **goose**-to
	How are you?	¿Cómo está usted?	**ko**-mo es-**tah** oo-**sted**
	Very well, thank you.	Muy bien, gracias.	**moo**-ee bee-**en**, **grah**-see-as
	And you?	¿Y usted?	ee oos-**ted**
	Hello (on the phone)	Diga	**dee**-gah
Numbers			
	1	un, uno	oon, **oo**-no
	2	dos	dohs
	3	tres	tress
	4	cuatro	**kwah**-tro
	5	cinco	**sink**-oh
	6	seis	saice
	7	siete	see-**et**-eh
	8	ocho	**o**-cho
	9	nueve	new-**eh**-veh
	10	diez	dee-**es**
	11	once	**ohn**-seh
	12	doce	**doh**-seh
	13	trece	**treh**-seh
	14	catorce	ka-**tohr**-seh

15	quince	**keen**-seh
16	dieciséis	dee-**es**-ee-**saice**
17	diecisiete	dee-**es**-ee-see-**et**-eh
18	dieciocho	dee-**es**-ee-**o**-cho
19	diecinueve	dee-**es**-ee-new-**ev**-eh
20	veinte	**vain**-teh
21	veinte y uno/ veintiuno	**vain**-te-oo-noh
30	treinta	**train**-tah
32	treinta y dos	train-tay-**dohs**
40	cuarenta	kwah-**ren**-tah
50	cincuenta	seen-**kwen**-tah
60	sesenta	sess-**en**-tah
70	setenta	set-**en**-tah
80	ochenta	oh-**chen**-tah
90	noventa	no-**ven**-tah
100	cien	see-**en**
200	doscientos	doh-see-**en**-tohss
500	quinientos	keen-**yen**-tohss
1,000	mil	meel
2,000	dos mil	dohs meel

Days of the Week

Sunday	domingo	doh-**meen**-goh
Monday	lunes	**loo**-ness
Tuesday	martes	**mahr**-tess
Wednesday	miércoles	me-**air**-koh-less
Thursday	jueves	hoo-**ev**-ess
Friday	viernes	vee-**air**-ness
Saturday	sábado	**sah**-bah-doh

Useful Phrases

Do you speak English?	¿Habla usted inglés?	**ah**-blah oos-**ted** in-**glehs**
I don't speak Spanish	No hablo español	no **ah**-bloh es-pahn-**yol**
I don't understand (you)	No entiendo	no en-tee-**en**-doh
I understand (you)	Entiendo	en-tee-**en**-doh
I don't know	No sé	no seh
I am American/ British	Soy americano (americana)/ inglés(a)	soy ah-meh-ree-**kah**-no (ah-meh-ree-**kah**-nah)/in-**glehs**(ah)
My name is . . .	Me llamo . . .	meh **yah**-moh
Yes, please/ No, thank you	Sí, por favor/ No, gracias	**see** pohr fah-**vor**/ no **grah**-see-ahs
Yesterday/today/ tomorrow	Ayer/hoy/mañana	ah-**yehr**/oy/mahn-**yah**-nah
This morning/ afternoon	Esta mañana/tarde	**es**-tah mahn-**yah**-nah/**tar**-deh
Tonight	Esta noche	**es**-tah **no**-cheh
This/Next week	Esta semana/ la semana que entra	**es**-tah seh-**mah**-nah/lah seh-**mah**-nah keh **en**-trah

This/Next month	Este mes/el próximo mes	**es**-teh mehs/el **prok**-see-moh mehs
How?	¿Cómo?	**koh**-mo
When?	¿Cuándo?	**kwahn**-doh
What?	¿Qué?	keh
What is this?	¿Qué es esto?	keh es **es**-toh
Why?	¿Por qué?	por **keh**
Who?	¿Quién?	kee-**yen**
Where is . . . ?	¿Dónde está . . . ?	**dohn**-deh es-**tah**
the train station?	la estación del tren?	la es-tah-see-**on** del **train**
the subway station?	la estación del metro?	la es-ta-see-**on** del **meh**-tro
the bus stop?	la parada del autobus?	la pah-**rah**-dah del oh-toh-**boos**
the bank?	el banco?	el **bahn**-koh
the hotel?	el hotel?	el oh-**tel**
the post office?	la oficina de correos?	la oh-fee-**see**-nah deh-koh-**reh**-os
the museum?	el museo?	el moo-**seh**-oh
the hospital?	el hospital?	el ohss-pee-**tal**
the bathroom?	el baño?	el **bahn**-yoh
Here/there	Aquí/allá	ah-**key**/ah-**yah**
Open/closed	Abierto/cerrado	ah-bee-**er**-toh/ ser-**ah**-doh
Left/right	Izquierda/derecha	iss-key-**er**-dah/ dare-**eh**-chah
Straight ahead	Todo recto	**toh**-doh-**rec**-toh
Is it near/far?	¿Está cerca/lejos?	es-**tah** sehr-kah/ **leh**-hoss
I'd like . . .	Quisiera . . .	kee-see-**ehr**-ah
a room	una habitación	**oo**-nah ah-bee-tah-see-**on**
the key	la llave	lah **yah**-veh
a newspaper	un periódico	oon pehr-ee-**oh**-dee-koh
a stamp	un sello	**say**-oh
How much is this?	¿Cuánto cuesta?	**kwahn**-toh **kwes**-tah
A little/a lot	Un poquito/ mucho	oon poh-**kee**-toh/ **moo**-choh
More/less	Más/menos	mahss/**men**-ohss
I am ill	Estoy enfermo(a)	es-**toy** en-**fehr**-moh(mah)
Please call a doctor	Por favor llame un medico	pohr fah-**vor** ya-meh oon **med**-ee-koh
Help!	¡Ayuda!	ah-**yoo**-dah

On the Road

Avenue	Avenida	ah-ven-**ee**-dah
Broad, tree-lined boulevard	Paseo	pah-**seh**-oh
Highway	Carretera	car-reh-**ter**-ah

Port; mountain pass	Puerto	poo-**ehr**-toh
Street	Calle	**cah**-yeh
Waterfront promenade	Paseo marítimo	pah-**seh**-oh mahr-**ee**-tee-moh

In Town

Cathedral	Catedral	cah-teh-**dral**
Church	Iglesia	**tem**-plo/ee-**glehs**-see-ah
City hall, town hall	Ayuntamiento	ah-yoon-tah-me-**yen**-toh
Door, gate	Puerta	poo-**ehr**-tah
Main square	Plaza Mayor	plah-thah mah-**yohr**
Market	Mercado	mer-**kah**-doh
Neighborhood	Barrio	**bahr**-ree-o
Tavern, rustic restaurant	Mesón	meh-**sohn**
Traffic circle, roundabout	Glorieta	glor-ee-**eh**-tah
Wine cellar, wine bar, wine shop	Bodega	boh-**deh**-gah

Dining Out

	de . . .	yah deh
A bottle of . . .	Una bottella de . . .	**oo**-nah bo-**teh**-yah deh
A glass of . . .	Un vaso de . . .	oon **vah**-so deh
Bill/check	La cuenta	lah **kwen**-tah
Breakfast	El desayuno	el deh-sah-**yoon**-oh
Dinner	La cena	lah **seh**-nah
Menu of the day	Menú del día	meh-**noo** del **dee**-ah
Fork	El tenedor	ehl ten-eh-**dor**
Is the tip included?	¿Está incluida la propina?	es-**tah** in-cloo-**ee**-dah lah pro-**pee**-nah
Knife	El cuchillo	el koo-**chee**-yo
Large portion of tapas	Ración	rah-see-**ohn**
Lunch	La comida	lah koh-**mee**-dah
Menu	La carta, el menú	lah **cart**-ah, el meh-**noo**
Napkin	La servilleta	lah sehr-vee-**yet**-ah
Please give me . . .	Por favor déme . . .	pohr fah-**vor** **deh**-meh
Spoon	Una cuchara	**oo**-nah koo-**chah**-rah

INDEX

Icons and Symbols

★ Our special recommen-
   dations
✕ Restaurant
🏠 Lodging establishment
✕🏠 Lodging establishment
   whose restaurant war-
   rants a special trip
▲ Archaeological site
☝ Good for kids (rubber
   duck)
☞ Sends you to another
   section of the guide for
   more information
✉ Address
☎ Telephone number
☉ Opening and closing
   times
🎫 Admission prices

Numbers in white and black
circles ③ ❸ that appear on
the maps, in the margins, and
within the tours correspond
to one another.

A

Addresses, *x*, 41
Air tours. ☞ *See* Plane tours
Air travel, *x–xii*
Campeche, 222
Cancún, 41
Caribbean coast, 136
Cozumel, 93–94
Isla Mujeres, 63
Mérida and State of Yucatán,
   184–185
Airports, *xii–xiii*, 41, 185
Aké (Maya site), 148, 163
Aktun-Chen caves, 121
Akumal, 104, 119–121
Alacranes Reef, 180
Alameda ✕, 155
Alberto's Continental Patio
   ✕, 154
All Natural Café ✕, 55–56
Amaro ✕, 155
Amigos Pizza ✕, 56
Anfitríon ✕, 155
Aniversario de Benito Juárez,
   xliii
Antillano 🏠, 32
Apartment rentals, *xxix–xxx*
Aquatic Procession, *xliv*
Archaeological sites, 5, 13,
   100, 121, 192. ☞ *Also*
   Maya sites and artifacts
Architecture (Campeche),
   192–193
Arrecife ✕, 80

Art galleries and museums
Campeche, 201
Cancún, 40
Mérida, 151, 152, 162
Arte Maya (workshop), 175
Arts
Campeche, 206–207
Cancún, 33–34
Caribbean coast, 115
Cozumel, 86–87
Isla Mujeres, 59
Mérida, 159–160
ATMs, *xxxii*
Autel Jardines 🏠, 218
Avalon Grand Resort 🏠, 29
Azul Cobalto Restaurant and
   Bar ✕, 81

B

Baal Nah Kah 🏠, 114
Bacalar, 104, 132–133
Baccará 🏠, 27
Bahamitas (beach), 221
Balamkú, 195, 216
Baluarte de la Soledad, 199,
   200
Baluarte de San Carlos, 199–
   200
Baluarte de San Juan, 203
Baluarte de San Pedro, 199,
   200
Baluarte de Santiago, 199,
   200
Baluartes 🏠, 205
Banco Chinchorro (national
   park), 132
Banks
business hours, *xiii–xiv*
Campeche, 224
Cancún, 45
Caribbean coast, 139
Cozumel, 96
Isla Mujeres, 65
Mérida, 187
Baseball, 160
Bazar de Artesanías
   Municipales (market),
   151–152
Beaches, 5
Campeche, 219, 220, 221
Cancún, 13, 17–18
Caribbean coast, 100, 105,
   109, 110, 111, 117, 118,
   119, 122
Cozumel, 70, 76–78
Isla Mujeres, 49, 53–54
Mérida and State of Yucatán,
   144
Becal, 209–210
Becán (Maya site), 195, 215
Bell of Dolores Hidalgo, 152
Bella Mar ✕, 182
Best Western María del
   Carmen 🏠, 158

Bicycling, *xii*
Caribbean coast, 116
Isla Mujeres, 63
Billfish tournaments, *xliii*
Bird Island, 132
Bird-watching, 5
Campeche, 207, 209
Caribbean coast, 111, 132
Isla Contoy, 62–63
Isla Mujeres, 49
State of Yucatán, 144, 177,
   183
tours, 178, 189
Bisquets Obregon ✕, 25
Blue Bay Club Cancún 🏠, 26
Blue Bayou ✕, 20
Blue Sky 🏠, 122
Boat tours
Cancún, 46
Cozumel, 97
Boat travel, *xiii*
Cancún, 41–42
Caribbean coast, 136–137
Cozumel, 94
Isla Mujeres, 63–64
Boca Paila Fishing Lodge
   ✕🏠, 129
Bookstores, 162
Bullfights
Cancún, 36
Mérida, 160
Bus travel, *xiv*
Campeche, 222–223
Cancún, 42
Caribbean coast, 137
Cozumel, 94
Isla Mujeres, 64
Mérida and State of Yucatán,
   185–186
Business hours, *xiii–xiv*

C

Cabañas La Conchita 🏠, 125
Cabañas María del Mar 🏠,
   58
Cabañas Paamul 🏠, 117
Cabañas Xcalacoco 🏠, 110
Café Caribe & Backyard ✕,
   82
Café Cito ✕, 56
Café El Nopalito ✕, 56
Café La Habana ✕, 155–156
Café Olé International ✕,
   117–118
Café Sasta ✕, 112
Calakmul Biosphere Reserve
   (Maya reserve), 195,
   217–218
Calkiní, 208–209
Calle 59 (Campeche), 199,
   200
Cambalache ✕, 21
Cameras and photography,
   xiv–xv

Fodor's Key to the Guides

America's guidebook leader publishes guides for every kind of traveler.
Check out our many series and find your perfect match.

Fodor's Gold Guides
America's favorite travel-guide series offers the most detailed insider reviews of hotels, restaurants, and attractions in all price ranges, plus great background information, smart tips, and useful maps.

Fodor's Road Guide USA
Big guides for a big country—the most comprehensive guides to America's roads, packed with places to stay, eat, and play across the U.S.A. Just right for road warriors, family vacationers, and cross-country trekkers.

COMPASS AMERICAN GUIDES
Stunning guides from top local writers and photographers, with gorgeous photos, literary excerpts, and colorful anecdotes. A must-have for culture mavens, history buffs, and new residents.

Fodor's CITYPACKS
Concise city coverage with a foldout map. The right choice for urban travelers who want everything under one cover.

Fodor's EXPLORING GUIDES
Hundreds of color photos bring your destination to life. Lively stories lend insight into the culture, history, and people.

Fodor's POCKET GUIDES
For travelers who need only the essentials. The best of Fodor's in pocket-size packages for just $9.95.

Fodor's To Go
Credit-card–size, magnetized color microguides that fit in the palm of your hand—perfect for "stealth" travelers or as gifts.

Fodor's FLASHMAPS
Every resident's map guide. 60 easy-to-follow maps of public transit, parks, museums, zip codes, and more.

Fodor's CITYGUIDES
Sourcebooks for living in the city: Thousands of in-the-know listings for restaurants, shops, sports, nightlife, and other city resources.

Fodor's AROUND THE CITY WITH KIDS
68 great ideas for family days, recommended by resident parents. Perfect for exploring in your own backyard or on the road.

Fodor's ESCAPES
Fill your trip with once-in-a-lifetime experiences, from ballooning in Chianti to overnighting in the Moroccan desert. These full-color dream books point the way.

Fodor's FYI
Get tips from the pros on planning the perfect trip. Learn how to pack, fly hassle-free, plan a honeymoon or cruise, stay healthy on the road, and travel with your baby.

Fodor's Languages for Travelers
Practice the local language before hitting the road. Available in phrase books, cassette sets, and CD sets.

Karen Brown's Guides
Engaging guides to the most charming inns and B&Bs in the U.S.A. and Europe, with easy-to-follow inn-to-inn itineraries.

Baedeker's Guides
Comprehensive guides, trusted since 1829, packed with A–Z reviews and star ratings.

At bookstores everywhere.   www.fodors.com/books